Business analysis was something I simply did, rather than thinking of it as a profession; that was until I went to the launch of the first edition of *Business Analysis*. As the profession of business analysis continues to evolve and adapt to a changing environment, I'm delighted that this fourth edition continues to lead the way. It remains the 'go-to' book and most important guide for professional business analysts. Indispensable and invaluable.

Dylan Jones, *Deputy Director, Department for Work and Pensions*

In its fourth edition, *Business Analysis* continues to incorporate emerging concepts, clearly presented and easily read, reflecting the evolution of business analysis. It is the benchmark publication for any business analyst, to which readers will continue to return for reference and reassurance.

Mark Wilson, *Business Analysis Practice Manager, Allianz Insurance plc*

This updated edition supports the continued evolution of business analysis and remains the go-to resource for practicing business analysts to turn to throughout their careers. The inclusion of the Business Analysis Service Framework and a wealth of Lean and Agile techniques reflects the customer-centricity of business analysis in today's world.

Michelle Shakesheff, *Head of Business Analysis, Close Brothers*

Business Analysis has long been the key book for every self-respecting business analyst. After six years of excellent service in its third edition, I am delighted that this fourth edition introduces a service framework and has captured advancements such as Agile, SIPOC and Design Thinking whilst maintaining the core integrity of traditional business analysis.

Ian Richards, *Director, Business Analysis, Capita*

The book that no business analyst should be without gets an up-to-the-minute update that maintains its status as the primary reference on business analysis for change professionals everywhere. The wealth of material and scope of the updates ensure this edition is an invaluable addition to any business analyst's bookshelf regardless of their experience! I heartily recommend it to anyone wishing to know more about this vital and rewarding role.

David Beckham, *Principal Consultant, ChuDo Consulting*

This much anticipated new edition does not disappoint! The BA Service perspective moves the profession forward in our understanding of how business analysis can be used to best effect within our organisations. From aspiring BAs to highly-experienced practitioners, this book is a must-read for all business analysts.

Christina Lovelock, *Co-Author of* Delivering Business Analysis *and* Business Analysis Manager, *University of Leeds*

BUSINESS ANALYSIS

BCS, THE CHARTERED INSTITUTE FOR IT

BCS, The Chartered Institute for IT, is committed to making IT good for society. We use the power of our network to bring about positive, tangible change. We champion the global IT profession and the interests of individuals, engaged in that profession, for the benefit of all.

Exchanging IT expertise and knowledge
The Institute fosters links between experts from industry, academia and business to promote new thinking, education and knowledge sharing.

Supporting practitioners
Through continuing professional development and a series of respected IT qualifications, the Institute seeks to promote professional practice tuned to the demands of business. It provides practical support and information services to its members and volunteer communities around the world.

Setting standards and frameworks
The Institute collaborates with government, industry and relevant bodies to establish good working practices, codes of conduct, skills frameworks and common standards. It also offers a range of consultancy services to employers to help them adopt best practice.

Become a member
Over 70,000 people including students, teachers, professionals and practitioners enjoy the benefits of BCS membership. These include access to an international community, invitations to a roster of local and national events, career development tools and a quarterly thought-leadership magazine. Visit www.bcs.org/membership to find out more.

Further information
BCS, The Chartered Institute for IT,
3 Newbridge Square,
Swindon, SN1 1BY,
United Kingdom.
T +44 (0) 1793 417 417
(Monday to Friday, 09:00 to 17:00 UK time)
www.bcs.org/contact
http://shop.bcs.org/

BUSINESS ANALYSIS
Fourth edition

Debra Paul and James Cadle

Published by BCS Learning and Development Ltd, a wholly owned subsidiary of BCS, The Chartered Institute for IT, 3 Newbridge Square, Swindon, SN1 1BY, UK.
www.bcs.org

Paperback ISBN: 978-1-78017-5102
PDF ISBN: 978-1-78017-5119
ePUB ISBN: 978-1-78017-5126
Kindle ISBN: 978-1-78017-5133

Ebook available

British Cataloguing in Publication Data.
A CIP catalogue record for this book is available at the British Library.

Disclaimer:
The views expressed in this book are of the authors and do not necessarily reflect the views of the Institute or BCS Learning and Development Ltd except where explicitly stated as such. Although every care has been taken by the authors and BCS Learning and Development Ltd in the preparation of the publication, no warranty is given by the authors or BCS Learning and Development Ltd as publisher as to the accuracy or completeness of the information contained within it and neither the authors nor BCS Learning and Development Ltd shall be responsible or liable for any loss or damage whatsoever arising by virtue of such information or any instructions or advice contained within this publication or by any of the aforementioned.

Publisher's acknowledgements
Reviewers: Katie Walsh
Publisher: Ian Borthwick
Commissioning editor: Rebecca Youé
Production manager: Florence Leroy
Project manager: Sunrise Setting Ltd
Copy-editor: Gillian Bourn
Proofreader: Barbara Eastman
Indexer: Matthew Gale
Cover design: Alex Wright
Cover image: iStock/Grafner
Typeset by Lapiz Digital Services, Chennai, India

CONTENTS

LIST OF FIGURES AND TABLES

AUTHORS/CONTRIBUTORS

AUTHORS

Debra Paul

Debra Paul is the Managing Director of Assist Knowledge Development, a training and consultancy company specialising in business analysis and business architecture. Debra co-authored the publications, *Business Analysis*, *Agile and Business Analysis*, *Business Analysis Techniques* and *Delivering Business Analysis*. Debra conducted doctoral research into the role of the business analyst and developed the Business Analysis Service Framework.

Debra is a regular speaker at business seminars and IS industry events and is a Chartered Fellow of BCS. Debra is a founder member of the BA Manager Forum and was the chief architect for the BCS Advanced International Diploma in Business Analysis. She is also a sessional lecturer at Henley Business School.

James Cadle

James Cadle is a Chartered Fellow of BCS and has worked in business analysis and project management for more than 40 years. As a director of Assist Knowledge Development, he has created and presented a range of courses in his specialist subjects. James is a BCS oral examiner and the co-author of several books including *Business Analysis Techniques*, *The Human Touch*, *Developing Information Systems* and *Project Management for Information Systems*.

CONTRIBUTORS

Craig Rollason

Craig Rollason heads up the IT Planning, Performance and PMO team at National Grid. Prior to this role he was head of National Grid's Business Analysis Practice for five years, investing in recruitment, coaching, training and development of business analysis at all levels of the organisation. He has worked across a number of sectors as an analyst including manufacturing, government and utilities. He is a BCS member and was a keynote speaker in 2018 at the Business Analysis Conference Europe, presenting on the topic of building capabilities. Craig contributed to Chapter 2 (The competencies of a business analyst).

Jonathan Hunsley

Jonathan Hunsley has worked in numerous senior business analysis roles across a variety of industries including consultancy, insurance and banking. Jonathan is a director of Assist Knowledge Development and focuses on training, consultancy and mentoring apprentices for the AssistKD IS Business Analysis Apprenticeship programme. His training portfolio includes many Advanced International Diploma modules. Jonathan has presented at several business analysis and business change conferences and seminars. He is a BCS Chartered Member and is also a BCS oral examiner. Jonathan contributed to Chapter 3 (The strategic context for business analysis).

Malcolm Eva

Malcolm Eva has been involved in IS development since 1980, working as a programmer, systems analyst and then business analyst. As well as practising in the public and private sectors, he has taught at Greenwich University, Northampton University and Gloucestershire University, in the Information Systems departments, and spent several years delivering training in business analysis. He is the author of *SSADM – A User's Guide*, co-author with Steve Skidmore of *Introducing Systems Development* and of a number of papers on systems development, business analysis and requirements engineering. He is a BCS examiner in business analysis and solution development. Malcolm contributed to Chapter 5 (Investigating the business situation) and Chapter 10 (Establishing the requirements).

FOREWORD

The very first edition of *Business Analysis* was released in 2006. It is hard to believe that was 14 years ago now, and the business analyst (BA) role has certainly gained greater recognition in that time. Increasingly, companies are recognising that good quality business analysis can be a strategic enabler that contributes towards the successful delivery of change. As the authors quite rightly highlight, core BA skills are in high demand as organisations continually need to adapt in order to survive and thrive in a fast-changing world.

Yet there is still further for us to go as a global BA community. As any practitioner will tell you, even after 14 years of increasing recognition, business analysis is *not* always well-known or understood by stakeholders. This edition tackles this challenge head on with several important additional sections and frameworks. First, the Business Analysis Service Framework is a welcome addition that outlines the suite of services offered by business analysts and provides a suggested value proposition for each service. Thinking from the perspective of the customers and recipients of the business analysis work is crucial as it helps to articulate the benefits. Second, there is a clear acknowledgement that while business analysis is a broad discipline, BA roles themselves vary. Not *every* BA will cover the entire breadth – and some practitioners might specialise in particular areas.

The inclusion of 'T-shaping' will be of interest to both practitioners and teams that are considering future skills development. Specifically highlighting systems thinking, service thinking and design thinking provides a useful steer for those of us looking to develop and hone our skills further and bring in ideas from adjacent disciplines. A number of additional practical techniques have been included too, including the business model canvas, value stream mapping and customer journey mapping to name just a few.

This book has always been at the heart of the BA community and one that practitioners refer to time and time again. I cannot even begin to imagine how many times I have rifled through its pages. This updated edition shows that the BA community is continuing to learn, adapt and evolve. I have no doubt that the book will continue to be an extremely useful resource that will be utilised by new and experienced practitioners alike.

Adrian Reed, CBAP
Blackmetric Business Solutions

ACKNOWLEDGEMENTS

Every edition of Business Analysis benefits from the support offered by many business analysis professionals.

We must first of all thank Donald Yeates for suggesting that we write a book about business analysis all those years ago and for the many subsequent years of collaboration. Donald decided to 'leave the stage' for this edition but we are indebted to him for his longstanding guidance and friendship. In a very similar vein, we are keen to acknowledge the contribution made by Paul Turner to the success of this book. Paul was instrumental in exploring developments such as Business Architecture and Business Modelling, and has been a source of inspiration for us and many other business analysts.

This edition has benefitted from chapter contributions by Malcolm Eva and Craig Rollason, both of whom have been involved with this publication since the first edition. We are delighted that Jonathan Hunsley has provided his extensive experience and knowledge to contribute the strategic context discussion to this edition. We also wish to thank Adrian Reed for providing the foreword to this edition and for the numerous discussions about all matters related to business analysis.

Our colleagues at AssistKD have been a constant source of ideas and information, allowing us to formulate our thinking and never failing to challenge where they feel improvements are needed. We are extremely lucky to work with such a dedicated and supportive team. In particular, for this edition, we wish to thank Nicole Rayner for her terrific drawing skills, Neil Shorter for technical and security support, Peter Thompson for so many insights regarding business analysis and solution development topics, and Alan Paul for the extensive proofreading service that has proved essential during the production of this book. We also appreciate the insights about business analysis and business architecture work gained during numerous in depth conversations with senior consultants at Le Blanc Advies in The Netherlands.

We have benefitted enormously from the support offered by Lawrence Darvill and the BA Manager Forum members, who collectively represent over 200 organisations. There have been so many discussions with senior BA practitioners during Forum events over the last few years and we are indebted to everyone within this community for their ideas and insights. There are too many people to thank individually but we wish to give particular mention to Christina Lovelock, Hilary Catchpole, Ian Richards, David Beckham and Fraser Morris.

From the academic community, Dr Yin Leng Tan, University of Reading, has provided invaluable guidance about service science and other areas of research relevant to business analysis.

Finally, this book could not have been produced without the professional publishing know-how provided by Ian Borthwick and Becky Youé from BCS – we have benefitted greatly from their expertise during this collaboration.

ABBREVIATIONS

3Cs	card, conversation, confirmation
4Ms	manpower, machines, measures and methods or manpower, machines, materials and methods
4Ss	surroundings, suppliers, systems, skills
5Ws	why, what, who, when, where
6Ps	people, place, processes, physical evidence, product/service and performance measures
AI	artificial intelligence
APM	Association for Project Management
BA	business analyst
BAM	business activity model
BAMM	Business Analysis Maturity Model
BASF	Business Analysis Service Framework
BCG	Boston Consulting Group
BCM	business capability model
BMC	business model canvas
BPMN	Business Process Model and Notation
BRD	business requirements document
BSC	balanced scorecard
CARDI (log)	constraints, assumptions, risks, dependencies and issues (log)
CATWOE	Customer, Actor, Transformation, World View (*Weltanschauung*), Owner, Environment
CBAP®	Certified Business Analysis Professional
CCBA®	Certificate of Capability in Business Analysis
CI	configuration item
CIO	chief information officer
CMMI	Capability Maturity Model Integration
COTS	commercial off-the-shelf (software solution)
CPPOLDAT	Customer, Product, Process, Organisation, Location, Data, Applications, Technology
CRM	customer relationship management

CRUD	created, read, updated or deleted
CSF	critical success factor
CX	customer experience
DBMS	database management system
DCF	discounted cash flow
DMAIC	define, measure, analyse, improve, control
DSDM	Dynamic Systems Development Method
EA	enterprise architecture
ECBA™	Entry Certificate in Business Analysis
ERD	entity relationship diagram
GDPR	General Data Protection Regulation
HR	human resources
IIBA®	International Institute of Business Analysis
INVEST	independent, negotiable, valuable, estimatable, small, testable
IRR	internal rate of return
IT	information technology
ITT	invitation to tender
JRP	joint requirements planning
KPI	key performance indicator
MECE	mutually exclusive, completely exhaustive
MoSCoW	must have, should have, could have, want to have, but won't have this time
NPS	net promoter score
NPV	net present value
OMG	Object Management Group
OPOPOT	one person, one place, one time
OSCAR	objectives, scope, constraints, authority, resources
OTT	Over the Top
PESTLE	political, economic, socio-cultural, technological, legal and environmental
PID	project initiation document
PMI	Project Management Institute
POPIT™	People, Organisation, Processes, Information and Technology
RACI (chart)	responsible, accountable, consulted and informed (chart)
RAD	rapid application development
RAG	red, amber, green
RAID (log)	risks, assumptions, issues and dependencies (log)
RASCI (chart)	responsible, accountable, supportive, consulted and informed (chart)
RE	requirements engineering

ROI	return on investment
RoQ	re-order quantity
RPA	robotic process automation
SaaS	software as a service
SARAH	shock, anger, rejection, acceptance, hope
SDLC	systems development lifecycle
SFIA	Skills Framework for the Information Age
SIPOC framework	supplier, input, process, output, customer
SMART	Specific, Measurable, Achievable, Relevant and Time-bound
SME	subject matter expert
SSADM	Structured Systems Analysis and Design Method
SSM	Soft Systems Methodology
SUAVE	stable, unique, abstract, valuable, executives
SWOT	strengths, weaknesses, opportunities, threats
TIMWOODS	transport, inventory, motion, waiting, overproduction, overprocessing, defects, skills
TOGAF	The Open Group architectural framework
TOM	target operating model
ToR	terms of reference
TRM	technology reference model
UML	Unified Modeling Language
UP	unified process
VMOST (analysis)	Vision, Mission, Objectives, Strategy, Tactics (analysis)
VoC	voice of the customer
XP	extreme programming

PREFACE

Business analysis is at a critical point in its development. Despite recognition of the relevance of analytical thinking, questions have been raised for several years about the need for specialist business analysts amid suggestions that anyone can perform this role. Respect for business analysts has increased in many quarters but diminished in others. Comments that 'anyone can call themselves a business analyst' are still made all too frequently but, if this is accurate, where is the place for the professional business analysis practitioner and how does this impact recognition of the business analyst role? Further, what does this say about the work carried out by practising business analysts if they can be so easily dismissed and other roles feel that they could so easily carry out any business analysis themselves?

Clarity of definition is a key issue for many roles but seems to be a particular problem regarding the business analyst role, which has long suffered from ambiguity. Previous editions of this book have set out the landscape for business analysis – describing the areas where a business analyst contributes to change initiatives by offering distinct and much-needed services. However, it sometimes appears that every two steps forward come with one step back. The advent of new ways of working tends to give rise to new roles that promise much, although they are often doomed to fail due to high expectations and the recurring lack of clarity. The ongoing debate about the nature of the product owner role and how it overlaps or dovetails with that of the business analyst offers a good example of role confusion. There are many other examples such as the distinction between business analysts and business architects or solution architects or customer experience analysts. We are awash with roles but, while role identification seems to be very straightforward, clarity of role definition often eludes us.

Organisations across the globe are facing unprecedented rates of change arising from highly disruptive forces that are entirely outside their control. The global coronavirus pandemic is causing organisations to review their services and, in many cases, their entire business models. The use of digital technologies has changed how many people work and raises the potential for new or adapted products and services, where personalisation is a key differentiator. Data analytics offer novel, unexpected insights to which organisations need to respond. Customer-centricity is at the heart of what is offered – taking customers for granted is, thankfully, becoming increasingly unacceptable in today's connected world.

The picture for business analysis is complex. If organisations are to grasp the opportunities and deflect or manage the threats from their external environment, they need to employ analytical thinking skills more than ever and ensure that scarce investment funds are spent wisely. They need to consider the 'what if?' and also the 'what else?' questions if they are to really grasp the potential that digital technologies offer. Our business analysis experiences have confirmed that it is not the case that everyone can offer analytical thinking skills. The techniques used in business analysis are numerous and varied, and have to be applied with expertise if they are to offer innovations and insights, and enable beneficial outcomes. They also need to be accompanied by interpersonal competence and business domain understanding, coupled with the knowledge of how the organisation works.

This edition remains true to the essence of business analysis: the need to explore situations, determine where problems lie, engage with stakeholders, consider options and guide the development of relevant solutions. However, the business analysis landscape is constantly evolving and maturing so some topics have been introduced while others have been replaced. Key examples include:

- The introduction of the BA service and the service thinking world view.
- The recognition of digital technology and the impact upon business analysis.
- The integration of the Agile mindset and philosophy into business analysis approaches.
- The reference to contextual issues and the importance of adaptability to different contexts.

There remains a huge challenge for business analysts but this is accompanied by infinite opportunity. The frameworks, concepts, techniques and approaches described in this book offer a toolkit for business analysts. Our aim is to equip business analysts with the tools that will enable them to offer a clear value proposition and deliver the business analysis service their organisations need.

Debra Paul
James Cadle
July 2020

1 WHAT IS BUSINESS ANALYSIS?

INTRODUCTION

Business analysis aims to ensure that any business changes align with the needs of the organisation and are holistic, taking all relevant aspects into account. It is an important discipline that has evolved over several decades and offers a range of business improvement services. This book provides guidance to support professional business analysts and reflects the breadth of business analysis work, including the activities carried out and the extensive range of techniques used. The aim is to help business analysts deliver effective, relevant business analysis services, improve the quality of their business analysis work and, as a result, help organisations to deploy business improvements that ensure business success.

THE ORIGINS OF BUSINESS ANALYSIS

Developments in information technology (IT) have enabled organisations to create information systems that have improved business operations and management decision-making. In the past, this has been the focus of IT departments. However, as business operations have changed, the emphasis has moved onto the development of new services and products. The questions that now need to be asked are 'What can technology offer to enhance our portfolio of products and services?' and 'What needs to change in the organisation if the benefits from a new or enhanced IT system are to be realised?'

Technology has enabled new business models to be implemented through more flexible communication mechanisms that enable organisations to engage directly with customers, connect with suppliers and support global operations. The use of technology has also created opportunities for organisations to focus on their core capabilities without being distracted by peripheral areas of business requiring specialist capability. Established organisations that apply technology to enable and support well-defined enterprise architectures (EAs) are likely to develop significant competitive advantage while new organisations can gain considerable market share by investing in EAs that apply technology innovatively.

However, for many years there has been a growing dissatisfaction in businesses with the support provided by technology and the professional change and technology disciplines. This has been accompanied by a recognition on the part of senior management that investments in technology and change often fail to deliver the required business outcomes. While technology has the potential to deliver business improvements, it is often the case that the business requirements are not met in a timely fashion, resulting in limited competitive advantage to the organisation. *The Financial Times* reported in 2013 that this situation applies to all sectors, with IT projects continuing to overrun their budgets by significant amounts and poor communication between business and technical experts remaining problematic (Mance, 2013). The perception that, all too frequently, information systems do not deliver the predicted benefits continues to be well founded.

THE DEVELOPMENT OF BUSINESS ANALYSIS

The impact of outsourcing

In a drive to reduce costs, and sometimes in recognition of a lack of IT expertise at senior management level, many organisations have outsourced their IT services to specialist IT service providers rather than employ their own internal IT staff. This approach has been based upon the belief that specialist providers, often working in countries where costs are lower than the UK, are able to deliver higher quality at lower cost. In organisations that have outsourced their IT function, the IT systems are designed, constructed and delivered using staff employed by an external supplier. This has advantages for both the organisation purchasing the services and the specialist supplier. The latter gains an additional customer and the opportunity to increase turnover and make profit from the contractual arrangement; the customer organisation is no longer concerned with all the staffing, infrastructure and support issues and instead pays a specialist provider for delivery of the required service.

In theory this approach has much to recommend it but organisations with an outsourced IT function have experienced issues, for example, regarding supplier management and requirements definition. The issues relating to supplier management are not the subject of this book, and would require a book in their own right. However, the communication and clarification of requirements is key to ensuring the success of any IT system development and an outsourcing arrangement often complicates the communication process, particularly where there is geographical distance between the developers and the business. A breakdown in communicating requirements typically results in the delivered IT systems failing to provide the required level of support for the business.

The outsourcing business model has undoubtedly been a catalyst for the development of the business analysis function as more and more organisations recognise the importance of business representation during the development and implementation of IT systems.

Competitive advantage using IT

A parallel development that helped to increase the profile of business analysis and the business analyst role has been the growing recognition that three factors need to be present in order for IT systems to deliver competitive advantage. First, the needs of the business must drive the development of the IT systems; second, the implementation of an IT system must be accompanied by the necessary business changes; and, third, the requirements for IT systems must be defined and understood. While the advent of iterative systems development has provided a basis for deferring the detailed definition of the requirements to later in the development process, it is still important that there is sufficient understanding of the requirements prior to beginning this. All three of these factors must be addressed if the challenges facing business today are to be met.

The business change lifecycle

The need to adopt a broader view of business change rather than focusing purely on the IT element has been recognised by organisations for many years. The business change lifecycle reflects this, highlighting the need to ensure that change programmes focus on aligning with, and meeting, business needs. An overview representation of the business change lifecycle is shown in Figure 1.1.

Figure 1.1 The business change lifecycle (© Assist Knowledge Development Ltd.)

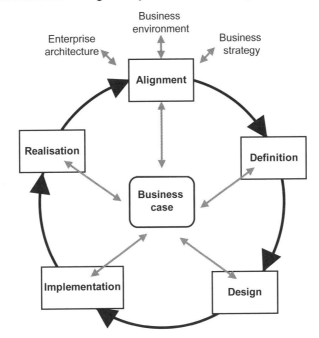

The early part of the business change lifecycle is concerned with ensuring alignment of business change initiatives with the external business environment and the EA and business strategy for the organisation. This provides a context for defining the change requirements that is based upon an analysis of the business situation and requirements in order to determine new ways of working that will improve the organisation's efficiency and effectiveness. Later business change activities are concerned with change design and development, business acceptance testing and, post implementation, benefits review and realisation.

Clearly, effective analysis is required throughout the lifecycle if the proposed changes are to be successful and deliver the desired benefits. The analysis work falls within the remit of business analysis yet, in many organisations, a coherent approach to business change, that necessitates the involvement of business analysts, remains unavailable. As a result, it is often the case that the business needs are not well understood, the requirements are unclear or ill-defined, and there is misalignment between them. All too often the focus, almost from the outset, is on a preferred technical solution rather than on understanding the problem to be addressed. The hasty selection of 'solutions' is often coupled with a lack of alignment of the proposed changes and can result in a failure to deliver business benefits and, accordingly, a waste of investment funds.

Business analysts as internal consultants

Many organisations use external consultants to provide expert advice throughout the business change lifecycle. The reasons are clear: they can be employed to deal with a specific issue on an 'as-needed basis' and they bring a broader business perspective and can provide a dispassionate, objective view of the company. On the other hand, the use of external consultants is often criticised, across all sectors, because of the lack of accountability and the absence of any transfer of skills from the external consultants to internal staff. Cost is also a key issue. Consultancy firms often charge daily fee rates that are considerably higher than the charge levied for an internal business analyst and while some firms provide consultants with a broad range of expertise steeped in best practice, this is not always guaranteed.

The experiences gained from using external consultants have also played a part in the development of the internal business analysis role. Many business analysts have argued that they can provide the services provided by external consultants and can, in effect, operate as internal consultants. Reasons for using internal business analysts as consultants, apart from lower costs, include speed (internal consultants do not have to spend time learning about the organisation) and the retention of knowledge within the organisation. These factors have been recognised as particularly important for projects where the objectives concern the achievement of business benefit through the use of IT as a prime enabler of business change. As a result, while external consultants are used for many business purposes, the majority of business analysts are employed by their organisations. These analysts may lack an external viewpoint across organisations but they are knowledgeable about the particular business domain and crucially have to live with the impact of the actions they recommend. Consequently, there have been increasing numbers of business analysts working as internal consultants over the last decade.

BUSINESS ANALYST ROLE DEVELOPMENT

The delivery of predicted business benefits promised from the use of technology and the implementation of IT systems has proved to be extremely difficult, with factors such as the outsourcing of IT services and the focus on technical rather than business solutions, serving to add complication to already complex situations. The potential exists for organisations to deploy technology as a means of gaining competitive advantage and yet this often appears to be just out of reach. Limited budgets are often spent on technology and change initiatives that fail to deliver the predicted benefits or, even worse, result in increasing levels of investment with little to show for it. Where software products are built or purchased that have the potential to meet business needs, they may not be deemed successful because changes to the broader business system have not been established, resulting in the emergence of further issues or a failure to address some of the root causes of problems.

For several decades, it has been apparent that business managers require support in analysing where their business areas need to change. Using investment funds wisely and delivering the business benefits predicted from IT and business change initiatives have become increasingly necessary for the survival of organisations. This is particularly the case given a global economic environment where budgets are limited and wasting financial resources carries significant risks for an organisation. There has also been increasing recognition that organisations need to take a holistic view when addressing business problems. A focus on technology without consideration of the broader business system has been accepted as one of the key reasons for dissatisfaction with IT projects.

These factors have led directly to the development of the business analyst role and the allocation of business system thinking responsibilities to this role. However, the development of the business analyst role has not been straightforward. Organisations have assigned business analysts to a variety of tasks and the expectations from the role have been inconsistent and unclear. Definitions provided by professional bodies have been vague, ambiguous and open to interpretation. Agile approaches, such as Scrum,[1] have questioned where and whether the business analyst is a necessary role for business change and IT projects. The rise of digital technologies has caused the skills possessed by business analysts to be questioned in the light of new and pressing requirements for the use of these technologies in business. While many organisations employ business analysts, there persists a lack of clarity about what the role entails. This issue needs to be addressed urgently.

Role clarity for business analysts

Clarity is extremely important for any role. Without such clarity, roles are misunderstood and there is a lack of awareness of what practitioners do and are able to offer. The 'customers' working with practitioners of ill-defined roles do not know what activities and behaviours to expect. This confusion can lead to dissatisfaction, an unwillingness to collaborate and disappointing outcomes.

Recognition of business analysis as a distinct and important discipline continues to be limited across the business community and this has been affected by the lack of role clarity. There are many misconceptions about business analysis and a lack of awareness of the contribution business analysts might make, raising questions such as:

- What do business analysts do?
- What skills do they require?
- How do they add value to organisations?

In the absence of a standard definition of the business analysis role and value proposition, problems have arisen:

- Uncertainty within organisations about where and how business analysis capability is best deployed. Many have introduced business analysis to make sure that business needs are paramount when new IT systems are introduced and that there is a holistic approach to business and IT change. However, recognising the importance of this in principle is easier than ensuring that it is achieved. Many business analysts report a continuing drive towards software solutions, whether developed in-house or purchased, without there being a clear understanding of the desired business outcomes.

- An understanding of the contribution business analysts may make within different change environments. The introduction of iterative ways of working, such as when using Agile approaches, has raised questions about the need for business analysts and has introduced uncertainty about whether or not a specific business analyst role is required within Agile development projects.

- The increasing need for business analysts to have strong technological and data skills given the advent of digital technologies and the change requirements they generate. Many business analysts have a business background and accordingly may have a limited understanding of these areas.

- The establishment of change projects without first ensuring that the issues to be addressed are understood, which has caused organisations to reject or ignore business analysts' advice. Many proficient business analysts, typically with extensive experience and knowledge, have felt that they could offer beneficial advice to their organisations but have been denied the opportunity to do this.

The definition of the business analyst role is a major issue, not only for business analysts themselves but also for the organisations that employ them. Empirical research into business analysis based on formal qualitative interviews and meetings (Paul, 2018), plus informal discussions with several hundred business analysts, across a range of business forums, have established that there is often ambiguity about the business analyst role and that this has contributed in no small measure to the lack of recognition that the role receives. This lack of role clarity has also meant that the potential benefits offered by business analysis capability is often overlooked and business analysts may be limited to work activities that do not exploit their full potential.

The Business Analysis Service Framework (BASF) (Paul, 2018) proposes an outline service catalogue that encompasses:

- The services provided by business analysts and the value proposition for each service.

- The activities conducted by business analysts in the delivery of these services. Much of this book provides guidance on how the services in the BASF may be carried out.

- The key techniques used to conduct each service. There are numerous business analysis techniques used during change projects and new techniques continue to emerge. Some techniques have been in use for far longer than the business analyst role has existed while others have been adapted having been used by other disciplines. For example, the strategy analysis techniques described in Chapter 3 have been used by senior executives for many years but understanding these techniques is beneficial for anyone working on business change projects.

This chapter examines business analysis as a specialist profession, considers how a service view can offer a clear definition of the business analyst role and introduces the BASF. Chapter 4 describes the BASF in further detail.

THE RANGE OF ANALYSIS ACTIVITIES

The term 'analysis' is used in many contexts and with regard to several different roles. Figure 1.2 shows three analysis disciplines that may be considered to be within the business analysis landscape.

Figure 1.2 The potential range of the business analyst role

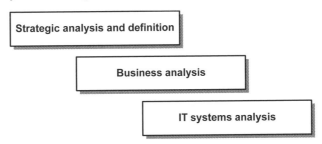

Inevitably, there are areas where these three disciplines overlap. For example, consultants may specialise in strategic analysis but also get involved in business process redesign to make a reality of their strategies, and good systems analysts have always understood the need to understand the overall business context of the systems they are developing. However, it is useful to examine them separately in order to consider their relevance to the business analyst role.

Strategic analysis and definition

Strategic analysis and definition is typically the work of senior management, often supported by business consultants, and is outside the remit of business analysts. While some business analysts may be required to undertake strategic analysis and identify business transformation actions, it is more likely that they are required to support this activity.

Business analysts often have to recommend, design and deploy the tactics that are needed to execute the business objectives and strategy; these typically concern the process and IT system solutions. Therefore, they need to understand the strategy analysis process and outcomes, and should be able to work within the strategic context for their organisations. This context encompasses the architectural domains that support the governance of an organisation and enable its growth. The business applications and data architectures are of particular relevance to business analysts as they need to ensure that these architectural domains support and align with any business change proposals. Business analysts have to work closely with their colleagues from the architectural disciplines and need to understand the impact of the architectural definitions.

It is also the case that some business analyst roles require strategic level thinking. The opportunities presented by digital technologies and the use of technology to enable business improvements need to be considered when conducting strategy analysis. Business analysts should offer specialist skills and be able to advise on the use of technology to drive business change. Again, this should be in collaboration with colleagues from the architectural disciplines.

Given these issues, while strategic analysis is not a core activity within business analysis, business analysts need a good understanding of how strategy is developed, the impact upon the enterprise and related architectures, and how it may be executed by technological and business changes. Chapter 3 discusses the strategic context for business analysis.

IT systems analysis

The long-established discipline of IT systems analysis is at the other end of the analysis spectrum shown in Figure 1.2. The systems analyst role has been in existence for several decades although the term 'systems analyst' tends to be used less often these days. Systems analysts are responsible for analysing and specifying the IT system requirements in sufficient detail to provide a basis for the evaluation of software products or the development of a bespoke IT system. Typically, systems analysis work involves the use of techniques such as data, process and event modelling, and requires detailed understanding of non-functional requirements and how they should be specified. This work is focused on describing the software requirements so the products of systems analysis define the data the IT system must hold, the processing to be applied to that data and the operation of the user interface.

Some organisations and individuals consider systems analysis to be of a technical nature to the extent that they perceive it to be completely outside the province of the business analyst. They have separated the business and IT analysts into different functions, with the latter having the responsibility for carrying out the detailed IT systems modelling and specification. Sometimes a technical business analyst role has been created where the primary focus is on the IT aspects of any business change project. Other organisations employ digital business analysts with a remit to focus on the use of digital technology. Variants of the business analyst role are discussed later in this chapter.

The essential difference between business analysis and IT systems analysis is that a business analyst has a business outcome focus and a systems analyst has a software focus. Business analysts are responsible for considering a range of business options to address a particular problem or opportunity; on the other hand, an IT business analyst, technical business analyst or systems analyst works within a defined scope and considers options for the software element of the business change solution.

The distinction is not always clear though and the advent of Agile approaches has often resulted in the restructuring of IT and change roles within organisations. This is discussed later in this chapter.

Business analysis

If the two analysis disciplines described above define the limits of analysis work, the area in the middle is the remit of business analysis. This is reflected in Figure 1.2, which shows the potential scope and extent of business analysis work. Typically, a situation or project is identified where changes are required and analysis is needed to determine the nature of those changes. However, the range and focus of any improvements can vary considerably, and may include the following:

- Investigation into a localised business issue. In such a case, the business analysts would need to recommend actions that would overcome a specific problem and achieve stated business benefits.

- A study with a broad business focus, requiring investigation into several issues or ideas for increased efficiency or effectiveness. Such work may necessitate wide-ranging analysis of the business area. The business analysts would need to make recommendations for business changes and these would need to be supported by a business case that evaluates the various options.

- The enhancement or replacement of an existing software product to meet new business requirements. In this case, the business analysts need to define the features and requirements to be delivered by the new product. The requirements may be defined in detail or at a more overview level, depending upon the software development approach adopted. It may also be the case that a software solution has been identified by stakeholders that the business analyst is required to evaluate for 'fit' with the business needs.

- The improvement of an entire work stream, probably using a service view and value realisation approach. This work is likely to require the business analysts to work with several processes and software applications and to apply a wide range of business and analytical skills including stakeholder relationship management.

Whichever situation applies, a business analysis assignment usually begins with the analyst gaining an understanding of the business situation in hand. A problem may have been defined in very specific terms and a possible solution identified, but in practice it is rare that the entire or actual problem has been identified and it is even less likely that any proposed solution will address all of the issues. More commonly, there is a more general set of problems that require a wide-ranging focus and in-depth investigation. Sometimes, the first step is to clarify the problem to be solved; without this, the analyst may examine the wrong area and identify unhelpful solutions. In the majority of situations, the business analyst needs to take a holistic view and consider all aspects, including the business processes, software products, job roles and employee skills that are needed to improve the situation successfully. Business analysis services such as situation investigation and problem definition, business process improvement and requirements definition may need to be delivered to identify the required business changes.

BUSINESS ANALYSIS PRINCIPLES

The key principles that underlie business analysis define the priorities for conducting business analysis work:

- **Root causes not symptoms:**
  - To distinguish between the symptoms of problems and the root causes.
  - To investigate and address the root causes of business problems.
  - To consider the holistic view.
- **Business improvement not IT system change:**
  - To recognise that IT systems should enable business opportunity or problem resolution.
  - To analyse opportunities for business improvement.
  - To enable business innovation and customer experience enhancement.
- **Options not solutions:**
  - To challenge pre-determined solutions.
  - To identify and evaluate options for meeting business needs.
- **Feasible, contributing requirements, not meeting all requests:**
  - To be aware of financial and timescale constraints.
  - To identify requirements that are not feasible and do not contribute to business objectives.
  - To evaluate stated requirements against business needs and constraints.
- **The entire business change lifecycle not just requirements definition:**
  - To analyse business situations.
  - To support the effective development, testing, deployment and post-implementation review of solutions.
  - To support the management and realisation of business benefits.
- **Negotiation not avoidance:**
  - To recognise conflicting stakeholder views and requirements.
  - To negotiate conflicts between stakeholders.

These principles clarify why business analysis is so relevant in today's business world and set out the responsibilities that business analysts should recognise and accept. The principles are underpinned by two key approaches:

- the holistic approach;
- the Agile philosophy.

The holistic approach

There is widespread agreement that business analysis requires the application of a holistic approach. Although the business analyst performs a key role in supporting management's exploitation of technology to obtain business benefit, this has to be done within the context of the entire business system. This means all aspects of the operational business system need to be analysed if the entire range of opportunities for business improvement are to be determined.

The POPIT™ model in Figure 1.3 shows the different views that must be considered when analysing business improvements and identifying required business changes.

Figure 1.3 The POPIT model showing the views of a business system (© Assist Knowledge Development Ltd.)

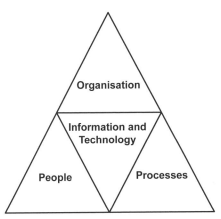

This model represents the different aspects, and the correspondences between them, that business analysts need to consider when analysing a business system. Example questions that should be asked about each area are shown below.

- **The processes:** Are they efficient, well defined and communicated? Do they meet the performance measures expected by customers? Is there good technology support or are there several 'workarounds' in existence? Do the processes require information or documents to be passed around the organisation unnecessarily? Is there the potential for delays or the introduction of errors?

- **The people:** Do they have the required skills and support to carry out the work? How motivated are they? Do they understand the business objectives that they need to support?

- **The organisation:** Are roles and responsibilities well defined? Is there a supportive management style? Is there collaborative cross-functional working? Does the culture enable productive work?

- **The information:** Do the staff have the information to conduct their work effectively? How is this information accessed? Are managers able to make decisions based on accurate and timely information?

- **The technology:** Do the software products support the business as required? Are they usable and accessible? Do they enable the organisation to meet staff and customer needs?

All of these areas should be analysed to uncover where problems lie and what improvements might be necessary if the business is to become more effective and efficient. A holistic view ensures that all aspects of the business system under investigation are considered and also supports the review of the linkages between these aspects. It is often the case that the primary focus of the business analysis work is on the software product, sometimes in conjunction with the analysis of the relevant business processes. However, even where there are effective business processes in place and high-quality software support is available, problems are likely to persist if issues with staffing, such as skills shortages, or the organisation, such as management style, have not been addressed.

A holistic approach can also address situations where a short-term administrative solution is needed. Organisations often have to respond rapidly to changing environmental circumstances and this can mean that there isn't the luxury of sufficient time to develop a fully automated solution. For example, a customer service problem may be overcome initially by defining a manual procedure or training members of staff. These solutions may then be superseded later by longer term, possibly more costly, solutions once any urgent business issues have been addressed.

Business analysis places an emphasis on improving the operation of the entire business system. While technology may enable improvements to the business operations, other possibilities also need to be considered. The focus should be on addressing business issues and achieving beneficial business outcomes rather than just using technology for technology's sake. Where business analysts think holistically, they are more likely to offer innovative ideas that deliver genuine business improvements and offer prudent investment of scarce financial resources.

Agile software development

Agile is a software development approach that emerged in the late 1990s following the advent of methods such as rapid application development (RAD), extreme programming (XP) and the Dynamic Systems Development Method (DSDM – now known as the DSDM Agile Project Framework). The application of Agile methods evolved as a reaction to the perceived shortcomings of the linear development lifecycles, in particular, their emphasis on completing each stage before moving on to the subsequent stage.

The Agile philosophy encompasses key principles and concepts including collaborative working, iterative software development and incremental software delivery. It does not support or require detailed definitions of requirements but instead uses evolutionary development techniques, such as prototyping, to explore outline product requirements in collaboration with end users. It is essential that business analysts understand these key principles and that they are able to adapt their skills and toolkit as necessary.

The Agile Manifesto,[2] which was published in 2001, states:

We are uncovering better ways of developing software by doing it and helping others do it. Through this work we have come to value:

Individuals and interactions over processes and tools

Working software over comprehensive documentation

Customer collaboration over contract negotiation

Responding to change over following a plan

That is, while there is value in the items on the right, we value the items on the left more.

Agile methods offer defined ways of working that embody the philosophy of the Agile Manifesto. However, organisations and projects tend to adapt their software development approach, even where a specific method is the prescribed standard, because of the context variables that exist (see Chapter 13). There is always a need for flexibility and adaptability, to ensure that the approach, techniques, deliverables and working practices are relevant and to vary them if required.

There has been much debate about the business analyst role within an Agile development environment. Some authors have suggested that there isn't a need for business analysts on Agile projects given that Agile development teams encompass co-located roles so enable ongoing conversations between developers and business staff. However, this is to overlook the investigative, analytical and modelling skills provided by professional business analysts and their ability to uncover tacit knowledge, challenge tacit assumptions and analyse scenarios and impacts.

Early engagement business analysis is essential to uncover the root causes of business problems and define the business requirements. It is also needed to support the definition, development and deployment of the solution. Within a software development team, the business analysts help the business staff to clarify, elaborate and prioritise their requirements at various points during the development process. Furthermore, they bring business domain knowledge and insight, and are able to ensure any proposed requirements align with the strategic business context.

Where organisations apply Agile methods, the product owner is the designated business representative who works alongside the development team. This raises further questions about the role of the business analyst, in particular about the relationship with the product owner role. The following alternative organisational models are typical:

- The business analyst works closely with the product owner to analyse the required features and also with the development team to clarify the detailed requirements as they evolve during the development process.

- The business analyst performs the product owner role, representing the organisation with regard to the development of the product and also providing analysis skills.

- The business analyst role is subsumed within the development team while the product owner represents the organisation and guides the development team's work.

Organisations need effective business analysis if change projects are to be successful in addressing business problems and developing solutions that meet business needs. Ultimately, this should be the aim of all business change and IT projects, and the way in which the projects are undertaken should be decided in line with the particular context. This contextual view is reflected in practice with some organisations, or projects, adopting an Agile approach while others apply linear lifecycles, such as the waterfall lifecycle or 'V' model. Any business analysts working within organisations where a linear approach is applied would still benefit from having an understanding of the Agile philosophy, principles and methods as they offer a range of techniques and skills that aid flexibility and adaptability when carrying out business analysis work.

While the Agile Manifesto and methods focus on software development, the stated philosophy and principles are also relevant within a broader business change context. Understanding that requirements can be defined at different levels and that the detail will tend to evolve, is helpful whether developing a software product, designing a business process, creating a new service or manufacturing a piece of equipment. Anyone who has needed to update a property or install a new kitchen will know that the detailed requirements often emerge later in the day. Why should requirements for software products or other business changes be any different?

THE BUSINESS ANALYSIS MATURITY MODEL

Business analysis began to emerge as a new discipline in the late 1980s and since this time has traversed a maturity development trajectory. The Business Analysis Maturity Model™ (BAMM) shown in Figure 1.4 was developed by Assist Knowledge Development to represent the development and maturity pathway for the business analysis discipline.

Figure 1.4 The Business Analysis Maturity Model™ (© Assist Knowledge Development Ltd.)

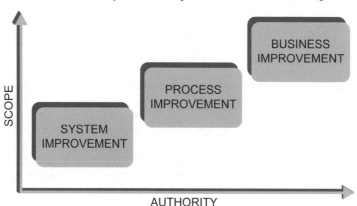

This model summarises information gained from discussions with several hundred, if not thousands, of business analysts working for numerous organisations across the UK, Europe and beyond. These business analysts have come from different backgrounds – some from IT, many from business areas – and have brought different skills and knowledge to their business analysis teams. The BAMM uses two axes: the scope of the work allocated to the business analyst and the authority level of the business analyst. The scope may be very specific if an initial study has identified the required course of action and the analyst now needs to explore and define a solution in greater detail. Alternatively, the scope may have been defined at only an overview level, or may be very ambiguous, with the business analyst having to carry out detailed investigation to uncover the issues before the options can be explored. The level of authority of the business analyst can also vary considerably, from a limited level of authority to the ability to influence and guide at senior management level.

The BAMM shows three levels of maturity during the development of business analysis. The first level is where the business analysis work is concerned with defining the requirements for an IT system improvement. At this level, the scope is likely to be well defined and the level of authority limited to the project on which the business analyst works. The next level is where the business analysis work has moved beyond a specific IT development so that the analysts work cross-functionally to improve the business processes that give rise to the requirements. The third level is where the scope and authority of the analysts are at their greatest. Here, the business analysis work is concerned with improving the business and working with senior management to support the delivery of value to customers.

These levels of maturity apply to three perspectives on business analysis: the individual analysts, the business analysis community within an organisation, and the business analysis profession as a whole. At each level, the techniques, skills and standards applied and the measures used to evaluate the work, can vary considerably. One of the points often raised about the BAMM is the link to the Capability Maturity Model Integration (CMMI). The CMMI[3] was developed by the Software Engineering Institute at Carnegie Mellon University and is an approach used for process improvement in organisations. When the BAMM is reviewed against the CMMI, it can be seen that the five levels of the CMMI apply at each level, for example:

- An organisation that is developing its business analysis practice may employ business analysts who are chiefly employed on requirements definition work. In doing this, the analysts may initially have to develop their own process and standards for each piece of work; therefore they would be at the system improvement level of the BAMM and the initial level of the CMMI, where work is likely to be carried out in an ad hoc manner.
- By contrast, an organisation that has employed business analysts for some time may have analysts that can work at all three levels of the BAMM. The analysts working at the business improvement level may have a defined process, standards and measures that are managed for each assignment. These business analysts are working at the managed level of the CMMI.

It is also useful to consider a version of CMMI, specifically adapted to evaluate the maturity of a business analysis service. This is an internal function that offers business analysis services within an organisation (Paul and Lovelock, 2019). Figure 1.5 shows a possible approach to this maturity assessment.

15

Figure 1.5 CMMI adapted for business analysis

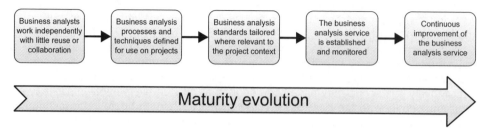

| Business analysts work independently with little reuse or collaboration | Business analysis processes and techniques defined for use on projects | Business analysis standards tailored where relevant to the project context | The business analysis service is established and monitored | Continuous improvement of the business analysis service |

Maturity evolution

THE BUSINESS ANALYSIS SERVICE

A clear definition of the role and responsibilities of a business analyst is needed if the role is to be recognised within organisations and the benefits of engaging business analysts is to be appreciated. Service science, management, engineering and design (abbreviated to 'service science') is an area of research concerned with examining the nature of 'service' and how entities, known as service systems, interact to co-create value from the delivery of service. Service science clarifies what is meant by 'value' and how value may be realised through the provision of service. The service perspective, often referred to as 'service thinking' in a business context, emphasises the importance of customer collaboration, so corresponds well with the nature of business analysis work.

A service view provides a strong basis for defining the business analyst role. The advantage of applying service thinking and adopting a service view is that a complex role, such as business analyst, may be clarified through the definition of a portfolio of services and understanding the key elements for each service. These are shown in Table 1.1.

Table 1.1 The definition of a service

Element	Description
Why?	The rationale for the service, in particular, the value proposition offered to customers
What?	The activities needed to perform the service in line with the stated value proposition
How?	The techniques and standards applied when performing the activities of the service

The nature of value is a key concern of service thinking. Service science clarifies that value is determined by the recipients of a service and, therefore, cannot be said to be 'delivered'. While a product or service may be delivered to customers, the realisation of value cannot be guaranteed as it does not result purely from the 'delivery'. This means an internal service provider, such as the business analysis (BA) service, cannot guarantee that value is delivered as a result of business analysis being performed.

A business analysis service portfolio should be defined such that the value proposition for each service is stated clearly. Each value proposition should inform business analysis customers about the intended beneficial outcomes from a given service. However, a statement of proposed value or intended outcomes is not a guarantee of value achievement. Value is always co-created by a service provider and customer working collaboratively. Accordingly, the realisation of value from business analysis imposes responsibilities on customers as well as the business analysts.

Figure 1.6 shows the three activities in the business analysis value co-creation process. Each activity requires the business analysts and their customers to work together to ensure that value is co-created.

Figure 1.6 Value co-creation process for business analysis (Source: Paul, 2018, © Debra Paul)

The three activities in Figure 1.6 enable the realisation of value from business analysis and focus on:

- Identifying the potential for value: investigating business problems and opportunities to identify options for beneficial change.

- Developing a potentially valuable solution: designing and creating a selected solution that has the potential to deliver benefits to the organisation.

- Embedding the solution within the organisation: supporting the deployment of a solution to ensure that a solution is used by the business staff to conduct their work and that benefits are realised.

Each of these stages reflects the need for value to be co-created and that it is achieved through collaboration between the business analysts and their customers.

The Business Analysis Service Framework

Research into business analysis (Paul, 2018) has identified that there is a suite of services offered by business analysts. Figure 1.7 shows the services of the BASF.

Figure 1.7 The BASF services (Source: Paul, 2018, © Debra Paul)

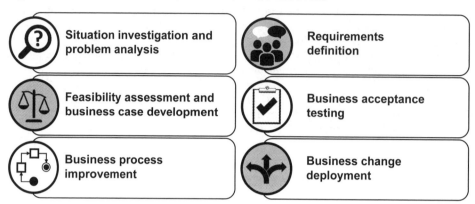

The BASF provides a basis for defining business analysis and the role of the business analyst as follows:

Business analysis is a specialist service that co-creates value for organisations through offering the following services:

- Situation investigation and problem analysis.

- Feasibility assessment and business case development.

- Business process improvement.

- Requirements definition.

- Business acceptance testing.

- Business change deployment.

These services are discussed in further detail in Chapter 4.

Some business analysts may perform work that is beyond the core services. Two additional services to accommodate such work are:

- **Strategy analysis and execution**: The business analysts work closely with senior management to help define the most effective business system to implement elements of the business strategy.

- **IT requirements specification**: The business analysts use modelling techniques, such as those from the Unified Modeling Language (UML), to specify functional and non-functional requirements.

While these services may be considered to be more relevant to other roles, such as management consultants (strategy analysis and execution) or systems analysts (IT requirements specification), there are organisational contexts where they may be carried out by business analysts.

VARIANTS OF THE BUSINESS ANALYST ROLE

The development of the business analyst role has led to the rise of variants, each of which imposes certain responsibilities, scope and focus. While the BASF sets out the core services offered by an internal BA Service, the ways in which these services form the basis for business analyst roles vary across organisations.

In some organisations, business analysts specialise in delivering a specific service or a subset of the services; in other organisations, business analysts may be required to have the skills to deliver any of the services, depending upon what is required by a particular assignment. For example, some organisations employ business analysts who specialise in feasibility assessment and business case development because this is particularly relevant to the work of their organisation; others allocate business analysts to change initiatives and expect them to adapt their work as necessary, which may extend into areas such as strategic or systems analysis as discussed earlier.

The extensive business analysis landscape and the emergence of technological and socio-cultural developments has led to the creation of several business analysis roles, each of which is a variant that focuses upon the delivery of particular services. Typical variants of the business analyst role are described in Table 1.2.

Table 1.2 Typical business analyst role variants

Role name	Description
Business BA / Enterprise business analyst	A business analyst role where the focus is on understanding the business situations to be improved and the business requirements to be met. This work is likely to require engagement with senior stakeholders as well as those at more junior levels and a focus on business system redesign. Requirements are defined from a business solution perspective and may be modelled using conceptual models such as business use case diagrams.
Technical business analyst / Business systems analyst	A business analyst role where the focus is on analysing the solution requirements and supporting the development of the software product. Where necessary, requirements may be specified using techniques to model system features (use case diagrams), data (class diagrams/entity relationship diagrams) and events (state machines and sequence diagrams).

(Continued)

Table 1.2 (Continued)

Role name	Description
Digital business analyst	A business analyst role that is concerned with the opportunities digital technologies offer organisations, both to improve operations and enhance the personalisation and customisation of customer services and experience. This role requires extensive understanding of the business domain, customer experience requirements and technology. The emergence of digital technologies has enabled extensive organisational change and has challenged existing ways of working. Business analysts are well positioned to exploit this trend. While core business analysis offers the fundamental skills required to exploit digital technologies, these need to be extended to engage with technology, data, innovation and a customer-centric service perspective. This trend connects to the IT systems analyst role, which has always required greater technical competence and understanding. However, the digital BA role extends beyond systems analysis and needs to embrace the pace of change, the opportunities provided by digital technologies, the availability of data and the insights offered by data analytics, and the focus upon enabling excellent customer experiences. Digital BAs need to think innovatively and embrace thinking approaches such as systems thinking, service thinking and design thinking.
Project business analyst	A business analyst role where the focus is on developing the software product. This typically involves elaborating user stories in collaboration with business staff and product developers. This role may also require the application of a range of techniques in order to elaborate and clarify business rules and non-functional requirements relevant to the software product.
Proxy product owner	A role where a business analyst takes responsibility for the management of the backlog of product requirements and features. This is the business representative during the development of a product who should be empowered to make decisions about the product, such as the priority of required features, on the organisation's behalf. This role is established within Agile software development environments.

Many organisations differentiate between different business analyst roles in line with those shown in Table 1.2. For example, an organisation may employ both 'technical' business analysts and 'business' business analysts, with the technical business analysts often performing a role more akin to that of a systems analyst. Another organisation may employ business analysts at enterprise and project levels; other organisations may set up a specialist team of digital business analysts to work on specific projects where the focus is on securing the advantages offered by technological innovations for the organisation. These variants reflect the broad landscape for business analysis and the extensive skill set possessed by many professional business analysts.

PROFESSIONALISM AND BUSINESS ANALYSIS

Business analysis has developed a great deal over the last three decades, to the extent that it is often referred to as a 'profession' and many practitioners view themselves as having a professional business analysis career. The factors that support professionalism in business analysis are as follows:

- **Professional body**: A body with responsibility for defining technical standards and the code of conduct, developing certifications and promoting the profession where possible. A professional body may remove membership from those who fail to comply with the behavioural standards required by the code of conduct. The major professional bodies for business analysts are BCS, the Chartered Institute for IT[4] and the International Institute of Business Analysis (IIBA®).[5]

- **Qualifications**: It is increasingly the case that organisations require business analysts to hold qualifications. These qualifications recognise the knowledge and expertise of individual business analysts and are recognised by employing organisations. Many business analysts hold qualifications such as:

  - BCS certifications: BCS offers a certification pathway for business analysts, which provides qualifications from entry level to expert. These include the BCS International Diploma in Business Analysis and the BCS Advanced International Diploma in Business Analysis.

  - IIBA certifications: IIBA offers a range of core qualifications including the Certified Business Analysis Professional (CBAP®), Certificate of Capability in Business Analysis (CCBA®) and Entry Certificate in Business Analysis (ECBA™), and specialist qualifications including the Agile Analysis Certification (IIBA-AAC) and Certification in Business Data Analytics (IIBA CBDA).

  - Business Analysis Manager Forum (BAMF): The seniority of some business analysts has also been recognised by the introduction of the Expert BA Award offered by the BA Manager Forum[6] (and endorsed by BCS).

  The BCS International Diploma in Business Analysis, the BCS Advanced International Diploma in Business Analysis and the IIBA CBAP qualifications are discussed further in Chapter 2.

- **Standards**: Techniques and documentation standards that are applied in order to carry out the work of the profession. Organisations typically have templates for documents and standardise on modelling techniques such as those provided by the UML. Books such as this one are used in many organisations as a foundation for standards of business analysis practice. The use of standards and the establishment of a BA Service within an organisation is discussed in depth in *Delivering Business Analysis: The BA Service Handbook* (Paul and Lovelock, 2019).

- **Continuing professional development**: Recognition of the need for the continuing development of skills and knowledge in order to retain proficiency in business analysis practice. BCS and IIBA both promote continuing professional development and IIBA requires this for recertification of its qualifications.

Business analysis has come a long way in 30 years. Gradually, the business analyst role is being defined with increasing clarity, individuals with extensive expertise are developing and enhancing their skills, best practice is flourishing across organisations, and a business analysis profession is becoming firmly established.

THE FUTURE OF BUSINESS ANALYSIS

Business analysis has developed into a specialist discipline that can offer significant value to organisations, not least by preventing unwise investments in ill-conceived solutions and enabling the delivery of business benefits. Business analysis offers an opportunity for organisations to ensure not only that technology is deployed effectively to support the work of the organisation, but also that relevant options for business change are identified that take account of budgetary and timescale pressures.

Business analysts can offer objective views that challenge conventional wisdom, uncover root causes of problems and define the changes that should accrue real business benefits. Most business analysts are passionate about their work and the contribution they can make. They continually develop their skills and extend the breadth of work they can undertake. Not only are they able to leverage technology to meet business requirements, they can also identify where the potential for enhancing products and services might lie. The increasing focus on personalising and customising products and services, and the need to ensure alignment between the stated organisational intentions and the customer experience encountered, also requires the application of business analysis skills.

The future of work and skills

The skills required by organisations in the future have been the subject of research conducted by the World Economic Forum (Gray, 2016). This research has identified the need for the following 10 skills for the workforce of 2020.

1. Complex problem solving
2. Critical thinking
3. Creativity
4. People management
5. Coordinating with others
6. Emotional intelligence
7. Judgement and decision-making
8. Service orientation
9. Negotiation
10. Cognitive flexibility

A similar list has resulted from research conducted by the Institute for the Future for the University of Phoenix Research Institute (2011). This research also identified 10 key skills for the future workforce, which are:

1. Sense-making: the ability to understand the meaning of what is being communicated.

2. Social intelligence: the ability to engage with others.

3. Novel and adaptive thinking: the ability to define innovative solutions.

4. Cross-cultural competence: the ability to work in different cultures.

5. Computational thinking: the ability to understand and use data through analytics.

6. New media literacy: the ability to use content from different forms of media.

7. Transdisciplinarity: the ability to work across different disciplines.

8. Design mindset: the ability to design processes and tasks to align with desired outcomes.

9. Cognitive load management: the ability to prioritise and manage information received.

10. Virtual collaboration: the ability to work as a member of a virtual team.

It is striking how many of the skills for the future align with those possessed by, and required of, business analysts. There are also skills that relate directly to business thinking approaches – systems thinking, service thinking and design thinking – that are becoming increasingly used during business analysis work. It is clear that there is an ongoing need for analytical skills to help organisations succeed across the constantly evolving global economy.

The future for the BA Service

The BA Service delivers the required business analysis portfolio of services to an organisation. While the nature of this portfolio is likely to be customised for relevance within a specific organisational context, the value propositions are constant. Value realisation relies on collaboration and co-creation so poses challenges for both business analysts and their employing organisations.

Business analysts need to ensure that they develop the extensive toolkit of skills – behavioural, business and technical – that enables them to engage with the issues facing their organisations, and support their resolution. The reports provided by the World Economic Forum and the University of Phoenix Research Institute identify clearly a range of skills of relevance to business analysts. Table 1.3 describes key categories of skill for business analysts that have been derived by combining the results from these reports and additional empirical research.

Table 1.3 Key skills required by business analysts for future working

Category	Description
Stakeholder engagement	The skills required to work effectively with people. In particular, collaboration, team working, emotional intelligence, cultural awareness and sense-making.
Analytical thinking	The skills required to work effectively with data – data analysis and modelling, evaluation and prioritisation of various forms of information and data, and analytical interpretation of data.
Innovative thinking	The skills involved in thinking innovatively – critical thinking, root cause analysis, problem solving, creativity and adaptive thinking.
Technical literacy	The knowledge and skills required to work effectively with technological innovations and developments such as artificial intelligence (AI), virtual reality and robotics.
Value co-creation	The knowledge and skills required to understand and achieve desired beneficial outcomes – service thinking, design thinking, lean thinking and systems thinking.

SUMMARY

Business analysis has matured as a discipline over several decades and offers a portfolio of services to support organisations with their business and IT change initiatives. The challenge facing organisations is to enable business analysts to develop the required skills, recognise the significant contribution business analysts can offer, and ensure they have the authority to conduct business analysis as appropriate to each business situation.

This book has been developed primarily for the business analysis community but it is also intended to help other business professionals face the challenges of working within an evolving economic and technological environment. The aim is that everyone involved in defining and delivering business changes finds the guidance within this book useful.

NOTES

1. www.scrum.org

2. https://agilemanifesto.org/

3. https://cmmiinstitute.com/

4. https://bcs.org

5. https://www.iiba.org

6. www.bamanagerforum.org

2 THE COMPETENCIES OF A BUSINESS ANALYST

INTRODUCTION

Good business analysts can make the difference between a poor and a great investment in business and IT improvement. They can also help to resolve issues without jumping to premature conclusions. But what exactly is a good business analyst and which competencies should a good business analyst possess? This chapter addresses these questions by identifying and describing the set of competencies that business analysts need in order to be effective in today's business environment.

Competence has been described as 'the ability to do a particular activity to a prescribed standard' (De Ville, 1986). For the purposes of this chapter, a business analysis competence is defined as: 'an ability needed to perform the business analyst role effectively'.

The T-shaped professional

Research into the nature of service, including internal service provision, has revealed the importance of highly skilled individuals who can adapt to different situations because of the range of skills they possess. These individuals are known as 'T-shaped professionals' because they hold deep skills in their specialist discipline and broad, generic skills across other disciplines. This mix of skills enables them to solve problems within their own specialism and to communicate effectively with colleagues and stakeholders from other areas. The horizontal bar of the T-shape may be used to represent the skills required to interact with those from another community, while the vertical bar represents the specialist skills needed to conduct the work of the particular discipline. The T-shaped professional concept is represented in Figure 2.1.

Figure 2.2 provides a partial view of a T-shaped business analyst.

The business analyst needs to develop generalist skills, which may apply to many different roles in organisations, and specific skills required to analyse business situations. Variants of the vertical bar may be developed to represent the skills required of business analysts who are delivering other business analysis services; for example, where analysts are working within an Agile development team or on business process improvement projects.

Business analyst competency definitions

The three broad groups shown in Figure 2.2 provide a basis for defining an extensive set of business analyst competencies. These are illustrated in Figure 2.3.

Figure 2.1 The T-shaped professional concept

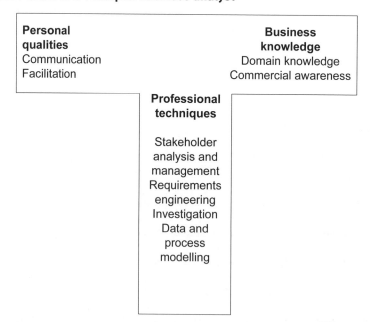

Multi-disciplinary breadth of knowledge and skill

Deep
knowledge
and skill of
specific
domain

Figure 2.2 Profile of a T-shaped business analyst

Personal qualities
Communication
Facilitation

Business knowledge
Domain knowledge
Commercial awareness

Professional techniques

Stakeholder
analysis and
management
Requirements
engineering
Investigation
Data and
process
modelling

Each of the competencies shown in Figure 2.3 is described in the following sections. Those marked with an * are covered in more detail in later chapters of this book.

Business analysis is a very broad discipline offering a range of services to organisations (see Chapter 4). Business analysts work closely with a range of stakeholders who may have varying levels of authority and different areas of concern. They may represent

Figure 2.3 The competencies of a business analyst

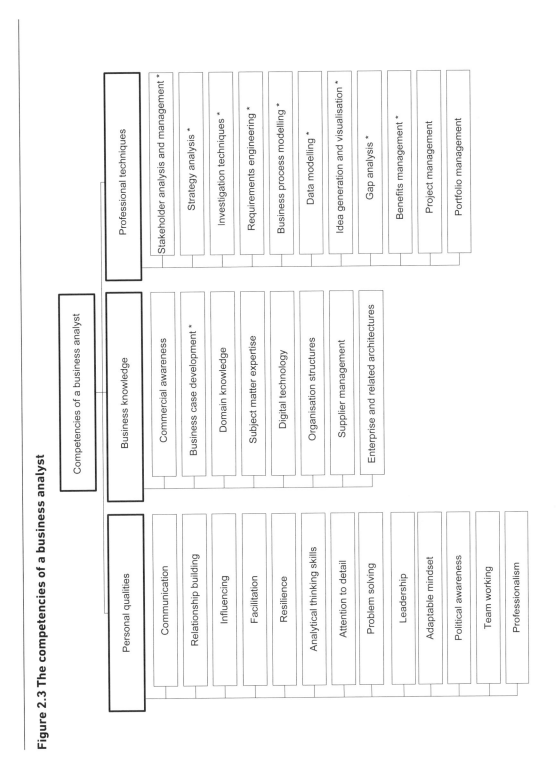

Competencies of a business analyst

Personal qualities

- Communication
- Relationship building
- Influencing
- Facilitation
- Resilience
- Analytical thinking skills
- Attention to detail
- Problem solving
- Leadership
- Adaptable mindset
- Political awareness
- Team working
- Professionalism

Business knowledge

- Commercial awareness
- Business case development *
- Domain knowledge
- Subject matter expertise
- Digital technology
- Organisation structures
- Supplier management
- Enterprise and related architectures

Professional techniques

- Stakeholder analysis and management *
- Strategy analysis *
- Investigation techniques *
- Requirements engineering *
- Business process modelling *
- Data modelling *
- Idea generation and visualisation *
- Gap analysis *
- Benefits management *
- Project management
- Portfolio management

operational business areas that are responsible for delivering the organisation's products and services, or they may provide input from the perspective of support functions such as finance or marketing. They may be stakeholders from governance areas such as the enterprise or business architecture functions or may have a more technical application or infrastructure focus. The area of concern for a particular stakeholder or stakeholder group will be reflected in the challenges faced during the course of their work. Therefore, business analysts may need to consider issues that relate to different domains, both business and technical. This wide-ranging context for business analysis requires business analysts to hold competencies in the three key areas indicated above: personal qualities, business knowledge and professional techniques. These areas are described in Table 2.1.

PERSONAL QUALITIES

These are the interpersonal skills and characteristics that are useful for a business analyst.

Table 2.1 Business analysis areas of competence

Area of competence	Description
Personal qualities	This area is concerned with how business analysts think and interact with people. They are not specific to business analysis but are generic skills that are needed to work collaboratively within any business environment. Behavioural skills are a prerequisite for working with other people. It is often said that it is easier to give a person with good behavioural skills the techniques they need for their job than to develop behavioural skills within a good technician who is lacking them. One of the main reasons for this is that good behavioural skills take time to develop and are as much concerned with attitude, personality and mindset as learning and development.
Business knowledge	Business analysts also require **business knowledge** as it helps them to develop a good understanding of their organisation and the business domain or sector within which it operates. This knowledge is vital if the business analyst is to offer the advice and insights that help to improve the organisation's performance. The primary source of business knowledge is through the experience of working within organisational and project environments. Additional business knowledge can be developed through reading relevant literature or studying for business qualifications.
Professional techniques	These techniques are those specific to the business analyst role and differentiate business analysts from other roles. There are numerous professional techniques that business analysts need to develop so that they can perform the role effectively and adapt to the range of situations they encounter.

Communication

Communication is perhaps the most important skill an individual can possess; it encompasses a wide range of skills such as building rapport, listening, influencing and building empathy. Much analysis work involves collecting and analysing data, eliciting and analysing requirements and presenting information to others. Poor communication skills are often cited as the root cause of problems during discussions between business and IT staff. Key issues concern the use of technical and business terminology, and failing to understand the other parties' points of view or motivation, during such discussions.

It is vital that business analysts communicate well with business colleagues and avoid using unfamiliar terms and references. Business analysts need to understand the business and the perspectives held by different stakeholders, possibly by conducting background research, and should avoid using technical language that may cause confusion. Spending time with business staff helps to increase understanding of the communication norms and relevant business terminology.

It is important to apply different communication styles to align with other participants in the discussion. For example, business analysts need to be aware of the interests and responsibilities of others and frame explanations and questions accordingly.

Relationship building

This competence concerns the ability to engage well with people, within a business context. Some individuals possess this ability naturally while others have to make efforts to develop it. Either way it is an essential skill for a business analyst. Business analysts need to encourage people to impart information and share opinions, and also to discuss ideas for change. This is very much easier if the discussions are held within a good working relationship. Those who are best able to build good working relationships demonstrate a genuine interest in the other person and offer open discussions that build mutual trust and respect. This is the basis for successful relationship building.

Influencing

Business analysts are often involved in suggesting options and possibly recommending a course of action. If that conclusion is at odds with preconceived ideas about what is required or if it calls for radical or unexpected action, then the ability to influence is essential.

Successful influencing requires careful consideration and a concerted effort to understand the individuals and issues involved. Identifying the stakeholders and understanding the amount of power they exert over the decision-making processes is vital to influence effectively. Some stakeholders are easily identified, such as the project sponsor, project management, governance committees, project boards and other steering groups. However, some are less obvious as there may be informal networks in place. It is important to consider any personal agendas, beliefs, priorities and commercial motives as these may be deeply held and are likely to flavour the positions taken by stakeholders. Where personal views are impeding progress, it may be necessary to involve other people, such as those in more senior positions.

Influencing activities need careful consideration and prior planning. Business analysts have to understand the range of views regarding a situation or proposal and any sources of resistance; this information helps to determine the influencing style needed to work with different stakeholders. For example, some managers require detailed information while others prefer a high-level summary. Some are interested in all the technicalities, others in the 'vision' or the 'big picture'. Having awareness of these preferences and tailoring the influencing approach is vital for a successful outcome.

The analysis itself may be questioned, requiring the business analysts to take or suggest another course of action. This may involve facilitating a round-table discussion or seeking support from senior colleagues on the best course of action. This is especially true when the business analyst is caught in the middle of opposing views. It also suggests that another personal quality that business analysts need from time to time is the ability to withstand pressure.

Facilitation

Effective facilitation requires extensive interpersonal and organisational skills and usually results from a combination of good preparation, clear understanding of the objectives, 'buy in' from senior stakeholders and the use of helpful techniques given the task, the participants and the organisational context. A good facilitator must possess several of the other personal qualities discussed in this chapter. However, some specific traits may be identified that are particularly relevant when facilitating.

Facilitators must have the ability quickly to evaluate the personality types and preferred learning style of a group of people who they may or may not have met before. Adaptability is another important quality, as facilitators need to be able to assess the progress of workshops and adjust the approach where necessary to keep on track. The ability to respond and adapt quickly is required because a facilitator is constantly processing what the participants are saying, formulating the questions that help to move the discussion forward and appraising whether the current techniques are working and what else might be tried instead. Facilitators also need to be assertive and to be able to establish their authority during the workshop.

One issue that often comes up in relation to facilitation is whether the facilitator needs to be a subject matter expert (SME) in the topic to be discussed. Some knowledge is required in order to follow the discussion but it is not necessary for a facilitator to be an expert in the subject matter. In many situations, this can help the facilitator to be objective and pose questions. The role of the facilitator is, after all, to help others reach a conclusion, not to impose a decision of their own.

Resilience

This quality is one that is often overlooked but is extremely important. It means having sufficient self-confidence to be able to withstand pressure, challenge proposals, analyse impacts and sustain arguments. Resilience is a key competence for working effectively with stakeholders and managing the broad range of situations that may be encountered by business analysts.

Analytical skills and critical thinking

Analytical skills form a major part of the business analyst role. It means digging deeper and deeper until the true situation is uncovered and the real problem has been defined.

It involves sifting through often-conflicting data and determining where data provides relevant insights and where this is not the case. It means not settling for the obvious, not accepting things at face value and not jumping to premature conclusions. Analytical thinking also involves presenting the results of the analysis in a form suitable for the relevant stakeholders. And it involves challenging received wisdom at every turn: asking 'Why do you do this?' 'What value does it add?' 'Where is it done?' 'How is it done?' 'Who is or should be responsible?' 'When should it happen?' 'Is there another way to do this?'

Some analysts appear to believe that the business analyst's role is straightforward and consists of recording what the business staff say they want and passing these 'requirements' to another team for delivery. However, this approach cannot reap the rewards offered by good analysis.

Analytical thinking does not, however, mean that every situation is analysed endlessly, taking significant resources and effort, as another key element of this competence is that those who can think analytically are able to assess the level of analysis required for a specific situation. This doesn't mean taking shortcuts on the analysis; it does mean recognising the key factors and the contextual constraints, and ensuring that the analysis is sufficient to address the business issues without trying to analyse everything.

Business thinking approaches, such as systems thinking (see Chapter 6), service thinking (Chapter 1) and design thinking (Chapter 8), can be invaluable aids to analytical thinking.

Attention to detail

Several aspects of the business analyst's work require detailed investigation. Whether it is uncovering the root causes of problems, defining the costs and benefits associated with a proposed option, defining business requirements and rules or identifying the impacts of proposed changes, the business analyst has a responsibility to ensure that key information is not missed. The key competence required is to have an attention to detail when necessary and to be able to identify when this is required.

Problem solving

Too often business analysts complain that a solution is decided upon without there being an appreciation of the problem it is to address. The focus on understanding the problem before rushing towards a solution is a key tenet and value proposition of business analysis.

The majority of business analysts are keen to solve business problems, and there are many problem-solving techniques and frameworks within the business analyst toolkit. Chapter 4 provides an overview of a model that helps to clarify the different stages required for creative problem solving. However, problem-solving competence requires more than just an understanding of how to approach a problem. There is also a need for a problem-solving mindset and this requires curiosity, tenacity and analytical ability plus the propensity to seek out and evaluate options. Pragmatism is another factor that is key to successful problem solving, as business analysts need to be realistic about what can be achieved given constraints such as a particular organisational culture and the availability of funds for investment in business change.

Leadership

Leadership is a skill that is often associated with line management job roles. However, the fundamental characteristics of leadership – developing a vision, taking ownership of that vision and ensuring the actions to achieve that vision are implemented – can be applied to all types of work. Thus, leadership is highly applicable to business analysis and in this context includes the following aspects:

- creating a vision of the approaches and options available to address a business issue;
- advising stakeholders in order to obtain agreement about the vision;
- driving the business and IT change process towards the achievement of that vision.

No two projects are the same. Each project has different objectives, constraints and stakeholders, and hence the required approach, skills and resources should differ. It is necessary to assess each situation on its own merits, decide what is needed and then design the analysis process. The business analyst needs to consider all aspects of the organisation or business area within which they work, including people, culture, processes, commercial and technical aspects. Leadership qualities are often required to ensure that the analysis encompasses the broad business system context rather than just focusing on IT systems. Getting the vision and actions right requires holistic thinking and careful analysis; this should also position the project successfully with key business stakeholders.

In recent years, the business analyst as a leader has emerged as a common theme in the business analysis and wider business and IT community. For example, the Expert BA Award developed by the BA Manager Forum requires candidates to demonstrate significant experience in leading analysis initiatives. The potential of business analysis to innovate and transform has, in some organisations, propelled the role to senior and executive levels.

There are different levels of leadership; Pullan and Archer (2013) recognised and defined four levels for the business analyst:

- **Self**: Having a positive mindset and being proactive. Recognising personal responsibility both for personal development and the work undertaken.
- **Project**: Supporting and influencing others to achieve project goals.
- **Organisation**: Helping the organisation to succeed at an enterprise service level.
- **Wider world**: Working with the business analysis community to enable excellence across the business analysis profession.

Adaptable mindset

Business analysts often work within contexts where the problems to be resolved and the desired outcomes are unclear or even not yet known. This requires a mindset that can cope with ambiguity and is adaptable and responsive.

Agile ways of working are well documented and when done well can produce excellent results. One of the traits of successful Agile projects is the mindset of the individuals who are conducting the work. Those with an adaptable mindset have the ability to:

- explore possibilities rather than just 'paint by numbers';
- be open to considering and trying out new ideas;
- be prepared to move beyond tried and tested ways;
- look for options and alternatives;
- work outside the job specification;
- 'see the world as it is, not as you want it to be'.

Political awareness

Political awareness is difficult to define but very apparent when observed or encountered. Alternative terms such as 'nous' or 'streetwise' are often used to capture the essence of this competence. Essentially, political awareness means the ability to work out what is and is not politically acceptable when working within an organisation and with particular individuals – and being able to use the right organisational levers to get things done. This requires analysts to know the sources of power and information within the organisation, understand what is acceptable or not and tailor their approach accordingly. Having political awareness does not mean agreeing with everyone or accepting the status quo; but it does mean using resourcefulness and being astute to get results, even in the face of opposition.

Team working

Business analysis involves working collaboratively to elicit information from a variety of stakeholders including colleagues from IT and change disciplines, suppliers, business staff and business managers. The ability to work in a team is an essential skill for a business analyst.

Business analysts benefit from understanding the nature of teams and how they develop. An appreciation of what makes a team successful enables business analysts to work well with colleagues, and to use their analytical skills to identify any issues and propose opportunities for developing the team.

Professionalism

Professionalism manifests itself in many ways but two key elements concern conduct and personal development. Professional conduct means possessing the knowledge and skills required of the particular role, working collaboratively and respectfully with other colleagues, having an ethical mindset and behaving appropriately in all business situations. Professional bodies, such as BCS, The Chartered Institute for IT, publish codes of conduct for members, all of whom are required to comply with their guidance.

Anyone working as a business change professional, including those undertaking a business analyst role, needs to possess a continuous improvement mindset that enables personal development. Various activities such as personal study, coaching, mentoring, training and engagement with professional forums help to build knowledge and understanding about industry trends and ensure currency. This competence is essential if a business analyst is to assist the organisation, enabling it to adapt to new challenges in today's fast-moving business and IT environment.

BUSINESS KNOWLEDGE

This section considers the range of business knowledge and understanding that business analysts need to conduct their work effectively.

Commercial awareness

All business analysts need to understand the sector and the industry that they work within. This helps them to ensure that any proposed courses of action or options for improvement align with the business environment for their organisation. All business domains develop to apply revised ways of working and to offer new products or services, and business analysts need to ensure that they are sufficiently aware of the commercial realities and pressures facing their organisations to support these initiatives.

Finance is the universal language of business. Whether the business analyst is working in the commercial, government or non-profit sectors of the economy, finance plays a key role in deciding what funds are available and what can and cannot be done. As a result, the business analyst needs to have a good working knowledge of the basics of business finance. This includes a general understanding of aspects such as the statement of financial position (balance sheet) and income statement (profit and loss account), financial ratio analysis, budgeting and cash flow, the nature of profit or surplus, and the principles of costing products and services. Without this understanding, it is not possible for an analyst to evaluate suppliers, deliver well thought through process improvements or evaluate options in business cases.

Business case development

Business analysts are often involved in identifying options to address a business problem, and assessing the costs and benefits of each option. Other specialists, such as management accountants, are usually involved in evaluating the options within a business case and analysing the financial impact on the organisation. However, business analysts require a basic understanding of the financial issues in order to engage in informed discussions with other specialists and business managers.

Business analysts need to understand the sources and types of costs and benefits, plus recognised investment appraisal techniques, such as break-even analysis and discounted cash flow (DCF); these techniques are explained in Chapter 9. Over recent years many business analysts have developed a greater understanding of the benefits and costs of technical solutions. This is a positive development as it enables analysts to disregard costly options quickly and ensure that they deliver value from their analysis work.

Domain knowledge

Domain knowledge concerns possessing a good general understanding of the business domain, or sector, in which the organisation operates. Apart from the general domain, such as 'retail' or 'local government', it is also necessary to have more specific domain knowledge, such as 'retail: supermarkets' or 'local government: social care'.

There are three reasons why this knowledge is required:

- Business analysts can use the terminology of the organisation and business domain. This enables effective communication with the business staff involved in the project.
- Business analysts have a greater understanding of what would, and would not, be acceptable or useful to this business domain.
- Business analysts may apply ideas, good practice and experiences from other organisations operating within the business domain or facing similar issues.

Subject matter expertise

Subject matter expertise is more specific, refining domain knowledge to a lower level of detail. If working in a particular area such as a specific product line or service, a good understanding of the particular terminology, processes and constraints is important to establish credibility with the customer. It also helps to guard against assumptions and to identify where there are errors of judgement or knowledge gaps.

Business analysts often specialise in particular business domains and have a strong understanding of the subject area. This enables them to collaborate more easily with the business staff, identify potential areas for change or further analysis, and challenge conventional wisdom and assumptions.

Digital technology

Many business analysts do not come from a technical background and are not expected to be specialists in technology-related matters. However, the original conception of business analysis was as a 'bridging' role, enabling communication between the business and IT staff, and this is still an important element of the role. The increasing use of Agile approaches has served to increase the need to facilitate this communication.

In today's business world, digital technologies are disrupting the products and services offered by organisations and the business processes adopted to deliver them. Competition and the opportunities offered by digital products are also driving improvement to the customer experience. Ross et al (2019) distinguish between two applications of digital technology: **digitization** – improving how the organisation operates and **digital transformation** – enhancing the organisation's value proposition. Business analysts need sufficient knowledge to be able to recognise where digital technology can be applied and facilitate improvements. While roles such as technical architect, developer and tester are responsible for the technical aspects of a solution, business analysts need to be able to identify where digital technology may be used to enhance their organisation's services and processes, and have informed discussions with their technical colleagues.

Given that the majority of business change projects require the development or procurement of software applications, a general understanding of technology, technological developments and software development approaches is necessary so that business analysts can communicate meaningfully with their technology-focused colleagues and appreciate their role and contribution to the solution architecture and development process.

The extent to which business analysts need technical knowledge depends on the nature of the analysis work being undertaken. The key requirement is for the business analyst to understand the potential offered by technology and the approaches and terms used by technical specialists. Some of the key areas that business analysts should understand are listed below:

- Trends and developments such as AI, robotic process automation (RPA), big data, software as a service (SaaS), visualisation, mobile technologies, and how these impact organisations and the potential they offer for new or improved products or services.

- Technical infrastructure components such as operating systems, application software, hardware, networks, cloud computing.

- Systems development lifecycles (SDLCs) and approaches such as the 'V' model and the unified process (UP) (see Chapter 13).

- Systems modelling approaches such as the UML.[1]

- Agile development approaches such as DSDM and Scrum.

- The relative pros and cons of developing software instead of buying off-the-shelf software products.

Organisation structures

Many business change projects involve restructuring divisions or teams to some degree in order to remove hand-offs, centralise tasks or improve the customer service. For these reasons, it is important for a business analyst to have a good understanding of the various organisation structures that may be encountered – functional, project, matrix, flat, virtual – and of their relative strengths and weaknesses.

Supplier management

Many organisations use external suppliers to deliver their IT systems, either on an ad hoc basis or through a more comprehensive outsourcing arrangement, which may cover whole business processes or even an entire business function. For example, many organisations have outsourced their payroll processes for several years but some have now extended this to cover much of the human resources (HR) work, from recruitment to record keeping.

The selection and contracting of suppliers tends to fall within the domain of the procurement function. However, for some outsourcing contracts the business analyst may be involved in ensuring that the business processes and systems continue to work efficiently. This requires business analysts to have a broad understanding of procurement and supplier management processes. As a minimum, business analysts should be aware of the different contractual arrangements that are available, in particular:

- **Time and materials**: Where the contracted party is paid on the basis of the time worked and deliverables completed; the time element does not concern the elapsed time on the project but the amount of effort employed.

- **Fixed price delivery**: Where the contracted party is paid the price that was agreed for the delivery of the work in line with the original specification.

- **Risk and reward**: Where the contracted party has agreed to bear some or all of the risk of the project. For example, by investing resources such as staff time, materials or office space, but where the potential rewards are greater than under other contractual arrangements.

Business analysts should be able to engage with suppliers to ensure that they deliver their services effectively. This requires personal qualities such as communication and relationship building, discussed earlier in this chapter.

Enterprise and related architectures

EA frameworks, such as those offered by Zachman[2] and The Open Group architectural framework (TOGAF),[3] set out the aspects of an enterprise that need to be defined, governed and coordinated. The key domains are business architecture, data architecture, applications architecture and infrastructure architecture (see Chapter 3).

Business analysts need to have awareness of the EA frameworks and domains in order to ensure that there is alignment between them and any proposed solutions. The artefacts provided by the domains, for example the business capability maps and value stream diagrams that form part of the business architecture, also offer insights and information that can help to identify and develop options for business improvement.

PROFESSIONAL TECHNIQUES

This section considers the range of business analysis techniques that are applied by business analysts in the course of their work.

Stakeholder analysis and management

Stakeholder management is a key element of business analysis. It involves the ability to identify stakeholders, assess the significance of the stakeholders, analyse stakeholders' perspectives and develop stakeholder management strategies. Stakeholder analysis and management is discussed in Chapter 6.

Strategy analysis

Business analysts need to understand their organisation's strategic context for the following reasons:

- To ensure that any recommended solutions align with the organisation's objectives and strategy.
- To determine the tactics required to execute the organisation's strategy.

Various techniques are used during strategy analysis and definition: for example, techniques to investigate the internal and external environments for an organisation. The strategic context and related techniques are explored in Chapter 3.

Investigation techniques

Business analysts are required regularly to investigate business situations and determine where the issues and problems lie. To do this, they need to be skilled in applying techniques that help to uncover and analyse the root causes of such problems. Investigation techniques are discussed in Chapter 5.

Requirements engineering

Requirements engineering (RE) is a framework of activities that are applied when defining requirements and encompasses a range of elicitation, analysis and modelling skills. Requirements provide the basis from which business and IT solutions are designed and developed so this is a key area of competence for business analysts. The RE stages, principles and techniques are discussed in Chapters 10, 11 and 12.

Business modelling

Business modelling is an approach to visualising business systems through the creation of conceptual models. A business system model represents an entire business system, typically in overview. There are several techniques that may be used to model a business system such as a business activity model (BAM), value chain, value stream, organisation model or capability map. Each of these models may be supplemented by more detailed models. For example, business process models provide a means of decomposing value chain or value stream activities, showing how the business processes actually work and where they might be improved. Capability models are discussed in Chapter 3, business activity modelling is described in Chapter 6 and value streams, value chains, organisation models and business process models are covered in Chapter 7.

Data modelling

Analysing the data stored and used within a business system affords valuable insights into how that system operates. A data model reflects the information requirements of the organisation and the business rules inherent within the structure of the data. There are several techniques used to model data. Entity relationship modelling and class modelling are widely used by business analysts and are discussed in Chapter 11.

Idea generation and visualisation

In addition to the 'Facilitation' personal quality described earlier, there are techniques that business analysts can use to stimulate discussion, generate ideas and represent outcomes during a meeting, workshop or focus group. These techniques include approaches such as dialogue mapping, open space technology, brainstorming, mind-mapping, the various uses of sticky notes and Edward de Bono's 'Six Thinking Hats'. An introduction to the key techniques is provided in Chapter 5.

Visualisation techniques are often used when facilitating. They are quick to understand and straightforward to explain, and help to engage workshop participants whether exploring business problems, strategic choices or requirements. Visual representations of information may be low fidelity drawings or may be produced using automated tools, where it is possible to model different scenarios without extensive redrawing.

Gap analysis

The ability to conduct gap analysis is core to the business analyst role. There are many situations where gap analysis is required. For example, to compare any of the following: 'as is' and 'to be' business process models; a current situation with conceptual BAMs, an off-the-shelf software product against a set of defined requirements; or capability needs against those currently available within the organisation. This technique is described in Chapter 8.

Benefits management

Benefits management involves the active planning, monitoring and evaluation of the benefits predicted in a business case for a business change initiative. Ultimately, business analysis aims to ensure that investments are made in relevant business changes and products, and predicted returns on investment are realised. A process for benefits management is discussed in Chapter 14.

Project management

Project management encompasses several areas of activity, in particular:

- project initiation and scoping;
- project planning and estimating;
- monitoring and control of the project work;
- resource allocation;
- reporting and communication.

The Project Management Institute[4] (PMI) and the Association for Project Management[5] (APM) are professional bodies representing project managers. Both organisations publish a body of knowledge that describe the work conducted by project managers.

Business analysts may be required to undertake the project manager role when working on small projects. Therefore, they should have project management skills and should be able to apply project management techniques and approaches. Larger projects often employ a specialist project manager but even in these cases, there are some project skills that an analyst should possess. For example, an appreciation of project initiation is vital as it allows the analyst to understand, or even define, the terms of reference (ToR) for the project. It is also important that the analyst understands project management planning approaches as they typically work within a defined plan. They may even be required to plan the analysis activity for a project so need to be aware of relevant aspects of project management such as task identification, dependencies between tasks, quality assurance and risk management.

Portfolio management

This encompasses the evaluation, prioritisation and delivery of a portfolio of business change projects. Business analysts require competence in this area if they have responsibility for the portfolio of analysis projects. This skill helps when assessing how the portfolio of projects fits together, analysing the dependencies and identifying where project priorities lie.

DEVELOPING BUSINESS ANALYSIS SKILLS

Personal development is based upon a gap analysis process: identify the required skills and the goals to be achieved; assess the current skills held; compare the two states; identify actions to attain the required skills and achieve the development goals.

The skill set defined earlier in this chapter provides a basis for conducting this gap analysis. However, business analyst roles vary across organisations so the skill set may need to be adapted. HR departments or line management may be able to provide an outline definition of the requirements for the business analyst role and an internal career development framework may be available that sets out the skill requirements for different roles and grades. The Skills Framework for the Information Age[6] (SFIA) may also provide helpful information. This framework is described in the next section.

Essentially, there are four ways in which business analysts can develop their competencies and these are listed in Table 2.2.

Table 2.2 Competency development approaches

Development approach	Description
Training	Classroom-based training can be an efficient way of acquiring skills and knowledge. It enables learners to practise applying skills with a tutor on hand to offer support, guidance and encouragement. The class environment enables knowledge-sharing and this helps to enrich the learning experience. Some training courses lead to industry qualifications, such as those offered by BCS, the Chartered Institute for IT (discussed later in this chapter).
Personal study	Personal study is an excellent way for analysts to develop their business and professional knowledge. There is a wide variety of resources available including online articles, blogs and videos, magazines and reference books. In addition to *Business Analysis*, other relevant BCS books include: *Business Analysis Techniques* (Cadle et al., 2014), *Business Analyst: Careers in Business Analysis* (Reed, 2018) and *Delivering Business Analysis: The BA Service Handbook* (Paul and Lovelock, 2019). IIBA also offer *BABOK V3: A Guide to the Business Analysis Body of Knowledge* (IIBA, 2015) a reference guide for business analysts.

(Continued)

Table 2.2 (Continued)

Development approach	Description
	Such self-study helps to broaden and deepen the analyst's understanding of business analysis and related areas such as technology developments, business change issues, strategy and the business environment.
Work experience	Work experience provides an opportunity to learn and apply techniques in practice and to extend understanding of the business analyst role. Given that business analysis requires extensive stakeholder engagement, it is usually the best arena to develop personal skills. The performance of most analysts improves over time as their experience grows but this can be heightened and accelerated if working within an organisation that operates a formalised skills development programme using coaching or mentoring. If this isn't available, it is useful to identify more experienced business analysts, possibly from other organisations, whose work is respected and who might be able to spare some time to provide support.
Industry engagement	The business analysis profession has expanded rapidly in recent years and this has led to increased support from professional bodies. BCS has offered certifications in business analysis since 1999 and published the first book (*Business Analysis*, 1st edition) on the subject. IIBA also offers certifications and networking opportunities. Representatives from BCS, IIBA and AssistKD organised the first conference dedicated to business analysts. Both BCS and IIBA run frequent events where business analysts can engage with their peers and each organisation runs an annual industry award to celebrate the work of business analysts. Attending events and conferences, obtaining certifications and promoting the business analysis profession through presentations and articles, are excellent ways to develop skills and acquire knowledge.

The ability to learn is greatly enhanced if learning experiences are supplemented by reflection. This involves thinking about the knowledge and techniques studied to relate them to experience, considering different scenarios, when they might be applied and making connections between them.

SFIA

SFIA is the standard skills framework for the IT industry. SFIA is owned and maintained by the SFIA Foundation, a not-for-profit organisation. BCS is a member of the SFIA Foundation.

SFIA is divided into six skill categories: Strategy and Architecture, Change and Transformation, Development and Implementation, Delivery and Operation, Skills and Quality, and Relationships and Engagement. Each category contains definitions of relevant skills and levels of competency in performing each skill. The levels are numbered 1 to 7 and the competence in a skill increases with each defined level. The levels are: 1 – Follow, 2 – Assist, 3 – Apply, 4 – Enable, 5 – Ensure, Advise, 6 – Initiate, Influence, 7 – Set strategy. Each skill is defined in overview and then for each relevant competence level. None of the skills is defined at all seven levels.

The SFIA definitions can be used to build descriptions of the skills and levels of competence that those performing a role should possess. Skills that are particularly relevant to the business analyst role are:

- Business Process Improvement: levels 5, 6 and 7.
- Business Analysis: levels 3, 4, 5 and 6.
- Business Modelling: levels 2, 3, 4, 5 and 6.
- Requirements Definition and Management: levels 2, 3, 4, 5 and 6.

A role definition for a relatively inexperienced business analyst may include a skills profile as follows:

- Business Analysis: level 3.
- Business Modelling: level 2.
- Requirements Definition and Management: level 3.

A role definition for a more senior business analyst may include a skills profile as follows:

- Business Process Improvement: level 5.
- Business Analysis: level 5.
- Business Modelling: level 4.
- Requirements Definition and Management: level 5.

The relevant SFIA skill definitions, including the competence levels required to conduct a particular role, may be used to develop a detailed profile of the role skill requirements. The SFIA definition of the Business Analysis skill, plus the levels of competency, are shown in the Appendix to this chapter.

SFIA is used worldwide in all sectors of industry and government and is the preferred framework for defining the skills required of IT professionals. The licence to use the framework is free of charge, although the Foundation requires a royalty from those using it to support a commercial offering such as consultancy services. The SFIA Foundation accredits consultants and partners, and provides training in the use of the framework. BCS offer an extended version of SFIA, called SFIA*plus*, to its members. SFIA*plus* provides additional information for each skill such as related skills, certifications and publications.

The right skills for the right situation

A key task for business analysis managers is to ensure that there is a good fit between the required analysis skills and the particular context. Putting a junior analyst in a situation where higher level skills are required can be demotivating. The reverse is also true where an analyst is over-skilled for the particular piece of work. Figure 2.4 offers a framework for thinking about the alignment between the situation and the required skill levels.

Figure 2.4 Skills analysis matrix

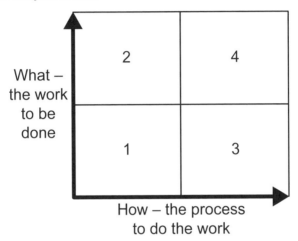

In quadrant 1, the analysis work to be done is well understood as is the process for doing it. For example, the business analysis work may involve defining the requirements for a system where the scope has already been agreed. This would be a good starting point for a new or inexperienced analyst and may equate to level 3 or 4 in the SFIA framework.

In quadrant 2, the analysis required is not clearly understood although there is a standard approach setting out how it should be done. For example, a new collaborative/social media technology has been proposed for an organisation and a business analyst has been engaged to conduct a feasibility study. The application of the collaborative technology is unclear but the organisation has a standard deployment approach. Typically, this work would be allocated to a more experienced analyst. This may equate to level 4 or 5 in the SFIA framework.

In quadrant 3, the analysis needed is understood although it is not clear how it is to be done. For example, an organisation wants to move from a variety of packaged systems solutions to a single enterprise-wide system but the way to achieve this is unclear. As with quadrant 2, this is likely to be assigned to a more experienced analyst. This work may equate to level 4 or 5 in the SFIA framework.

In quadrant 4, neither the analysis to be done nor how it is to be done are understood. This type of work is for the highly experienced and skilled business analyst and may require the analyst to adopt a consultancy approach. In this example, the brief can be as vague as 'we need to reduce costs', 'we need to improve sales', 'we need to innovate more' and so on. As a result, the analyst may need to define how the work is to be performed, manage senior stakeholders through the process and facilitate the organisation to think about what it is trying to achieve. This would equate to level 6 in the SFIA framework.

INDUSTRY QUALIFICATIONS

There are two key examination bodies that offer professional qualifications in business analysis. These are BCS and the IIBA.

BCS

BCS offers six levels of certification for business analysts: Foundation, Practitioner, Diploma, Professional, Consultant (Advanced Diploma) and Expert. There are several certifications available, as described in Table 2.3.

Table 2.3 Business analysis certifications offered by BCS

Level	Certification subject
Foundation	A Foundation certificate is awarded to a candidate who passes a multiple-choice examination that assesses knowledge and understanding of a particular subject area.
Practitioner	A Practitioner certificate is awarded to a candidate who passes an examination that assesses knowledge, understanding and practical application of the concepts and techniques within a particular subject area.
Diploma	BCS International Diploma in Business Analysis. Awarded to candidates who have passed written examinations in four subjects, two mandatory, one knowledge-based specialism and one practitioner specialism, and have passed an oral examination covering the Diploma syllabus.
Professional	A Professional certificate is awarded to a candidate who passes an examination that assesses understanding, practical application and analysis of the concepts, frameworks and techniques within a specialist subject area. Subject areas include: • Agile Business Analysis • Business Architecture • Data Analysis • Stakeholder Engagement

(Continued)

Table 2.3 (Continued)

Level	Certification subject
Consultant	BCS Advanced International Diploma in Business Analysis. Awarded to candidates who have passed examinations in four of the certificate modules and have submitted an Advanced Diploma application providing evidence of extensive business analysis experience and contribution to the business analysis profession.
Expert	Expert BA Award. Awarded in collaboration with the BA Manager Forum. Candidates are required to submit detailed evidence of extensive business analysis experience or to hold the BCS Advanced International Diploma in Business Analysis, and to have passed an assessment interview.

IIBA CBAP/CCBA

IIBA® has created the CBAP®, a designation awarded to candidates who have successfully demonstrated sufficient experience in business analysis and have passed the IIBA CBAP multiple-choice examination. The CBAP may be used towards the BCS International Diploma in Business Analysis as an exemption towards two of the modules.

IIBA also offers the CCBA® certification, which allows applications from candidates with lesser experience. The candidates need to pass a multiple-choice examination in order to be awarded the CCBA.

SUMMARY

This chapter has sought to categorise and describe the key skills required of a successful business analyst. Every organisation has a different interpretation of what a business analyst does and the services encompassed by business analysis, therefore business analysts need to possess the skills that align with the needs of their organisations. If business analysts wish to develop their skills and improve their performance, they need to understand the range of required skills, identify the levels of competence needed for each skill area and seek out relevant learning opportunities.

It is personal skills that can present the biggest challenge for business analysts. Anyone working in business change is only too aware of the apprehension and concerns that these projects create. This may even develop into resistance if these concerns are not met. Business analysts need to develop extensive personal skills in order to overcome any opposition to proposed business changes and work with their business colleagues to deliver the business improvements their organisations demand.

NOTES

1. https://www.uml.org/
2. www.zachman.com
3. www.opengroup.org/togaf
4. https://www.pmi.org/
5. https://www.apm.org.uk/
6. https://www.sfia-online.org/en

APPENDIX: SFIA DESCRIPTION OF BUSINESS ANALYSIS SKILL

SFIA describes the business analysis skill as follows:

The methodical investigation, analysis, review and documentation of all or part of a business in terms of business goals, objectives, functions and processes, the information used and the data on which the information is based. The definition of requirements for improving processes and systems, reducing their costs, enhancing their sustainability, and the quantification of potential business benefits. The collaborative creation and iteration of viable specifications and acceptance criteria in preparation for the deployment of information and communication systems. The adoption and adaptation of business analysis approaches based on the context of the work and selecting appropriately from predictive (plan-driven) approaches or adaptive (iterative/agile) approaches.

SFIA defines four levels of competence for the business analysis skill.

SFIA level	Description
Level 3	Investigates operational needs, problems and opportunities, contributing to the recommendation of improvements in automated and non-automated components of new or changed processes and organisation. Assists in defining acceptance tests for these recommendations.
Level 4	Investigates operational requirements, problems and opportunities, seeking effective business solutions through improvements in automated and non-automated components of new or changed processes. Assists in the analysis of stakeholder objectives, and the underlying issues arising from investigations into business requirements and problems, and identifies options for consideration. Works with stakeholders to identify potential benefits and available options for consideration, and in defining acceptance tests. Contributes to selection of the business analysis methods, tools and techniques for projects; selecting appropriately from predictive (plan-driven) approaches or adaptive (iterative/Agile) approaches.
Level 5	Takes responsibility for investigative work to determine business requirements and specify effective business processes, through improvements in information systems, information management, practices, procedures and organisation change. Selects, adopts and adapts appropriate business analysis methods, tools and techniques; selecting appropriately from predictive (plan-driven) approaches or adaptive (iterative/Agile) approaches. Collaborates with stakeholders at all levels, in the conduct of investigations for strategy studies, business requirements specifications and feasibility studies. Prepares business cases which define potential benefits, options for achieving these benefits through development of new or changed processes, and associated business risks.
Level 6	Takes full responsibility for business analysis within a significant segment of an organisation where the advice given and decisions made will have a measurable impact on the profitability or effectiveness of the organisation. Leads the selection of appropriate business analysis methods, tools, techniques; selecting appropriately from plan-driven/predictive approaches or more adaptive (iterative and Agile) approaches. Establishes the contribution that technology can make to business objectives, defining strategies, validating and justifying business needs, conducting feasibility studies, producing high-level and detailed business models, preparing business cases, overseeing development and implementation of solutions, taking into account the implications of change on the organisation and all stakeholders. Guides senior management towards accepting change brought about through process and organisational change.

3 THE STRATEGIC CONTEXT FOR BUSINESS ANALYSIS

INTRODUCTION

This chapter focuses on the strategic context for business analysis and includes an exploration of:

- what strategy is and why it is important;
- the relevance of the strategic context for business analysis;
- strategy development;
- internal and external environment analysis;
- strengths, weaknesses, opportunities, threats (SWOT) analysis;
- strategy execution;
- EA;
- strategic alignment.

The aim of the chapter is to provide awareness of the strategic development process and the key techniques used within this. Through application of the techniques discussed, an understanding of the strategic context within which the business analyst operates can be obtained.

WHAT IS STRATEGY?

The term 'strategy' originates from the military imperative to succeed in battle against the enemy. Some of the early uses of the term describe it as being the 'generals' knowledge' for the 'tricks of war'. These 'tricks' might have included:

- selecting and preparing the terrain for battle;
- planning, preparing and positioning troops, weaponry and supplies;
- cultivation and maintenance of supply chains (e.g. armour, medical supplies, food/ water);
- formation and maintenance of alliances with other military powers;
- ensuring appropriate use of available resources;
- selecting the appropriate time to engage in battle.

The term 'tactics' relates to the making of decisions once battle has commenced. Tactical decisions should be aligned to strategy and are specific in nature. For the military, tactics would include selecting the specific timing of deployment of troops and weaponry during battle and orchestration of responses to enemy attacks. Both 'strategy' and 'tactics' are key to overall battle success; they are also key for success within an organisational context.

Academic and business literature offer many competing definitions of the term 'strategy'. For example, Porter defined strategy as:

> An integrated set of actions aimed at increasing the long-term wellbeing and strength of an enterprise.
>
> (Porter, 1980)

Chandler argued that strategy is:

> The determination of the basic long-term goals of an enterprise, and the adoption of courses of action and the allocation of resources necessary for carrying out these goals.
>
> (Chandler, 1962)

Johnson et al. state that strategy is:

> The long-term direction of an organisation.
>
> (Johnson et al., 2017)

Each of these definitions emphasises that strategy concerns the 'long-term'. However, what constitutes 'long-term' is variable as it depends on the context provided by the environment, industry and organisation. For example, a small technology start-up might consider 'long-term' to mean a one- to two-year horizon. However, a power generation firm, perhaps one that commissions nuclear power stations, may consider 'long-term' to mean a period spanning 50 to 75 years. The timespan for strategy is therefore context dependent.

In contrast to original use in the military context, strategy is an organisation's long-term plan for success within the context of its environment.

THE IMPORTANCE OF STRATEGY

Strategy provides a foundation for the organisation to succeed through aligning execution with the context of its internal and external environment. It can be a means of providing an organisation with business advantage and sustainable success.

Effective strategy provides a foundation for the health and performance of the organisation over the long term. Effective strategy is much like the concept of clean air – its existence may be taken for granted until it ceases to be available.

An ineffective strategy damages the long-term health of the organisation and can cause a multitude of different problems. Using the 'air' analogy, ineffective strategy, for the organisation, can be seen to be akin to breathing polluted air. While this doesn't necessarily have an immediate negative consequence, over the long term it damages organisational performance. Unless the situation is rectified it can lead to the demise of the organisation entirely.

In an age of global competition, increased complexity, continually changing customer expectations and enhancements in the availability and performance of ever-changing technologies, it is perhaps of no surprise that strategy as a subject remains very much in demand.

Organisations that develop and maintain effective strategy are provided with a foundation from which to execute their plan for success. Execution typically encompasses the development and configuration of capabilities and the delivery of strategically aligned change. It is typically within execution that the business analyst role comes to prominence.

BUSINESS ANALYSIS AND THE STRATEGIC CONTEXT

Understanding the strategic context helps to clarify the environment in which the business analyst operates. This insight allows for the business analyst to contribute positively to the organisation's strategic journey through the delivery of business analysis services.

Many benefits arise if the business analyst is aware and can apply knowledge of the strategic context. These include the ability to:

- analyse and discuss strategic approaches and priorities;
- build credibility when discussing the organisation with stakeholders;
- question the appropriateness and alignment of decisions taken prior to and during the execution of change;
- analyse the effectiveness of the approach, outputs and benefits expected from a change initiative;
- provide leadership and influence for the delivery of strategically aligned change.

If the business analyst can apply knowledge of the strategic context, they are able to contribute positively to the organisation's strategic change journey, typically through the enhancement of the organisation's capabilities. If business analysts are not aware of the strategic context, they can potentially deliver outputs that harm or cause damage to the capabilities of the organisation.

Each business analyst essentially has a choice. Do they support senior executives in the execution of strategy or conduct their work without reference to the strategic context? If the latter is the case, then the effectiveness of the business analyst is diminished and the effectiveness of the outcomes from delivery of business analysis services is reduced.

DEVELOPING STRATEGY

While there is a degree of overlap, the approach adopted by organisations towards the development of strategy often varies. Common influencing factors include organisational culture, decision-making processes, domain complexity and overall organisation size. The environment in which the organisation operates and the ambitions, beliefs, wants and needs of key stakeholders are also influential.

Adaptive strategy development

Some organisations develop strategy in an iterative way based upon market and stakeholder feedback. While some authors describe this as 'adaptive', others describe this as a 'lean' strategic development approach.

Hofer defines adaptive strategy as being:

> Concerned with the development of a viable match between the opportunities and risks present in the external environment and the organization's capabilities and resources for exploiting these opportunities.
>
> (Hofer, 1973)

Many new start-up organisations develop strategy this way. Their aim is to deploy, often at low cost, viable products or services into a market. Through these deployments they aim to learn quickly through feedback what it is that the market wants. Products and services then evolve in alignment with this feedback.

Adaptive strategy development is often associated with non-hierarchical organisations where employee ownership and empowerment are high. Other traits associated with this approach are the acceptance of feedback, objective decision-making, continuous improvement and the valuing of knowledge.

There are several drawbacks to the adaptive strategic development approach. If an organisation is risk averse or there are major consequences of failure it is unlikely to be culturally acceptable. Adaptive strategic development may not be appropriate if obtaining market feedback is not perceived to be helpful, such as within a government department. Also, the constant adaptation may result in difficulties when communicating the strategy.

Linear strategy development

Historically, many large, successful organisations and government departments have developed strategy in a linear manner. Chandler's definition (shown earlier in this chapter) is often cited as reflecting linear strategy development:

Linear strategy development may be adopted where environmental conditions are stable and immediate market feedback is not deemed to be particularly valuable. This approach provides the advantage of a relatively unchanging strategy that can be communicated to the organisation's stakeholders.

This approach is often associated with organisations that are hierarchical in nature or are risk averse. Often organisations using this approach are seen to have lower employee ownership and empowerment compared with organisations applying an adaptive strategic development approach.

The approach is criticised as leading to slower reactions by the organisation to changes in the internal or external environment; if consumer preferences change, the organisation may not respond quickly for instance. This can lead to the loss of market share to competitors.

Hybrid strategy development

Some organisations blend the approaches and apply a hybrid mix of adaptive and linear strategy development. This may even be the case within different departments or divisions of the same organisation. Some of the organisation's departments, perhaps those focused on developing new products or services, may use 'adaptive' strategic development while other departments, perhaps those maintaining the traditional suite of products or services, use linear strategic development.

UNDERSTANDING THE STRATEGIC CONTEXT

To begin to understand the strategic context, relative to an organisation, it is first necessary to ask and understand the answers to several questions. These provide the foundational building blocks for strategic development. The questions are:

* What is the organisation's 'current state'?

* What is the organisation's desired 'target state'?

* What is the plan to move between the current state and target state? (aka strategy execution. This is often referred to as the strategic mission or roadmap.)

Figure 3.1 Core building blocks for understanding the strategic context

There are several techniques that are used to supplement the analysis of the building blocks shown in Figure 3.1. This includes techniques that aid with:

- analysis of the current state of the internal and external environment;
- definition of the target state;
- performance measurement of progress towards the target state.

Techniques associated with the core building blocks for the strategic context are explored throughout this chapter, beginning with the analysis of the internal and external environment for an organisation. The techniques that assist with this analysis are shown in Figure 3.2.

Figure 3.2 Internal and external environment analysis

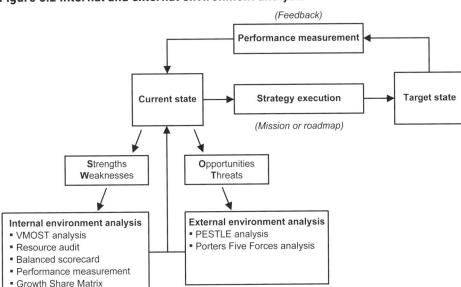

STRATEGY ANALYSIS: EXTERNAL ENVIRONMENT

The external environment presents 'opportunities' and 'threats' for the organisation. This stimulates changes to the organisation's strategy and tactics. The two main techniques used to analyse the external environmental analysis are PESTLE and Porter's Five Forces analysis.

PESTLE analysis

PESTLE is a framework used to assess the factors in the macro strategic environment that are beyond immediate control, but in some way influence the organisation. The factors considered within PESTLE are described in Table 3.1.

Table 3.1 PESTLE factors

Political	Forces within the international, national and local political environments. Examples include: • Policies and decisions made by national and local governments • Policies and decisions made by transnational political organisations such as the African Union, Arab League, European Union, United Nations, North Atlantic Treaty Organization (NATO) • Trends and policies advocated by associations looking to further their political cause such as Amnesty International, Greenpeace, WWF
Economic	Forces within the international, national and local economic environment. Examples include: • Interest rates. This impacts the cost of borrowing • Inflation. This indicates the rate at which prices are stable or increasing within the economy • Levels of employment. This impacts the availability of labour for an organisation • Levels of disposable income. This impacts consumer spending power and can negatively or positively impact spending levels within the economy • Availability and cost of resources. For example, an increase in the price of energy can impact costs throughout the economy • Growth trends in national and international economies (high economic growth, stagnant growth and recessions). This impacts investment and consumer confidence as well as other economic considerations • Fluctuations in currency exchange rates. This impacts the cost of imports and the prices of exported goods and services
Socio-cultural	Trends within society and culture. Examples include: • Changes to demographics. This includes changes to characteristics of the population such as ethnicity, gender, age, education levels, occupation, religion, marriage and birth/death rates • Changes in preferences and habits. For example, the trend towards using smart devices (such as voice-enabled devices, smart watches, smart home devices)

(Continued)

Table 3.1 (Continued)

	• Changes within popularly held viewpoints and opinions. For example, the increased prominence of speaking about mental health issues by celebrities or the increased discussion and focus on environmental concerns
Technological	Trends within technology.
	Examples include:
	• The availability of new technologies such as AI, self-driving vehicles, smart devices, voice-enabled devices
	• The increased connectedness of technologies (for example, the increased prominence of intra-technology communication standards)
	• The increased use of RPA
	• Availability of skills to build and maintain technology platforms
	• The movement towards digital products and services
Legal	Trends and expectations that have legal or regulatory impact.
	Examples include:
	• Employment law
	• Data protection law
	• Competition law
	• Health and safety law
	• Taxation rules and regulations
	• Disability discrimination and or equality law
	• Intellectual property law
	• Market specific legislation and regulation (for example, legislation that targets a specific sector such as finance or health)
Environmental	Trends and influences that are concerned with the natural environment.
	Examples include:
	• Carbon emissions and climate change
	• Changes to natural habitats (e.g. deforestation, shrinking of polar ice caps)
	• Animal welfare
	• Waste disposal and recycling

Over time PESTLE has evolved from what was originally known as PEST analysis. Some commentators describe the technique as PESTEL analysis while others add in an additional 'E' for **E**thical, making the technique either 'PESTLEE' or 'STEEPLE'.

Whichever acronym is used, the approach is a core technique that enables assessment of the wider macro environment within which an organisation operates.

If changes occur within the external environment, and these are not detected or responded to appropriately, a negative impact on the organisation may result. For example, there is a social–cultural trend of consumers purchasing environmentally friendly white goods that use digital technology to connect to other devices. If a white goods manufacturer doesn't respond to this change, then it is at risk of losing market share to competitors. While detecting and responding to this trend would not guarantee success, understanding the trend would enable the executives for the manufacturing organisation to make informed strategic decisions.

Porter's Five Forces Model

Successful organisations retain an awareness of the marketplace in which they operate. This is true for those that operate in the competitive and the not-for-profit sectors. The Five Forces Model (Porter, 1980) aids with the analysis of the relative positioning and power of the organisations that participate in a particular industry or business domain. The forces identified by Porter are as follows:

- competitive rivalry between existing competitor organisations;
- bargaining power of suppliers;
- bargaining power of buyers;
- threat from potential new entrants;
- threat from possible substitute products or services.

An example Five Forces Model for the fast food burger restaurant industry is shown in Figure 3.3.

Industry competitors and rivals
This force concerns the degree of rivalry among the industry competitors; the higher the degree of rivalry, the more difficult it is to operate and compete. Actions taken by rival firms can influence the actions taken by others in the market. Some industries have a high degree of competition and others are less competitive. Where there is a single dominant provider, this is known as a monopoly. Where there are two dominant providers this is described as a 'duopoly'. Example considerations for this force include:

- The volume of industry competitors.
- The relative size, power and influence of competitors to each other.
- The degree of differentiation between the product and service offers made by industry rivals. For example, is there a high degree of product commoditisation?
- The extent of growth in the overall market.
- The barriers to leaving the industry.

Figure 3.3 Porter's Five Forces Model

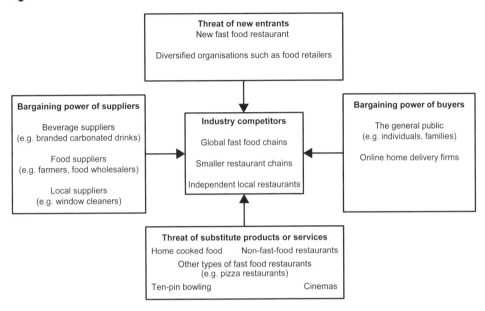

The fast food burger restaurant industry, shown in Figure 3.3, is highly competitive given that there are many global fast food restaurant chains, a vast number of much smaller independent local restaurants and a growing number of smaller restaurant chains.

Bargaining power of suppliers

This force looks at the relative power and influence of the suppliers to industry competitors. Suppliers may provide tangible items such as raw materials and equipment; they may also provide services involving people and may be sources of finance. Considerations for this force include:

- The relative size of suppliers compared with the industry rivals. Where the supplier is larger than the organisation they are supplying, it may be that they have an advantage in negotiations. Where the supplier is smaller, the opposite is true and influence may reside with the organisation being supplied. For example, Figure 3.3 shows suppliers of window cleaning services and they are likely to have much lower bargaining power when negotiating with global fast food restaurant chains.

- The strength of the suppliers' branded products or services. If there is significant brand awareness of particular branded soft drinks products the bargaining power of the drinks supplier is likely to be high. Failure to provide the branded drinks may damage both the reputation and revenue for the fast food restaurant. Where there is limited recognition of a supplier's products or services, the bargaining power of the supplier is reduced. In the example in Figure 3.3, customers are unlikely to change their chosen restaurant if there is a change to the provider of 'salt' or 'sugar' sachets.

- The cost of switching between different suppliers. This depends on the industry and the product or service in question. Where switching costs are high this may put the supplier in an advantageous position: for example, an organisation that has a highly complex IT platform supplied by an incumbent provider. For this organisation to switch to an alternative provider could cause significant business disruption and risk business continuity. The supplier is aware of this risk and can use this to its advantage within negotiations.

- The degree of alignment between organisations when purchasing products and services. Where fragmentation in purchasing decisions is high this can lead to an increased degree of power or influence from suppliers. Where there is alignment between competitors, perhaps through some use of industry forums or standards, this can lead to a reduction in the power of suppliers relative to industry rivals.

Figure 3.3 shows that there may be some suppliers, such as the branded drinks suppliers, who may wield significant power in this marketplace.

Bargaining power of buyers

This force looks at the relative power and influence between the buyers and the industry competitors. Considerations for this force include:

- The relative size of buyers compared with the industry rivals. Where the buyer is larger than the organisation that is supplying goods or services, they are likely to have an advantage during any negotiations. Where the buyer is smaller, the opposite is true, and the industry organisations are likely to hold the balance of power.

- The cost of switching between different suppliers. This can be relatively low or high depending on the industry and the product or service in question. Where switching costs are high this may put the industry firm in an advantageous position. Where it is easy to switch between different suppliers, the buyer could have a higher degree of power and influence during negotiations.

- The degree of buyer choice. Where there is limited choice for buyers, perhaps due to limited supply or due to a high concentration of power within the industry firms, the degree of buyer power and influence is limited.

- The threat of buyer competition. Some buyers may have the capability to provide the products or services. Where this is the case, the buyers tend to have additional power in negotiations with their suppliers.

In the example shown in Figure 3.3, the general public have relatively low bargaining power when contrasted with the restaurant providers. In contrast, the providers of home delivery services may have higher bargaining power when negotiating with the independent local restaurants and smaller restaurant chains.

Threat of new entrants

Threats from new entrants provides stimulus to industry firms to enhance product and service offerings. In addition, the threat causes existing organisations to consider increasing barriers to entry into the marketplace. Examples of barriers to entry for new entrants include the need to:

- Meet industry legislation and compliance obligations.

- Create market awareness of the new brand or product or service.

- Create a compelling and unique value proposition that will entice buyers.

- Gain access to supply or distribution channels (for example, securing landing/ take-off slots at an airport where no such slots are available, obtaining access to a trading platform or space on the shelves of retail outlets).

- Secure sufficient capital (funds) to develop and deploy the product or service offering into the marketplace.

- Create, deploy and maintain physical and virtual resources to enable capability. This includes:

  - people with the necessary skills and knowledge;

  - processes to support the new business operation;

  - effective EAs (including the domains of business, application(s), data and infrastructure);

  - industry knowledge (for example, the blueprints from which to build or deploy product or service offerings).

Figure 3.3 shows that there are relatively high barriers to entry for firms seeking to gain a prominent international position. For example, investment capital would be needed to establish:

- the global chain of restaurants (e.g. land acquisition costs, building or renovation costs);

- a compelling menu and brand proposition to entice buyers;

- robust processes to deliver consistent outputs across the globe;

- sufficient staff;

- supplier relationships;

- licences to operate.

In contrast, for a provider looking to establish a single local fast food restaurant, barriers to entry into the local marketplace would be considerably lower.

Threat of substitute products or services

This force looks at the availability and convenience of substitute products or services. Example considerations include:

- Could a buyer select to live without the product or service? For example, could a chocolate enthusiast simply decide to stop eating it altogether?

- Could a buyer choose a different means of sourcing the outcome desired or meeting the need or want behind purchasing decisions? Examples include:

  - The need to obtain transportation. Could buyers decide to use public transport, lift sharing or other transport services as opposed to the purchase of a vehicle from a motor manufacturer? Could virtual working or shopping remove the need for a vehicle?

- The need to obtain energy. Could electricity buyers decide that they no longer need to purchase this because they have independent means of generating energy (e.g. wind turbines, solar panels)?

- The need to be entertained. Could avid theatre enthusiasts stop going to live performances and instead watch these at home via streaming platforms?

Figure 3.3 reflects that the substitutes may be extensive and varied. For example, 'Ten-pin bowling' and 'Cinemas' are shown as substitutes because they offer alternative ways of spending time with family or friends, while also providing food.

Beyond the Five Forces Model

Porter's Five Forces Model provides a framework that may be used to analyse an industry where the organisation supplies products and/or services. If used in combination with PESTLE analysis it provides a mechanism for exploration of the external business environment for an organisation.

Critics of the Five Forces Model highlight that it is difficult to apply to not-for-profit organisations and to complex market environments. Examples include situations where an organisation is competing internationally across many different national markets and where complex relationships exist between firms operating in the marketplace, such as where an industry rival is also a supplier, or a new entrant is also a buyer.

Historically, within some highly competitive marketplaces, there has been a false confidence that the barriers to entry would be insurmountable for new entrants. However, there are many examples of where this has proven to be incorrect. Digital technologies offer the opportunity for 'Over The Top' (OTT) product or service offers. For example, a company may provide video or audio streaming services using available industry architecture despite not owning any video or audio content. While the term originates from the media industry, OTT as a business model can also be used for other types of industries. Examples include the provision of accommodation or transportation services by organisations that do not own accommodation or have a transportation infrastructure.

The threat and opportunity that may result from disrupting or reshaping a marketplace should not be neglected if an organisation is to survive in the long term. In their book *Blue Ocean Strategy*, Kim and Mauborgne (2015) suggest an approach for creating uncontested marketplaces. They argue for redefining market boundaries through the creation of new and compelling business models. Instead of a focus on individual product or service offers, they suggest the creation of an entirely new marketplace (initially without industry rivals). The exploration of this dimension of the external environment is also a component of external environmental analysis.

STRATEGY ANALYSIS: INTERNAL ENVIRONMENT

Internal environmental analysis also provides stimulus to the strategy and tactics of the organisation. In contrast to external environmental analysis, it provides insight that enables the organisation to identify 'strengths' and 'weaknesses'. There are a variety of techniques that can be used here, including:

- VMOST analysis;
- resource audit;
- balanced scorecard (BSC);
- performance measurement;
- growth share matrix (Boston Consulting Group (BCG) matrix).

Each of these techniques is discussed in this section.

VMOST analysis

Vision, Mission, Objectives, Strategy, Tactics (VMOST) provides an approach for the development and assessment of strategy. The technique provides a framework for analysing and defining the following:

Vision: Defines the target state for the organisation without regard to how this will be achieved. The target state is realised through the completion of the 'mission'.

Mission: Describes what the organisation does or will do.

Objectives: The specific objectives or outcomes that the organisation wants to achieve. These are used to guide and measure progress towards the organisation's vision and the completion of the mission.

Strategy: The long-term approach that is going to be taken by the organisation to achieve the 'vision', 'mission' and 'objectives'.

Tactics: The specific and detailed means by which the strategy should be executed. The tactics are often adapted when feedback regarding the success of the strategy is received.

Table 3.2 shows an example VMOST for an organisation looking to develop private tuition services for local school children.

Table 3.2 VMOST example

Vision	To be the leading provider of private tuition for school children
Mission	To improve educational outcomes for all our students
Objectives	• To enhance examination performance of students within 6 months of their engagement with our private tuition service
	• For at least 50% of parents to recommend the organisation to a friend within 1 year of engagement with the service
	• To increase operating profit by at least 10% per annum

(Continued)

Table 3.2 (Continued)

Strategy	• To recruit and retain the best available private tutors
	• To instigate a recommend a friend scheme for parents
	• To deliver tuition in modern, comfortable and safe surroundings
	• To build and share expertise among tutors to enhance student examination success
Tactics	• To work proactively and collaboratively with our network of tutors
	• To pay above the market rate for tuition services provided by tutors
	• To make our service offering as easy to use for tutors, parents and students as possible
	• To instigate a rigorous approach towards continuous improvement
	• To provide a 10% discount to parents for a recommendation that leads to private tutor engagement
	• To lease state of the art offices for the provision of tuition
	• Obtain access to and distribute past examination papers and teaching materials to our network of tutors

Figure 3.4 demonstrates how the components of VMOST relate to the core building blocks for understanding the strategic context shown earlier within Figure 3.1.

Figure 3.4 VMOST and the core building blocks for the strategic context

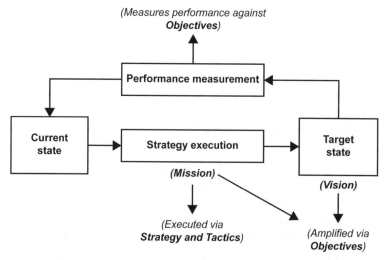

When using VMOST to assess the internal strategic environment the goal is to assess whether the elements within VMOST are a source of strength or weakness to the organisation.

To do this it is useful to consider several questions relative to the VMOST for the organisation including:

- Does a VMOST for the organisation exist?
- Are the elements of VMOST clearly defined?
- Is the VMOST communicated to and understood by leadership, management and employees?
- Are the 'Vision' and 'Mission' elements aligned?
- Do 'Objectives' align to and amplify the 'Vision' and 'Mission'?
- Are the objectives SMART (Specific, Measurable, Achievable, Relevant and Time-bound)?
- Are the Objectives balanced (see 'BSC')?
- Does the 'Strategy' align to the 'Vision', 'Mission' and 'Objectives?'
- Do the 'Tactics' align to the 'Strategy'?

Resource audit

A resource audit aids with the identification of strengths and weaknesses. The technique can be applied to an organisation, department or team.

When analysing each of the resource types it is useful to consider whether they are a source of strength or weakness for the organisation.

Physical
Example physical resources include:

- buildings;
- land;
- machinery;
- physical computer equipment;
- vehicles.

To assess the relative degree of strength or weakness, questions to be asked include:

- Are the physical resources appropriate and fit for purpose?
- Do physical resources impede or constrain the organisation in meeting strategic goals and objectives?
- Are the costs for development and maintenance of physical resources appropriate?

Financial

Example financial resources include:

- all financial assets and liabilities;
- cash flow;
- profitability;
- credit rating;
- overdraft and loan facilities;
- ability to generate capital (e.g. through obtaining shareholder investment, obtaining access to grants and or government funds).

To assess the relative degree of strength or weakness, questions to be asked include:

- How strong is the overall financial position of the organisation?
- What is the balance of assets and liabilities for the organisation?
- Are income streams growing/declining?
- Are costs growing/declining?
- How strong is the cash flow position of the organisation?
- Is the organisation able to raise finance through borrowing?

Human

Example human resources include:

- leadership and management;
- full- and part-time employees;
- temporary workers.

To assess the relative degree of strength or weakness, questions to be asked include:

- Are the human resources willing and able to execute against strategic objectives?
- How strong are the succession plans within the organisation?
- How adaptable and skilled are the human resources of the organisation?
- Where are the human resources geographically?
- How motivated are the human resources within the organisation?

Know-how

Example know-how resources include:

- patents, copyright and other intellectual property;
- knowledge resources (e.g. operating procedures, processes, internal knowledge repositories);

- knowledge of supplier and customer preferences;
- acquisition, retention and analysis of data.

To assess the relative degree of strength or weakness, questions to be asked include:

- How strong is the know-how of the organisation?
- Is know-how documented and retrievable?
- Is the organisation reliant on the know-how of key individuals? What is the risk associated with this?
- What unique abilities does the organisation have?
- What abilities do the suppliers and customers of the organisation have?

Reputation
This resource concerns the reputation of the organisation among stakeholders.

Example reputational resources include:

- the reputation of the brand(s) that the organisation owns;
- the reputation of the organisation as an employer;
- the reputation of the organisation as a partner, supplier or customer;
- the reputation of the organisation as a supplier of goods or services;
- benchmark information, accreditations and awards;
- the level of goodwill towards the organisation from customers and potential customers.

To assess the relative degree of strength or weakness, questions to be asked include:

- What is the reputation of the organisation?
- What positive or negative reviews of the organisation are available?
- What feedback do regulators, partners, suppliers, customers or employees provide about the organisation?
- What do competitors say about the organisation?
- What do regulators say about the organisation?
- What benchmarking information is available about the organisation?
- Has the organisation obtained any accreditations or awards?

The BSC

The BSC (Kaplan and Norton, 1996) provides a means by which to assess the breadth and balance of 'goals' and 'objectives' that the organisation uses to measure strategic performance. The BSC should align to the vision and strategy of the organisation. The structure and elements of the BSC are shown in Figure 3.5.

Figure 3.5 Balanced scorecard (BSC)

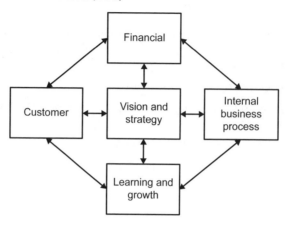

The four performance areas measured within the BCS are described in Table 3.3.

Table 3.3 Elements of the BSC

BSC element	Description
Financial	Measures that relate to financial performance (e.g. profitability, liquidity, turnover, share price)
Internal business process	Measures that relate to processes (e.g. error or defect rates, lead time, performance against service level agreements, process variability)
Learning and growth (innovation)	Measures that relate to investment in the organisation for future learning and growth (e.g. employee skill development, new product/service development, meeting benchmark targets, continual improvement initiatives)
Customer	Measures that relate to the customer (e.g. complaints, recommendations, loyalty, customer feedback ratings, reviews)

In line with other internal environmental analysis techniques, it is necessary to assess whether the organisation's objectives are a source of strength or weakness. Historically, many organisations have placed a great deal of emphasis on the financial measures of performance. This has led to a limited amount of focus on process, learning and growth, and customer-based performance measurement. All of these aspects are important if the organisation is to succeed in the long term.

Performance measurement

The approach adopted towards performance measurement is guided and informed by an organisation's 'vision' and 'mission'. Objectives 'amplify' the vision and mission as they allow for measurement of progress towards the target state vision and the accomplishment of the organisation's mission.

Essentially, performance measurement is looking to answer two fundamental questions. The first question is 'How well is the organisation executing against its chosen strategy?' Aligned to this, performance measurement also leads to the question 'How well is the organisation performing against chosen objectives?' If the organisation is executing strategy effectively and is meeting targets, this may indicate an area of strength. Conversely, if the organisation is not executing strategy effectively or is falling short of targets, this would indicate an area of potential weakness.

In addition to informing the view of the organisation in its current state, performance measurement is used to guide and inform, as well as provide feedback, on the effectiveness of the chosen 'strategy' and 'tactics' of the organisation. Performance measurement provides feedback to the organisation and, if designed well, can provide valuable inputs into objective and evidence-based strategic decision-making. Table 3.4 clarifies key terms used to discuss performance measurement.

Table 3.4 Performance measurement terminology

Objectives	• The specific objectives or outcomes that the organisation wants to achieve
	• These are used to guide and measure progress towards the organisation's 'Vision' and the completion of the 'Mission'. They should be **S**pecific, **M**easurable, **A**chievable, **R**elevant and **T**ime-bound (SMART)
Critical success factors (CSFs)	• Qualitative descriptions of the critical factors that must be in place for the organisation to achieve defined objectives
	• CSFs are ideally balanced (see BSC) and should align to the 'Vision' and 'Mission' of the organisation
	• Multiple CSFs can be relevant to any individual objective
Key performance indicators (KPIs)	• Quantitative (SMART) measurements of performance that track the achievement of CSFs.
	• Multiple KPIs can be used to measure a single CSF
	• KPIs can be used to measure multiple different CSFs
Targets	• These are specific in nature and provide an objective measurement of performance against 'Objectives' or 'KPIs'
	• Often the red, amber, green status is used to indicate the current status of defined targets:
	▪ Red: performance significantly below target
	▪ Amber: performance slightly below target
	▪ Green: performance in alignment with or above target

The example below explores one of the objectives of the private tuition business mentioned above:

To enhance examination performance of students within 6 months of their engagement with our private tuition service.

CSFs are defined that help to monitor the progress towards achieving this objective. In this instance, the following factors have been deemed to be critical:

- quality of private tuition;
- student engagement;
- parent engagement.

Relevant KPIs and associated targets are determined for each CSF to provide quantitative measures that support progress tracking.

Quality of private tuition

- **KPI:** Star rating provided by pupil per private tuition session.
  - **Target:** At least 95 per cent of private tuition sessions score 4 stars or above over a 6-month period.
- **KPI:** Exam grade performance.
  - **Target:** Exam grade performance to increase by at least one grade within 6 months.

Student engagement

- **KPI:** Star rating provided by pupil per private tuition session.
  - **Target:** At least 95 per cent of private tuition sessions score 4 stars or above over a 6-month period.
- **KPI:** Student attendance of scheduled tuition sessions.
  - **Target:** Zero unplanned absences from scheduled tuition sessions over a 12-month period.

Parent engagement

- **KPI:** Number of parent home observation slips completed.
  - **Target:** At least one home observation slip completed per month.
- **KPI:** Attendance of parent at tutor bi-monthly meetings.
  - **Target:** 100 per cent attendance over a 12-month period.

One of the KPIs in this example, 'star rating provided by pupil per private tuition session', has been used to assess performance for two CSFs: quality of private tuition and student engagement. This is a helpful and sensible approach as it ensures consistency and alignment with the objective.

Performance measurement and VMOST

When considering performance measurement, it is useful to consider the explicit alignment with the wider VMOST technique. Figure 3.6 shows the key areas of alignment with VMOST.

Figure 3.6 Performance measurement and VMOST

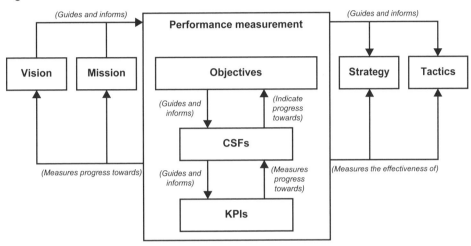

Growth share matrix

The growth share matrix (also known as the BCG matrix or Boston box) was developed by BCG and provides a means of conducting an analysis of the portfolio of products or services that an organisation offers. The matrix, shown in Figure 3.7, is used to categorise the organisation's products relative to the level of both market share and market growth.

Figure 3.7 Growth share matrix (Source: Adapted from the BCG Portfolio Matrix from the Product Portfolio Matrix, © 1970, The Boston Consulting Group)

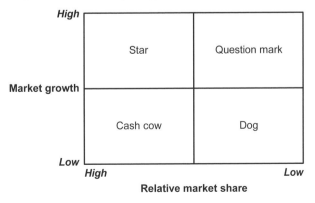

The four quadrants of the grid are explained in Table 3.5.

Table 3.5 Quadrants of the growth share matrix

Growth share matrix quadrant	Description
Star	Products or services that have a high degree of relative market share within a market that has high growth. These offer positive and growing revenue contributions.
Question mark	Products or services that have low relative market share in high growth markets. These require careful examination, and this may lead to product/service redesign, reconfiguration or repositioning.
Dog	Products or services that have low relative market share in low growth markets.
Cash cow	Products or services that have a high degree of relative market share within a market that has low growth. As their name suggests, these offer positive revenue contributions. Cash cows do not require much investment so the extra funds they generate can be invested in Stars or Question marks

The growth share matrix helps to identify the strengths and weaknesses derived from an organisation's portfolio of products.

STRATEGY ANALYSIS: SWOT ANALYSIS

A SWOT analysis summarises the results of the internal and external environment analysis and highlights the key factors identified. It is essential that the SWOT is developed using the techniques described for internal and external environmental analysis as this ensures that it accurately reflects the organisation's strategic position. Failure to do this could lead to ill-considered strategic decision-making based on insufficiently robust information.

A SWOT analysis is often represented as a two-by-two matrix as shown in Figure 3.8.

The content and language used in SWOT analysis is important. Overall the SWOT should be accurate, complete, brief and clear. It should also align with the VMOST of the organisation.

For example, a SWOT could contain the following entries:

Strengths:

- Strong levels of customer satisfaction. The organisation has exceeded annual targets for all customer-focused objectives.

Figure 3.8 SWOT analysis

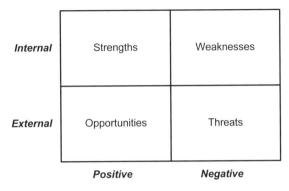

	Positive	Negative
Internal	Strengths	Weaknesses
External	Opportunities	Threats

- Accommodation and facilities. The organisation is located in an accessible area and the offices and equipment are of a high standard.

Weaknesses:

- Unclear direction set for the organisation.

- Weak financial position. The organisation has high levels of debt relative to assets and is experiencing poor cash flow.

- Leadership succession planning. The organisation has identified a gap in the succession plans for several key roles.

Opportunities:

- The availability of technology advancements and the popularity of digital service offerings.

- Demographic changes in Europe and the US opening up a large potential market for the organisation's products.

Threats:

- Increased likelihood of stringent regulatory interventions following several high-profile supervisory failures.

- Increasing propensity for fraud.

A key point that emerges from these examples is that strengths and weaknesses are found from within the organisation. They are discovered following an analysis of the VMOST, performance, the resource audit and the portfolio of products. In contrast, opportunities and threats are from outside the organisation and are found using the PESTLE or the Five Forces Model. The external factors that present opportunities and threats cannot be influenced by the organisation. It is the decisions about whether or not to grasp opportunities or deal with threats that are within the control of the organisation. The ability of the organisation to make decisions on how to respond to factors presenting opportunities and threats depends upon the internal strengths and weaknesses. Typical decisions may be:

- to develop new products and services for the existing market;
- to move into new markets;
- to introduce a new marketing or sales strategy and increase the share of existing markets;
- to diversify into new product areas that open up new markets.

Enabling decisions on the way forward for the organisation is the essence of strategy analysis.

STRATEGY EXECUTION

There are various aspects to consider when executing an organisational strategy. These include the results of the internal and external environment analysis and the gap between the organisation's current and desired target state. There are several techniques that may be used to inform strategy development and execution, in particular:

- business model canvas (BMC);
- business capability model (BCM);
- value stream modelling;
- target operating model (TOM).

These techniques are discussed below.

Business model canvas

The term 'business model' has several meanings. It is used to refer to the way an organisation is designed to deliver products and services to customers. This provides a means through which to develop and execute strategy.

Business models help to align the work of the organisation with desired outcomes. They can be used to assess the current and target state and to identify and plan changes.

In the book *Business Model Generation*, the following definition for a business model is offered: 'A business model describes the rationale of how an organisation creates, manages and delivers value' (Osterwalder and Pigneur, 2010).

Osterwalder and Pigneur offer an overview generic business model template known as the BMC. An overview representation of the BMC is shown in Figure 3.9.

The questions addressed by the BMC elements are described in Table 3.6.

Figure 3.9 Structure and components of the BMC

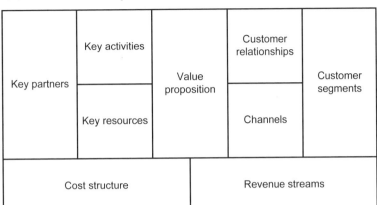

Table 3.6 The elements of the BMC

BMC element	Questions addressed
Customer segments	Who are the organisation's important customers? For whom is value proposed?
Value propositions	What value does the organisation offer? Which customer problems or pains does it propose to solve? Which customer opportunities or gains do the products or services support or satisfy? What are the qualities (e.g. price, availability, choice, quality, functions supported) offered by the products or services? What is the relative value of the organisation's brand or image?
Channels	How does the organisation interact and communicate with customers? Is there variance in customer experience across different channels? Which channels work best? What additional channels do customers expect? How do customers pay?
Customer relationships	What is the nature of the relationship that the organisation has with each customer segment? Where might it be possible to enhance the customer experience?
Revenue streams	What are the organisation's revenue streams? How profitable are each of these revenue streams? How much does each revenue stream contribute?
Key resources	What key resources do the organisation's value proposition, channels and customer relationships require?
Key activities	What key activities do the organisation's value propositions, channels and customer relationships require?
Key partners	Who are the organisation's key partners and suppliers? Which key resources or key activities do they provide?
Cost structure	What are the costs of the key resources, key activities and key partners employed in the business model? Is the cost structure sustainable?

Through consideration of the major components of the business model, ideally with their stakeholders, the business analyst has an opportunity to help shape and influence the outcomes of the change initiatives and ensure that they are strategically aligned.

Business capability model

A BCM provides a pictorial view, which is both abstract and conceptual, of what it is that an organisation can do. The model is not sufficiently detailed to represent how the capabilities are enacted in the physical environment. Capabilities are typically defined using the noun/noun naming convention and would be expected to exhibit the following characteristics, summarised using the acronym SUAVE:

Stable: Each capability represents a business activity that persists over time

Unique: Each capability is unique

Abstract: Each capability is abstracted from the real world

Valuable: Each capability is of value to the organisation and its stakeholders

Executives: Each capability is important to the organisation and captures senior leadership interest

Business capability taxonomy

A taxonomy provides a basis for organising and representing capabilities. The following two levels are helpful when building a capability taxonomy.

- **Capability groups**:
  - Contains a minimum of two lower level business capabilities.
  - May include multiple other capability groups (known as nested capability groups).
- **Business capability**:
  - The lowest level building blocks of the capability model.

Figure 3.10 provides an example where the capability taxonomy has been used without 'nested capabilities'. This example shows a capability group that encompasses five business capabilities.

Figure 3.11 provides an example where the business capability taxonomy has been used to show nested and non-nested capability groups. In addition, it shows business capabilities existing outside a capability group and indicates those capabilities that require additional decomposition and/or clarification.

BCM strata

Capability models are typically organised using separate layers known as 'strata'. The strata are as follows:

- **Strategic: direction setting** – capabilities that are critical to the organisation's long-term success. These typically command senior leader attention.

Figure 3.10 Example business capability taxonomy

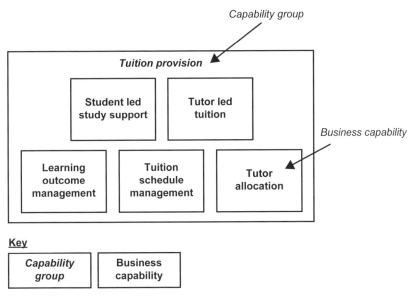

Figure 3.11 Example business capability taxonomy showing nested capability groups

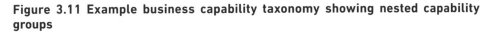

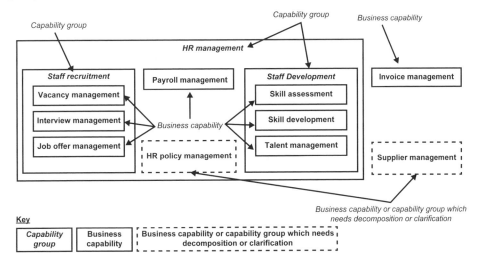

- **Primary or core strata: customer facing** – capabilities with which customers interact directly.

- **Support strata** – capabilities that contribute towards the organisation's operation and long-term success that support the internal working of the organisation rather than being customer-facing.

Why model business capabilities?

A BCM provides a common language to support and enable discussions throughout the organisation. This language is particularly useful when considering the development or execution of strategy. The capability model can also be used:

- to analyse the differences between the current and target state of the organisation;

- to help shape and scope proposals for change;

- to identify opportunities to extend the organisation's products and services;

- to identify opportunities to improve organisational performance;

- to support the analysis of change investment decisions.

BCMs offer executive managers information about what the organisation is able to offer. This can help with strategic idea generation and decision-making, for example, through leveraging capabilities to move into new markets or to extend existing markets.

Value stream modelling

In contrast to the capability model, the value stream shows an active view of the organisation interacting with either an internal or external stakeholder through the provision of a 'value item'. The model is abstract and conceptual. It can be used to help formulate ideas for the target state of the organisation, including identifying products and services that the organisation does not currently offer. Value stream models therefore provide a basis for discussion, common understanding and more detailed analysis. An example value stream is shown in Figure 3.12.

Figure 3.12 Example value stream

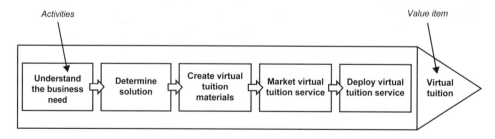

Value streams may be aligned with more detailed process views by providing an overview of an end-to-end process that is then decomposed (see Chapter 7). This provides a useful framework from which to guide and shape strategy execution and product/service delivery.

Target operating models

The term 'Target Operating Model' (TOM) is used to describe 'how' a business needs to be established to support the execution of strategy. TOMs are more detailed and less abstract than the content provided within many of the business architecture blueprints such as the BCM and value stream models. Where a TOM and the business architecture artefacts are used in alignment with each other, they help to improve understanding of what is required within the target state and can be used as a basis for gap analysis with the current state. This informs the roadmap to achieve strategic objectives.

There are many different definitions of a TOM or the term 'operating model', including the following:

- The Business Architecture Guild® emphasises that an operating model is focused on business processes, people and IT (BIZBOK® Guide, 2020).

- An alternative view is that the TOM should cover the full range of elements across POPIT™. These are People, Organisation, Processes, Information and Technology.

It is useful to agree with stakeholders what is intended by this term in order to avoid any potential confusion. The POPIT model shown in Figure 3.13 offers a clear representation that often helps to provide clarity.

Figure 3.13 The POPIT model (© Assist Knowledge Development Ltd.)

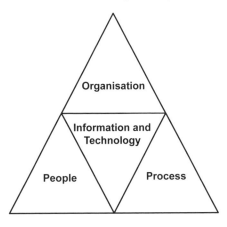

Some example considerations for each of the elements of POPIT in relation to TOMs are shown in Table 3.7.

Table 3.7 Elements of the POPIT model

POPIT element	Considerations
People	What knowledge and skills will people need in the target state? What levels of motivation will be required? How will people communicate?
Organisation	Who will be the key partners and suppliers? What business model or organisation structure will be adopted? What culture will pertain within the organisation? What leadership and management approaches will be used? How many people are needed and in what roles?
Process	Which processes will be used in the target state? Are the processes optimal? What efficiency gains will be obtained?
Information	What change will be made to the capture, storage and analysis of data and information? How secure will the organisation's information and data be?
Technology	What technology will be used in the target state? How well will this align to the organisation's processes? Will the technology be scalable? Will the technology be interoperable?

Addressing the elements and considerations of the POPIT model provides a firm basis for developing an effective TOM.

EA

All organisations have an EA. An EA represents the core building blocks of the organisation and demonstrates how it is organised. The term 'enterprise' is used in this context to mean the entire scope of the organisation. The term architecture is defined as:

> The fundamental concepts or properties of a system in its environment embodied in its elements, relationships, and in the principles of its design and evolution.
>
> (ISO/IEC/IEEE 42010:2011).

This definition, when used relative to the enterprise, means that every concept and property of the organisation relative to its environment is within the scope of EA.

There are competing definitions for the term EA. The publication *Enterprise Architecture as Strategy* offers the following definition:

> The enterprise architecture is the organizing logic for business processes and IT infrastructure, reflecting the integration and standardization requirements of the company's operating model. The enterprise architecture provides a long-term view of a company's processes, systems, and technologies so that individual projects can build capabilities – not just fulfil immediate needs.
>
> (Ross et al., 2006).

This definition indicates that EA is directly relevant to strategic discussions and decision-making and suggests that individual projects should build capabilities rather than just focusing on immediate needs. This is highly relevant to business analysts. If business analysts focus on short-term 'fixes', it is possible that they can diminish or harm the long-term development of capabilities and, accordingly, cause damage to the organisation during strategy execution. Conversely, if business analysts can clarify and define business needs that enhance and contribute to the long-term development of capabilities, they can contribute positively to the execution of the organisation's strategy.

EA domains

A further means of understanding EA is to look at the domains that this discipline covers. These domains are shown in Figure 3.14.

Figure 3.14 EA domains (© Assist Knowledge Development Ltd.)

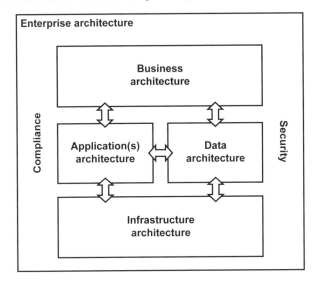

The domains encompassed by EA are described in the overview below.

Business architecture
The Business Architecture Guild® originally defined business architecture as:

> A blueprint of the enterprise that provides a common understanding of the organization and is used to align strategic objectives and tactical demands.
> (BIZBOK® Guide, 2020)

Blueprints relate to conceptual and abstract views of the organisation and can cover many different areas including:

- business motivation and strategy;
- organisation structure and design;

- operating model;
- organisational culture;
- value propositions for products and services;
- processes;
- capabilities;
- information.

For a seller of goods at a local market, the business architecture might relate to the processes used to acquire, transport and sell products. This would include the relationships with suppliers, partners, regulators, competitors and customers. The business architecture would encompass all of the processes used by the market seller to trade and all the capabilities inherent within the business.

For a global seller, the business architecture is likely to contain information similar to that of the market seller. However, the complexity and volume of the blueprints is likely to be much more expansive.

Application(s) architecture
This domain includes the portfolio of applications used within the enterprise and their alignment to the business architecture.

For a seller of goods at the local market, this might include any spreadsheets used to maintain a record of stock. Perhaps the seller uses an application to support customer payments and has a separate financial management system to maintain accounting information. Any paper-based lists or documents are also part of the application architecture.

For the global seller, an applications catalogue should be maintained to demonstrate the alignment between software applications and the respective business processes and capabilities that they support. This could potentially include a vast array of different software applications, particularly if the countries have made independent decisions regarding the selection of software. Paper-based lists and documents are also part of the application architecture.

Data architecture
Data architecture includes all of the data held and used within the business. The data architecture should represent the alignment between the data and business architecture, and should include information on where data is stored within the portfolio of applications.

For the seller of goods at the local market this would include any data captured on spreadsheets, customer payment data and accounts information. The data architecture would also include any data captured within paper-based lists or documents.

For the global seller, the data architecture should encompass all of the data captured and maintained across the business. This would include the data stored within any software applications and paper documents.

Infrastructure architecture

This domain encompasses the hardware, operating system software, networks, and so on that enable the applications and data to be run and stored.

For example, a seller of goods at a local market may make use of a terminal to support customers making card-based payments. This device is likely to be connected to the seller's phone; both constitute elements of the infrastructure architecture. The connectivity to the seller's telecommunications provider and to any cloud-based service offerings also form part of the infrastructure architecture. It is likely that there are other infrastructure components such as the seller's personal laptop or other device. If a cloud-based software application is utilised for the completion of accounts, the infrastructure on which this resides also forms part of the infrastructure architecture.

For the global seller, the infrastructure architecture is likely to be much more complex. Components should include any cloud-based infrastructure services consumed, hardware supplied to employees, internal networks and data centres to name just a few.

Compliance architecture

The compliance architecture domain covers all compliance obligations for the enterprise and the means by which they are met. This includes the building blocks across all other EA domains that enable the enterprise to meet and manage both external and internal compliance expectations. External compliance obligations tend to be legal and regulatory whereas internal obligations relate to internal policies. Compliance architecture should ensure that any taxation, employment or other trading laws relevant to the business operation are met.

For the seller of goods at the local market, this might include meeting any permit requirements associated with continuing to trade. For example, where a local organisation issues permits to traders based upon an annual review of public liability insurance, fire precautions and compliance with health and safety inspections. The trader can obtain insight into how compliance obligations are met through the domains of 'business', 'application(s)', 'data', 'infrastructure' and 'security' architecture.

As with the other domains, for the global seller the compliance architecture is likely to be of much greater complexity. However, the domains of 'business', 'application(s)', 'data', 'infrastructure' and 'security' architecture should help to clarify how compliance obligations are met.

Security architecture

Security architecture encompasses all components and systems through which the enterprise protects its assets from harm, loss or danger. This includes items such as security-focused applications or infrastructure, security policies and processes, access controls, vetting and training of people.

For the seller of goods at the local market, the security architecture might relate to the alarm and locking systems installed on vehicles and on any physical premises used to store stock. Security architecture would also include the protection of data stored on any of the organisation's applications.

For the global seller of goods, the security architecture is likely to cover many assets that require protection. Similarly to compliance architecture, it should be possible to gain insight into the components of the security architecture through understanding the 'business', 'application(s)', 'data', 'infrastructure' and 'compliance' architecture domains.

EA and the core building blocks of strategy

It is useful to consider how the EA domains relate to the current and target state of the organisation. This view helps to provide the business analyst with contextual awareness relative to the change initiative on which they are working.

Figure 3.15 shows how EA relates to the core building blocks of the strategic context. Effective strategy execution ensures that changes are made to the EA in a manner that allows the organisation to progress towards its desired target state. This progress is aligned to and monitored through performance measurement.

Figure 3.15 EA and the core building blocks of the strategic context (© Assist Knowledge Development Ltd.)

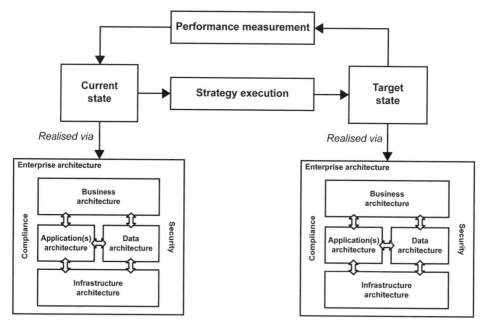

THE IMPORTANCE OF STRATEGIC ALIGNMENT

If a strategy is to be successful, it is imperative that it is aligned with the philosophy of the organisation. To understand the philosophy of the organisation it is useful to ask some fundamental questions as shown in Figure 3.16.

Figure 3.16 Foundations for strategic alignment

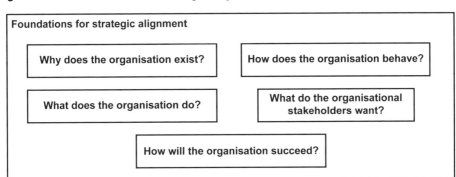

Alignment between the answers to these questions and the organisation's strategy is likely to have a positive impact on the organisation's health over the long term. Each question is addressed below.

Why does the organisation exist?

The answer to this question should align with the organisation's vision, mission and objectives. However, this is not always the case.

For example, a café has been set up that reflects the owner's passion for providing nutritional vegan and vegetarian meals. Meat-based products are not sold within the café even though this may present an opportunity for profitable growth. Within this example, what Lencioni (2012) describes as the organisation's 'core purpose' is clear. External and internal stakeholders understand the purpose of the business and decisions are made in alignment with this.

A second example concerns an established business that was set up by its original owners to focus on the provision of nutritious and balanced meals. The business has since been acquired by an entrepreneur looking to increase personal wealth. The entrepreneur decides to leverage the established brand and reputation of the business while minimising investment and maximising profit. The core purpose of this business is stated in marketing literature as being focused on the provision of nutritious meals. However, the new non-explicit or non-communicated purpose of the organisation is to increase wealth for the owner. Within this café, all business decisions are driven by this profit motive. If an opportunity arises to grow the business via acquisition of a fast food outlet serving unhealthy non-nutritionally balanced meals, this opportunity may well be taken forward. This is despite the stated 'core purpose' that the business exists to provide 'nutritious' meals.

So long as it remains profitable, the fast food outlet may be left to operate separately and to take independent decisions from the core café business. If at a later stage someone asks the head of the original café outlet and the head of the fast food outlet why the business exists, different answers are likely to be provided. In this instance, the core purpose and direction of the organisation is not clear. Misalignment between strategy and execution is apparent.

Persistent misalignment can confuse leaders, managers and employees while they attempt to make decisions and execute strategy. Although diversification is not in itself a damaging strategy, if this strategy is not recognised and communicated, it is potentially detrimental to the organisation's long-term success.

The context described above would be problematic for business analysts should they be required to execute changes that oppose the organisation's stated purpose. For example, a business analyst is tasked with supporting an initiative that aims to reduce supplier costs and a decision is made to replace suppliers of nutritionally balanced ingredients with lower cost suppliers of non-nutritious ingredients. If the business analyst doesn't realise that the actual purpose of the organisation is to maximise profits, they may well raise questions and challenges regarding whether this is an appropriate decision given the stated purpose of provision of 'nutritious' meals. However, if the business analyst is aware of the change in the organisation's 'core purpose', they may be able to navigate the situation effectively.

What does the organisation do?

The answer to this question is also foundational to the organisation's strategy and should align to the organisation's mission, strategy and tactics.

While elements of the answer to this question may change over time, particularly in response to changes to the external environment, the essence of what the organisation does should not change without careful and considered review. For example, the café that wants to sell nutritional vegan and vegetarian meals could develop to become an organisation that continues to sell meals to customers visiting its cafés, but also delivers meals to people's homes and supplies frozen ready meals to supermarkets. Later, the organisation could also diversify and develop a series of cookbooks or host workshops on the preparation of nutritional and vegan meals. Throughout these changes in direction, the 'core purpose' of the organisation has not been contradicted. Also, what the organisation does at a conceptual level has not changed.

Internal conflict may result where there is misalignment between the views held by the organisation and those held by the internal departments. This is especially the case where there are competing priorities. For example, the café has diversified through acquisition of a fast food outlet and now wishes to use digital technologies to allow online ordering via smartphone or tablets. The intention is to reduce costs and enhance customer experience. However, if each area of business wishes to invest in technologies that enable customers to order meals via mobile or tablet applications, there is likely to be internal competition for investment and resources. There may be competing views from each of the businesses regarding which technology platforms to use, which features to support and which products and services should be offered. This may lead to a situation where independent decisions are made to build mobile or tablet applications, leading to two variants in use, and resulting in the development and maintenance of two separate applications that support different processes for viewing menus, ordering, order fulfilment and payment.

For the business analyst working within these organisations this presents a challenge. The business analyst should be able to quickly see the duplication of processes, data capture and supporting technologies. Divergence in accountability for the respective applications and any involved partners should also be clear. The long-term cost of these independent decisions is likely to be higher than the creation of a single and consistent process and supporting suite of applications. One of the root causes of misalignment is disagreement among the businesses when answering the question 'What does this organisation do?'

How does the organisation behave?

This question is not explicitly covered by VMOST but misalignment when answering this question can perhaps have the most damaging effect on long-term organisational health. This is particularly the case when the implicit and explicit values of an organisation are not aligned with the behaviour of the leadership, management and employees. Where an organisation has a stated set of values that do not align to the behaviours of the individuals within the organisation, it is likely that confusion over strategy and misaligned execution will result.

For example, an organisation states that it is 'passionate about great customer service'. If this is a true belief of the individuals within the organisation it can be regarded as what Lencioni (2012) would describe as a 'core value'. The core value exists even if it's not written down and impacts every single decision that the organisation makes. All stakeholders are aware of the organisation's desire to offer 'great customer service'. This should in turn lead to an enhanced customer service offering that is not provided by competitors who do not share this core value.

Alternatively, if the stated value is used solely for marketing purposes and the behaviour demonstrated by members of staff is aligned with beliefs about minimising costs and maximising profits, stakeholders are likely to become disillusioned. Customers may have raised expectations regarding great service so are left disappointed when this is not delivered by the organisation. Employees are also likely to be disillusioned as they are forced to justify decisions that the organisation takes, such as the removal of product choices or the reduced quality of service.

While customer service has been used in this example, value misalignment can occur in many other areas of business.

The business analyst needs to understand the answer to the question 'How does this organisation behave?' in order to recognise if misalignment of values and behaviours exists. Considering this foundational question helps analysts to contribute positively and influence the decisions of the organisation.

What do the organisation's stakeholders want?

Organisations need to understand what stakeholders want in order to inform decisions on what value proposition should be offered. This position should be reviewed regularly to ensure that changes in stakeholder expectations are identified and considered.

Organisations typically have a broad range of stakeholders including customers, owners, partners, regulators, employees, managers, competitors and suppliers (see Chapter 6 for further information on stakeholder categories). Analysing expectations across these categories should ensure that all stakeholder wants and needs are considered in the development of strategy and in any subsequent execution.

If the organisation can accurately anticipate stakeholders' responses to what it does it is better able to plot a path for successful stakeholder interactions. This is particularly key if stakeholder interaction is important for the organisation's success. For example, the café that markets itself as being focused on providing nutritious meals is, in reality, focused on increasing profit. If within this organisation it does not anticipate the expectations of health and safety regulators, it may fail to meet food hygiene standards. This could in turn lead to the withdrawal of permission to trade, causing the organisation to close. This may be only a temporary setback but it will do little to enhance the prosperity of the business or its reputation. Where an organisation does not anticipate when customers are likely to respond negatively to changes, it may choose a direction leading to negative consequences.

Long-term strategic performance is enhanced if the organisation can obtain feedback from stakeholders and respond positively to their wants and needs. There are many techniques available that help business analysts to understand stakeholders and their views; these are covered in Chapter 6.

How will the organisation succeed?

The final question that forms the basis for strategic alignment is perhaps the most difficult to answer. The leaders of the organisation have to decide the pathway to organisational success. The pathway chosen is influenced by the strategic context, the external and internal environment and the chosen approach towards strategy execution as well as the answer to the questions raised above.

SUMMARY

Business analysts need to understand each of the component parts of the strategic development process if they are to contribute positively to strategically-aligned business change initiatives. This includes an appreciation of business philosophy, EA and each of the elements shown within Figure 3.17.

Figure 3.17 The strategic context for business analysis

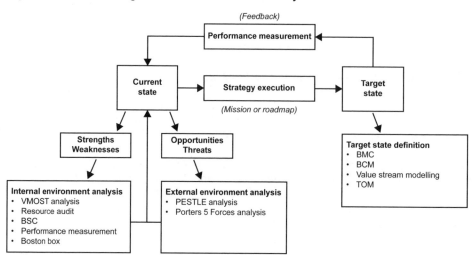

4 THE BUSINESS ANALYSIS SERVICE FRAMEWORK

INTRODUCTION

The breadth of the business analyst role has resulted in the development of an extensive toolkit of skills and techniques. However, clarifying business analysis itself is critical if the role and the benefits it can bring are to be recognised by organisations. Chapter 1 introduced the BASF, which proposes a portfolio of services that may be offered by business analysts. The BASF also provides a basis from which the business analyst role may be adapted to align with any organisational or project contexts. These contexts may impose standards that determine the required approaches to the business analysis work, the modelling techniques applied when analysing business situations and system requirements, and approved documentation templates.

The BASF service definitions state what business analysts do and why this is of benefit. The framework also suggests how the work is to be done, by identifying relevant activities and techniques that should be considered to determine the most appropriate approach for each situation and context. This provides a basis for competency development and career progression.

THE BUSINESS ANALYSIS SERVICE FRAMEWORK

One of the aspects that makes business analysis work so interesting is the range and nature of business change projects. The business systems investigated and the approaches required to conduct the business analysis work can be very varied. Within different project contexts, business analysts may need to adapt the activities they carry out and select which techniques they should apply. They may also need to engage with and influence stakeholders who hold views that differ considerably.

This variety is reflected in the BASF and the six business analysis services. Figure 4.1 (repeated from Chapter 1) shows the service portfolio defined within the BASF. This chapter describes these services and the value proposition, activities and techniques relevant to each service.

SITUATION INVESTIGATION AND PROBLEM ANALYSIS

The **situation investigation and problem analysis** service is represented in Figure 4.2.

Figure 4.1 The BASF services (© Debra Paul)

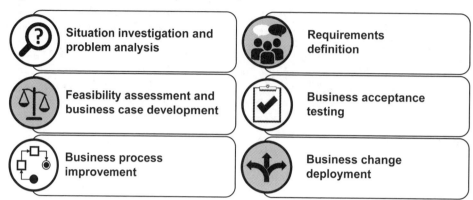

Figure 4.2 Situation investigation and problem analysis overview (© Debra Paul)

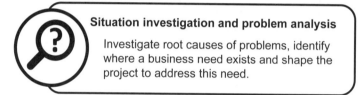

Service description

This service is concerned with uncovering issues, defining problems and shaping the change project. During this service, the analyst may be presented with a formal or informal statement of 'the problem'; however, this statement is rarely correct or complete. Business analysts have to investigate business situations in order to determine where the root causes of problems lie and ensure that symptoms of these problems are not confused with the underlying real issues.

To do this, the business analyst has to be open-minded and needs to avoid making assumptions or accepting without question any information provided. The ability to challenge is key to the success of this service, as is recognising that different stakeholders are likely to have different perspectives on a business situation. Contrasting, or even conflicting, perspectives typically give rise to different views on the problems to be addressed, the desired outcomes and the priorities for the future business system. The business analyst also needs to be knowledgeable about the business context for the area under investigation.

The focus of this service is to identify where problems lie and what actions may be taken to improve the business system. A 'gap analysis' is conducted whereby a current or 'as is' view is compared with a desired, future or 'to be' view. The objective is to identify areas where action is needed to deal with the gaps. This may require changes to the organisation, people, processes, information or technology. The target views may be developed using business activity models (see Chapter 6) or business process models (see Chapter 7).

A business activity model provides a conceptual picture of the desired business activities and allows the business analyst to see where the current business system is lacking. When examining the model, the range and extent of the gaps found will vary from activity to activity. Some activities may be in place and operating satisfactorily, while others may be inadequate in the current business system and some may not exist at all. There may be good support for the activity from the organisation's information systems or this may be poor and in need of improvement. Identifying the gaps at this level helps to determine the potential for change to the business system and the degree to which this is required.

At a more detailed level, gap analysis focuses on the business processes that are applied within the business system. Whereas the activities represented on the business activity model provide a conceptual view of *what* activities should be within the desired business system, business process models enable consideration of *how* the work is carried out. The analysis is therefore conducted at a more specific level of detail and, rather than being conceptual, is much closer to the physical reality of the business system. Chapter 8 discusses gap analysis and the means of evolving an overview of a desired solution.

Architectural artefacts such as capability models and value streams (see Chapter 3) may also be used to define a target view of the business system.

Service value proposition

The **situation investigation and problem analysis** service offers the following value proposition:

- State a clear definition of the problem to be addressed and the business needs to be met.
- Define the scope of the work to achieve this.
- Where undertaking a project is relevant to addressing the business issue, clarify in outline the investment objectives and business benefits to be achieved by the project.

Service activities

The activities required to carry out the **situation investigation and problem analysis** service are as follows:

1. Investigate the situation and the problem or opportunity
2. Understand the strategic context for the situation
3. Identify and articulate the business needs
4. Define the problem
5. Define the scope of the business change project
6. Define the rationale for rejecting a project proposal

Service techniques

This service often takes place within a context that is ambiguous and the potential exists for uncertainty and complexity. It is important to consider the various techniques that may be used and choose those that are most appropriate to the particular business situation. There are two areas required to deliver this service and the key techniques for each area are as follows:

- Investigating situations: interviewing, workshops, surveys, observation, focus groups, document analysis, scenario analysis, prototyping, wireframing. Techniques such as activity sampling, record searching and surveys may also be used where it is necessary to quantify information.

- Recording information: rich pictures, mind maps, problem statements, Fishbone (or Ishikawa) diagrams, five whys, context diagrams, brainstorming/brainwriting, Post-it™ exercises. Fishbone diagrams can also be very useful to uncover the root causes of problems.

Situation investigation and recording techniques are described in Chapter 5.

FEASIBILITY ASSESSMENT AND BUSINESS CASE DEVELOPMENT

The **feasibility assessment and business case development** service is represented in Figure 4.3.

Figure 4.3 Feasibility assessment and business case development overview
(© Debra Paul)

Feasibility assessment and business case development

Evaluate the options to meet the business need and support the development of the business case for change.

Service description

This service is concerned with examining the problem or opportunity and the potential solutions identified, developing business options to address these issues and evaluating the options for acceptability and feasibility. These options may include proposed changes in a number of areas. For example, they may include changes to the business processes, the job roles, the management structure or the IT systems. At this point, the changes are likely to be defined in outline only, but in sufficient detail for a business case to be developed to support the recommendations and provide a basis for decision-making. Once the work to define the changed areas begins in earnest, there may be a need for further consideration of options. For example, where changes are required to the supporting IT systems, these may be agreed in principle at this stage but it is likely that the detailed options for the new IT system will need to be evaluated, and the business case revisited, at a later date.

All of the options to be considered in detail need to be evaluated for business, technical and financial feasibility. Chapter 9 explores these aspects of evaluation in further detail. In addition, areas such as the impact of options on the organisation, and the risks that may be associated with an option, also need to be considered as they will affect the acceptability of that option. Impacts and risks may give rise to additional costs that need to be fed into the cost/benefit analysis for the option. Consideration of the business values and VMOST should also form part of this work as any new business system will need to be aligned with the organisational values and strategy, and support delivery of the business objectives.

Service value proposition

The **feasibility assessment and business case development** service offers the following value proposition:

- Define the rationale for a proposed business change.
- Generate, describe and evaluate the options to achieve the business requirements.
- Quantify and/or describe the investment objectives and predicted business benefits.
- Support informed decision-making regarding business change investment.

Service activities

The activities required to carry out the **feasibility assessment and business case development** service are as follows:

1. Generate and describe options to resolve the problem
2. Remove unviable options
3. Identify and analyse impacts and risks for each option and what may be done about them
4. Identify and analyse costs and benefits for each option
5. Evaluate financial, technical and business feasibility of options
6. Evaluate alignment of options with strategic goals
7. Support comparison and selection of solution

Service techniques

Key techniques required to conduct this service include: business options identification, cost/benefit analysis, including quantification of costs and benefits, investment appraisal, impact analysis and risk analysis (see Chapter 9).

BUSINESS PROCESS IMPROVEMENT

The **business process improvement** service is represented in Figure 4.4.

Figure 4.4 Business process improvement overview (© Debra Paul)

Business process improvement

Research, analyse and define current and proposed business processes; apply gap analysis to identify actions required to implement the revised processes.

Service description

A business process is initiated by a business event and concludes when the goal of the process has been achieved. The business process view of a business situation cuts across departments and job roles in order to show a more results-oriented view that is focused on meeting customer needs. Models of existing business processes – the 'as is' processes – are developed and are used as a basis for identifying where changes might be made to improve the efficiency and effectiveness of each process. The 'as is' processes are redesigned to create 'to be' processes. Business process modelling and improvement is explored in further detail in Chapter 7.

Service value proposition

The **business process improvement** service offers the following value proposition:

- Describe and redesign existing business processes.
- Define required process changes that will enable business improvement and business benefit realisation.
- Identify the actions to be undertaken to deploy the improved processes.

Service activities

The activities required to carry out the **business process improvement** service are as follows:

1. Model existing processes
2. Define required (new or revised) processes
3. Identify gaps between existing ('as is') and required ('to be') processes
4. Analyse gaps between existing and required processes
5. Identify and analyse business process measures
6. Identify actions to implement new processes
7. Ensure alignment between IT systems and processes

Service techniques

Key techniques used to conduct this service include: business process modelling (using UML or Business Process Model and Notation (BPMN)[1]), business rules analysis, value chain/value stream analysis, activity diagrams, event analysis (see Chapter 7) and gap analysis (see Chapter 8).

REQUIREMENTS DEFINITION

The **requirements definition** service is represented in Figure 4.5.

Figure 4.5 Requirements definition overview (© Debra Paul)

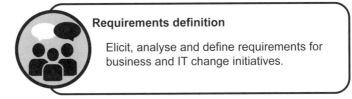

Requirements definition

Elicit, analyse and define requirements for business and IT change initiatives.

Service description

This service is concerned with eliciting, analysing and defining the requirements that are to be fulfilled by a new or enhanced business or IT system. It is sometimes the case that the requirements can be met through limited changes, such as introducing well-defined job descriptions or additional training for the staff. However, it is often the case that extensive change is needed. For example, if redesigned business processes are to be introduced, it is likely that this will also necessitate enhancements to existing IT systems, or even the introduction of a new IT system.

The **requirements definition** service and the corresponding business analyst role are likely to vary between projects and organisations, depending upon the required standards. There are many techniques that may be used to define the requirements and, while this may be dependent upon the approach adopted by an organisation, the business analyst is also responsible for selecting the most appropriate approach.

The RE framework defines the key activities to ensure that requirements work is carried out effectively. This framework highlights the need for proactive elicitation, analysis and management of requirements. However, the RE framework does not prescribe the techniques that should be applied or which of the many requirements modelling and documentation techniques available to business analysts should be used.

RE is described in Chapters 10, 11 and 12. Lifecycles and approaches for delivering the requirements are discussed in Chapter 13.

Service value proposition

The **requirements definition** service offers the following value proposition:

- Elicit, analyse, describe and manage requirements that are to be addressed by business and IT changes, at the level of detail relevant to the context.

- Define requirements that will enable business improvement and business benefit realisation.

Service activities

The activities required to carry out the **requirements definition** service are as follows:

1. Define requirements definition approach and quality standards

2. Elicit and interpret the requirements

3. Record requirements

4. Build models and prototypes to represent the requirements

5. Collaborate and communicate with internal stakeholders in the business and IT functions, and external stakeholders to clarify requirements

6. Analyse, prioritise and assure the quality of the defined requirements

7. Support stakeholder review of requirements

8. Conduct user analysis and profiling

9. Ensure requirements are aligned with project scope and strategic business goals

10. Establish traceability of requirements from the business need to the solution

Service techniques

Key techniques used to deliver this service include: user role modelling, data modelling, process modelling, requirements elicitation (see Chapter 5), requirements analysis and prioritisation (see Chapter 10), requirements definition and modelling (see Chapter 11), requirements management (see Chapter 12) and requirements delivery (see Chapter 13).

BUSINESS ACCEPTANCE TESTING

The **business acceptance testing** service is represented in Figure 4.6.

Figure 4.6 Business acceptance testing service overview (© Debra Paul)

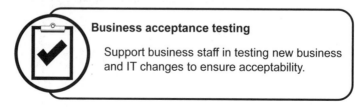

Business acceptance testing

Support business staff in testing new business and IT changes to ensure acceptability.

Service description

This service is concerned with supporting the business staff in testing the solution. The testing may relate to any aspects of the business system, such as a redesigned business process or the features of a new software product. The objective is to identify where a change solution does not accurately reflect the defined requirements or provide what the business needs.

The responsibility for business acceptance testing rests with the business staff but, often, they face difficulties in discharging this responsibility. Such difficulties often include a lack of understanding of what is required and limitations on the time available for the testing work in the face of the day-to-day pressures of business-as-usual.

Business analysts can assist this work by:

- making sure that business managers understand the importance of testing;
- encouraging managers to allocate time for their staff to participate;
- assisting business staff in designing test scenarios and test cases, carrying out the tests and documenting the results.

Service value proposition

The **business acceptance testing** service offers the following value proposition:

- Define acceptance tests for a business solution.
- Collaborate with stakeholders to support business acceptance of a business solution.

Service activities

The activities required to carry out the **business acceptance testing** service are as follows:

1. Agree scope for testing activity
2. Define test scenarios and test cases
3. Provide support to stakeholders when testing for business acceptance

Service techniques

Key techniques used to conduct this service include: test scenario analysis and test case definition (see Chapter 14).

BUSINESS CHANGE DEPLOYMENT

The **business change deployment** service is represented in Figure 4.7.

Figure 4.7 Business change deployment service overview (© Debra Paul)

Business change deployment

Support the deployment of business and IT changes to ensure a smooth transition.

Service description

The **business change deployment** service is concerned with the delivery and adoption of the business change solution and providing support for realising the business benefits. Ensuring the successful deployment of a business change solution is not solely the responsibility of the business analyst but there are several tasks, such as providing support to the stakeholders and delivering training in the new work practices, that fall within the business analyst's remit. The delivery of the business solution needs to consider aspects such as the emotional impact of change and the realisation of the business benefits. These issues are discussed in Chapter 14. The business analyst may be heavily involved in designing and documenting any new roles, tasks and procedures, and reviewing benefits to support their realisation.

Service value proposition

The **business change deployment** service offers the following value proposition:

- Define transition requirements for the business changes.
- Collaborate with stakeholders to support the deployment of the required business changes and enable their adoption.

Service activities

The activities required to carry out the **business change deployment** service are as follows:

1. Assess business readiness
2. Support transition planning
3. Support the adoption of the IT and business changes
4. Develop and deliver training in the new IT and business systems
5. Support the benefits and post-implementation reviews
6. Support the realisation of the business benefits

Service techniques

Key techniques used to deliver this service include: user role modelling, training needs analysis, training material development, business readiness assessment using techniques such as POPIT or Customer, Product, Process, Organisation, Location, Data, Applications, Technology (CPPOLDAT), and post-implementation and benefits review (see Chapter 14).

STAKEHOLDER ENGAGEMENT

This service is not included in the BASF because it is an auxiliary service. The value proposition, activities and techniques involved in stakeholder engagement are relevant whenever a business analyst is conducting any of the other services.

Service description

Every business change initiative has an impact on many individuals and business areas and, among those affected, there are likely to be different levels of interest and power regarding the changes. There may be a direct impact on some stakeholders while others may be affected only indirectly. Some stakeholders may hold strong views on why problems exist and where the focus of a business change initiative should lie. Others may be less concerned. Some individuals have clear opinions on how the systems and working practices should be changed. Others believe strongly in the importance of maintaining the status quo. Sometimes, stakeholders are able to influence the changes but it is often the case that organisations enforce regulations, impose constraints or set specific objectives for a change initiative.

The complexity of business change is often reflected in the variety of discernible stakeholder perspectives. These are often contradictory and can lead to hidden agendas, conflicts and inconsistent priorities. Understanding these differences allows the business analyst to approach issues and problems from an informed position and, hence, have an improved chance of resolving the situation.

Business analysts have to work with people whether they represent their own views or that of their organisation, and this requires extensive interpersonal skills. The range of possible stakeholders and techniques that help with stakeholder analysis and management are discussed in detail in Chapter 6.

Service value proposition

The **stakeholder engagement** service offers the following value proposition:

- Support the achievement of business change and IT project success through stakeholder collaboration, communication and effective stakeholder relationship management.

Service activities

The activities required to carry out the **stakeholder engagement** service are as follows:

1. Identify stakeholders
2. Challenge and inform stakeholders
3. Negotiate stakeholder conflicts
4. Engage with stakeholders
5. Communicate with stakeholders verbally and in writing
6. Support stakeholders
7. Facilitate meetings and workshops and record outputs

Service beneficiaries

Business analysis is concerned with business improvement, whether through process, software or other forms of organisational change. The 'value' realised from such improvements is determined by those who stand to benefit from such changes. However, the beneficiaries vary depending upon the business or project context, and there may be several for each change solution. Also, business analysts often work with both internal and external stakeholders and, in some situations, the ultimate beneficiaries are not stakeholders in direct contact with the business analysts. For example, if the desired outcome from a change is a more efficient process that offers an improved customer experience, the business analysts may be working with the internal business staff to define a business solution that will achieve this. However, it is the internal staff carrying out the business process who will actually deliver the customer experience to the external customers of the organisation.

Figure 4.8 shows how the business analysis service is intended to benefit – or offer value – to both internal and external recipients.

Service techniques

The key stakeholder management techniques include: Customer, Actor, Transformation, World View, Owner, Environment (CATWOE), root definition, world view analysis, stakeholder wheel, stakeholder assessment, power/interest grid, social network analysis and RACI/RASCI (see Chapter 6).

THE STRATEGIC CONTEXT FOR THE BA SERVICE

The services within the BASF are not conducted in isolation; they all need to relate to the strategic context for the organisation. This context may be documented using a VMOST and/or TOM, supported by artefacts such as value stream diagrams and capability models (see Chapter 3). In addition, the overall objectives for the organisation may be expanded into CSFs and KPIs. These definitions state the strategic context within which business analysts deliver their services. However, the detailed tactics required to execute the VMOST are typically defined by business analysts in the course of their work.

Figure 4.8 Recipients of business analysis services (© Assist Knowledge Development Ltd.)

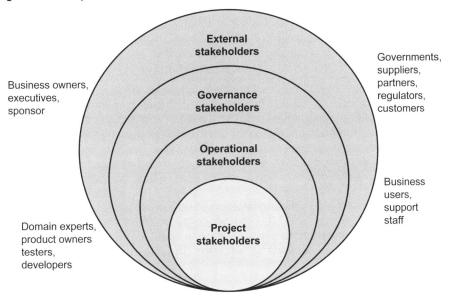

Organisations need to investigate and improve business situations or processes, explore business options, and define the requirements to be fulfilled by business change solutions, if they are to instigate change projects that will enable them to execute their strategy, achieve their objectives and turn their TOM into reality.

This view of the BASF is represented in Figure 4.9.

Figure 4.9 The BASF within the strategic context (© Debra Paul)

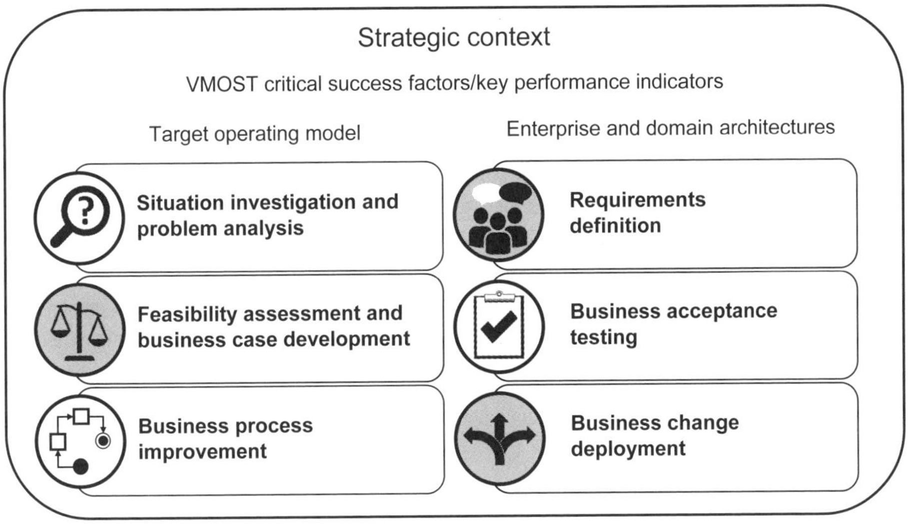

Strategic context

VMOST critical success factors/key performance indicators

Target operating model   Enterprise and domain architectures

Situation investigation and problem analysis

Requirements definition

Feasibility assessment and business case development

Business acceptance testing

Business process improvement

Business change deployment

The impact of the strategic context is that all business analysts need to have two areas of focus during their work:

- Ensuring that the business analysis is conducted to the depth and extent required for the particular assignment or project. For example, it is important that root causes of problems are uncovered, business rules are defined accurately and acceptance test scenarios have sufficient coverage.

- Ensuring that the overall required business outcomes are kept in focus. There are too many examples of project failure where the project team have been overly concerned with the immediate detail and haven't kept the overall goals in mind. For example, methods or approaches are followed slavishly without asking if this is beneficial or relevant to the situation at hand. This is often the case where technology is involved, as too often the project becomes about implementing a software product rather than achieving the desired business outcome.

The ToR should be confirmed before conducting a business analysis service. The ToR are needed to set out clearly the context within which the business analysis work will take place. The OSCAR acronym can be very useful when clarifying what should be included within the ToR. The OSCAR elements are described in Table 4.1.

Table 4.1 The OSCAR elements

OSCAR element	Description
Objectives	The business and project objectives to be achieved. If the ToR relate solely to a business analysis service, the objectives may be defined in line with a particular value proposition or specific change artefacts such as business process designs, requirements definitions or training plans.
Scope	The area of the business to be investigated and the required deliverables. This may also be defined in terms of the business analysis service(s) to be performed. Any areas that are specifically excluded should also be defined.
Constraints	The time, budgetary and policy constraints within which the work must be conducted. The organisational standards, such as methods, approaches, techniques and tools, may also be defined as constraints; this is particularly relevant for business analysis.
Authority	The person who is responsible for approving the delivery of the project objectives. The authority should receive and agree the deliverables and confirm that the work has been completed.
Resources	The human, financial and physical resources available to perform the work. For example, the business staff available to provide information for the business analysis service or support tools that may be used.

A key responsibility for the analyst is to clarify the objective of the study and tailor the approach accordingly – often a task that requires a good deal of skill. The ability to tailor the approach depends upon experience and the development of an extensive toolkit of techniques and skills. It also requires a flexible, adaptive attitude coupled with a preparedness to explore alternatives where a selected approach is not delivering the desired results.

AN APPROACH TO PROBLEM SOLVING

Business analysts have a responsibility to investigate business situations and offer an analytical consideration of which aspects require change and the nature of those changes. This requires a thoughtful, even creative, approach to investigating business issues and developing ideas for solutions. While this is supported by the services within the BASF, a formal problem-solving approach is also helpful to understand:

- the overall process for creative problem solving;
- the importance of establishing the problem before moving towards a solution;
- the need to distinguish between opinion and data;
- the availability of options and the need to identify and evaluate them objectively.

Creative problem solving is vital in the business world as, increasingly, organisations need to develop innovative ideas in order to respond to changes in their business environment, including the actions of competitors. However, many people find this to be difficult, often because they feel under pressure to produce ideas very quickly. In this context, Isaksen and Treffinger's creative problem-solving model (Isaksen and Treffinger, 1985) provides a useful framework for understanding problems and developing creative solutions. An adapted version of this model is shown in Figure 4.10. This model is particularly useful for business analysts as it emphasises the need to investigate and analyse rather than leaping to quick, possibly premature, solutions.

The first stage, **mess finding**, is concerned with finding out about the complexity of the problem situation. Many problems are poorly defined or ambiguous, and each problem situation is likely to be complex and contain various issues and concerns; in other words, there is likely to be a 'mess' and different situations will have different components to that mess. Identifying this as the starting point in this model emphasises the need to understand the situation fully before leaping to options and solutions.

The rich picture diagram, described in Chapter 5, is particularly useful to help document and analyse the 'mess' in problematic business situations. Rich pictures do not use a defined notation set so this offers a great deal of flexibility when representing business situations. Mind maps and fishbone diagrams are also described in Chapter 5 and are similarly helpful.

Data finding, the second stage of the model, is concerned with analysing the opinions, concerns, knowledge and ideas uncovered in the previous stage, in order to identify where this information can be quantified and supporting data obtained. It is often useful to examine the rich picture, mind map or fishbone diagram to clarify thinking about

Figure 4.10 A problem-solving model (Source: After Isaksen and Treffinger, 1985)

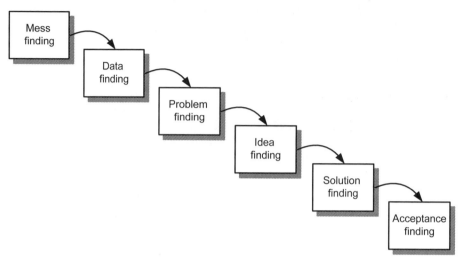

the situation. It is particularly important to consider which information is factual and which is based on opinion. This helps to identify the aspects that need to be verified and also emphasises the need to distinguish opinion from provable fact. Chapter 5 describes techniques, such as surveys and activity sampling, that may be used to collect quantitative data.

The **problem finding** stage uses the work of the previous two stages to help uncover the heart of the problem. At this point, the complexity of the situation has been understood through eliciting opinions and personal views, and this understanding has been supplemented by quantifiable data. A statement of the problem may have been provided at the outset but, having carried out the previous two stages, it is important to revisit this statement and ensure that there is a clear definition of the problem to be addressed. Finding the right problem to solve is often a necessary part of business analysis as analysts are often pointed at symptoms that they have to explore in depth in order to find out where the real problems lie.

These first three stages are concerned with understanding the problem to be addressed and they provide a structure for gaining this understanding. The next two stages focus on developing solutions.

First, there is **idea finding** during which business analysts try to generate a wide range of ideas. Analysts often use brainstorming approaches to uncover ideas but this can be difficult as it requires a group to generate ideas 'cold'. Sometimes this works but often different approaches need to be used with brainstorming to stimulate ideas, so during this stage it may be useful to use some creative thinking techniques. Two examples of techniques that can provide stimuli for creative ideas are 'assumption reversal' – where assumptions about a situation are listed and reversed – and 'analogies' – where a problem is considered within a different context (Thomas et al., 2012). What is important at this stage is that no ideas are ruled out prematurely; suggestions that seem outlandish or unlikely to be acceptable may provide insights or stimulate thoughts that lead to valid solutions.

Once some ideas have been identified, they can be evaluated to explore in further detail those that could provide solutions to the problem. This is the focus of the **solution finding** stage and it is significant that this stage appears so late in the model. Business analysts are often expected to define solutions quickly. However, it is important to resist the pressure to do this as such solutions are often based upon reactive judgements and fail to recognise where assumptions have been made. Isaksen and Treffinger stress the importance of defining criteria to help evaluate potential solutions and this would not be possible without the earlier work. Working through the earlier stages enables the development of more relevant, creative solutions that are likely to be more beneficial for the organisation.

The final stage in the model is **acceptance finding**, which is concerned with gaining business acceptance of the solution. This aspect is critical to the success of any change project and relates directly to all of the BASF services.

SUMMARY

Business change projects are concerned with improving or transforming how organisations carry out their work and deliver their services. Changes may be made to a range of aspects including the organisational structure, staff resources, business processes and supporting IT systems. Increasingly, business analysts are also required to support the development of software products, delivery of business changes and realisation of business benefits.

The BASF defines the range of services provided by business analysts and suggests the value proposition, activities and techniques for each service. Business analysis can vary considerably across different organisations and projects so each service should be customised to meet the needs of the particular context.

The BASF was developed to help clarify the business analyst role and support business analysts with their skill development and career progression. The development of a BA Service, and the recognition of business analysis as an internal value co-creating service with a customer focus, is vital to ensure the continued ability of business analysts to support organisations to achieve their VMOST and deliver their TOM. The application of the BASF and the service concept is further described in the BCS publication *Delivering Business Analysis: The BA Service Handbook* (Paul and Lovelock, 2019).

NOTE

1. www.bpmn.org/

5 INVESTIGATING THE BUSINESS SITUATION

INTRODUCTION

This chapter discusses the techniques relevant to the **situation investigation and problem analysis** service (see Chapter 4). This service aims to uncover issues within a business area, diagnose the underlying causes of those issues and offer suggestions for improvement.

When business analysts investigate a business area, they need access to a range of tools and techniques to help them understand the issues to be resolved. While they should use both qualitative investigation techniques, such as background research, workshops and interviews, and quantitative data collection and analysis methods, they also need to deploy diagnostic tools that help to visualise any findings and identify the root causes of problems.

The techniques described in this chapter also apply to other business analysis services. For example, **business process improvement** requires business analysts to investigate existing processes from the triggering event to the desired outcome; **requirements definition** requires business analysts to elicit, analyse and model requirements. Business analysis work can be complex and variable so a toolkit approach is likely to be much more beneficial than the application of a strict checklist method. The more tools available, the greater the likelihood that the analyst can be flexible and responsive to the needs of the business and each particular situation.

BACKGROUND RESEARCH

Business analysts should spend time researching the background and context for a new assignment. There are various sources of information available to business analysts, both formal and informal. Some are internal documents and reports that derive from the organisation itself, while others are available using online access. Access to background information has never been more straightforward and, as a result, stakeholders expect analysts to be informed to at least some degree when they begin their work. Four key sources of background information as discussed below are:

1. Website for the organisation
2. Company reports
3. Procedure manuals and documentation
4. Organisation chart

Website for the organisation

This is often the most straightforward way to obtain a view of what the organisation does, its values and mission, how it presents its brand and how it wants to be perceived by potential customers. Depending upon the nature of the organisation and the sector it belongs to, there may be access to information about its products or services, reports on its performance, and opportunities to interact by placing an order, making a query or providing feedback.

Particular areas that are relevant to business analysts include the organisation's branding, stated or apparent values and priorities, the ease with which interactions with the organisation may be made, and the descriptions of the products and services. One other area to consider concerns information that is not provided. For example, organisations often have website pages that describe the management team but while some provide information about the individuals within the team, others just offer a high-level overview that reveals very little. Some organisations display feedback or reviews from customers, and these can be worth reading, particularly those that are less than whole-heartedly positive. However, such reviews are likely to be selected to show the company in its best light and it may be worth exploring customer reviews on industry feedback sites, such as those that provide reviews of hotels or restaurants.

One useful inference from the design of a website is how the company views its place strategically, in terms of the balance between cost of its products and the perceived quality. The design of the website often indicates the level of quality of the products or services offered. Primary colours, flashing icons, liberal use of exclamation marks and free use of suggestive words like 'Bargain!' imply a more populist approach, while a more subtle background, relevant photographs, moderated colours, all indicate a desire for a perception of quality. Interpreting a website this way can provide an early insight into the business imperatives for the organisation.

It is also helpful to evaluate the ease of navigating around a website, placing an order or making an enquiry. These aspects provide insights into the level of professionalism of the site and expected standards of technology presentation and achievement. This in turn can provide clues about the technological maturity of the company; for example, is the technology aligned to the business values and mission or does the way in which technology is used undermine this?

Company reports

Some situations require the business analysts to review company reports in order to understand the organisation's financial health. This may be where business analysts are delivering services to external companies or are working with suppliers of services to their organisation. Companies with limited liability are required to file statutory documents reporting on their financial position. For example, UK companies are required to file their annual income statement (profit and loss account) and statement of financial position (balance sheet) with Companies House, from where they may be accessed by the public and company representatives. These documents can provide much rich information about the levels of debt, liquidity, gearing, trends in growth or stagnation over the previous years, and a first insight into where there may be problems.

The shareholders' reports also set out the future direction of the company as agreed by the directors, and state the targets and aims for the next year. Company reports should explain the target market and strategic intentions, which offer business analysts insights into the perspectives held by senior stakeholders.

Studying these reports at the outset of a project can save unnecessary effort later and avoid financial loss. As an example, following an invitation to carry out consultancy work for a new client, an examination of the company's entry at Companies House revealed that it was about to be suspended for non-submission of accounts over the previous two years. A failure to carry out this research could have ended with unpaid invoices and wasted effort.

Procedure manuals and documentation

The scope of many business change projects relates to a particular business area, suite of processes or software product. The prior research for such projects should include studying current system documentation and any procedures manuals. These documents offer information about the current processes and procedures. However, over time, such documentation is likely to become unrepresentative of the way in which each actual process operates, failing to describe the 'as is' process and instead offering a description of the 'what-we-thought-it-ought-to-have-been' process.

Studying the documentation is not a substitute for investigation and analysis; rather it enables a prior understanding of the domain in question that gives the analyst an entry point for various lines of investigation.

The organisation chart

An organisation chart sets out the management structure of the organisation and can offer insights into its style and culture. Understanding the job roles and reporting lines provides valuable preparation for the more detailed investigation to follow. The types of information shown on an organisation chart are:

- The shape of the organisation – for example, is it hierarchical with several levels of management or is it a 'flat' structure where each manager is responsible for many staff.

- The span of control (the area and people for whom a manager has oversight).

- The way in which the organisation is structured – is it according to function, product/service, geography? If geography or product, are some functions duplicated, or centralised?

- Whether the organisation has a centralised or decentralised business model.

Chapter 3 describes some other architectural artefacts that, alongside the organisation chart, can help to illuminate the intentions and capacity of the company. They include the following (note the precise titles of these artefacts may change from company to company):

- **Principles:** These are high-level policy statements that have a significant impact on both business and IT operations. Typically, there should be between 10 and 20 defined principles that are reviewed regularly by architects and senior business leaders. Their aim is to reach agreement on basic rules, values and aims.

- **BCMs:** BCMs are concise views of the capabilities of a business and are used mainly for strategic analysis and for evaluating and planning IT and business change initiatives. They are generally static models and are independent of such matters as organisation structure.

- **Roadmaps:** These are used in conjunction with a BCM, to determine the route towards a TOM. They help to determine where future investment in the infrastructure and applications architecture will be most beneficial, given the organisation's strategic plans. The roadmaps are developed jointly by senior business leaders and enterprise architects.

- **Technology reference models (TRMs):** These reference models represent standards for technology, in terms of platforms and infrastructure technologies to be used in IT projects within the organisation. They also show the applications used within the organisation. The TRMs are developed by solution architects, and regularly reviewed. All IT projects need to be aligned to these TRMs, and regular reviews should be carried out to ensure that this is the case.

This preliminary research by the business analysts enables them to understand a great deal about the target organisation or business area, in particular, its priorities, structure, guiding principles and architecture, before beginning the detailed investigation. Such research also helps to identify and resolve assumptions that may otherwise lead to problems at a later stage in the project.

INVESTIGATION TECHNIQUES

There are many reasons why a business analysis investigation is required. For example, a study might be required to investigate a general concern, diagnose a weakness in the business processes or compile the requirements for a new system. After the background research has been done, the business analyst needs to consider how to conduct the more detailed investigation. There are a variety of techniques available, depending upon the size of the domain to be investigated, its location, the numbers of stakeholders to be consulted and the nature of the information to be ascertained.

Investigation techniques can be categorised broadly as **qualitative**, gaining impressions and opinions about what is needed, and **quantitative**, concerned with volumes and frequencies. Qualitative techniques can be categorised as one-to-one sessions and collaborative sessions. Collaborative investigation approaches include workshops and focus groups. The most commonly used qualitative one-to-one approaches are interviews, meetings with individual stakeholders and shadowing sessions.

WORKSHOPS

Workshops provide an excellent collaborative forum in which issues can be discussed, conflicts resolved and requirements elicited. They are also a useful environment for carrying out other activities, such as compiling process models (see Chapter 7), understanding data requirements (see Chapter 11), eliciting CSFs and KPIs (see Chapter 3) or analysing the quality of a requirements set before they are formally documented (see Chapter 10). Given the various reasons for running workshops, this technique may be used at many different points during a study or project. Workshops are especially valuable when time and budgets are tightly constrained and several viewpoints need to be explored or reconciled.

Advantages and disadvantages of workshops

The advantages gained from using workshops include the ability to:

- **Gain a broad view of the area under investigation:** Having a group of stakeholders in one room allows the analyst to gain a more complete understanding of the issues and different views at play. Some of these issues may well be political or cultural, and the analyst has to pay attention to the interactions and dynamics of the group to get early insight into the prevailing business and stakeholder perspectives.

- **Increase speed and productivity**: It is less time-consuming to have one extended meeting with a group of people than interviewing them one by one, cross-referring responses for agreement or divergence and conducting follow-up sessions.

- **Obtain buy-in and acceptance for the project:** When stakeholders are involved in a collaboration, they are not only more accepting of any suggestions for change, they are also more likely to be champions for the agreed ways forward.

- **Gain a consensus view or group agreement:** If all of the stakeholders are involved in the decision-making process, there is a greater chance that they will take ownership of the results. If two or more stakeholders have different viewpoints at the outset, there is a better chance of helping them move to an agreement in a well-facilitated workshop, as long as they feel that their concerns and views have been listened to respectfully and any particular concerns have been addressed.

Although workshops are extremely valuable, there are some disadvantages to using them, including:

- **Extensive preparation time:** Workshops can be time-consuming to organise. For example, it is not always easy to arrange for all of the key stakeholders to be together at the same time.

- **Undue influence of dominant personalities:** If a workshop is not facilitated carefully, forceful participants can tend to dominate the discussion. In extreme cases, such a participant may be able to impose a decision because the other members of the group feel disempowered and unable to raise their objections.

- **Authority limitations:** It can be difficult to ensure that workshop participants have the required level of authority – which sometimes means that decisions are reversed after the workshop has ended. This can be a problem especially in an organisation with a culture where power radiates from a few central people or where there is a strong hierarchical structure. If there are two authoritative stakeholders with opposing views, the facilitator may have to use a range of skills to keep the workshop on track and moving towards achieving its objective.

Gaining the advantages, and avoiding the disadvantages, is only possible if a workshop is well organised and run; the means of achieving this is discussed in the rest of this section.

Preparing for the workshop

The success or failure of a workshop session depends in large part upon the preparatory work done by its facilitator and its business sponsor. They should spend time before the event planning the following areas:

- **The objective of the workshop:** This has to be an objective that can be achieved within the time constraints of the workshop. Where this is a sizeable objective, the workshop duration needs to reflect this – possibly running the workshop over several days. In this case, the overall objective should be broken into sub-objectives, each of which should form the basis for an individual workshop session. For example, a two-day workshop may be broken into four sessions, each of which is focused upon a particular sub-objective.

- **The people to be invited to participate in the workshop:** It is important that all stakeholders interested in the objective of a workshop should be invited to attend or be represented. It is the facilitator's responsibility to ensure that all stakeholders are able to contribute, which may mean performing many of the key tasks by using break-out groups or other techniques, and reporting back to a plenary session to collate the individual results. It can also be useful to consider in advance the personalities, concerns and viewpoints of those to be invited to the workshop.

- **The structure of the workshop and the techniques to be used:** These need to be geared towards achieving the defined objective and should take into account the nature of the group, the needs of the attendees and their preferred participation style. For example, a standard brainstorming session may not work very well with a group of people who have never met before as they may not all have the confidence to contribute when required to shout out ideas. Alternatively, some attendees may prefer to work in smaller groups or even to think through ideas individually before contributing to a group discussion.

- **Arranging a suitable venue:** It is important to ensure that the venue provides an environment for focused participation. This may be within an organisation's premises but it is sometimes useful to use a neutral venue, particularly if the issues to be discussed are contentious, or there is a danger that a participant could be interrupted by a colleague or manager who wants to call them away.

Facilitating the workshop

The workshop should start by discussing the objective and endeavouring to secure the participants' buy-in to its achievement. Where there are strongly held views about a situation and it is anticipated that the workshop will be difficult to facilitate successfully, it may be useful to invite a senior manager or the project sponsor to open the workshop. This person can define the ground rules and expectations for behaviour, confirm support for the facilitator and demonstrate commitment to achieving the workshop objectives.

During the workshop, the facilitator needs to ensure that the issues are discussed, views are aired and progress is made towards achieving the stated objective. The discussion may range widely so the facilitator needs to ensure that, while everyone has an opportunity to express their concerns and opinions, it remains on track.

A record needs to be kept of the key points emerging from the discussion. This is often done by the facilitator keeping a record on a flipchart, but it is better practice to appoint someone else to take the role of scribe during the workshop. The presence of a scribe allows the facilitator to concentrate fully on running the workshop, applying the agreed techniques and ensuring that progress continues towards achieving the objective. The use of a scribe also enables the facilitator to focus on the workshop participants and evaluate their expressed views and non-verbal behaviour, and ensure that everyone feels able to contribute. Where a facilitator is spending time writing or drawing, such cues can be easily missed.

It is not uncommon for the scribe to take notes on a tablet or laptop linked to a projector so that participants can see what is being typed at the time. This is not desirable for two main reasons: it is distracting for attendees who tend to watch what is happening on the screen rather than following and contributing to the discussion; and, as only the most recent notes will be displayed on the screen, important points from earlier in the workshop may be forgotten. It is much better for the conduct of the workshop for the scribe to use a flipchart or whiteboard and ensure all of the items noted are on display so that the workshop participants can refer back to a model or discussion point when necessary.

At the end of the workshop, the facilitator needs to summarise the key points and actions. Each action should be assigned to an owner and allocated a timescale for completion.

Workshop techniques

There are two main categories of technique required for a workshop: techniques for discovery and techniques for visualisation (see Figure 5.1). The purpose of the workshop helps in the selection and use of techniques. For example, if the purpose is to elicit requirements for a new system, brainstorming and round robins are less likely to yield relevant sets of requirements than a sticky (Post-it™) note exercise, process model or break-out group discussions that concentrate on specific functions of the system. If the workshop is to explore a series of customer complaints, or reasons for a fall off in business, then brainstorming could well generate useful threads to examine in more depth.

Discovery techniques are those that help a facilitator to elicit information and views from the participants. Facilitators need to consider which technique is most suitable for a particular situation and group of participants. Examples of discovery techniques and when they are particularly appropriate are discussed below.

Figure 5.1 Workshop techniques

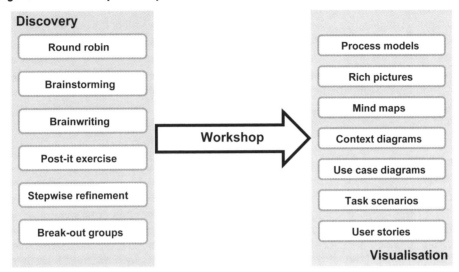

- **Brainstorming (sometimes known as idea storming):** Participants are asked to call out ideas about a given topic. All of the ideas are written on a flipchart or whiteboard as they are suggested. It is important that all suggestions can be seen by all of the participants as this allows them to build on each other's ideas. Evaluation of the ideas is suspended until everyone has finished making suggestions. This technique is particularly relevant for groups where the participants know each other well and are comfortable calling out ideas in an open forum. It is less useful where participants lack the confidence to call out suggestions or prefer a more reflective approach.

- **Round robin discussions:** Participants are asked to provide their ideas in turn. This can be very useful to encourage participation from those who do not like brainstorming because they are uncomfortable when required to interrupt others in order to call out ideas. Round robin discussions provide each participant with an opportunity to speak without fear of interruption or being ignored. One difficulty is that during the 'round' participants may want to comment on an earlier contribution rather than offer their own idea, and without good facilitation it can turn into a discussion on just one or two points without all participants having the opportunity to offer their own idea.

- **Brainwriting:** This technique has similarities with brainstorming but requires participants to write down ideas rather than call them out. Each person writes an idea on a sheet of paper and then puts it in the middle of the table. Everyone then takes another sheet with an idea already written on it, writes down another idea and then returns the paper to the centre. This continues until there are no more ideas being generated. This approach overcomes the problem where participants are not sufficiently confident to interrupt others and call out their ideas but still enables them to build on the ideas of others.

- **Sticky (Post-it) note exercises:** Ideas are written down, but the participants work individually or in pairs. Each individual or pair writes down their suggestions – one per sticky note – and, once everyone has stopped writing, displays them to the group, usually by sticking them on a wall or board. Once all of the suggestions have been displayed, those that are similar are grouped together using affinity mapping and broader themes are identified.

- **Stepwise refinement:** The facilitator proposes a statement or idea and asks 'why?' continually until the heart of a problem, idea or situation has been uncovered.

- **'Break-out' or 'syndicate' group exercises:** Many workshop participants prefer to work in small groups as it is easier for them to make suggestions or develop their ideas. Typically, a volunteer from each smaller group reports back to the larger group. This is a powerful way to manage a larger workshop, particularly where there is a range of skills and knowledge. It can also be useful for each break-out group to have its own sub-facilitator.

Once all the ideas and suggestions have emerged, they need to be evaluated and reduced to an acceptable number to manage. One approach to evaluating them, which has had considerable success, is De Bono's Six Hats technique (De Bono, 2016). The six hats help the facilitator to structure workshop discussions by ensuring that only one perspective is discussed at a time. The six hats are:

- **Green hat:** Generate ideas, typically using one of the techniques described above.

- **Red hat:** For each idea, record the emotional response from each participant. Any that arouse strong emotions, such as nervousness or excitement, may be discussed further to understand the reactions. Those that provoke strong dislike, or even those with no strong emotional reaction, may be candidates for removal.

- **White hat**: If any facts are needed to support or clarify either the advantages or disadvantages, they should be obtained. Looking at information from a white hat perspective helps to distinguish between those that are factual and those that are subjective opinion. Where it is important to confirm or clarify information, it may be necessary to postpone a workshop until the data is available.

- **Yellow hat:** The group examines the ideas using a positive critical perspective. For example, what would be the advantages of implementing a suggestion? What forces would encourage its success?

- **Black hat:** The group examines the ideas using a negative critical perspective. What are the drawbacks, disadvantages and penalties of implementing a proposal? What are the forces that militate against its success?

- **Blue hat:** The facilitator's perspective, which should focus on the process to run the workshop.

Another approach is to structure discussions and capture the outcomes using recognised organisational analysis techniques (see Chapter 3). For example, if the workshop is concerned with the implementation of the business strategy, a performance management approach, such as CSF analysis, can be employed. This could begin by considering the company objectives, agreeing the CSFs for the part of the organisation under discussion, developing the associated KPIs and their associated targets, and then considering the information requirements needed to monitor the achievement of the CSFs and KPIs. This can then lead to the definition of more detailed requirements in areas such as data capture and management reporting.

A variety of visualisation techniques are suitable for use in a workshop. They are quick to understand and to explain, and help workshop participants to understand the information being captured. Several useful pictorial or diagrammatic techniques are explored in this book including process models, data models, use case diagrams, rich pictures and mind maps. Some of these are discussed later in this chapter while modelling techniques are explained in Chapter 11. Diagrammatic techniques help the workshop participants to visualise the area under discussion. Diagrams may be supplemented by text-based lists that record suggestions, agreed action points or issues for further discussion.

Following the workshop

After the workshop any key points and actions should be transcribed and sent to the relevant participants and stakeholders. This should be done as quickly as possible in order to keep up the momentum and highlight the need for timely action.

Hothouse workshop

Hothouse workshops were originally devised within BT, the UK telecoms company, as a way to focus concentration on one goal at a time, rather than have analysts, project managers and developers assigned to multiple projects with multiple goals. The goal was to involve customers in all stages of a product development project and to deliver the product within 90 days. The hothouse was the first step in the 90 days.

A CSF for a hothouse workshop is to engage the right mix of people in the workshop. Senior business staff, possibly at chief information officer (CIO) level, are desirable members as are the project sponsor, solution architects, testers and developers.

A hothouse workshop is a specific type of workshop that applies Lean and Agile principles to a business problem. In Agile environments a project, or phase of a project, may be initiated by a hothouse workshop, bringing the business and development teams together to solve business problems and using prototypes to define the functionality and scope of the solution. The business participants are ideally at executive level.

The idea of a hothouse workshop originated from the work of James Martin at IBM in the 1980s, when a joint requirements planning (JRP) workshop brought senior executives and analysts together to define functionality, scope and timeframes for new developments. Hothouses combine this JRP approach with Lean techniques where the focus is on removing waste.

As the name suggests, hothousing can be an intense experience, often with participants working into the night, to produce prototype models of how the new solution might look. Hothouse workshops typically take place over 2–3 days and are primarily used for innovation projects rather than those focusing on enhancements to existing processes and systems. The group of workshop participants is usually split into smaller teams and each team develops a prototype solution during a series of iterations. At the end of each iteration, the output is reviewed and feedback given, which is used during the next iteration and so on.

A hothouse may be run as a competition between the participating groups. Ultimately, the outcome should be a prototype solution to a business problem accompanied by additional analyses of the corresponding metrics, processes, costs and benefits required to enable the delivery of the full solution.

FOCUS GROUPS

Focus groups tend to be concerned with business and market research. They bring together a group of people with a common interest or area of understanding to discuss a topic. While such a meeting has similarities with a workshop, they are not the same because the desired outcomes are different; workshops aim to achieve consensus about an issue whereas focus groups aim to elicit information and opinions (which may differ significantly).

A focus group could be used to understand people's attitudes to any current shortcomings with the business system; for example, to uncover reasons why customers are unhappy with a service, or why a website is failing to convert accesses into sales. A focus group may also be used to suggest ideas for future developments and directions or as part of an information-gathering exercise.

A focus group may be used for the following purposes:

- To understand people's attitudes to any current shortcomings with the business system. For example, the reason why customers are unhappy with a service, or why the website is failing to turn hits into sales.
- To suggest ideas for future developments and directions.
- To gather information about a subject.
- To uncover opinions. For example, to find out what customers think about the organisation's products or services.

As in a workshop setting, the facilitator must be clear at the outset about objectives and ground rules. This is probably more important in a focus group that includes customers as it may be that many have never been involved in this type of discussion before and don't understand the usual protocols and what constitutes acceptable and unacceptable behaviour.

The preparation process for a focus group is similar to that for a workshop so the approach discussed in the previous section is usually relevant to ensure that:

- the rationale for the focus group is clear;
- the participants are selected carefully;
- the approach to the discussion has been thought through and decided upon;
- the timing, duration and location have been agreed.

A focus group does not necessarily result in findings that should be acted upon as they may need to be evaluated against the business strategy. Some opinions or information may already be known but may not align with how the organisation wants to work or the services it wants to deliver.

Focus group participants should represent a sample of the target constituency. They may be external customers or suppliers, or internal staff from different locations or business areas. They are given an opportunity to express their opinions and views, and to discuss them. Given that there is no intention to form a consensus during a focus group discussion or for the group to acquire a sense of ownership of any decisions made or solutions identified, the participants may express their view freely and without fear of evaluation.

The facilitator must take care with the way in which a question is worded when inviting discussion from a focus group. If the question is too open, such as 'What do you think of Customer Service?' this may close down discussion rather than elicit helpful responses. It is better to frame the issue in a way that directs the participants' attention to concrete examples, such as 'What left you satisfied when you called Customer Service? What left you dissatisfied?' These are still open questions but within a specific context.

Advantages and disadvantages of focus groups

Focus groups can be a cost-effective way of obtaining views and ideas, but are unlikely to offer significant insights regarding the solution to a problem or an agreed way forward. The information gleaned from focus groups is essentially qualitative and it is not suitable for eliciting quantitative data. The success of a focus group session depends largely upon the skill of the facilitator in allowing all members to express their thoughts and opinions, and to explore the reasons for any strong feelings that are offered.

Focus groups are discussion forums and, as with a workshop, there is a danger that strong personalities may dominate and a diffident member of the group may feel intimidated. It is the facilitator's responsibility to recognise this behaviour and ensure that all members feel safe to express dissenting views without being attacked or feeling belittled. This, after all, is an information-gathering exercise to help the analyst understand the business situation; differing views and dissent can reveal important information that sheds light on a problem area.

A focus group of customers from one location cannot be expected to describe all customers' concerns, particularly where an organisation has a national or even international presence. Collaboration tools are available that provide features that support online focus groups and, using AI technology, can offer both qualitative and quantitative analysis. For example, through offering analytic data that summarises employee concerns and feedback about customer experiences.

OBSERVATION

Observing the workplace and the staff carrying out their work, particularly when done early in an investigation, is very useful to obtain information about the business environment and work practices.

It is important that before any work is observed, the person being observed should be reassured that the objective is to understand the task, not to judge their performance. Care is needed in organisations where there is a unionised work-site as approval must be sought from the trade union representatives and any required protocols must be observed.

There are several different approaches to observation, depending upon the level and focus of interest. The key approaches are: formal observation, protocol analysis, shadowing and ethnographic studies. These are all explained in detail later in this chapter.

Advantages and disadvantages of observation

The views of the stakeholders involved in a project may have been sought during interviews, but to really obtain a feel for the situation the analyst needs to see the workplace and business practices. Apart from collecting factual information, it is also possible to clarify and increase understanding about areas where the stakeholders possess 'taken-for-granted' knowledge that they do not recognise the need to express (this is known as 'tacit knowledge' and is discussed in Chapter 10). Observation has the following advantages:

- A much better understanding of the problems and difficulties faced by the business users is obtained.

- Seeing a task performed helps to identify relevant questions for a follow-up interview with the person responsible for that task.

- The depth of understanding gained from observation helps in identifying workable solutions that are more likely to be acceptable to the business.

However, there are a number of caveats that need to be kept in mind when using observation to understand a situation:

- Being observed can be rather unnerving so people tend to behave as they feel is expected rather than how they would under normal work conditions. The saying 'you change what you observe' needs to be factored into the approach taken and the findings obtained.

- When observing a task being performed, the analyst just sees what happens on that particular occasion. The routine activities are likely to be performed but there may be other aspects of the process that are carried out infrequently and, if they are not needed during the observation session, the analyst may be unaware of them. For example, conducting an observation on a Wednesday morning would mean that the final summarising task performed each Friday afternoon is not observed.

Formal observation

Formal observation involves watching a specific task being performed. While this form of observation runs the risk of staff following standard practices without demonstrating any of the everyday variances, this is still a useful technique to increase understanding of the business situation. It is important that the staff members being observed are prepared beforehand and are aware that the focus is on understanding the task rather than assessing competence and performance. Self-consciousness can influence how the staff member performs and a lack of prior notice serves to accentuate this problem. If the staff members perceive the observer as having been sent by management, they are more likely to perform the task according to the rulebook, rather than how it has evolved over time.

When observing a task, it is acceptable to ask those being observed about the sequence of steps they are following, so long as the question does not:

- sound critical of the way the person is working, either in words or tone of voice;
- distract from their performance of the job. The analyst must position themselves in such a way that they can see clearly all that is happening but do not interfere with the completion of the task.

To obtain full value from the observation, it is beneficial to watch the staff members perform the task several times in order to understand the standard sequence, any possible exception situations and how they are handled, timings for the task and any ergonomic factors or physical working conditions that may enhance or hinder performance.

Physical tasks such as handling goods in a warehouse, or despatching consignments to customers are likely to be more amenable to formal observation than sedentary tasks such as data entry. However, observing tasks such as manning a customer services helpline or telesales can still provide a lot of useful information, enable understanding of where problems exist or help to elicit requirements for a new system. When watching a physical task, it can be helpful to develop a sketch of the workplace showing where the various actors are located as this helps with later reflection and analysis of the results.

Protocol analysis

Protocol analysis involves asking business staff to carry out a specified task and describe each step they perform while doing this. It helps to elicit information about the skills required to complete a task when they cannot be described in words alone. The higher the level of unconscious skill involved in a task, the harder it is to explain verbally. Protocol analysis uses a 'performing and describing' approach that can help analysts to gain detailed understanding of a task and the way in which it is carried out. A similar approach may be used to train a new member of staff or someone unfamiliar with a task. For example, rather than teaching new learner drivers in a classroom before they try driving on the roads, the drivers learn by watching the task being both performed and explained simultaneously, and they then perform it for themselves.

Shadowing

Shadowing involves following a member of staff for a period, such as one or two days, to find out what a particular job entails. This is a powerful way to understand a specific user role. When shadowing someone, the analyst can request explanations of various aspects of the work performed in order to clarify what the individual actually does to perform the role. These aspects include how the work is done, the information used or the workflow sequence.

There are often aspects of a role that are taken for granted by the individual carrying out the work. Shadowing helps to uncover these aspects and the longer the analyst spends shadowing someone the greater the opportunity to build rapport and capture the additional details that are unlikely to be elicited during a single interview. Shadowing key staff is a useful approach when investigating a business situation as it helps to highlight the nature of problems and why they have arisen. It also improves requirements definition work since it provides a visual context for processes described during interviews or workshops.

Ethnographic studies

An ethnographic study is often beyond the budget of business analysis projects but could yield high returns if conducted. It is derived from the discipline of anthropology and involves spending an extended period of time – from a few weeks up to several months – within the target environment. This approach enables the analyst to gain a thorough understanding of the business system as, in a short space of time, the business community becomes used to the analyst's presence and behaves more naturally and authentically. The main value gained from ethnography is an appreciation of intangible aspects such as the organisational culture in which any proposed change must be embedded, including recognising where both formal and informal power and influences reside. This approach can also be very useful when analysing complex business systems where the staff members are highly expert in conducting their work and the business rules are difficult to assimilate. In this situation, extended interaction with the experts as they make decisions can be invaluable to acquire in-depth understanding of the rules applied.

INTERVIEWS OR MEETINGS

The meeting or interview is a key tool in the business analyst's toolkit. The term 'interview' can imply a formal one-to-one meeting but in practice is a meeting with any number of stakeholders. There is no reason for an interview to concern just one stakeholder; three or four stakeholders may be interviewed simultaneously in order to save time and encourage openness. It is possible that, during a meeting with several stakeholders, the analyst senses that one or more of the stakeholders are not able to be open about the situation when their colleagues are present. This may be because one stakeholder is dominant and inhibits others' participation, or that they disagree with something said and feel unable to express that openly. When in the early stages of an investigation, this may indicate political or cultural issues that the analyst must take into account. Where this is the case, a follow-up session is advisable to ensure that all relevant information has been elicited.

Well-run interviews can help the business analyst to achieve a number of objectives. These include:

- Making initial contact with key stakeholders and establishing a basis for the business analysis work.

- Building and developing rapport with different members of staff and business managers.

- Acquiring information about a business situation, including any issues and problems.

- Discovering different stakeholder perspectives and priorities.

Interviews tend to take place on a one-to-one basis, which is a key reason why they can be invaluable in obtaining personal concerns. They focus on the views of an individual and provide an environment where the interviewee has an opportunity to discuss their concerns and feel that they are given individual attention. However, interviewing can be quite time-consuming, so the analyst has a responsibility to ensure that the interviewee's time is not wasted, the required information is acquired in a timely fashion and a good degree of understanding and rapport is achieved.

There are three areas that are considered during investigative and requirements elicitation interviews:

- The current functions that need to be fulfilled in any new business system.

- The problems with the current operations or performance that need to be addressed.

- The additional features required from the new business system.

The last point can be the hardest part of an interview as interviewees are asked to think beyond their experience and identify features that are not currently available but may be of use in the future. This may result in vaguely worded suggestions and the skill of the interviewer is needed to assess the implications of the initial suggestions and draw out more detailed information.

Advantages and disadvantages of interviewing

One of the major benefits of conducting an interview is that it provides an opportunity to build a relationship with the individual stakeholders. Whether enabling the business to improve operations, solve a specific issue or replace a legacy IT system, it is critical that the business analysts understand the perspectives of the people working within the business system. This requires an appreciation of what they do, their concerns and what they want from any new processes or systems. For their part, business staff need to have confidence that the analysts are aware of their concerns, behave in a professional manner and do not attempt to implement a solution that overlooks their needs and worries. The opportunities to understand the business context and the concerns and needs of the staff are likely to increase where good relationships are developed early in the project.

The second major benefit is that the interview can yield important information. The focus of the information varies depending upon the needs of the project but usually includes details about the current operations, difficulties in carrying out the work, the impact of problems and where improvements are needed. It is also possible to elicit requirements during an interview. Where the interview is conducted as part of an initial investigation study, these requirements are likely to be general in nature and may reflect the wishes of senior managers. However, it is often the case that such requirements are key indicators of successful business outcomes and recording them at an early stage helps when identifying options for business improvement.

Additional advantages of interviews include the following:

- They help the analyst to understand different viewpoints and attitudes across the user group.
- They provide an opportunity to investigate new areas that were not previously mentioned.
- They enable the analyst to identify and collect examples of documents, forms and reports used by the clients.
- They allow an appreciation of political factors that may affect how the business performs its work.
- They provide an opportunity to study the environment in which the business staff carry out their work.

While interviewing is an effective investigation technique, it does have some disadvantages:

- Interviews can require significant investment of time and budget, particularly if the business staff are widely dispersed. They require interviewees to allocate sufficient time if the interview is to be of use and this may prove difficult within a busy schedule. This may mean that interviewees try to speed up the interview and may resent the time required to participate.
- The information provided during interviews is often based upon opinion and is likely to derive from the interviewee's perspective on the situation. Therefore, quantitative data may be required to confirm the information elicited during interviews before any firm conclusions can be drawn.
- Different interviewees often hold different views and, where this is the case, the business analyst needs to analyse the information gathered in order to identify conflicts. This may create a need for follow-up interviews or meetings to investigative the situation further and attempt to build consensus.

Preparation for interviewing

The interviewing process is improved significantly when the interviewer has prepared thoroughly. Good preparation saves a lot of time as it ensures that the best use is made of the interview time allocated. It also demonstrates a professional approach to the interviewee, which can help to establish mutual respect and rapport.

The 'Why?', 'What?', 'Who?', 'When?' and 'Where?' structure, known as the 5Ws, provides an excellent basis for preparation as it ensures the key elements of an interview are considered.

- **Why?** This involves considering why a particular interviewee is to be interviewed and the nature of the information the interviewee may be able to provide. The objectives of the interview may range from establishing a good rapport and working relationship with a key stakeholder to eliciting detailed requirements. The forms of questioning and of notetaking differ significantly depending upon the objectives of the interview.

- **What?** This involves considering the information that could be provided by a particular interviewee and identifying the areas to be explored during the interview. Answering the 'What?' question provides the foundation for the interview agenda.

- **Who?** This involves identifying which stakeholders to interview and the order in which they should be interviewed. It is typical to begin with the more senior stakeholders as this helps to obtain information about the business context before exploring the situation in further detail. A senior person will also be able to identify the key business staff to interview and may make any necessary introductions.

The level of authority of the interviewee dictates the nature of the questioning. The STOP model (Figure 5.2) illustrates a hierarchy for different levels of management and corresponding questions.

Figure 5.2 'STOP': the organisation hierarchy

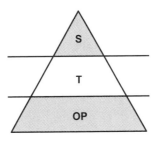

- The 'S' represents the strategic level of management. The discussion when interviewing stakeholders at this level should concern:

  - confirmation of the ToR;

  - management information needs;

  - the approach to the investigation;

  - the alignment of the project with the business objectives and strategy.

- The 'T' represents the tactical level, or middle management. The discussion when interviewing stakeholders at this level should concern:

  - Issues related to performance, targets and management control. There are likely to be defined CSFs and KPIs (see Chapter 3) plus any associated reporting requirements.

- The processes that are carried out within the business area and the members of staff responsible for this work. This is unlikely to include detailed descriptions of how the processes are executed.

- New business requirements to aid alignment of the tactics with the organisational strategy.

- The 'OP' level represents the operational level, the business staff who perform the actual tasks of the department. These are the people who can describe accurately the existing business situation and can identify problems and workarounds to deal with the current procedures. They have information about source documents, bottlenecks and the flow of the work, and are likely to provide suggestions about the volume of transactions handled (although these need to be treated with caution and should be confirmed using quantitative investigation techniques).

The questioning strategy for the interview depends upon several factors, including where the prospective interviewee sits in the STOP hierarchy, the objectives of the project and the nature of the issues to be investigated.

- **When? and Where?** These questions are concerned with the venue, timing and duration of the interview. Some interviewees dictate the exact timing and duration as this is dependent upon their availability. It is good practice to limit interviews to a maximum length of one hour since:

  - The majority of interviewees have many work commitments so may not be able to reserve more than one hour for an interview.

  - It can be very difficult to concentrate for more than an hour so longer interviews are often unproductive. This applies to both interviewer and interviewee.

  - Longer interviews typically generate more information so it is often difficult to write up the notes accurately.

  The 'where' is restricted to three possibilities: the interviewee's place of work, the interviewer's place of work or a neutral third location. An interviewee's work location is usually recommended for an initial interview for the following reasons:

  - Interviewees are more likely to be more at ease and less apprehensive during the meeting. Meeting interviewees at their place of work also indicates a degree of respect.

  - The interviewer has an opportunity to observe the working environment, the culture of the organisation and the frequency and nature of any interruptions.

  - The interviewee should have all relevant information at hand.

  Should it be necessary to arrange a subsequent interview, a mutually convenient location may be used as the analyst should have established a good working relationship during the first interview session, making the venue choice less important.

The decisions made when considering the who, why, what, when and where questions help the business analyst to produce an agenda for an interview. This should be sent to the interviewee a few days in advance of the interview to aid preparation for the forthcoming discussion.

Conducting the interview

Interviews should be structured if the maximum amount of information is to be elicited. The standard structure consists of three parts: the introduction, the body of the interview and the interview close. This structure is shown in Figure 5.3.

Figure 5.3 The structure of an interview

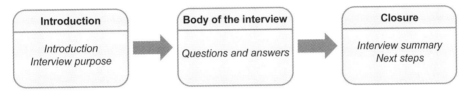

The introduction

In addition to making personal introductions, it is also important that the analyst makes sure an interviewee understands the purpose of the project in general and the interview in particular. Ideally, the interviewee should already understand why the interview has been requested but this cannot be relied upon. Explaining the interview context helps to put an interviewee at ease and increases the likelihood that relevant information is provided. It is also important to make sure that the interviewee has received the agenda and had the opportunity to add any points they wish to raise.

Body of the interview

The body of the interview is where the facts and issues are uncovered. It is useful to think about how this might be structured. A good approach is to begin by obtaining an overview explanation of the interviewee's concerns and responsibilities. This provides a context for the interview and helps to identify the areas where more detailed discussions are required to uncover specific issues and requirements.

It is essential to take notes during an interview. Even those with an excellent memory are unlikely to remember the key points discussed and the information provided. If the purpose of the interview is to understand a current task or process, a diagram such as a flow chart or other visual representation such as a rich picture or mind map (see later in this chapter) are often beneficial. If the purpose of the interview is to discuss a number of broad issues, a structured diagram, such as a context diagram or fishbone diagram, can help to identify the key points clearly, organise the discussion and, at a later stage, provide a visual check on the areas to explore further and the problems to address. An outline structure helps to keep the discussion on track as interview conversations always take unexpected diversions. While is important to allow detours into other areas, using a diagram to help keep the interview structure in mind can be invaluable.

In some situations it is appropriate to record an interview in preference, or as a supplement, to taking notes. This can be very useful if it is important that all details are captured. However, many people feel self-conscious when being recorded and this may affect what they say and how they express themselves. It should also be remembered that reviewing a recorded interview can be very time-consuming and it can take up to an hour to transcribe ten minutes worth of conversation.

Closure
It is important to bring an interview to a formal close. The analyst should:

- Summarise the points covered, the actions agreed and the timescales for completion.

- Explain what happens next, both with regard to the particular interview and the project.

- Ask the interviewee how any further contact should be made. Managing an interviewee's expectations of future behaviour can be invaluable if additional information or clarifications are required at a later point. This approach helps to 'keep the door open', which can be vital when working with some stakeholders, particularly those who work at a senior level.

Following-up the interview
It is always a good idea to write up the notes of an interview as soon as possible – ideally straight away and usually by the next day. If it is not possible to write up the notes immediately, reading through them immediately after the interview and extending them where they are unclear helps to commit the key points to memory. Once the notes are completed, they should be sent to the interviewee to confirm that they reflect accurately what was discussed. After they have been approved, they should become a formal part of the project documentation and may assist with later work including understanding stakeholder perspectives, defining requirements and ensuring traceability of the features offered by delivered solutions.

SCENARIOS

Scenario analysis involves telling the story of a task or transaction. Scenarios are useful when analysing or redesigning business processes as they help both the staff member and the analyst to think through the steps followed to carry out a piece of work. This enables them to visualise the steps more clearly and to identify where the standard approach may need to deviate.

A scenario description includes the business event that triggers the transaction, the set of actions that have to be completed in order to achieve a successful outcome, the exception situations to be handled, plus other aspects such as the actor responsible for carrying out the task, the preconditions and the post-conditions. The preconditions are the characteristics of the business or state of the IT system that must be true for the scenario to begin. Post-conditions are the characteristics that must be true following the conclusion of the scenario.

One of the key strengths of scenarios is that they provide a framework for discovering the exceptions that require alternative paths to be followed when carrying out a task. The transition from each step to the next provides an opportunity to analyse what else might happen or be true. This analysis often uncovers additional information or tacit knowledge. For these reasons, scenarios are extremely useful in requirements elicitation and analysis.

Advantages and disadvantages of scenarios

Scenarios offer significant advantages to the analyst:

- They require the member of staff to identify each step required to carry out a transaction, and the transitions between the steps; this reduces, or even removes, the opportunity for omissions.
- The step-by-step development approach helps to ensure that there are no taken-for-granted elements and the problem of tacit knowledge is addressed.
- They are developed using a 'top-down' approach, starting with an overview scenario and then refining this with further detail. This helps the member of staff to visualise all possible situations and removes uncertainty.
- A workshop group with responsibility for refining a scenario should identify those paths that do not suit the corporate culture or are not congruent with any community of practice involved.
- They provide a basis for developing prototypes.
- They provide a painstaking basis for preparing test scripts.

The disadvantages of scenarios are that they can be time-consuming to develop and some scenarios can become very complex, particularly where there are several alternative paths. Where this is the case, it is easier to analyse the scenarios if each of the alternative paths is considered as a separate scenario.

Scenario development process

Each scenario is developed using a standard process that enables the achievement of the advantages described above. This process is shown in Figure 5.4.

Figure 5.4 Process for developing scenarios (© Assist Knowledge Development Ltd.)

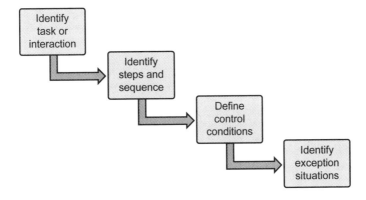

Figure 5.4 shows an overview approach to developing scenarios and includes the following steps:

- Identify the task or interaction to be modelled as a scenario and the trigger, or event, that causes that interaction to take place.

- Identify the steps that are carried out during the usual progress of the interaction and the flow of these steps.

- Define the control conditions that must be met in order to move from one step to the next, following the typical sequence of steps.

- Identify alternative paths that would be required to handle situations where the control conditions are not met.

The first three steps of this approach establish a default path for the scenario that assumes there are no complications and everything is working as expected. This path is often known as the main success scenario, or sometimes, the 'happy day' scenario. Scenarios are powerful when eliciting information.

Once the default steps have been identified, it is then necessary to ask the questions 'What needs to be true to continue with this path?' and 'At this point, what might happen instead?' These questions cause the business user to think about the situations where the standard procedure would not apply and identify alternative courses of action through asking the question, 'What should we do if this happens, or if this is true?'

Consider an example scenario where a customer wishes to place an order over the telephone. The precondition might be that for the process to happen the sales assistant is already logged in to the sales system.

The default steps for the sales assistant could then be:

(i) Enter customer reference number

(ii) Confirm customer details

(iii) Record order items

(iv) Accept payment

(v) Advise customer of delivery date

In order for this scenario to flow in the sequence shown, the control conditions to go from step (i) to step (ii), step (ii) to step (iii), and so on must be true; for example, the order items recorded in step (iii) must be available for step (iv) to take place. However, if there were insufficient stock then the next step to be followed would not be step (iv) but an alternative step. There may be several possible actions to be taken following this alternative step, such as:

- delaying order fulfilment until stock arrives;

- allocating a substitute item;

- advising the customer that the item is not available and concluding the call.

At the (successful) conclusion of the process the post-condition might be: The customer order is recorded, payment is received and stock levels have been adjusted.

All of the possibilities for diversion from the default scenario should be explored and documented as alternative paths; these are termed 'extensions' to the default scenario. This process helps to ensure that all possible situations and exceptions are anticipated and managed.

The example above is of a generic, abstract scenario. Another possible approach is to develop a 'concrete' scenario where a specific narrative or story is developed and then tested against the requirements already identified to find any gaps.

Here is an example of a concrete scenario for a restaurant booking system:

> A phone call is received from a customer wishing to book a table in the restaurant for the following Saturday. This is a highly valued customer who eats in the restaurant regularly. The customer tells the receptionist that they need a table for four people at 8 p.m. The table plan shows that there is a table available at this time so the receptionist records the customer's name and contact details, and books the table.

There is a possible extension to this concrete scenario where a table is not available at 8 p.m. but there is one available at 7.30 p.m. This extension requires the receptionist to offer the alternative time and ask if this is acceptable. This adds a further step to those reflected in the 'happy day' scenario. Another possibility is that there are no tables available for the evening and other dates are explored with the customer.

Concrete scenarios such as this example are extremely useful to uncover where possible extensions lie during one-to-one discussions or workshops. It can be helpful for the analyst to present a prepared concrete 'happy day' scenario and then use this as the basis for the scenario analysis. An exercise that helps to encourage business stakeholders to contribute wholeheartedly to this process involves placing them in break-out groups with the instruction to produce a concrete scenario that does not conform to the 'happy day' path. Experience shows that this exercise increases creativity and can produce many valid extensions that increase understanding of the task.

Documenting scenarios

A popular way of documenting scenario descriptions is to develop use case descriptions to support use case diagrams (see Chapter 11). This technique is part of the UML and is a text-based approach. However, there are a number of graphical methods that may be used to document a scenario such as activity diagrams (see Chapter 7) and decision tables (see Chapter 14). It is also possible to use drawings to create a 'storyboard' setting out a visual scenario.

PROTOTYPING

Prototyping is helpful when eliciting, analysing, demonstrating and validating requirements. Analysts often complain that the business staff do not know what they want from a system or process, and that as a result it is difficult to define the requirements. However, it can be very difficult for anyone to envisage requirements for the future without having a sense of what is possible. It is much easier to review a suggested solution and identify where there are errors or problems.

Prototyping involves building simulations of a process or system in order to review them with the business representatives and thereby increase understanding about the requirements. There are several approaches that may be used to build prototypes:

- They may be built using the organisation's software development environment so that they exactly mirror the future system.

- Images of the screens and navigations may be built using presentation software products such as Microsoft PowerPoint.

- They may be mocked up using flipchart sheets, pens and packs of sticky notes and developed in collaboration with business staff. This enables the business staff to build prototypes of screens or reports, identify navigation paths, define the data they must input or refer to and prepare lists of specified values. This approach can also be used to develop prototypes of a business process.

It is therefore important to consider the context and application of the prototype before building it as this helps to determine how it should be developed. There are three aspects to be considered:

- What is the **scope** to be covered by the prototypes? Is it to demonstrate how a particular screen should look or is it a prototype of an entire system or process?

- Should the prototypes be high or low **fidelity**? Prototypes can range from sketches drawn on paper to detailed simulations of actual screen displays developed using the application software.

- How extensive should the **functionality** of the prototypes be? Should the prototype access and use data and, if so, will the data be created solely for the purpose of the demonstration or should the prototype access fully operational system data?

Wireframes offer a similar approach to prototypes although they are created primarily to show the layout of a screen, document or website page and to indicate how the elements, and any navigation between them, might work. Wireframes usually lack images, colours or graphics so may be viewed as outline prototypes. They may be created using software applications designed for drawing purposes or may be created by hand using paper or a whiteboard. Collaboration tools, such as digital whiteboards, may also be used to create wireframes.

Building a prototype often releases the blocks to thinking because they provide a concrete visualisation that often results in greater understanding and clarity. Prototypes also offer a way of demonstrating how the new processes or system might work and provide a concrete basis for evaluation and discussion. They can be useful for several specific reasons:

- If the business staff are unclear about their requirements, prototypes can help to visualise a new process or system and thereby provide insight into possible requirements. A workshop can be an excellent forum for doing this. These prototypes tend to be low fidelity with minimal scope as they are usually 'mocked up' using flipcharts, whiteboards and sticky notes.

- Prototypes can be used to analyse or confirm requirements. Typically, these prototypes are high fidelity in that they are developed using software that is able to demonstrate how the actual solution might look. Where the prototypes are purely for demonstration purposes, the scope tends to be specific to a particular area and actual data is not used so they are often discarded once the prototyping exercise has been concluded.

- Agile software development approaches, such as DSDM and Scrum, use evolutionary prototyping as an integral part of their development lifecycle. These prototypes are used for elicitation, analysis, validation and development purposes, usually within the context of a development team where the software developers and users have direct conversations. Prototypes built as part of evolutionary software development tend to be high fidelity and may use actual data.

There is a strong link between scenarios and prototyping because scenarios can be used as the basis for developing prototypes. In effect, a prototype mirrors a scenario, providing a visual representation of how the scenario should be enacted in practice. As well as confirming requirements, prototyping can often help the users to identify some that they had not considered previously.

Advantages and disadvantages of prototyping

There are several advantages gained from using prototypes:

- They clarify any uncertainty on the part of the analysts and confirm to business staff that their requirements have been understood.

- They help the business staff to identify new requirements as they gain an understanding of how the system will operate and what the system will do to support their work.

- They demonstrate the look and feel of the proposed system and elicit usability and accessibility requirements.

- They enable business staff to validate the requirements and identify any errors.

- They provide a means of assessing the navigation paths and system performance.

Prototyping also has a number of hazards, most of which can be avoided by setting clear objectives for the prototyping exercise and managing the stakeholders' expectations. The hazards include the following:

- The prototyping cycle can spin out of control with endless iterations taking place.

- If the purpose of the exercise has not been explained clearly, business staff may make false assumptions about the progress of the work and believe that the solution is almost ready for delivery on the basis of an agreed prototype.

- Expectations can be raised unnecessarily by failing to match the final appearance of the system, or its performance. A system that is on a stand-alone machine that is accessing six dummy data records is likely to be more responsive than a machine that is accessing a shared resource with thousands of other users. If there is likely to be a delay in the real response time, it is important to build that into the prototype.

Agile prototyping

In an Agile software development environment, prototyping sessions are used to elicit and analyse requirements, and to construct and test working functionality. The development work is conducted iteratively, with each iteration using the concept of a timebox or sprint, typically lasting a specified number of weeks, within which pre-planned functionality is delivered. During the timebox, the selected requirements for delivery are validated, coded, tested and released. Contingency is provided by the prioritisation of the requirements, whereby some are designated a lower level of priority and may be postponed to a later timebox if necessary. In this approach, the tension between time and quality is resolved in favour of time but, because Agile encourages iterative development, the quality aspect is merely postponed, not sacrificed.

The evolutionary prototyping approach delivers the most critical pieces of functionality into the business operations at the point when it is needed, leaving the less urgent functionality to be delivered in future releases.

USER ROLE ANALYSIS

Techniques such as scenario modelling emphasise why it is important to understand the people who engage with a business area or system. A starting point for understanding these individuals is to define generic titles such as 'customer', 'supplier' or 'regulator'. These titles reflect the roles adopted by individuals or organisations when they interact with the business system.

While there is a relationship with stakeholder analysis (see Chapter 6), user role analysis is concerned with identifying specific groups of individuals where all of the members of a group need to access a particular set of services from a business system. For example, the employees of an organisation all require access to the HR services; the customers for a manufacturing organisation all require access to product-related services.

Individuals are said to take on a 'role' when interacting with a system. It is possible for an individual to adopt more than one role where they wish to access two distinct sets of services. For example, an individual may be a customer of a food store and take on a customer role for certain transactions but may also work within the food store and perform a sales assistant user role for other transactions.

Advantages and disadvantages of user role analysis

There are several advantages gained from analysing user roles as they provide:

- a means of identifying where stakeholders have common interests or requirements;
- a more efficient approach to eliciting and analysing requirements;
- a strong basis for analysing scenarios, stakeholder perspectives (see Chapter 6), use cases and user stories (see Chapter 11).

However, a disadvantage of user role analysis occurs when generic user role names cover a very wide stakeholder group, which makes it difficult to envisage how and why individuals might want to use particular system. For example, 'Customer' is a very broad term that may not capture the variety of characteristics displayed by actual customers of an organisation. This disadvantage may be overcome using the supplementary technique of persona analysis. In the case of the 'Customer' user role, a good way of understanding the nature of different customers is to create 'personas' for them.

Personas

Figure 5.5 represents the customer user role and three typical customer personas for a banking system. These personas are described below.

- **George:** George is a man in his mid-70s who has banked with us for 50 years. He is not particularly familiar with computers, which he mainly uses for email to keep in touch with his grandchildren in Australia. He prefers face-to-face contact with the bank rather than using its online services, although he might be induced to use these if they could be made intuitive enough.

- **Emma:** Emma is a professional woman in her 30s who combines a fairly high-pressure job with looking after two small children. She is very conversant with computers and prefers to do her banking in spare moments or late in the evening and rarely, if ever, visits a physical bank branch.

- **David:** David is a high worth businessman who makes extensive use of the bank's wealth management services. He is extremely busy but nevertheless likes to have a personal relationship with his financial advisers. He demands a high-quality standard of service.

Figure 5.5 Customer user role with personas

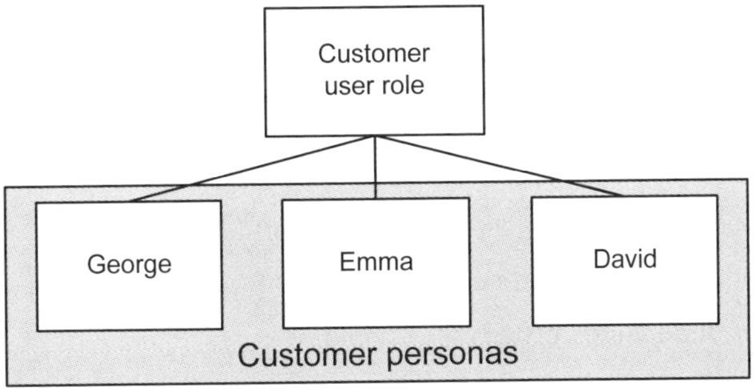

Although these personas are archetypes, they nevertheless help to envisage why and how these different customers might want to access the bank's services. This information helps when designing processes and services to ensure that they meet the needs of the personas who wish to access them. Personas can also be useful when analysing users of the business system who have particular accessibility requirements. For example, a persona representing customers who have a specific disability might be defined in order that their accessibility requirements may be fully explored and understood.

STORYTELLING

The storytelling approach is useful to supplement the structured techniques used to understand the issues within the business situation. Inviting stories from stakeholders is a powerful way to uncover layers or patterns of information that may help or hinder progress. Staff at all levels have anecdotes of disaster or triumph and these stories can be highly illuminating, offering insights into their expectations and experiences. The anecdotes may concern customer experience – good or otherwise – or their own experiences resulting from a change in the company, which may also be positive or negative.

Eliciting stories can be carried out either one to one or in a group forum but if it is done with a group, it should be less formal than a workshop or focus group discussion.

Humans enjoy telling stories of horror or woe, so a good way to introduce this is to ask about something that has happened in the past, perhaps a difficult customer or an unsatisfactory supplier, a failed reorganisation, or an incident that caused difficulties for the company or members of staff. The purpose is not to solve any problems mentioned but to gain an insight into what has caused unhappiness or dissatisfaction in the past, and find out how to avoid those problems. The business analyst must be careful not to allow blame to be allocated as this may alienate some of the stakeholders.

After talking about difficulties or frustrations, the analyst can invite stories and episodes that show success or are causes of pride, whether it was meeting a deadline against the odds, winning a difficult contract or evidence of good teamwork to deal with an emergency. Any anecdote about such experiences is likely to provide strong indications about the culture and expectations of the stakeholders.

QUANTITATIVE APPROACHES

Quantitative approaches are used to obtain data that is needed to quantify the information that has been collected during workshops, interviews or when using other qualitative techniques. Quantitative data may include the following:

- the number of people using a particular system;
- the number of complaints received during a set period;
- the number of bookings processed each day.

Quantifying data helps to ensure that assumptions are not made during the analysis and definition of a solution. These assumptions concern information provided by business staff that prove to be inaccurate at a later stage. It is important to identify where information is merely opinion and confirm whether or not it is accurate. To do otherwise can raise the risk of a delivered solution failing to provide what is needed by the organisation and its staff.

Surveys or questionnaires

Surveys can be useful to get a limited amount of information from a lot of people as interviewing them individually or running a series of workshops is not practical or cost-effective. There are many software applications that may be used to create online surveys but, despite the ease of development and access offered by these tools, surveys are not always successful in obtaining data. This is because many surveys are poorly designed so discourage the participants from completing them. Effective survey design is needed if the survey is to generate the required volume of accurate data.

The exact design of a survey depends upon its purpose but there are three main areas to consider: the heading, classification and data sections.

Heading section

This is where the purpose of the survey is explained. It is important that the heading section explains the rationale for the survey, how the data is intended to be used and, where appropriate, any incentive for its completion. A well-formed heading section helps the respondents to understand why the information is needed and as a result may significantly increase the volume of responses.

Classification section

This is where the details about the respondent are captured. This data provides the basis for categorising the respondents using pre-defined analysis criteria, like age, gender or length of service.

Sometimes, surveys are anonymous in that they do not require identification information about respondents, perhaps because some controversial opinions are requested. If this is the case, it is necessary to ensure that the respondents cannot be identified by other means. When individuals are asked to complete a survey where anonymity is essential, they become acutely aware of any risk to that anonymity. If they feel that this cannot be guaranteed, confidence in the process is lost and either the response will be untruthful or no response will be forthcoming. Compromising anonymity is usually unintentional; sometimes just asking for data such as job role, age and gender would enable the identification of a respondent, so care must be taken in these circumstances.

If there is a need to identify respondents, it is important to be aware of the provisions and stipulations of data protection legislation and not keep the data any longer than is necessary for the purpose of the survey.

Data section

This is where the main body of questions is posed. It is vital to think carefully about the phrasing of the questions. They must be unambiguous and, ideally, allow for straightforward answers such as 'yes/no', 'agree/neutral/disagree' or 'excellent/satisfactory/inadequate'. Where opinions are sought, the Likert scale is often used. This scale asks for an answer within the following range: strongly agree, agree, neither agree nor disagree, disagree, strongly disagree.

This is a five point Likert scale; it is also possible to extend or reduce the scale. For example, a four point scale could be achieved by removing the 'Neither agree nor disagree' option; a seven point scale could be achieved by adding 'somewhat agree' and 'somewhat disagree' as options.

It is better to structure the questions and answers using a consistent format as it helps when analysing the responses. It also helps if the same range of answers is required for each group of questions.

Every set of potential responses to a question should be thought through carefully using the 'mutually exclusive, completely exhaustive' (MECE) approach. MECE involves checking each set of defined, alternative responses to ensure that:

- only one response would apply to each survey participant;
- the range of responses cover every possible situation.

Surveys must be designed carefully to ensure that meaningful data is obtained. Analysts need to be able to build a summary of the responses to each question, allocate percentages to each response to a question, observe patterns and trends, analyse responses using the classification data, and thereby draw relevant conclusions. Online survey products often offer helpful features that may support this analysis. However, for the conclusions to be meaningful, the survey must provide clear, unambiguous questions and well-defined possible responses so that the data can be collated and analysed properly.

A frequent error used in surveys involves framing questions that are ambiguous. For example, if the question 'Have you used our website recently?' was posed and the response was 'No', what would that mean? Would it mean that the respondent:

- Is not interested in the purchasing the company's products and services so has not visited the website?
- Is unaware that the products and services are available via the company website?
- Is uncomfortable using technology so has never used this or any other website?
- Last used the website six months ago but does not consider that that counts as 'recently'? In this example, the term 'recently' is ambiguous and needs to be quantified.

The question could be rephrased to ask when the website was last used, and the responses should offer specific time periods that align with the MECE approach. This would need to include a response of 'never' to ensure that those who have not used the website are accommodated.

The key drawback with using surveys is that people find it difficult to find the time and motivation to complete a survey unless it is a topic of significant interest to them. This may be countered by providing clear clarification of the reasons why the survey exists and why the data is needed. In some situations, a 'prize' or other type of reward may be offered as an inducement to complete the survey. Ultimately, though, it can be very difficult to obtain the desired number of responses and that needs to be considered when adopting a survey approach. A limited sample of responses may provide misleading information and erroneous conclusions.

A common weakness of surveys, particularly when used for marketing purposes, is that they can take a long time to complete with the result that respondents give up after a few sections and abandon the effort. If it is going to take more than 10 minutes out of their working day, many people get impatient and either enter mischievous answers (assuming anonymity) or don't bother to complete the survey. Either way, the quality and quantity of data is compromised.

Special purpose records

Special purpose records are data-gathering documents used to collect data about specific situations. For example, the number of complaints about a specific issue received in a day or the number of times it is necessary to access a website over a period of time. The format for a special purpose record is usually decided by the analyst and tends to be informal. At the simplest level, a special purpose record may be a number that increments each time a situation occurs. They can be completed either by the analyst during an observation session or given to the relevant members of staff to complete over a period of time, as follows:

- The analyst may spend a period of time in a department shadowing one of the staff, compiling a special purpose record in order to document the number of customer requests received each day. It may also be necessary to classify the requests according to whether they are complaints, queries or returned goods. It is also possible to extend the information recorded to show aspects such as the nature of customer calls, their duration and how long it takes to retrieve the data needed to answer the query. This information could help the analyst to understand the problems with the business process and where there is scope for improvement.

- Another approach is to give the form to the business staff to complete as they perform their work. For example, they could keep a five-bar gate record about how often they need to transfer telephone calls. Again, this could provide the analyst with information about the problems with the business process.

There are difficulties with using special purpose records, chief of which is that it is extremely easy to forget to record each occurrence. Where a special purpose record is required, two important criteria have to be satisfied if the data gathered is to be of use:

- The people undertaking the recording must be induced to 'buy-in' to the exercise. This may be done by persuading them of the need or benefits. Another possibility is that they are instructed to do this by their manager.

- The survey must be realistic about what people can reasonably be expected to record while performing their work.

Some software applications are able to track the work of the business staff, for example by recording the duration of telephone calls automatically. This may not always be possible, however, and special purpose records can provide a low fidelity but speedy way of obtaining data. These records can help to avoid the problems associated with observation as, in effect, business staff are conducting the observation themselves. Creating and analysing special purpose records can be an effective use of the analyst's time.

Activity sampling

Activity sampling is also a quantitative form of observation and is used when it is necessary to know how people divide their work time among a range of activities. For example, how much time is spent on the telephone? How much time spent on reconciling payments? How much on sorting out complaints?

One way to find out how people spend their time would be to get them to complete a special purpose record. However, in some situations, the results need to have a guaranteed level of accuracy, such as where they are to be used to build a business case. In situations where accuracy is important, activity sampling may be used in preference to observation or special purpose records.

An activity sampling exercise is carried out in five steps. The analyst has to:

1. Identify the activities to be recorded. This list should include a 'not working' activity as this covers breaks or times away from the desk. It might also include a 'not-related' task, such as first aid or health and safety officer duties.
2. Decide on the frequency and timings, that is, when and how often to record the activities being undertaken.
3. Visit the study group at the times decided upon and record what each group member is doing.
4. Record the results.
5. After a set period, analyse the results.

An activity sampling exercise provides quantifiable data about the number of times an activity is carried out per day by the group studied. By analysing that figure against other data, such as the total amount of time available, it is possible to calculate the total length of time spent on that activity and the average time one occurrence of the activity takes. This information can be useful when developing business cases and evaluating proposed solutions. Also, it generates other questions such as whether the average time is reasonable for this task or whether it indicates that there is a problem somewhere in the process.

Document analysis

Document analysis involves reviewing samples of source documents or reports to uncover information about an organisation, process or system. The documents may be in physical form or may be software-based. Analysts sometimes need to define questions to ask about a business area or problem situation and this can be difficult. Document analysis helps to identify many questions, each of which helps to develop the analyst's understanding.

The following questions may be asked about each document:

- How is the document completed?
- Who completes the document?

- Are there any validations or controls on the document?
- Who uses the completed document?
- When is the document used?
- How many are used or produced?
- How long is the document retained by the organisation, and in what form?
- What are the details of the information shown on the document?
- Where is the data or information obtained?
- Are other names used in the organisation to refer to any of the items of data?
- Are all the data items on the document still needed, or are any redundant?
- Is there other data that is not entered on the document, but would be useful for this process?

Document analysis is useful to supplement other techniques such as workshops, interviews and observation. For example, analysing the origin and usage of a document can prove very enlightening when investigating a process. Samples of completed documents or reports also help to clarify the key items of data used to carry out the work of the business area and can offer an excellent basis for modelling data (see Chapter 11).

APPLICABILITY OF INVESTIGATION TECHNIQUES

Some of the techniques described in this chapter are suitable for general investigation of the problem situation while others are useful when eliciting requirements for a new system. Some are more suitable to elicit requirements when using a linear, analysis approach, others are more relevant when applying an Agile software development approach. Some techniques are suitable in all situations. Table 5.1 gives a guide to the suitability of these techniques for the different situations.

Table 5.1 Relevance of techniques for different BA services/environments

Investigation technique	BA service: Situation investigation and problem definition	BA service: Requirements definition	
		Linear requirements elicitation	Agile requirements elicitation
Activity sampling	HR	HR	LR
Document analysis	R	HR	R
Focus group	HR	R	LR
Hothousing	LR	LR	HR
Meeting/Interview	HR	HR	HR

(Continued)

Table 5.1 (Continued)

Investigation technique	BA service: Situation investigation and problem definition	BA service: Requirements definition	
		Linear requirements elicitation	Agile requirements elicitation
Observation	HR	HR	R
Prototyping	LR	HR	HR
Scenario analysis	LR	HR	HR
Shadowing	HR	HR	R
Special purpose records	HR	HR	LR
Storytelling	HR	LR	R
Surveys	HR	R	LR
User role analysis	HR	HR	HR
Workshops	HR	HR	HR

Key: HR = highly relevant; R = relevant in many situations; LR = limited relevance

RECORDING BUSINESS SITUATIONS AND ISSUES

While the investigation of the current situation is underway, the analyst needs to record the findings in order to understand the range of issues and the business needs. Meeting reports should be produced for each interview and workshop so that they can be agreed with the participants. It is also helpful to use diagrams to record the findings about the business situation. This section suggests four diagrammatic techniques that help the analyst to understand the information that has been obtained and find the root cause of any problems.

Rich pictures

The rich picture technique is one of the few that provide an overview of an entire business situation. Whereas modelling approaches such as data or process modelling provide a clear representation of a specific aspect of a business system, rich pictures show all aspects. The technique does not have a fixed notation, but allows the analyst to use any symbols or notation that are relevant and useful. For this reason, the rich picture can show the human characteristics of the business situation and can reflect intangible areas such as the culture of the organisation.

Many problems in the current business system may have originated with the people performing the tasks rather than being caused by poor process design or inadequate IT systems. There could be differing viewpoints, misunderstandings, stress from too many tasks, personal differences with co-workers, dissatisfaction with management or frustration at inadequate resources. Any of these factors could impair the performance of a task, but the standard analysis models do not offer a means of recording them.

A rich picture allows the analyst to document all of the organisational, human and cultural aspects as well as process and information flows of a business system. The unstructured nature of the technique allows the analyst to build a personal visualisation of the information using pictorial representation. Its strength is that the process of building the rich picture helps the analyst to form a mental map of the situation and see connections between different issues. The rich picture can also be enriched further as more information about the situation comes to light.

Figure 5.6 shows an example of a rich picture for a business system called Simply Juices. Simply Juices sells fruit juices and smoothies to retail outlets, including supermarkets and local shops. They have a telesales operation and five years ago set up an online sales system to supplement this. Since then, sales have actually declined, and the volume of customer complaints increased. The rich picture presents a graphic summary of the business analyst's investigation. Unlike a model that uses a formal notation set, such as a process model, the rich picture shows elements of the process, the people involved, organisation structure and information and technology.

Figure 5.6 Example of a rich picture

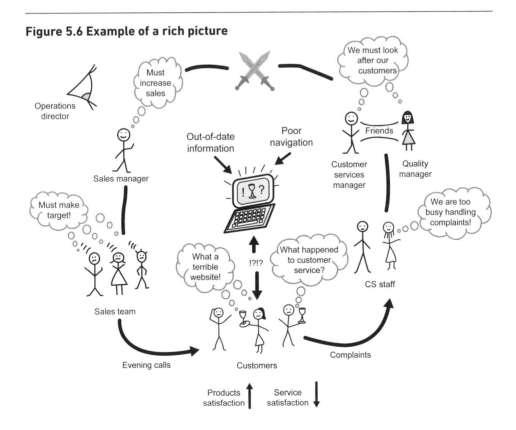

Mind maps

Mind maps (Buzan and Buzan, 2000) are a useful tool for summarising a lot of information in a visual form. The information is structured to highlight connections between ideas and topics. They provide a means of representing all of the issues that have been uncovered about the situation but in an organised manner. The business system or problem under consideration is drawn at the centre of the diagram with the main topics or issues shown as the first level of branches radiating from the central point. Each of these branches is labelled to indicate the nature of the particular issue. The labels should use as few words as possible and ideally should be just one word. The branches might represent particular processes, equipment and systems used, relationships between the staff who conduct the work and so on.

The first level branches are extended to support second level branches that are concerned with more detailed areas. For example, the level one branch 'equipment' might be expanded with second level branches indicating problems with the printing or photocopying equipment; the level one branch for systems might show second level branches, each of which records a key failing of the IT support.

A mind map helps to structure the information gathered about a business area into a recognisable and manageable set of connections. They are extremely useful in helping analysts to order their thinking and they work well both on their own and when used in conjunction with rich pictures. The mind map in Figure 5.7 for Simply Juices relates to the rich picture shown in Figure 5.6.

Business process models

In order to understand fully how a process is carried out, it is helpful to draw a flow chart diagram showing the tasks in a process, the actors responsible for carrying them out and the process flow. These models are relatively straightforward to draw and business stakeholders find them accessible. Accordingly, they are effective when used to support communication between analysts and business staff. Business process models are also invaluable as a diagnostic aid since they help to identify problems such as delays, bottlenecks and duplicate tasks. However, such models show only one aspect of the situation – the logical workings of the process. They do not show the human interactions, culture, politics, conflicts or harmonious interactions, the frustrations or ergonomics involved in performing a process. To gain a full understanding of the situation, business process models should be used in tandem with the other visualisation techniques discussed above. Business process models are described in detail in Chapter 7.

Fishbone diagrams

One of the major objectives in investigating and modelling a business system is to identify where there are problems and discover their underlying causes. Some of these causes may be obvious or the stakeholders may be aware of the root causes of their problems; however, sometimes it is only the symptoms that are highlighted by the stakeholders because the causes are deep-rooted or have proved difficult to isolate.

Figure 5.7 Example of a mind map

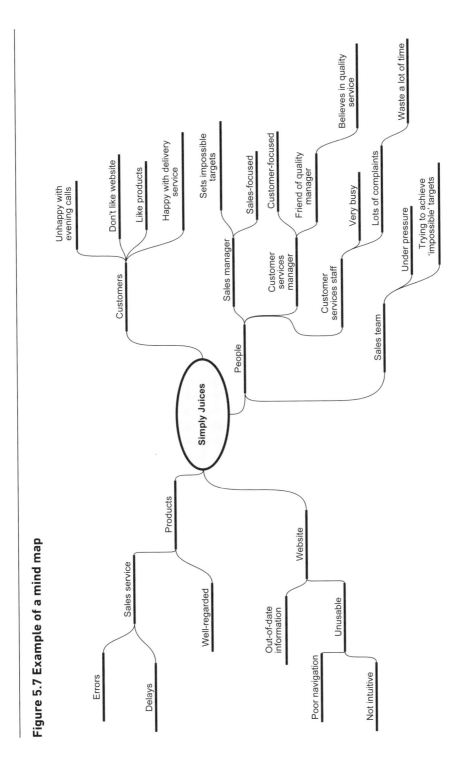

Figure 5.8 Example of a fishbone diagram

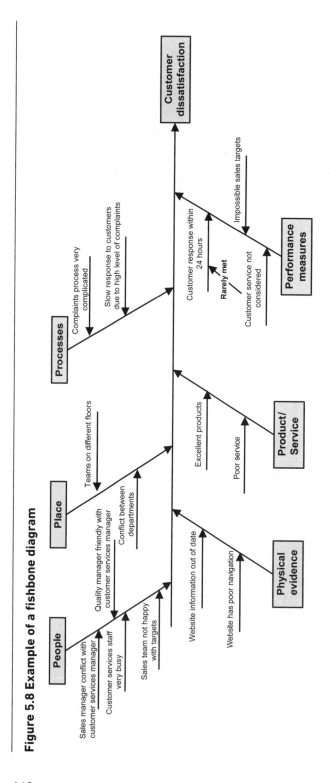

The fishbone diagram is a problem-analysis technique designed to help uncover the underlying causes of an inefficient process or a business problem. It has similarities to a mind map but its purpose is strictly diagnostic rather than recording. The technique was invented by Dr Kaoru Ishikawa (Ishikawa, 1985) and the diagrams are sometimes known as Ishikawa diagrams. They are often used to analyse the root causes of a specific business problem, which is drawn in a box at the right-hand side of the diagram. A line is drawn from this box towards the left of the page and represents the backbone of the 'fish'. Radiating up and down from this backbone are spines, each of which suggests possible areas where the causes of the problem may be found. A number of approaches may be used when labelling the spines:

- **The 4Ms:** manpower, machines, measures and methods

- **An alternative 4Ms:** manpower, machines, materials and methods

- **The 6Ps:** people, place, processes, physical evidence, product/service and performance measures

- **The 4Ss:** surroundings, suppliers, systems, skills

These categories help because they list areas that have been found to be the sources of inefficiencies in many business systems. In practice, the range of categories may be a combination of the most relevant elements from the approaches listed above, or the analyst may even define some categories that are particularly relevant to the particular business area. Data for this analysis can be found from workshops, interviews, observation, activity sampling and special purpose records. The categories used to produce a fishbone diagram may also be used as a structure for a workshop discussion about a particular problem.

As with mind maps, the spines may have more detailed elements associated with them. Each category along a spine is examined, and the factors within that category that may be affecting the problem are added to the diagram. The resultant diagram is shaped like a fishbone – hence the name 'fishbone diagram'. An example is shown in Figure 5.8.

Once the diagram has been completed, the results are analysed to seek out the key causes of problems. These tend to be the items that are listed several times or those that appear to have the most impact upon the situation. Such items should be prioritised so that action to address the issue is undertaken promptly.

SUMMARY

Business situations need to be investigated to clarify where problems exist and the root causes that underlie these problems. To do this effectively, business analysts need to be able to apply a range of investigative and visualisation techniques and need to be able to identify when these techniques are relevant. A toolkit of such techniques combined with an understanding of their relevance forms a key competency for a business analyst.

6 ANALYSING AND MANAGING STAKEHOLDERS

INTRODUCTION

Effective stakeholder management is crucial to the success of any business analysis project. Knowing who the stakeholders are, and understanding what it is they expect from the project and delivered solution is vital if they are to remain involved and supportive of the business changes. One of the major reasons why business analysis projects do not succeed – or do not succeed fully – is poor stakeholder management. For example, a project team may not recognise the importance, or even the existence, of a key stakeholder and accordingly may find that their plans are constantly frustrated. On the other hand, if the relevant stakeholders are identified and managed properly, most obstacles can be cleared.

Much of the groundwork for stakeholder management takes place during project initiation and inception and this work must be revisited constantly as the project progresses. The key steps involved in stakeholder management are illustrated in Figure 6.1.

Figure 6.1 Stakeholder management in the project lifecycle (© Assist Knowledge Development Ltd.)

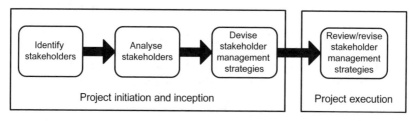

The main responsibility for stakeholder management may rest with the project manager or with a senior business analyst. However, all team members have important roles to play in identifying stakeholders, in helping to understand their needs and by helping to manage their expectations of the project.

STAKEHOLDER CATEGORIES

As Figure 6.1 illustrates, the first step in stakeholder management involves finding out who the stakeholders are. A good working definition of a stakeholder is: anyone who has an interest in, or may be affected by, the issue under consideration. This means, more or less, anyone affected by the project or who may be in a position to influence it.

Of course, each project has its own distinctive set of stakeholders, determined by the nature of the project and the environment in which it is taking place. However, some 'generic' stakeholder categories can be identified that may apply to many projects, as illustrated in Figure 6.2.

Figure 6.2 The stakeholder wheel (© Assist Knowledge Development Ltd.)

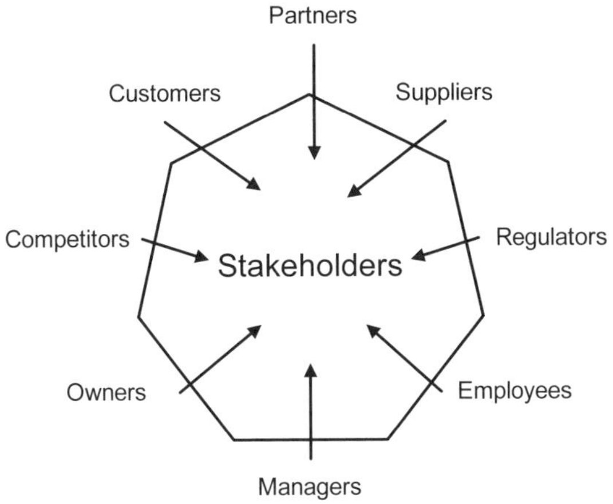

Customers

These are the people or organisations for whom the organisation provides products or services. They are stakeholders because anything done in the way of change has a potential effect on them. The project team must consider how to manage that change most effectively so as not to lose customers that they wish to retain. It may be useful to subdivide the term 'customer' into specific categories, such as:

- large or small;
- regular or occasional;
- wholesale or retail;
- corporate or private;
- commercial, non-profit or public-sector;
- civilian or military;
- domestic or export.

There may be categories that are specific to an organisation. For example, 'local customers' and 'regional customers', however these are defined. Customer categories are discussed further in Chapter 7.

Partners

These are the organisations that provide specialist services to the organisation or work on its behalf. Examples of partner organisations may be a reseller of products or services, or an outsourcing company that provides catering services.

Suppliers

These provide the organisation with the goods and services that it uses. They may be subdivided into the following categories:

- major or minor;
- regular or occasional;
- domestic or overseas.

Suppliers are stakeholders because they are interested in the way the organisation does business with them, what it wishes to buy, how it wants to pay and so on. Many change initiatives have the effect of altering the relationships of organisations with their suppliers and, as with the customers, such changes need to be managed carefully to make sure that they achieve positive and mutually beneficial results.

Regulators

Many organisations are now subject to regulation or inspection by external authorities. Regulators are concerned that any changes proposed by an organisation comply with the rules they enforce. For example, laws and regulations that govern an organisation's financial conduct, or professional standards, such as those required of the medical profession.

Employees

The people who work in an organisation clearly have an interest in the way it is run and in changes that it makes. In a small firm, the employees may be regarded as individual stakeholders in their own right but, in larger organisations, they are probably best considered as groups. Sometimes, employees belong to trades unions, whose officials therefore become stakeholders too.

Managers

There are also the professional managers of the organisation, those to whom its direction is entrusted. In a large organisation, there may be many layers of management and each may form a distinctive stakeholder grouping, for example:

- board-level senior managers;
- middle managers;
- junior managers;
- front-line supervisors.

As with many aspects of stakeholder management, it is an error to assume that a group is homogeneous in its views and concerns; junior managers may well have a very different perspective, and a different set of values and priorities, from those on the Board who take the major strategic decisions.

Owners

For a commercial business, the owners are just that – the people who own it directly. The business may be, in legal terms, a sole trader or partnership, or it could be a limited company, in which case the owners are the shareholders. For public limited companies, the majority of shares are held by institutions such as investment companies and pension funds and so the managers of these share portfolios become proxy owners.

Competitors

Competitors vie with the organisation for the business of its customers and, therefore, they have a keen interest in any changes made by an organisation. Their reactions to any changes have to be considered; for example, how a competitor might react and whether they might try to block an initiative or to produce a form of counterproposal.

Other stakeholders

The groups shown in Figure 6.2 are generic and, in particular cases, there may well be other stakeholders. For example, the insurers of an organisation may be interested in any areas that could affect the pattern of risk that is covered. Alternatively, the police might be interested in the law and order implications of some actions. In some organisations, the views of staff associations are also significant.

It is important for each project that the identification of stakeholders is as complete as possible, as it will otherwise be impossible to develop and implement effective management strategies for them. It may be useful to conduct some sort of workshop with people knowledgeable about the organisation and the proposed project to make sure that the coverage of stakeholders is comprehensive.

ANALYSING STAKEHOLDERS

Having identified the stakeholders, the next step is to make an assessment of the weight that should be attached to their issues. No stakeholder should be ignored completely but the approach to each will be different depending on (i) their level of interest in the project and (ii) the amount of power or influence they wield to further or obstruct it.

The power/interest grid (adapted from Newcombe, 2003), shown in Figure 6.3, offers a useful technique for analysing stakeholders.

In using the power/interest grid, it is important to plot stakeholders where they actually *are*, not where they should be. Strategies can then be explored for managing them in their positions or, perhaps, for moving them to other positions that might be more advantageous for the success of the project.

Figure 6.3 The power/interest grid

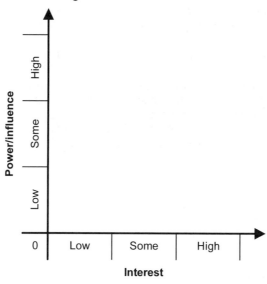

STAKEHOLDER MANAGEMENT STRATEGIES

There are many positions that could be taken on the power/interest grid but it is usually sufficient to consider the nine combinations of power and interest illustrated in Figure 6.4.

Figure 6.4 Key stakeholder management strategies

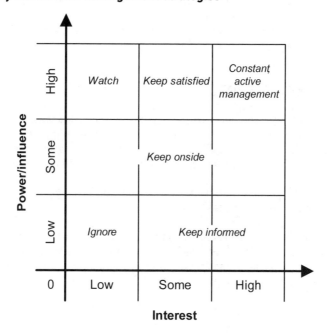

No or low interest and no or low power/influence

These are stakeholders who have neither a direct interest in the project nor any real power to affect it. For practical purposes, they can be ignored as regards day-to-day issues on the project and there needs to be no special effort made to 'sell' them its benefits. However, as stakeholders do change positions on the grid (see below), it is usually wise to inform them occasionally about progress and the latest position. A periodic newsletter can be a helpful mechanism for these updates.

Some or high interest but no or low power/influence

These groups can be very difficult to manage effectively as, although they may be very directly affected by a change project, they feel powerless to shape its direction in any way. This can result in frustration and a sort of passive resistance to change that, though overcome by positional power, can lead to delay and less-than-optimal results.

The management strategy for these stakeholders is to keep them informed of what is going on and of the reasons for the proposed change. However, this can be a rather passive approach and, in many circumstances, more effort should be devoted to 'selling' the benefits of the project. This can best be done by being as honest as possible about the need for change, and highlighting the positive aspects of the change and the negative consequences of not making them. Frequent and focused communication regarding progress is also necessary when managing these stakeholders.

No or low to high interest but some power/influence

This is a rather varied group. It includes some stakeholders like middle or senior managers who do have some power or influence but, because their interests are not directly affected, are not very concerned about the direction a project is taking. Regulators may also fall into this category although they will only become involved if there is a suspected breach of their rules. This group can also include those with a higher level of interest in the project but who have only limited power or influence.

The best approach with this group is to keep them supportive of the project, possibly by issuing frequent information updates to them, and also by increasing their involvement with the project. As the old saying has it, it is better to have them inside the glasshouse throwing stones out than outside throwing them in.

No or low interest but high power/influence

These are probably very senior managers who, for one reason or another, have no direct interest in the project. This may be because it is too small or unimportant for them to bother with or it may be that it is in an area that doesn't interest them. For example, the marketing director for an organisation is unlikely to be concerned about a project to streamline the stationery purchasing procedures and it may be assumed that this stakeholder can be ignored. However, this is actually a rather risky approach. The marketing director may become very interested in the stationery procurement system if items such as pens or sticky notes are unavailable in time for an important meeting or conference.

Where a situation arises that might cause these stakeholders to take a greater interest in the project, it might be prudent to address their needs directly, possibly via one-to-one meetings, in order to ensure that they do not start to raise concerns or even decide to exert their influence. In some situations, the project team may wish to encourage the increased interest of influential stakeholders, for example, if it was felt that their support would help achieve the project objectives. Where this is the case, it may be necessary to highlight any aspects of the project that have a direct impact upon the stakeholder's business area; some form of discussion will be required that, with very influential stakeholders, would typically involve a meeting.

Some interest and high power/influence

These stakeholders have some interest in the project, and they have actual power over what happens. The key strategy to manage these stakeholders is to keep them satisfied, so that they do not take a more direct (and hence, possibly, more obstructive) interest in the project. However, in some circumstances, the strategy may be to encourage these stakeholders to become more actively involved in a project. For example, if the finance director for an organisation can be persuaded to be positively involved in a project, they may be a powerful force for success, since they can make resources available that would otherwise be hard to obtain.

High interest and high power/influence

These are the key players, the people who are both interested in the project and have the power to make it work or not. Often, the key players are the managers of the functions involved in a project. Initially, it is important to determine if individual key stakeholders are positive or negative in their approach to a project. If positive, then their enthusiasm must be sustained, especially during times of difficulty. It is also important to appreciate the concerns and opinions of key stakeholders and these will need to be taken into account when making any recommendations. For example, if one of the key stakeholders has a particular solution in mind it is important to know about this as early as possible in order to ensure that, at the very least, the solution is evaluated as one of the options. It is also vital that the key stakeholders understand the progress of the project and why certain decisions have been made. These are the people to whom any final recommendations will be presented and who will have the final say on any decisions. They need to be kept informed at all stages of the project so that none of the recommendations comes as a shock to them.

Those key players who are negatively inclined towards a project can be managed in various ways, depending on the circumstances:

- By far the best approach is to find some personal benefits for them in the proposed course of action. The stakeholder perspective analysis techniques described later in this chapter can be very useful here.

- Alternatively, a more powerful counterforce must be found to outweigh their negative influence. This may mean engaging the interest of someone in one of the high power areas of the grid.

Individuals and groups of stakeholders

An individual customer may not be of much concern to an organisation such as a big supermarket chain. But if they post a negative review using social media, write to newspapers, organise petitions or complain to consumer groups, they can increase their level of power considerably. A lot of 'people power' can damage even large organisations considerably and force them into major reversals of course. The classic business example of this concerns the case from the 1980s when Coca-Cola was impelled to reintroduce its traditional drink formula in the face of a massive worldwide customer revolt against a new formula. Similarly, individual employees can be marginalised by an organisation but, if they are members of a trade union, their power is greater. A single government employee who objects to a policy may be relatively powerless but if they 'blow the whistle' to national newspapers, they can cause considerable difficulty.

These examples illustrate the dangers of ignoring the weakness of an individual or mistaking individual weakness for collective weakness. Stakeholders must be considered not just as individuals but as potential groups as well. Their ability to gain strength, particularly with the availability of social media mechanisms, should never be underestimated.

Summary of stakeholder management strategies

The key strategies for stakeholder management are summarised in Figure 6.4. However, individual stakeholders do not necessarily fit neatly into one of the nine types, so management approaches must be tailored for each. Also, as is discussed in the next section, stakeholders do not stay in the same place over time and so the ways they are managed must be adapted accordingly.

MANAGING STAKEHOLDERS

Stakeholders' positions on the framework in Figure 6.4 do not remain static during the life of a project. For example, a manager may be promoted and move from being in the high interest/low power situation to becoming both interested and powerful. Alternatively, the manager may lose interest in a project if promoted into a job with a wider remit. The circumstances of an organisation may change so that senior managers begin to focus more or less on IT projects. A scandal within a competitor organisation may cause a regulator to take a closer interest in all companies in a sector. This means that stakeholder analysis must be a continuing activity throughout the project – and even afterwards, to find out what the stakeholders thought of the final outcome. The project team and project manager should be constantly on the lookout for changes in stakeholders' positions and should be re-evaluating their management strategies accordingly. Once stakeholders' initial positions have been plotted, a plan should be drawn up for managing each of them and how to approach it. A one-page assessment can be made for each stakeholder, but a more useful approach would be to see all stakeholders at a glance by setting up a spreadsheet with the following headings:

- **Name of stakeholder**: It may also be useful to record their current job title(s).
- **Current power/influence**: From the power/interest grid.

- **Current interest**: From the power/interest grid.
- **Issues and interests**: This is a brief summary of the interests each stakeholder is thought to have and what are believed to be their main issues with the project.
- **Current attitude**: A classification scheme is needed to determine the attitude of a particular stakeholder. The following categories may be used:
  - **Champion**: will actively work for the success of the project.
  - **Supporter**: in favour of the project but probably will not be very active in promoting it.
  - **Neutral**: has expressed no opinion either in favour or against the project.
  - **Critic**: not in favour of the project but probably not actively opposed to it.
  - **Opponent**: will work actively to disrupt, impede or derail the project.
  - **Blocker**: someone who will just obstruct progress, possibly for reasons outside the project itself.
- **Desired support**: This is the level of support that would be useful from this stakeholder. A basic scale of high, medium or low may suffice to indicate the desired level of support.
- **Desired role**: It can be useful to clarify the role to be undertaken by a stakeholder. For example, by providing a definition of the role and responsibilities of the business representatives on the project. A responsible, accountable, consulted and informed (RACI) chart (see the following section) is an excellent technique for clarifying an individual's role and responsibilities. It may also be helpful to take action to increase a stakeholder's active involvement in the project, possibly by designating them the domain expert or project sponsor, or by involving them in a particular committee.
- **Desired actions**: These are the actions that stakeholders should carry out, where possible, in order to benefit or advance the project.
- **Messages to convey**: This is where the emphasis to be put on any communications to this stakeholder is defined. For example, there might be a need to identify and highlight any issues that are of particular interest to this stakeholder. The messages are likely to be tailored to each stakeholder and so the more that is known about them and their concerns, the more effective the communications will be.
- **Actions and communications**: This is the most important part of the plan, where the actions to be taken with regard to this stakeholder are defined. It may be just to keep them informed, in a positive way, about the project and progress to date. Alternatively, it may involve a more active approach, such as meeting stakeholders to engage their interest in the project. Where a strategy has been devised to change a stakeholder's position – possibly to encourage the person to take a closer interest – then its success must also be evaluated and other approaches developed if the desired results are not being achieved. As mentioned earlier, the high interest/low power stakeholders are the key players and require positive management, such as frequent meetings and discussions about the direction the project is taking. This helps to make sure that they are kept informed about a project and are happy with the approach being taken. This also helps to detect where opinions or issues have changed, which may be reflected in changes to the project direction and work practices.

STAKEHOLDER RESPONSIBILITIES: RACI AND RASCI CHARTS

As well as deciding on the management strategy for the various stakeholders, it can also be very useful in a business change project to consider the tasks or deliverables and the extent to which the stakeholders are involved with them. A RACI chart offers an effective method for achieving this, as illustrated in Figure 6.5.

Figure 6.5 Example RACI chart

R = Responsible A = Accountable C = Consulted I = Informed	Project sponsor	Senior user	Business actor (user)	Domain expert	Project manager	Business analyst
Business case	A	C	I	C	R	C
Project initiation document	A				R	
Interview notes	I	C	C	C	A	R
Notes from workshops	I	C	C	C	A	R
Requirements catalogue	I	C	C	C	A	R
Use case diagram	I	C	C	C	A	R
Use case descriptions	I	C	C	C	A	R
Class diagram	I	C	C	C	A	R

A RACI chart – sometimes known as a 'linear responsibility matrix' – lists the main tasks or deliverables down the side and the various stakeholders along the top. Where a stakeholder is involved with the work to conduct a task or create a deliverable, this is indicated using one of the RACI categories:

- **Responsible:** This is the person or role responsible for creating or developing the deliverable or performing the task. For example, Figure 6.5 shows that a business analyst is responsible for creating the interview notes.

- **Accountable:** The person or role who is answerable for the quality of the deliverable or task. For example, the project sponsor must ultimately be accountable for the business case for a project.

- **Consulted:** This person or role provides information relevant to the deliverable or task. In Figure 6.5, the senior user, other business actors and the domain expert are shown as being consulted during the interviews and workshops.

153

- **Informed:** These stakeholders are informed about a deliverable or task, though they may not have contributed directly to them. For example, the project sponsor has the right to be kept informed about any of the products being produced during the project.

A RASCI chart, shown in Figure 6.6 uses a similar approach but has an additional category; 'S' for 'supportive'. This person (or role) will provide assistance, and sometimes resources, to whoever is responsible for carrying out the work of the task or producing the deliverable. For example, Figure 6.6 shows that the business analyst supports the project manager in the creation of the project initiation document (PID) and the database administrator supports the business analyst in developing the class diagram.

Figure 6.6 Example RASCI chart

	Project sponsor	Senior user	Business actor (user)	Domain expert	Project manager	Business analyst	Database administrator
R = Responsible A = Accountable S = Supportive C = Consulted I = Informed							
Business case	A	C	I	C	R	C	
Project initiation document	A				R	S	
Interview notes	I	C	C	C	A	R	
Notes from workshops	I	C	C	C	A	R	
Requirements catalogue	I	C	C	C	A	R	
Use case diagram	I	C	C	C	A	R	
Use case descriptions	I	C	C	C	A	R	
Class diagram	I	C	C	C	A	R	S

Yet another scheme that could be used on a linear responsibility matrix includes I (initiation), E (execution), A (approval), C (consultation) and S (supervision).

SOCIAL MEDIA AND STAKEHOLDER MANAGEMENT

Social media can be an integral part of a stakeholder communication and management strategy. In addition to publicly available platforms, such as LinkedIn and Twitter, there are several software products that are used primarily for organisation-specific communications. These products support a wide variety of functions including direct instant messaging, collaborative working, online meetings, and audio and video recording. Some products offer shared document and knowledge repositories, typically with cloud storage facilities.

Often, the communication approach taken within social media is less formal than traditional communication methods. As with other communications though, care should be taken to consider the desired outcome and the appropriateness of the content and format of the communication. For example, putting sensitive or confidential information onto public or social media messaging boards, whether external or internal to the organisation, is likely to risk negative consequences. If, in contrast, the messaging boards are used to provide appropriate, useful, timely and accurate updates, such as on the progress of a change initiative, this may have a positive effect.

Care should be taken when considering conducting research into stakeholders through publicly available social media platforms. For example, reviewing an individual's personal photographs and messages is likely to be deemed intrusive. That said, researching an individual through company websites and professional networking platforms may be helpful in providing a context and background for the person and may provide insight into an individual's role, professional interests, network and career history.

UNDERSTANDING STAKEHOLDER PERSPECTIVES

While it is essential to identify the stakeholders and understand the influence that they may have on a project, it is also important to understand their attitudes, values and beliefs. In other words, what are their perspectives on the situation or project? in other words, what are their business perspectives? For example, in a commercial organisation, one stakeholder might feel that any activities are allowable as long as they are not actually illegal, whereas other stakeholders may feel that the organisation has some responsibility towards society at large and therefore conclude that some activities should be avoided on ethical grounds.

To help understand these stakeholder perspectives, and to model the different business systems that would fulfil them, some of the elements from Peter Checkland's Soft Systems Methodology (SSM) (Checkland, 1999) can be utilised.

Systems thinking and SSM

Systems thinking offers a way of looking at situations holistically, considering interrelationships between different aspects and identifying where properties emerge from such interconnections. It has been defined as follows: 'Systems thinking is a discipline for seeing wholes ... a framework for seeing interrelationships rather than things' (Senge, 2006).

SSM was developed by Peter Checkland and his colleagues at Lancaster University, as a way of applying systems thinking to help understand real-world situations. The basic premise underlying SSM is that real-world situations are rarely straightforward and are often very complex. An approach to business analysis, based upon elements and concepts from the SSM, is illustrated in Figure 6.7.

Figure 6.7 Business analysis using SSM concepts (© Assist Knowledge Development Ltd.)

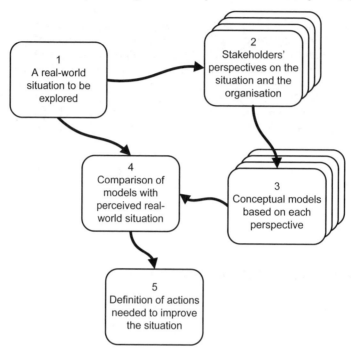

When investigating business situations, it is often the case that stakeholders have different views about what the 'problem' is and also about what needs to be done. As Figure 6.7 shows, there are five main stages that should be applied:

1. A problem situation is identified. For example, the loss of market share by a company or the poor public perception of a public body.

2. Stakeholders' views – perspectives – are sought about what the organisation is about, what it should be doing and so forth.

3. From each stakeholder's perspective, a conceptual model is created to show how the organisation should look.

4. These conceptual models are compared with the real-world situation and a consensus model is generated, possibly by combining elements from various stakeholders' perspectives.

5. Actions are defined to address the situation by implementing the consensus model in place of whatever is happening currently in the organisation.

Analysing the perspectives – CATWOE

SSM provides a very useful tool that can be used to explore the stakeholders' perspectives. Although the technique is known as CATWOE, experience shows that exploring the CATWOE elements is actually best done in the following order:

- **World view** (or *Weltanschauung*): A summary statement of a stakeholder's beliefs about the organisation or business system, which explains why it exists. Two possible world views for the Simply Juices example discussed in Chapter 5 might be: the newly appointed sales manager believes that success in this business results from contacting potential customers proactively to convince them to buy their products; or the customer services manager believes that success results from establishing close links with regular customers and providing them with excellent service.

- **Transformation:** The core business activity of the business system; in other words, what lies at the heart of its operations. (Checkland used the term 'transformation' because, at the highest level of abstraction, all systems exist to transform some form of input into some form of output.) In the case of Simply Juices, the sales manager's world view leads to a transformation that consists of making one-off 'point sales', whereas the customer services manager thinks that it is about providing a high quality of service throughout the sales process, in order to establish relationships with customers.

- **Customer(s):** The beneficiaries or recipients of the system outputs according to the stakeholder's world view. One way of thinking about customers is to ask: 'Who is on the receiving end of the transformation?' Stakeholders with different world views may hold different beliefs about who their customer is (or should be). In the example, one view might be 'anyone willing to buy juice products from us' whereas another might be 'established regular customers who appreciate excellent customer service'.

- **Actor(s):** The people who are required to carry out the transformation. For example, knowledgeable sales staff or customer services staff who are skilled in establishing long-term relationships with customers.

- **Owner:** The person or group who ultimately controls the system envisaged by the world view and who could instigate change, or even closure of the system. For example, the owner may be the business's chief executive, as shown for Simply Juices in Figure 6.8. However, in other situations, it could be a group, such as a board of directors or trustees.

- **Environment:** All organisations operate within the constraints imposed by their external environment. PESTLE analysis – discussed in Chapter 3 – can be used to identify key external factors that may constrain the operation of the system envisaged by the stakeholder's world view. There may also be internal constraints, such as governance policies, that may need to be considered as part of the environment surrounding a system.

Disagreements between the stakeholders emerge when analysing the world views they hold. Where there are differences of world view, the remaining CATWOE elements are also likely to differ; for example, a particular world view is inextricably linked with the transformation and usually targets customers with a related profile. Figure 6.8 presents CATWOE analyses for Simply Juices from the two stakeholders' perspectives.

In Figure 6.8, the owner and environment for both perspectives is the same. This is sometimes the case when using CATWOE, although different perspectives may yield

Figure 6.8 Contrasting perspectives for Simply Juices

	Perspective of Karen Thorne, Customer Services Manager	Perspective of Jason Shore, Sales Manager
C	Established regular customers who appreciate a personal touch	Anyone who is willing to buy juice products from Simply Juices
A	Knowledgeable sales and customer service staff who develop long-term relationships with customers	Telesales team set challenging sales targets
T	Repeat selling of soft drinks to long-term customers	Proactive 'point' sales of juice products to customers
W	Success in the juice products trade results from establishing close links to customers and providing excellent service	Success in the juice products trade results from the aggressive selling of juice products to a wide customer base
O	Tom Rake, CEO of Simply Juices	
E	PESTLE factors include government taxes on juice products (P); fierce competition from supermarkets (E); flavoured water and other branded soft drinks now popular in the UK (S); online purchasing of products (T); driving laws increasing the market for branded soft drinks (L); pressure to cut out use of plastics and reduce use of glass (E)	

alternatives in these areas. For example, a further environment constraint might be the willingness of people to buy drink products on receipt of an unsolicited telephone call.

Although at first sight CATWOE may appear to be a rather abstract technique, experience shows that differences in business perspectives are often at the root of the problems faced by an organisation. Where this is the case, stakeholders may pursue different business objectives that are in conflict with each other. An example concerns a large organisation where the senior management team had concluded that it was too centralised and that its services could be improved by delegating more authority to front-line managers. The problem was that many of these managers were not convinced that this approach would be successful and so continued to pursue a very centralised organisational structure. This resulted in confusion and inertia.

In this example, the different managers knew that they disagreed so could take steps to improve matters. The situation would have been more problematic if the stakeholders had not realised that they were in disagreement. If an organisation does not have frequent, open and frank discussions about its direction, managers are apt to think they are pursuing the same objectives when they are not. It is in such situations that business analysts can help to uncover areas of disagreement and encourage the stakeholders to analyse their differences of view in order to consider the future direction for the organisation or business area.

If stakeholder disagreements concern fundamental issues – such as if they relate to the values and vision for the business – then it is unlikely that progress will be made unless decisive action is taken by the business system's owner (as revealed in the CATWOE analysis).

Business analysts can often help stakeholders to better understand their differences by analysing each CATWOE perspective and building a representative set of BAMs. These models are described in the next section.

Illustrating the perspectives: BAMs

BAMs provide conceptual models of the activities that would be conducted within a business system in order to fulfil a particular stakeholder perspective. A BAM shows *what* the organisation should be doing, as opposed to a business process model (discussed in Chapter 7), which explores *how* it does these things.

Creating a BAM requires the business analyst to think about the activities that each stakeholder's perspective implies. Initially, there will be one BAM for each distinct perspective. At a later point, these are examined in order to identify where there is agreement or conflict between the BAMs. Ultimately, the aim is to combine them and, in discussion with the stakeholders, achieve a consensus BAM.

The approach for creating a BAM is as follows and a completed BAM for Simply Juices (drawn from the perspective of the sales manager) is shown in Figure 6.9.

1. Identify the **Doing** activities (D) that are at the heart of the model. These are derived from the transformation element of CATWOE and reflect the organisation's principal business activities. In the case of Simply Juices, there is one doing activity: 'Sell soft drinks'.

2. **Enabling** activities (E) are next added. These lead into the doing activities on the model and acquire or replenish the resources needed to carry them out. For example, Figure 6.9 shows that there are activities to recruit and train salespeople and to advertise the company's products.

3. All of the activities of the organisation should follow on from **Planning** activities (P). The strategic planning activities that set the general direction of the organisation are not usually represented as the model is concerned with the planning required for the particular business system (which will support the strategy execution). Figure 6.9 shows activities to plan how many salespeople are needed and the skills they require, and how to market the organisation's products to customers. Planning activities also include setting targets, such as KPIs (discussed in Chapter 3) against which the performance of the business system can be measured.

4. The actual evaluation of the performance is done within the **Monitoring** activities (M). Figure 6.9 includes an activity that is concerned with monitoring the performance of the salespeople.

5. Finally, if the monitoring activities reveal that performance is not what was expected in the plans, **Control** activities (C) may be required to institute the necessary remedial actions.

Figure 6.9 BAM for Simply Juices

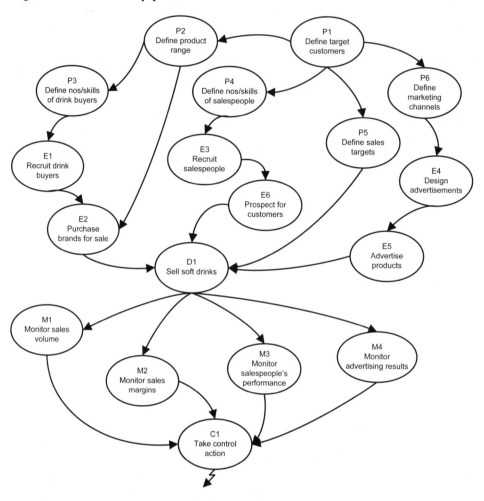

With regard to control activities, two observations are relevant:

1. A control activity may be associated with each monitoring activity on a BAM, and some users of the technique show these activities this way. However, managers often consider a range of measurements so a less cluttered model can be created by feeding all of the monitoring activities into one control activity, as shown in Figure 6.9.

2. The control activities themselves could feed back into any of the other activities on the model. Since trying to show this would create a diagram that is impossible to understand, the convention is to show a 'lightning strike' symbol emanating from the control activity, to indicate that it feeds back into the model wherever relevant.

The model shown in Figure 6.9 represents Simply Juices as seen from the perspective of Jason Shore, Sales Manager. However, the Customer Services Manager, Karen Thorne, sees the organisation rather differently. Both managers agree that 'Sell soft drinks' is at the heart of the business but, for Jason Shore, this means proactively contacting new customers and pushing them to buy Simply Juices' products; Karen envisages selling to existing customers who contact Simply Juices to ask for advice and guidance on what to buy. If the model had been built from Karen's perspective, it would probably not contain the enabling activity E6 'Prospect for customers' but it would have included activities to recruit and train customer service staff, who could help with customer queries about the product range.

It should be understood that a BAM does not (or does not necessarily) reflect what a particular stakeholder believes the organisation is doing. It shows the set of business activities that would be needed to fulfil a stakeholder's CATWOE. Where there are differences in perspective, they are reflected in a stakeholder's CATWOE and will be reflected in the corresponding BAM. For example, the Doing activities will be based upon the relevant Transformation; the Enabling activities may state the need for certain resources in line with the needs of the Doing activities; and the Monitoring activities should reflect the areas of importance to the particular stakeholder.

Having modelled the organisation from the perspective of each key stakeholder or stakeholder group, the models may be used to create a consensus BAM that represents an agreed way forward. Ideally, this is achieved through negotiations involving the stakeholders and the business analysts, so that the stakeholders all 'buy in' to this consensus view. Realistically, however, sometimes stakeholders just cannot agree and this is where identifying the 'owner' of the business system (as in CATWOE) is important. The owner may choose between the perspectives represented in the BAMs or may decide to impose one that is a hybrid. This is less desirable than securing all the stakeholders' agreement, as some people may not necessarily accept the agreed BAM, but it may be the best that can be achieved in some situations.

The consensus BAM is an extremely valuable product for a business analyst as it provides a model of *what* the business system *should* look like and *should* be doing given an agreed perspective. Where the actual situation on the ground differs from this conceptual view, the differences provide a basis for considering opportunities for improvement. Examination of the difference between the current situation (perhaps reflected in a range of documents including meeting reports, a rich picture or fishbone diagram – see Chapter 5) and the conceptual view provided by the BAM is an important part of gap analysis and is discussed in Chapter 8. As part of the gap analysis, business analysts may wish to explore *how* the activities are currently carried out, and how they should be performed in the future; this can be achieved through business process modelling covered in Chapter 7.

Notation for BAMs

There is no universally agreed notation for BAMs. Many users of the technique like to use 'cloud' or 'thought' symbols to emphasise that this is a *conceptual* model and not a representation of what the organisation looks like now. In Figure 6.9, ovals have been used for the practical reason that they take less space than clouds and are easier to draw free hand. It is probably not a good idea to use boxes, as then the models may be confused with business process models, which illustrate *how* an organisation works rather than *what* it does.

Activity 'threads' in BAMs

Sometimes, rather than considering individual business activities, it is more useful to group them into 'threads' of related activities. For example, in Figure 6.10, those activities from Figure 6.9 relating to the recruitment and training of salespeople have been extracted. (Activities E6 and D1 are shown for completeness although may not be considered directly relevant to this aspect of the business system.) This extract provides a means of considering the way in which the organisation recruits, trains, measures and controls their salespeople (and possibly other staff too). For example, it may be found that the jobs are poorly defined, ineffective recruitment processes are being used or salespeople are being set the wrong targets.

Figure 6.10 Thread of business activities relating to staff management

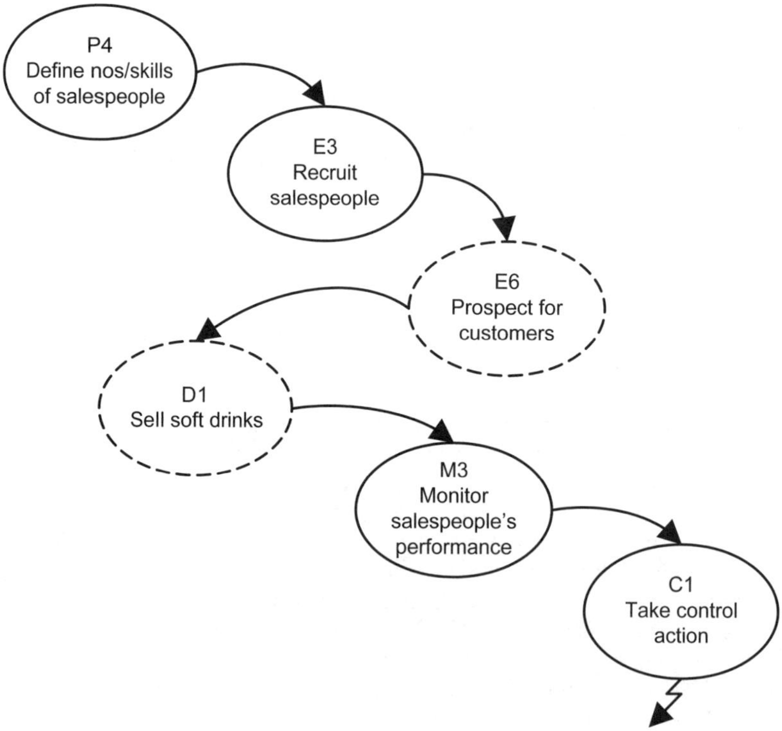

SUMMARY

Effective stakeholder management is key to the success of any business analysis project. It should begin during project initiation and inception, and should be continued throughout the project – and even afterwards to ensure that the changes are implemented effectively and the benefits are realised. Stakeholders can be assessed according to their level of interest in the project and the power or influence they wield, and strategies must be defined to actively manage them in accordance with this assessment.

Clarifying the role and responsibilities of stakeholders is extremely useful when analysing business changes. RACI and RASCI matrices provide a formal basis for defining roles within a business system.

Stakeholder perspective analysis, using the CATWOE and BAM techniques, helps to uncover personal beliefs, values and priorities and identify potential conflicts. Understanding the root causes of differences between stakeholders, and the impact these differences can have, can prevent issues from arising at a later stage in a project and can support attempts to build consensus, thus providing a firm basis for defining the desired changes.

7 IMPROVING BUSINESS SERVICES AND PROCESSES

INTRODUCTION

Business processes are the means by which an organisation carries out its work and delivers its products and services to customers. This chapter describes the use of value streams to analyse and document the delivery of organisational services, the business process hierarchy and the techniques used to model and improve business processes at all levels of this hierarchy.

The business process hierarchy comprises three levels:

- Enterprise level: the **value stream** required to deliver products or services. An organisation may identify several value streams, each of which comprises a set of activities that together offer a value proposition to customers. The customers' value expectations should be understood when analysing a value stream.

- Event-response level: the **business process** that forms the organisation's response to a business event and encompasses a set of tasks, each of which is performed by a designated actor. Together these tasks deliver the defined outcome from the business process. There may be several event-response level business processes for each value stream activity.

- Actor-task level: the **task**, which is formed of a set of steps, that is carried out in response to a task-initiating event. Each task may require access to information, may be subject to performance measures and may be constrained and governed by business rules.

These levels are represented in Figure 7.1 and are described in further detail throughout this chapter.

There are many reasons for modelling value streams and business processes:

- To clarify the core activities required to deliver products and services to customers and the nature of the value proposition offered to those customers.

- To understand how a business process is carried out. This helps to illustrate the actors and tasks that form the process and clarify the current response to a business event.

- To represent how each task relates to a business process and how each process relates to a value stream. The insight offered by these hierarchical connections helps business managers to take a holistic view of process and business staff to

Figure 7.1 Business process hierarchy

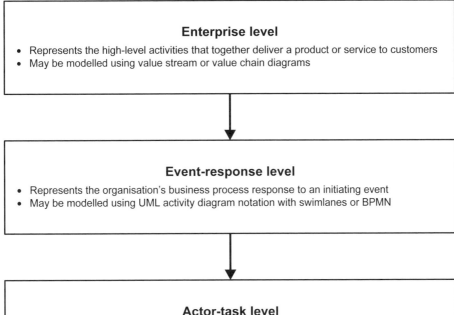

Enterprise level
- Represents the high-level activities that together deliver a product or service to customers
- May be modelled using value stream or value chain diagrams

Event-response level
- Represents the organisation's business process response to an initiating event
- May be modelled using UML activity diagram notation with swimlanes or BPMN

Actor-task level
- Represents the sequence of actions performed by an actor in one place at a point in time
- May be defined using both text and UML activity diagram notation

understand how their work relates to others. The existence of a business process hierarchy may be used to train existing staff when changing roles or to induct new staff when joining the organisation.

- To embed consistency and standardisation within the organisation so that everyone follows the same process and customers receive the same level of service and a uniform experience whoever they contact.

- To recognise where an existing or 'as is' business process is inefficient or ineffective in order to identify where improvements may be made. A model of an improved business process is known as a 'to be' model.

- To demonstrate compliance with regulatory or standards bodies. A well-documented business process hierarchy helps to confirm how an organisation is ensuring compliance with legal regulations or criteria used to evaluate enterprise performance.

There is a standard structure that is used to model and analyse processes. This structure is shown in Figure 7.2 and reflects that there has to be an input, a process that responds to this input and produces an output, and the output itself.

Each level of the process hierarchy should be modelled in line with this standard.

Figure 7.2 A process receiving input and producing output

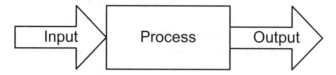

THE ENTERPRISE LEVEL

Chapter 3 explored different architectural views of the enterprise, each of which concerns a particular area. The traditional view of an enterprise represents how divisions, functions, departments and teams are organised and shows the line management reporting and staff allocation. This view is illustrated using an organisation chart as shown in Figure 7.3.

Figure 7.3 Organisation chart based upon business functions

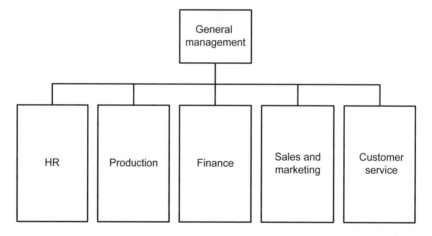

The organisation chart view shows the management and staff how the organisation is structured and where they fit within it. It may also be used to explain the structure to external partners and suppliers. However, as with any view of an enterprise or business system, there are some limitations with this view given that it:

- focuses on the internal structure and reporting lines of the organisation;
- does not show where there is communication and collaboration across different business areas;
- fails to identify where there are links to the external world; for example, the customers are not represented in an organisational structure view;
- provides a static view and does not represent what the business does over time to respond to an event and deliver a service.

The internal, static organisation chart view is in contrast with the value stream view (discussed in Chapter 3), which is often cross-functional, requiring activity across various business areas, and focuses on the customer experience. The value stream view reflects that there is collaboration between different areas of activity and that this collaboration is needed if the desired level of customer experience is to be achieved. Where an organisation is viewed primarily from an internal structure perspective, it is probable that the staff employed within each area focus solely on the work they perform and may fail to see the holistic process and the customer viewpoint.

Business analysis is best conducted if different views are modelled and analysed. While an organisation chart can be extremely helpful, it needs to be augmented by other views such as that offered by a value stream diagram and the other levels of the business process hierarchy.

Modelling the enterprise level processes

An enterprise level process model shows the core areas of process that together deliver a product or service to the customer and fulfil the stated value proposition of the enterprise. Figure 7.2 provides an outline structure that may be used to model an enterprise view, but to be of use when analysing processes, this structure needs to be explored in greater depth and has to be specific to the particular end-to-end process. Figure 7.4 shows an outline order processing enterprise level model.

Figure 7.4 Order processing model

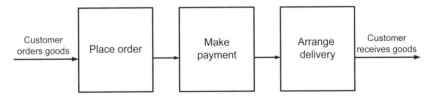

This view shows sets of related business processes, and their interactions, in a single diagram. Each process area is represented as a box with the arrows connecting them reflecting the interdependencies. An example interdependency is that the 'Make payment' activity cannot take place unless an order has been placed. The diagram helps to identify the boundaries of each process area by showing where each process begins and where it passes to the next process.

The value stream diagram (discussed in Chapter 3) also shows the customer or beneficiary from the output – those for whom the value proposition is offered. The supplier, input, process, output, customer (SIPOC) framework extends the diagram to ensure that all five key elements are explored at this level of the process hierarchy. A worked SIPOC example is shown in Figure 7.5.

Figure 7.5 SIPOC for a sales organisation

Supplier	Inputs	Process	Outputs	Customer
Consumers	Orders for products	Record order and take payment ↓		
Product suppliers	Products to be sold	Collate, package and deliver products	Delivered products	Consumers in receipt of products

Figure 7.5 extends the order processing diagram in Figure 7.4 to incorporate the other areas defined within SIPOC:

- the suppliers of resources;
- the processes that provide input to the core processes, for example, providing products to be sold;
- the processes that deliver the output to the customer, for example, deliver products;
- the customers receiving the outputs.

Value chain analysis

Michael Porter's value chain (Porter, 1985) provides an alternative framework for building an enterprise view of processes. The value chain is helpful to structure thinking about the areas of process required to deliver a value proposition. The value chain comprises two areas of activity: primary and support. The areas of activity and how they may be used to model enterprise level processes are explained in Table 7.1.

The concept of a value chain is similar to that of a value stream although the defined areas of activity within Porter's value chain provide a more precise foundation for the analysis. It is often helpful to consider the value chain primary activities when constructing a value stream diagram. However, the support activities are usually disregarded when modelling the enterprise level of the process hierarchy because they do not contribute directly to the delivery of the value proposition. An example of a value chain of primary activities for a sales organisation is shown in Figure 7.6.

Table 7.1 Areas of activity within Porter's value chain

Value chain area	Activity	Description
Primary activities: Activities handling business processes and tasks that together deliver the value proposition	Inbound logistics	Activities that enable the performance of the operations. For example, procuring resources or registering customers.
	Operations	Activities that conduct the core work of the value chain. For example, manufacturing goods or creating services.
	Outbound logistics	Activities that deliver the products or services to the customers. For example, distributing goods or providing services.
	Marketing and sales	Activities concerned with researching and informing the potential customers, and selling the enterprise's products and services. For example, conducting market research or promoting products.
	Service	Activities concerned with supporting customers, both before and after product or service purchases have been made. For example, responding to customer queries or complaints.
Support activities: Activities handling business processes and tasks that support the primary tasks	Firm infrastructure	Activities concerned with the establishment and maintenance of the physical infrastructure that enables the enterprise's work. For example, managing building facilities or equipment features.
	HR management	Activities concerned with recruitment and management of the enterprise's employees. For example, recruiting new staff or managing the performance of existing staff.
	Technology development	Activities concerned with the provision of technological services to the enterprise. For example, setting up the technical and applications architectures.
	Procurement	Activities concerned with managing suppliers of resources and services to the enterprise. For example, selecting preferred suppliers or managing supplier performance.

Figure 7.6 Example value chain for a sales organisation

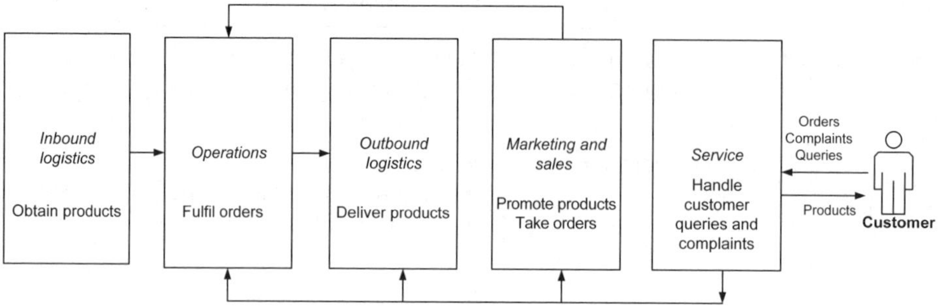

When drawing a value chain it is usually easiest to start with the operations – the core activity of this value chain – and then progress to the other areas. The example in Figure 7.6 shows a sales organisation, which means that the following activities are identified:

- The Operations primary activity is 'Fulfil orders'.

- The next step is to consider the resources required to carry it out. This results in the Inbound logistics 'Obtain products' activity.

- The Outbound logistics activity concerns delivery to the end customers so 'Deliver products' is identified.

- In the Marketing and sales area, the organisation needs to 'Promote products' and 'Take orders'.

- Finally, the Service activity involves providing support to customers by responding to queries and dealing with complaints.

The value chain concept was published in 1986 when the manufacturing context was prevalent. This has resulted in a model that is more relevant to this context. However, it remains relevant in today's service-oriented world as the activities within the framework may be applied to service organisations, albeit with some adjustment. The nature of service organisations is such that the core activity concerns service delivery and, therefore, the Operations and Outbound logistics areas usually need to be combined when using the framework to develop a value stream representation.

This enterprise level process model may be developed as a value stream, a value chain or a SIPOC diagram. Whichever approach is used, the model provides a contextual view from which more detailed business process models at the event-response level may be developed.

Value propositions

A value proposition is a key concept for organisations and has three areas of focus:

- Clarifying the outcomes offered by an organisation from the delivery of its products or services that the organisation believes will be perceived by customers to be beneficial.

- Demonstrating to customers that what is delivered will achieve what they desire or need.
- Differentiating organisations from their competitors. A value proposition can be a powerful mechanism where an organisation understands what customers require and value, and aligns this understanding with their values.

Perceptions of value vary between customer groups and understanding those perceptions, and attempting to fulfil them, lies at the heart of value proposition analysis and definition. Low-cost airlines provide a good example as they do not pretend to compete with airlines offering a more extended service but instead focus on the core needs of the travelling customer such as safety, cost and efficiency.

While organisations offer value propositions, customers have requirements and expectations. Customers usually know what they expect and the value they hope to realise, and wish to work with organisations that offer value propositions that meet their needs. Understanding the customers' value expectations, and the extent to which they are met by the organisation's value proposition, can help to identify the areas of the business processes that would benefit from improvement and the nature of the required changes.

Organisations often produce poor or misleading value propositions that may not be aligned with the needs of their customers or may promise benefits that they cannot fulfil. This can be a risky approach as value delivery is determined by the recipient rather than by the organisation and a failure to meet the value expectations held by customers is likely to result in lost business.

Kaplan and Norton (1996), the architects of the BSC, have identified the main attributes that make up successful value propositions, as a means of overcoming the problem of unhelpful value propositions. These attributes are the drivers that lead to increased customer satisfaction, acquisition and retention. The proposition attributes cover three areas:

- product/service attributes that define the product itself;
- customer relationship aspects;
- image and reputation aspects.

The elements of a value proposition are illustrated in Figure 7.7.

Figure 7.7 Elements of a value proposition (© Assist Knowledge Development Ltd.)

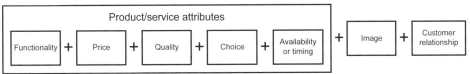

The product/service attributes concern the item purchased and the aspects of performance related to timeliness. These attributes cover the following areas:

- **Functionality**: The features offered by the product or service.
- **Price**: The amount charged for the product or service.
- **Quality**: The level of performance offered by the product or service. This includes many performance areas such as robustness, accuracy and speed – these vary depending upon the functionality of the product or service.
- **Choice**: The potential for customising and personalising the product or service.
- **Availability or timing**: The level of responsiveness when faced with a customer request or purchase.

The image of the organisation and its products or services form a key part of the value proposition. Endorsements by market influencers may develop a perception of value that enhances the key features offered. Customers may wish to engage with an organisation and purchase its products or services because of these perceptions.

Customer relationship aspects concern the relationship between the organisation and its customers. This relates directly to the experience offered by an organisation (and encountered by customers) throughout the entire customer journey. Awareness of the need to ensure a consistent customer experience that aligns with the values of the organisation and the stated value proposition has increased significantly in recent years. Guidance on analysing customer experience is provided later in this chapter.

An alternative view of a value proposition is provided by Osterwalder and Pigneur (2010). Again, this approach suggests the need to ensure alignment (or 'fit') between the organisation's value proposition and the value expectations held by customers, focusing on defining the product or service in order to address two key areas of concern:

- **Pain relievers**: How would this product or service help to alleviate the 'pains' customers are experiencing? For example, what will it help them to overcome that is not possible at the moment?
- **Gain creators**: How would this product or service help customers to achieve the 'gains' they are seeking? For example, what will it help them to achieve that they cannot at the moment?

Value propositions help to define what the organisation believes it needs to deliver to its customers in order to meet their value expectation needs. The business processes performed across the organisation help to deliver the organisation's value propositions.

When conducting a business process improvement project, an understanding of the organisation's value proposition is essential as it helps the analysts to understand the focus and objectives of the business process hierarchy. It is not enough to state 'we pride ourselves on our excellent customer service'; the organisation has to know what this means in terms of the attributes offered by Kaplan and Norton and the 'gains and pain' suggested in Osterwalder and Pigneur's approach. The business processes delivering the overall service to the customer, which includes the particular products and services themselves, need to be designed to ensure that this value proposition matches what is delivered.

AN EXTENDED SIPOC VIEW OF THE ENTERPRISE

Harmon (2019) developed a view of the enterprise that includes both the SIPOC elements and factors from the external business environment. An adapted version of Harmon's model is shown in Figure 7.8.

Figure 7.8 Organisation model (Source: Adapted from Harmon, 2019)

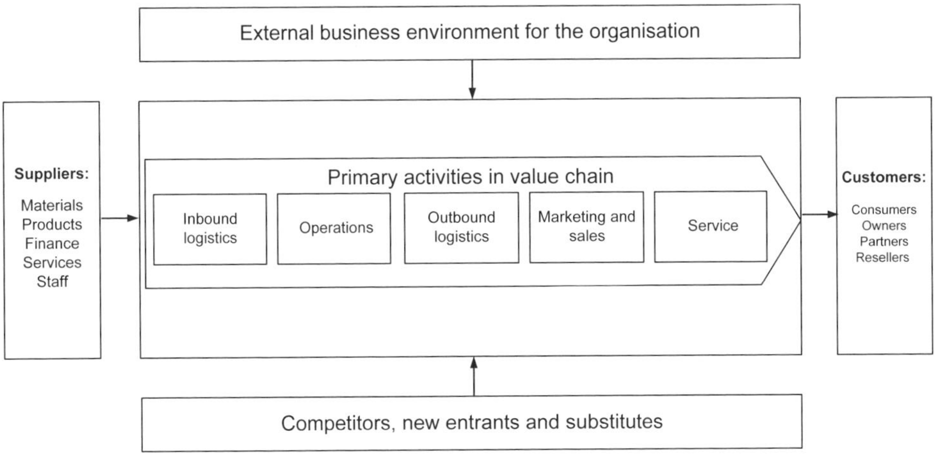

The four areas shown outside the organisation in Figure 7.8 highlight those aspects of the external environment that need to be considered and define the business context within which the organisation operates. These four areas are:

- The suppliers of the resources that are required to perform the business process. Suppliers may provide a variety of resources including raw materials, people, finance and services such as production and distribution.

- The customers who are the intended beneficiaries of the business process. There are four categories of customer that should be considered if a holistic view of those benefiting from the organisation's output is to be understood. These four categories are discussed later in this chapter.

- The competitors operating within the same industry or business domain. Traditionally, this is interpreted to mean other organisations competing in specific markets. In the organisational model, the range of competitors is extended to include those organisations competing for the supply of resources such as materials, finance, services and skilled staff, as well as those competing for customers. Competitors may also include firms with the potential to enter the market as new entrants.

- The generic business factors that may affect the organisation such as proposed legal regulations, economic matters or environmental sustainability issues. These are the types of factors covered by a PESTLE analysis (discussed in Chapter 3).

The categories of customer are represented in Figure 7.9 and are described in Table 7.2.

Figure 7.9 Four categories of customer (Source: Adapted from Paul and Lovelock, 2019)

Consumer	Owner	Partner	Reseller
A beneficiary or recipient of the product or service	A senior executive or shareholder for the organisation	A representative of an organisation that works in partnership with the organisation	A representative of an organisation that sells the organisation's products or services

Table 7.2 Descriptions of customer categories

Category of customer	Description
Consumer	Consumers of the organisation's products or services. The organisation has to understand their needs in order to support their success. 'Voice of the customer' (VoC) techniques help business analysts to understand all categories of customer but are particularly useful when considering consumers and clarifying their expectations and perspectives. Key VoC techniques include value network analysis and customer journey mapping, and are discussed later in this chapter.
Owner	The owners vary depending upon the type of organisation. Their particular context determines the needs they have as customers. Some business owners are the ultimate financial beneficiaries from organisational success; others may be those responsible for the performance of the organisation; in some cases, they may have both financial reward and performance responsibility; for example, there may be individual shareholders requiring dividends or trustees of charities who are responsible for ensuring the financial wellbeing of the organisation. In some organisations, the owners are responsible for the executive decisions of the organisation so also require information about the organisation's performance.
Partner	Many organisations work with partner companies to deliver their products and services. In these situations, the partners may require information in order to be able to work effectively with the organisation.
Reseller	Resellers are intermediary organisations who resell products or services to consumers. Resellers are often the 'sales force' for the organisation so are the representative of the consumers (who are typically their customers). The resellers define their own value proposition and require that the organisation's business processes support this.

The end consumers, who purchase the products and services, often form the most visible customer group so the value proposition is largely directed at them. However, it is important to take this broader view as different types of customer have different value expectations. For example, business process improvements may be made at great expense and so may impact upon the financial requirements of the owners and senior executives of the organisation; other process improvements may impact upon the quality of the product or service and could undermine the value proposition offered by the reseller organisations providing a sales channel to the customers.

It is also possible that the value chain may relate to a service delivered to internal customers. In this situation, there may be two additional customer categories to consider:

- **Business employees**: Those responsible for delivering the organisation's products or services. These are internal customers and so are customers of support services offered within the organisation.

- **Managers**: Executive managers who have perspectives about the products and services. These individuals need the business processes to work effectively and are likely to be assessed on the performance of the areas under their control. They require management information to support their decision-making.

The organisation's value proposition and the customers' value expectations are often in conflict. For example, customers would like prices to be as low as possible while shareholders would like to have high dividends, which they may see resulting from higher prices.

Analysing the external context on the organisation model encourages the business analyst to think carefully about the context for the business processes and question the various external perspectives. For example:

- What are the factors in the external environment that need to be considered? Will they constrain proposed improvements to the business processes?

- Which resources are required? Are there many suppliers or is supply limited? Which competitors are competing for scarce resources?

- Who are the major competitors that offer products or services to the consumers? Are their processes more efficient? Is it possible for this organisation to offer a more efficient or effective service to consumers?

- Who are the owners of the organisation? What information requirements do they have? What are their financial requirements and do they constrain or affect how the business processes may be improved?

- Who are the consumers of the products and services? What are their value expectations? How diverse are they with regard to their requirements?

The organisation's business processes need to operate within the constraints and factors inherent in the external environment. An example organisation model for a sales organisation, showing both the internal enterprise level business process and the external environment, is shown in Figure 7.10. It is important to understand this context when carrying out a business process improvement project, as forces within the external environment may have an impact upon the organisation and may highlight where process change is likely to be required.

Figure 7.10 Organisation model for sales organisation

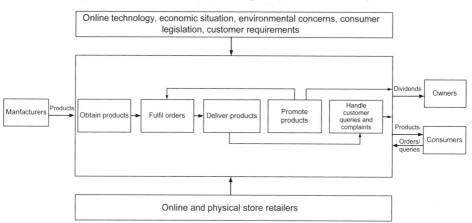

BUSINESS PROCESS MODELS: EVENT-RESPONSE LEVEL

Each area of business activity shown at the enterprise level is executed by business processes and procedures. These business processes may cross several business functions or departments. When defining a business process hierarchy, the enterprise-level activities should be decomposed by first considering the business events that each activity handles.

Business events

Business events take place outside the business process under consideration and trigger the process to begin. The events may occur outside the organisation or may be internal. Some events are time-related where a business process is automatically initiated at a pre-defined point. Examples of these three types of event are shown in Table 7.3.

A business process is triggered by a business event and provides the organisation's response to the event. The business process is not concerned with how the business event arose, that is the matter of the stakeholder or the point in time; it is merely reacting to the receipt of the event. The business process should also deliver the required outcome(s) from the event.

A model of a business process contains six key components: the event that triggers the process, the tasks that make up the process, the process flow, the decision points, the actors that carry out the tasks and the outcome of the business process. Unfortunately, there is no universally agreed set of terms in business process modelling and the

Table 7.3 Examples of business events

Type of event	Description	Examples
External	Events that occur outside the area of business under consideration. Typically, these events originate from the consumers or suppliers.	Customer-initiated business events: booking made, order placed, purchase order received, complaint received. Supplier-initiated business events: goods received, invoice received.
Internal	Events that occur within the business area under consideration. Typically, these events originate from senior members of staff.	Business manager-initiated: grade review finalised; product change decided; new supplier requested; staff recruitment requested.
Time-based	Events that occur at a given point in time. These events are predictable in advance and are likely to occur with a time-based frequency.	End of month; 2 p.m. each Friday; midnight each day; end of financial reporting period.

terms 'process', 'activity', 'task' and 'step' are often used interchangeably. For the sake of consistency, the following conventions have been adopted in this book:

- '**Process**' refers to a set of tasks, each of which may be conducted by a different actor. The process starts with a triggering event and ends with the delivery or achievement of an outcome related to that event. For example, if the triggering event is 'Recruit member of staff', the outcome would be the acceptance by an applicant of a job offer.

- '**Task**' refers to an individual activity within the overall process. Tasks are triggered by events that are internal to the process such as where one actor passes a piece of work to another or where a point in time is reached where a task has to be conducted as part of the overall process. Each instance of a task is carried out by an actor in one location at a single point in time. This convention is applied to aid the clarity and readability of a process model as it avoids the need to draw each step in a task as an individual box. The convention is sometimes referred to as 'OPOPOT' (one person, one place, one time). Where an actor conducts a task in two parts because there is an inherent time delay, a need to move to a different location or both, this would be represented on a business process model as two tasks. For example, a business analyst may prepare to run a facilitated workshop and may run the workshop at a later point and possibly in a different location; this would be shown as two tasks on a business process model.

- '**Step**' refers to an action carried out within an individual task; these are discussed further in the actor-task section later in this chapter. Each step may be subject to business rules that determine how the work is done and which outcomes are achieved. Task descriptions define the steps within each task and the business rules that govern any decision points.

Creating business process models

Business process models may be developed for many reasons, as explained earlier in this chapter. Business analysts often build models that represent a current process, for the purpose of documentation, training or process improvement. This model is known as an 'as is' business process model. Analysis of an 'as is' model may be carried out to identify problems and weaknesses within the business process. Business analysts are often required to analyse the problems within an 'as is' process to identify potential improvements. This may lead to the creation of alternative process models and ultimately to the development of an improved process; this is documented in a 'to be' business process model.

There are many standards for modelling business processes and they may be applied to both 'as is' and 'to be' business processes. Each standard has a defined notation set, that includes the following common elements:

- the overall layout of the model;
- the symbols used to denote the elements of the model, such as an event or task;
- the sequencing of the symbols.

Two popular notation standards are provided by the Unified Modeling Language (UML) activity diagram and the Business Process Model and Notation (BPMN).

UML activity diagrams
The notation set for a UML activity diagram consists of the elements defined in Table 7.4.

Table 7.4 Elements of a UML activity diagram

Element	Description
Event	The event that triggers the business process. This is shown as a filled-in circle.
Actor	A named person, group or IT system with responsibility for carrying out one or more tasks.
Task	A round-cornered rectangular box that represents work conducted by an actor in one place at one time.
Swimlane	A 'row' of tasks that are conducted by one actor; a boundary is shown for each swimlane to distinguish the work of one actor from that conducted by another actor. Where a task is completed by two actors together, for example, where a hotel booking is made by telephone, a task should be shown straddling both swimlanes.

(Continued)

Table 7.4 (Continued)

Element	Description
Decision point	A diamond-shaped box that represents the application of a business rule in order to determine the next task to be performed. Each process flow emerging from a decision point is clarified using a 'guard expression', which is shown in square brackets. The guard expression represents the business rule that determines whether or not the process can progress in a particular direction of flow. There may be several flows emerging from a 'decision diamond', each of which has a guard expression stating the rule that has to be satisfied.
Fork and join	Two lines are used to indicate where parallel processing is taking place.
Outcome	The situation resulting from the completion of the business process. This is shown as a bullseye – a filled-in circle within an outer circle.
Process flow	An arrow shown from an initiating event to a task, between tasks or from a task to a final outcome.
Timeline	A timeline indicating the length of time taken to conduct tasks within the process. This is an optional element but can be very helpful when considering organisational or customer timing requirements.

Several of these notation elements are identified in Figure 7.11; other elements are shown in Figures 7.12 to 7.15.

Several investigation techniques support the development of a business process model. These include group discussions or workshops with business staff, analysis of documentation or observation of the work carried out. Sometimes, business analysts 'walk through' a business process, moving from one actor or task to another in order to gain a detailed understanding of what is done. Each actor would need to provide:

- the information used to conduct a task and the source of this information;
- an overview of the work conducted within a task;
- the destination of the output from a task.

Further detail about the work of a task should be elicited once an overall view of the business process has been developed.

A typical approach to building a business process model is as follows:

- Identify the event that triggers the business process.
- Identify the business actors responsible for carrying out the work.
- Starting with the initial task initiated by the event, represent each of the tasks required to carry out the work of the process and the process flows between the

Figure 7.11 Diagram showing elements of a UML activity diagram

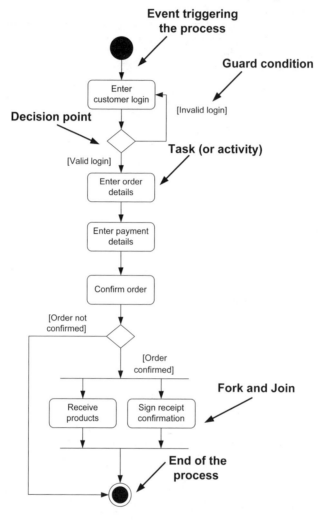

tasks on the model. Where an actor is responsible for a task, the task must be shown in the swimlane for that actor. The customer swimlane is often placed at the top of the diagram but other swimlanes usually appear on the diagram in the same sequence as the actors' become involved in the process.

- Add decision points or fork and join points where relevant during the business process.

- Add a timeline for the business process if required.

A UML activity diagram is usually drawn with horizontal swimlanes when it represents a business process. Each swimlane is added beneath the preceding swimlane as a new actor becomes involved in the process. This results in a model where the business process tasks progress from left to right and from top to bottom as the different actors become involved. To reinforce the representation of the work moving forward over time, it is useful to show a process flow from Task A to Task B as the process flow arrow originating from the right-hand edge of Task A and ending at the left-hand edge of Task B.

This flow is reflected in Figure 7.12 where the process flows from *Send information to customer* (Task A) to *Receive response to query* (Task B).

Figure 7.12 Business process model showing swimlanes

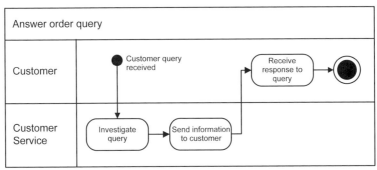

A decision point requires more than one process flow, each of which depends upon the application of a business rule. Figure 7.13 shows a decision point, the alternative flows with corresponding conditions and the two tasks required to handle each situation.

Figure 7.13 Business process model showing decision point

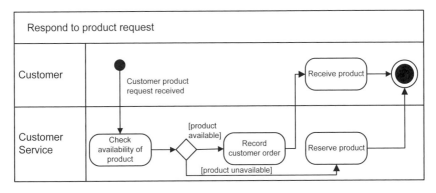

The alternative paths that could be taken are controlled by a diamond symbol representing the decision point. The business rule conditions that determine the alternative process flows are indicated by placing a guard expression alongside each flow arrow. For example, Figure 7.13 uses the guard expression [product available].

It is not always possible to show the process flow from left to right as it may be necessary for a task to be repeated. For example, where a decision point is encountered and a task has to be repeated as it has not fulfilled the requirements of a business rule. Figure 7.11 shows this situation when the customer login is not confirmed so the task *Enter customer login* has to be repeated.

A separate business process may interact with the business process that is under consideration. In this case, the other business process may be included to reflect where that process provides input into a task. Figure 7.14 shows this situation where the action that follows *Investigate request* is carried out in the *Accept product delivery* process from the higher-level model. Within this process there is a check each time a product delivery is received. The check is made to determine whether or not a customer has reserved the product and, if so, an order is recorded and the product is issued to the customer.

Figure 7.14 Business process model with link from another process

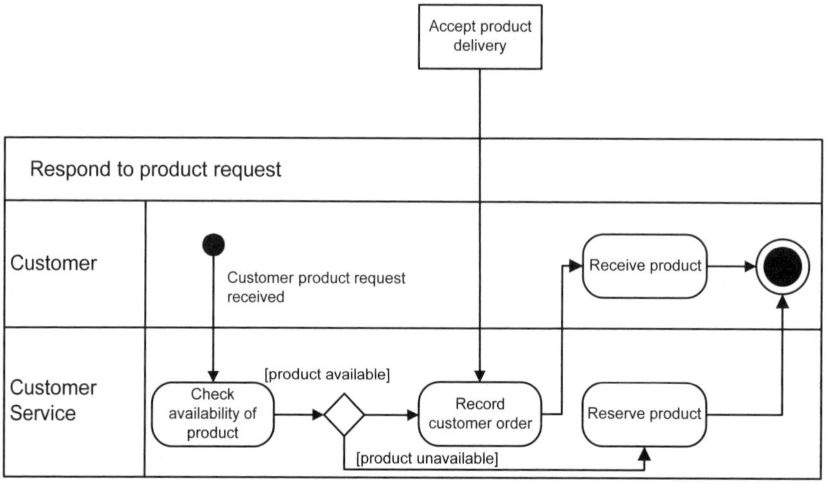

Figure 7.15 shows the situation where a business employee and a customer complete a task together. This is represented as a single task shown crossing the boundary between the two actors' swimlanes.

The end of a process is represented by a bullseye symbol. Usually processes have multiple pathways and hence multiple ways in which they can end. A retailing organisation, for example, would normally expect its order process to end with the successful delivery of the order to the customer. The order could, however, be checked and rejected. It is necessary to know the state of the order when the process ends because that determines what can happen next. If an order has been successfully delivered to a credit customer, for example, the next thing is to invoice them for the order amount. For a rejected order on the other hand, the customer must resubmit it. As a guideline, there should be a separate end for each significant end state. Some modellers label the end symbol with the name of its state.

Figure 7.15 Business process model with task conducted across two swimlanes

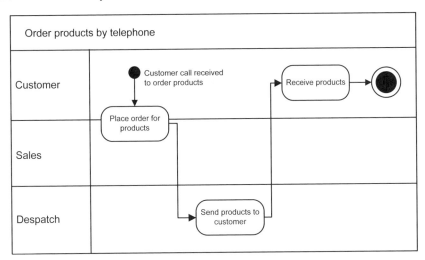

The limited notation set offered by the UML activity diagram approach aids the clarity and readability of business process models and, in turn, supports business analysts when communicating with their customers and other stakeholders. The adoption of a consistent approach when naming the various elements of the business process model helps this communication process. Typical naming conventions are as follows:

- Each task should be named using a 'verb/noun' structure and the verb should take the imperative form. For example, 'draw diagram', 'evaluate performance' or 'deliver order'. The name should use the business language as far as possible so if the business staff use terms such as 'issue instructions' this should be the task name rather than the more generic 'send details'. Words such as 'handle' or 'process' should be avoided. The task wouldn't be on a process model if the work didn't involve processing something. A task named 'handle payment' does not offer a clear view of the work involved; 'pay invoice' is more specific.

- Each event should be named using either of the following structures: '[verb] of [noun]' or 'noun/verb'; for example, 'receipt of application' or 'application received'.

- Each guard condition should be named to reflect the outcome from applying a business rule condition. For example, where there is a business rule to check whether or not there is enough money in an account to make a purchase, the guard conditions could state: [sufficient funds] for one process flow and [insufficient funds] for the alternative process flow.

A major advantage of a well-drawn business process model is that the actors are able to understand their contribution to the overall process and the point at which they need to be involved. This helps when reviewing the diagram for correctness and also when exploring individual tasks in further detail.

Business analysts should avoid delving into the detailed steps and rules within the individual task until they have a model of the entire business process that shows the set of tasks and the process flows between them. While some actors may wish to describe everything about their work, and this is likely to be helpful information, a 'top-down' approach usually results in a more complete and consistent understanding.

BPMN

BPMN provides a comprehensive, detailed and unambiguous approach to drawing business process models. It is an Object Management Group (OMG) standard, as is the UML.

The notation set provided by BPMN is attractive to business analysts because it may be used and transferred across a range of modelling tools so may be applied in different organisations. BPMN is extensive and enables analysts to represent precise process logic that can be executed by workflow or other process automation software products.

In a similar vein to UML activity diagrams, BPMN business process models help business analysts to understand the problems with processes and consider how they may be improved. However, the precision offered by the notation set also enables the business analysts to specify how the processes should be deployed into operation.

BPMN provides a notation set that has numerous concepts and symbols in order to achieve both of these outcomes. While some symbols are appropriate for process modelling as carried out by business analysts, others are more relevant for use by technical specialists.

The fundamental BPMN set is similar to that used in UML activity diagrams. Tasks are drawn within swimlanes and are connected by process flows. Initiating events and process outcomes are also shown on BPMN diagrams. However, there is an extensive notation set available that provides additional detail regarding processes. The additional notation includes the following:

- Pools where lanes (the BPMN name for a swimlane) are combined. Each lane contains the tasks performed by a particular actor. The actor that initiates the process is regarded as external to the process so is shown as a 'black-box pool', containing one lane only. No activities are shown in this pool (hence the black-box title) as the work of the external actor is invisible to the process being analysed.

- Gateways that control the flow of the process. Each gateway is represented using the same diamond symbol as that used in the UML activity diagram. However, it is possible to enter further notation within the diamond, providing additional information about the process flow. If a + is shown within the diamond, this indicates a parallel process flow. If a letter O is shown within the diamond this represents a number of pathways following the decision point and the flow progresses along one or more of the pathways.

- Messages that reflect how processes may communicate with each other and how they collaborate.

An example representation of a business process is shown in Figure 7.16. This process represents an organisation's response to the receipt of an invitation to tender (ITT) for a consultancy assignment.

Figure 7.16 Example BPMN diagram showing the response to an ITT

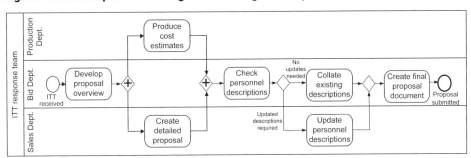

While BPMN provides an extensive set of symbols and concepts, business analysts need to take care that BPMN diagrams retain the clarity required to communicate with business stakeholders. The notation set is also intended to define a process in sufficient detail that the model may be implemented as a workflow, but this can result in a model that is difficult to understand. Some BPMN specialists recommend that business analysts only use a subset of the BPMN facilities. *BPMN Method and Style* (Silver, 2011) provides details of a 'Level 1' palette of facilities that can be helpful to business analysts who are intending to build BPMN business process models that can be discussed and agreed with business stakeholders. This can avoid the risk of applying notation that is unnecessarily complex for analysis purposes and is unhelpful when improving or confirming process models.

BUSINESS PROCESS MODELS: ACTOR-TASK LEVEL

A business process model shows the work carried out to complete the business process but at an overview level of description. The actor-task level of the process hierarchy concerns the work conducted within each individual task, which is the next aspect business analysts need to explore. While an 'as is' business process model provides insights into some issues, such as the process flow between tasks, business analysts need to investigate further to understand exactly where improvement is needed.

Each task within the business process model needs to be analysed in turn, with consideration given to the aspects described in Table 7.5.

Investigating these areas provides an opportunity for detailed analysis of a task and helps to identify aspects that are problematic or would benefit from improvement. An example of a task analysis is shown in Table 7.6.

Table 7.5 Analysis considerations at actor-task level

Area for analysis	Description
Actor	The role, the group or the system with responsibility for performing the task.
Event	The event that triggers the task; other than the initial task in the business process, each task is initiated by a sub-event.
Input	The information required to conduct the task. This may be the same as the event but, in most situations, the input is the information used rather than the trigger to start work.
Output(s)	The deliverable(s) produced from conducting the task. This may be a tangible deliverable, such as a product, or may be less tangible, such as information.
Costs	The costs associated with the performance of the task.
Performance measures	The measures used to evaluate the performance of the task. These are concerned with two areas: 1. Accuracy: what are the areas where accuracy is to be assessed and what is the required level of accuracy? 2. Timeliness: was the task performed within the required timescale?
Steps	The individual actions taken when conducting the task. The actor may be required to apply business rules when performing a step. The business rules determine how the task, or possibly the business process, is to be carried out following the completion of the step. For example, a business rule may determine the nature of the output from a task or may determine that a different task should begin. Some steps may apply business rules that could result in the termination of the entire process.

Table 7.6 Analysis of 'Check availability of product' task (see Figure 7.13)

Area for analysis	Description
Actor	Customer service
Event	Customer product request received
Input	Details of product the customer requires
Outputs	Order requirements to be fulfilled or reserved
Costs	Average time to handle call is 3 minutes; equates to 1/20 of hourly rate for customer service call handler

(Continued)

Table 7.6 (Continued)

Area for analysis	Description
Performance measures	1. Complete call within maximum of 5 minutes; on average, complete call within 3 minutes.
	2. Check customer identity at outset of 100% of calls.
	3. Advise customers of company policies and regulations once customer identity confirmed during 100% of calls.
Steps	1. Greet customer
	2. Perform customer identity check
	a. If customer fails identity check, terminate call
	b. Else continue with call
	3. Ask for customer requirement
	a. If product available proceed to *Record customer order* task
	b. Else proceed to *Reserve product* task
	4. End task

The example shown in Table 7.6 provides a textual description of the steps involved in completing the task; a simplified form of Structured English (If ... Else ...) has been used to clarify the steps. While this is acceptable for tasks where the steps and business rules are straightforward, a diagram can help to define more complex tasks. The notation offered by the UML activity diagram offers a helpful notation for such diagrams. A UML activity diagram representing the steps and rules in a task is shown in Figure 7.17; as there is only one actor involved, swimlanes are not required.

THE BUSINESS PROCESS HIERARCHY

The set of business process models – from enterprise level to event-response level to actor-task level – provides an organised, clear hierarchy of the value stream and the business processes and tasks. A representation of this hierarchy, with examples at each level, is shown in Figure 7.18.

This multi-levelled approach to business process modelling requires an iterative approach to the analysis. Initially, a top-down view is developed whereby the enterprise level model is expanded to the event-response level. This is then expanded further as each individual task is investigated and analysed. However, at this point, it is likely that changes should be made to the higher level models to take account of the new information that has emerged as more detailed analysis is undertaken.

Figure 7.17 UML activity diagram showing steps in a task

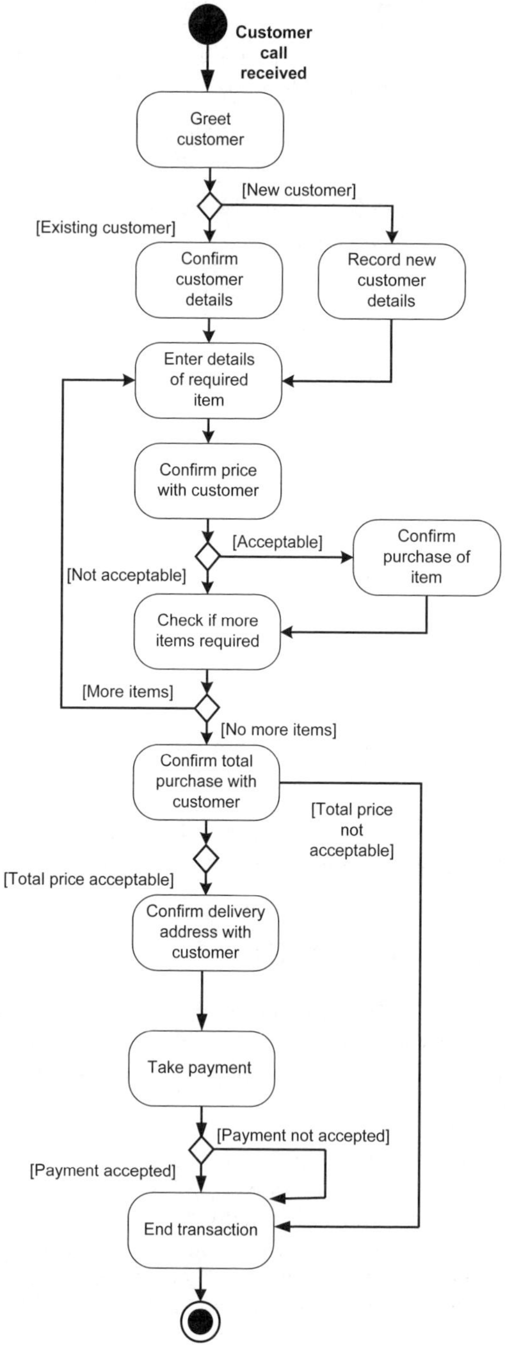

Figure 7.18 The business process hierarchy (expanded) (© Assist Knowledge Development Ltd.)

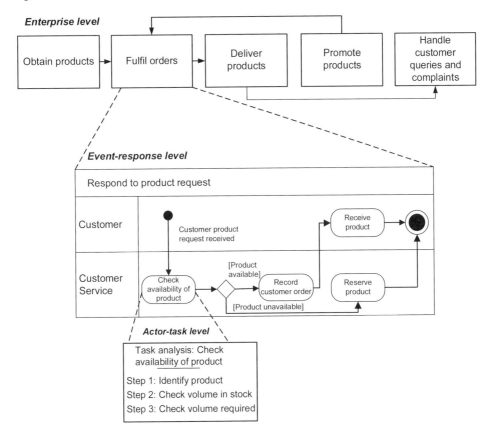

ANALYSING 'AS IS' BUSINESS PROCESSES

Organisations have to respond to changes in their business environment. Chapter 3 explored the sources of environmental change, discussing techniques such as PESTLE and Porter's Five Forces analysis. These techniques help organisations to identify where they need to address issues such as legal, demographic, economic or competitive changes. There may also be changes that emerge from within the organisation. A new senior executive may be appointed who has a different perspective, possibly resulting in a new strategy or tactical changes. Whatever the origin of change, organisations have to decide on their response and this often involves a need to make business process improvements or adaptations.

Most processes change over time and often these are incremental changes to adapt to new circumstances. Unfortunately, these changes can occur in an ad hoc and uncontrolled way, and may result in unnecessarily cumbersome business processes. Actors often know about their part of the overall business process but do not understand the role that others play. There may be a perception that a change only impacts a single task, which may result in a failure to communicate changes across the business process.

A defined process hierarchy that encompasses a set of 'as is' business process models and tasks is extremely helpful as it imposes order on a messy situation. Typically, the models highlight where problems lie and provide a clear basis for improvement. They also clarify process flows that are often unknown or misunderstood.

Identifying problems

Problems with business processes tend to fall within the following categories:

- **Lack of customer focus**: The process does not consider customer requirements and expectations so fails to provide what is needed; for example, there may be issues with the accuracy, timeliness or costs relating to the products or services offered. The business processes may focus on meeting the needs of the organisation rather than the needs of the customers.

- **Lack of organisation focus**: The process meets customer needs but at significant expense to the organisation. For example, there may be a lack of technological support, requiring excessive manual intervention in the process or some tasks may be redundant or duplicated for historical reasons.

The needs of customers and the organisation must be considered when identifying problems with an 'as is' process. The organisation model at the top of the process hierarchy can help to clarify the value proposition offered and the value expectations of the customers. This information helps to determine the performance levels required of the business process and to establish where there are gaps. Any gaps between the required and actual performance levels should be analysed and improvements identified.

There are two key aspects that should be analysed when considering how to address performance gaps: the 'hand-offs' between the tasks on the business process model and work conducted within the tasks.

Analysing the hand-offs

A 'hand-off' occurs when one actor passes control of the process to another actor. This is clearly identified on a business process model where the process flow can be seen crossing from one swimlane to another. Figure 7.14 shows a hand-off from Customer Service: *Record customer order* to Customer: *Receive product*.

Hand-offs are often a cause of problems in business processes as they may cause information to be lost, communication to fail or work bottlenecks to occur as one actor relinquishes responsibility but the next actor fails to act in a timely manner – or even at all! Actors are often busy completing their own tasks and assume that any outputs they produce are dealt with immediately, but, in practice, this may not be the case. A common bottleneck occurs when an email or other notification is sent to an actor who fails to act but also fails to notify the originator that no action has taken place. The originator is in blissful ignorance and doesn't realise there is a problem. This can result in unhappy customers and colleagues.

Queues can form at hand-offs because the two actors involved are not working to the same timescale or do not have the same priorities. There can be situations where improvements have been made to an individual task, but the increased productivity cannot be matched by other actors. As a result, attempts to optimise work in one task have diminished the performance of the entire process.

Hand-offs are often the root cause of process problems in all types of organisation. Identifying where hand-offs occur, and analysing them to identify potential problems, is a key element of business process improvement.

Analysing the tasks and procedures

Where 'as is' processes have been in place for some time and changes have been made in an incremental way, problems may have been introduced inadvertently. The problems may concern the ways in which different actors perform their individual tasks. The business analyst should consider the following areas to identify where tasks contain inefficiencies and inconsistencies:

- **Duplication**: Changes to tasks may have caused them to duplicate part or all of the work carried out elsewhere.

- **Redundancy**: Tasks, or steps within some tasks, may have been required at one time but are now unnecessary.

- **Lack of standardisation**: Different templates and standards are used when carrying out the work of the tasks.

- **Inefficient work practices**: Additional information or outputs have been required of the task, but these features have only been provided through the efforts of individuals and IT system workarounds.

- **Inappropriate measures**: Over time, the measures used to control the work of the tasks have become less relevant.

Each of these task-related issues offers an opportunity for business process and task improvement. However, even where a process is well-designed, other issues may undermine the achievement of the process performance objectives. There is a variety of reasons why this might be the case:

- The people working on the process may not have the required skills, training or motivation to produce the desired results.

- There may be insufficient resources available to carry out the process. These resources may include staff or equipment.

- The process may not be managed well, resulting in a lack of ownership for the process performance and poorly defined actor roles.

- The systems supporting the process may not provide the required features or performance levels.

- The business rules applied during the process constrain how the work is done and the decisions that are made. There may be assumptions underlying the business rules that are no longer relevant and would benefit from being challenged.

IMPROVING BUSINESS PROCESSES

The analysis of the hand-offs and tasks is likely to identify several areas that need improvement. Some improvements may be relatively straightforward, such as training and development to address a skills gap, while in other situations the entire process may require revision.

In addition to more formal business process improvement approaches, such as Six Sigma (described later in this section), it is helpful to consider generic improvement strategies, such as simplification or reengineering.

Generic improvement strategies

Generic business process improvement strategies may be applied individually, in combination or within a more formal framework such as Six Sigma. Six generic strategies are described in Table 7.7.

Table 7.7 Generic business process improvement strategies

Generic improvement strategy	Description
Simplification	Eliminate redundant tasks either by combining or removing them. The general principle is that all tasks should contribute to the overall success of the process. Any task that does not contribute to achieving the process objectives should be eliminated.
	This strategy reduces the running costs and resources used by the process, and removes the hand-offs and any related delays. This can result in further improvements such as a reduction in errors and duplication.
Redesign	Workarounds are often created to deal with business scenarios that are not covered by the 'as is' process. These workarounds are likely to be inefficient as they are developed to adapt tasks in ways that were not originally intended. It is also possible that different actors handle such scenarios in different ways.
	The process may be improved by redesigning the work carried out within tasks to incorporate the scenarios.
Bottleneck removal	Bottlenecks result when there is a mismatch in the capacities of related tasks. For example, there is a mismatch if task A deals with 50 transactions per hour and these are passed on to the actor carrying out task B, which can only deal with 40 transactions per hour. In this example, the bottleneck may be removed by increasing the resources undertaking task B or by analysing the tasks to see if it is possible to simplify the work. Real life processes are often very complex and require detailed analysis to identify such capacity mismatches. It may be necessary to use process modelling tools to simulate tasks and examine the performance and resource requirements of proposed process redesigns.

(Continued)

Table 7.7 (Continued)

Generic improvement strategy	Description
	It is often worth asking whether the bottleneck results from a checking process and whether that check is really necessary. For example, if a manager has to sign off expenditure above a certain figure, might it be practical to raise that figure and give the actor proposing the expenditure greater authority and discretion? In this type of situation, the risk of fraud or error must be compared with the cost and delay resulting from the checking process.
Change task sequence	The sequence of the tasks within a business process can be changed to improve performance. It is also possible to define a 'to be' process where tasks are carried out in parallel in order to improve productivity and timing.
Redefine boundary	The boundary of an 'as is' process may be changed in order to improve the process. This may involve extending or reducing the tasks within a process; for example, by outsourcing tasks or even complete business processes to specialist organisations. Technology may also be used to redefine the boundary of processes so that external stakeholders, such as customers or suppliers, carry out tasks in place of the business staff. Examples of such boundary redefinition involve placing orders or booking rooms online.
Automate processing	Automation can carry out processing with greater reliability and speed. It can also result in the standardisation of data that supports the processes. Process automation may be achieved through the following approaches:
	Bespoke software development. The business process model and the task descriptions provide an excellent basis to define the detailed requirements of a bespoke IT solution.
	Software products. Off-the-shelf software products incorporate best practice processes. They are typically used to support standard functions such as finance or HR.
	Workflow management systems. These systems control the flow of electronic documents or transactions through the various tasks of a process.

Six Sigma

The Six Sigma method offers a set of techniques that are used to improve process performance through applying statistical process control. While this approach was used within manufacturing organisations originally, it is now used across a wide variety of industries. The overall aim of a Six Sigma approach is to eradicate performance deficiencies in business processes, particularly those that are critical to meeting customer expectations, which include complaint handling and order fulfilment.

Six Sigma follows a five step approach known as DMAIC:

- **D**efine the problem. Investigate the situation to understand the objective of the change project and to find out where the symptoms and problems lie. There may be more than one problem, some more serious than others.

- **M**easure the data. Collect data that illustrates the problems, including data that identifies where they occur within the process. The focus should be on those areas that are more serious.

- **A**nalyse the problem. Analyse the data to understand why problems are occurring. Identify and test propositions that explain the causes of the problems. Identify the root causes of problems.

- **I**mprove the process by addressing the root causes of the problems. Define options for improving the situation and evaluate these options. Design, test and implement the chosen solution.

- **C**ontrol the effectiveness of the solution. Monitor it to ensure that the process has been improved and to prevent the original problem from reoccurring.

Six Sigma is a highly methodical and structured approach to process improvement that uses data and statistical measurement to identify where improvements should be made to obtain the greatest business benefit. The aim is to reduce errors so that all processes meet or exceed customers' expectations and that there are no more than 3.4 defects per million occurrences. In a distribution company example, this would translate into performance that delivers the right package to the right place at the right time 99.997 per cent of the time!

Customer experience (CX) analysis and design

Chapter 1 explores the nature of service and explains that value cannot be delivered but must be co-created. An organisation's products and services are intended to be beneficial to customers, possibly by offering the ability to work more efficiently or to do something new. However, beyond the delivered products and services, it is increasingly the case that customers have value expectations of the experience they have when engaging with an organisation. The nature of the experience encountered can either enhance or diminish a customer's perception of the organisation's products and services.

The service view, represented in Figure 7.19, encompasses the following aspects of a service:

- The nature of the service offered: what are the core values and objectives that underpin the service?
- The processes required to offer the service: how is the work to deliver the service carried out?
- The value proposition offered to customers: what is the value – the beneficial outcome – that is intended to be co-created with customers?
- The customer experience required to co-create value: how should the customers feel from engaging with the organisation?

Figure 7.19 The service view (© Assist Knowledge Development Ltd.)

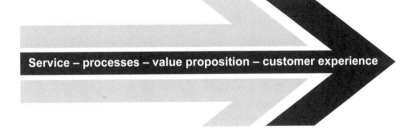

Organisations design and deploy processes to deliver their products and services to customers. However, an effective process that provides the required information and quality product or service may not be sufficient to ensure customer satisfaction. Customers expect to have an experience that fulfils emotional as well as purchasing needs and these expectations should be considered when improving business processes. The expressed customer needs and expectations are sometimes referred to as the VoC, as mentioned in Table 7.2.

One VoC approach that may be used to improve processes and the overall customer experience, considers the instances when customers and the organisation are in contact; these instances are known as 'touchpoints'. Each touchpoint may be analysed to identify whether the experience offered is aligned with the values of the organisation and the expectations of the customers.

Two techniques used to analyse touchpoints and establish where the service offered by an organisation may be improved are:

- **Value network analysis**: This technique is used to show the roles involved in delivering a service and the value exchanges between the roles.
- **Customer journey mapping**: This technique is used to represent all of the touchpoints a customer has with an organisation while they are receiving the products or services provided.

Together these techniques offer a view of process improvement that focuses on how the organisation presents itself externally to customers. They help organisations to ensure that proposed process improvements keep the customers in mind and to identify where the service offered to customers may be improved.

Value network analysis

Verna Allee (2002) defined a value network as 'a web of relationships' between different groups and individuals in order to generate value. Allee developed the value network analysis technique to represent the information flows, dependencies and exchanges that occur between different participants within a value network. These value exchanges may be tangible or intangible, for example:

- Tangible exchanges involve items that are paid for, so form part of the contracted deliverables within the business area under investigation. Examples are goods, services and payments.

- Intangible exchanges involve items that are not part of the commercial contract but are additional and help to build the relationships between participants. Examples are information, reactions and requirements.

A value network diagram is created as follows:

1. Identify the roles involved in the value network and represent them as ovals on the diagram. The roles may be external customers or internal roles that have responsibility for conducting the work of the organisation. Examples for a retail organisation may include consumers, sales staff, manufacturers, distribution companies, financial services organisations and customer service staff.

2. Identify the tangible exchanges that occur between the roles to enable the delivery of the organisation's products and services and represent these exchanges on the diagram using solid arrows. Examples for the retail organisation may include products, price communication, payment, credit check and complaint.

3. Identify the intangible exchanges that occur between the roles to enable the delivery of the organisation's products and services and represent these exchanges on the diagram using dotted arrows. Examples of intangible exchanges for the retail organisation are product information, requirement, knowledge and smile.

An example value network diagram for a retail organisation is shown in Figure 7.20.

Value network analysis provides insights into the interactions that take place between an organisation and its customers in the delivery of goods, services or related aspects such as advice or guidance. The value network diagram shows a holistic view of a business area and highlights the 'touchpoints' that occur when the organisation carries out its operational processes. The analysis of each touchpoint can help to identify where the service provided is lacking in some way and the organisation needs to make process improvements. The value network analysis technique may be combined with a red, amber, green (RAG) categorisation to identify clearly where exchanges and touchpoints need improvement and should be subject to more detailed investigation.

Figure 7.20 Value network diagram for a retail organisation

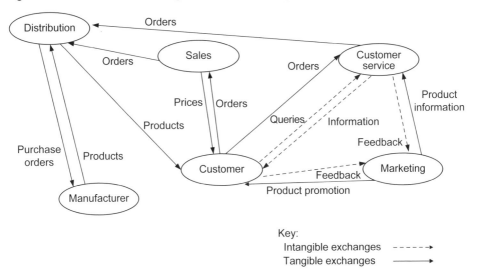

Customer journey maps

A customer engages with an organisation during many stages and each stage offers an opportunity for the organisation to provide service and for the customer to evaluate the service received. Sometimes, the organisation demonstrates a level of service that is satisfactory, on occasion the service offered may be exemplary; in other situations, the service may fall short of the customer's expectations. However, there may be instances where the service provided is extremely poor.

Where a customer's experience is positive, it is likely that they will engage with the organisation again and purchase further products or services. Where the experience is negative, customers may respond to the service delivered by deciding never to purchase from the organisation again or, if at the outset of the purchasing journey, may decide not to purchase at all. Dissatisfied customers may also mention the poor experience to their friends and colleagues, damaging the organisation's reputation.

Process improvement can run the risk of placing a focus on the organisation's needs for efficiency and productivity, but at the expense of the customer experience. Therefore, when improving processes, there should be a focus on the external customer view – a failure to do this can result in reduced customer engagement and purchasing.

Customer journey maps examine processes from the customer's perspective. There are some key elements that should be considered when developing a customer journey map and a hierarchical approach, in line with the process hierarchy described earlier in this chapter, is helpful. The key elements are described in Table 7.8.

Table 7.8 Elements considered within a customer journey map

Role	The customer role, which typically includes types of customer, for example, consumer, purchaser (on another consumer's behalf) or reseller (intermediary).
Persona	It is helpful to consider different personas of the particular role. For instance, 'consumer' is a very broad grouping and it is likely to improve the analysis if different personas within this group are identified and analysed. A summary of persona characteristics helps to gain more detailed understanding of the customer experience requirements and perceptions.
Persona goal	The outcomes required by the persona; these may include tangible product or service outcomes and intangible emotional outcomes.
Stages of customer journey	Value stream or value chain definition of the high level stages when there is customer engagement.
Touchpoints	Decomposition of high level stages into specific touchpoints between the customer and the organisation.
RAG assessment of touchpoints	Customer experience perceptions are colour coded using a RAG categorisation: green (positive); amber (neutral); red (negative).
Emotional responses of persona	Statements made by personas or summary comments on feedback that reflect the emotional response to the customer experience at each touchpoint.
Potential opportunities for improvement	Opportunities for improvement at each stage.

An example customer journey map for a retail organisation is shown in Figure 7.21.

There are some key aspects to consider when building a customer journey map, as summarised in Table 7.9.

Customer journey maps show an end-to-end view of the touchpoints where customers engage with an organisation and the perceptions of the customer experience offered during the delivery of the organisation's operational processes. Each touchpoint offers an opportunity for an organisation to excel and the analysis of a customer journey map helps to identify where the service provided is lacking and process improvements are needed.

Business process engineering

The typical approach adopted for business process improvement involves the following steps:

Figure 7.21 Customer journey map for a retail organisation

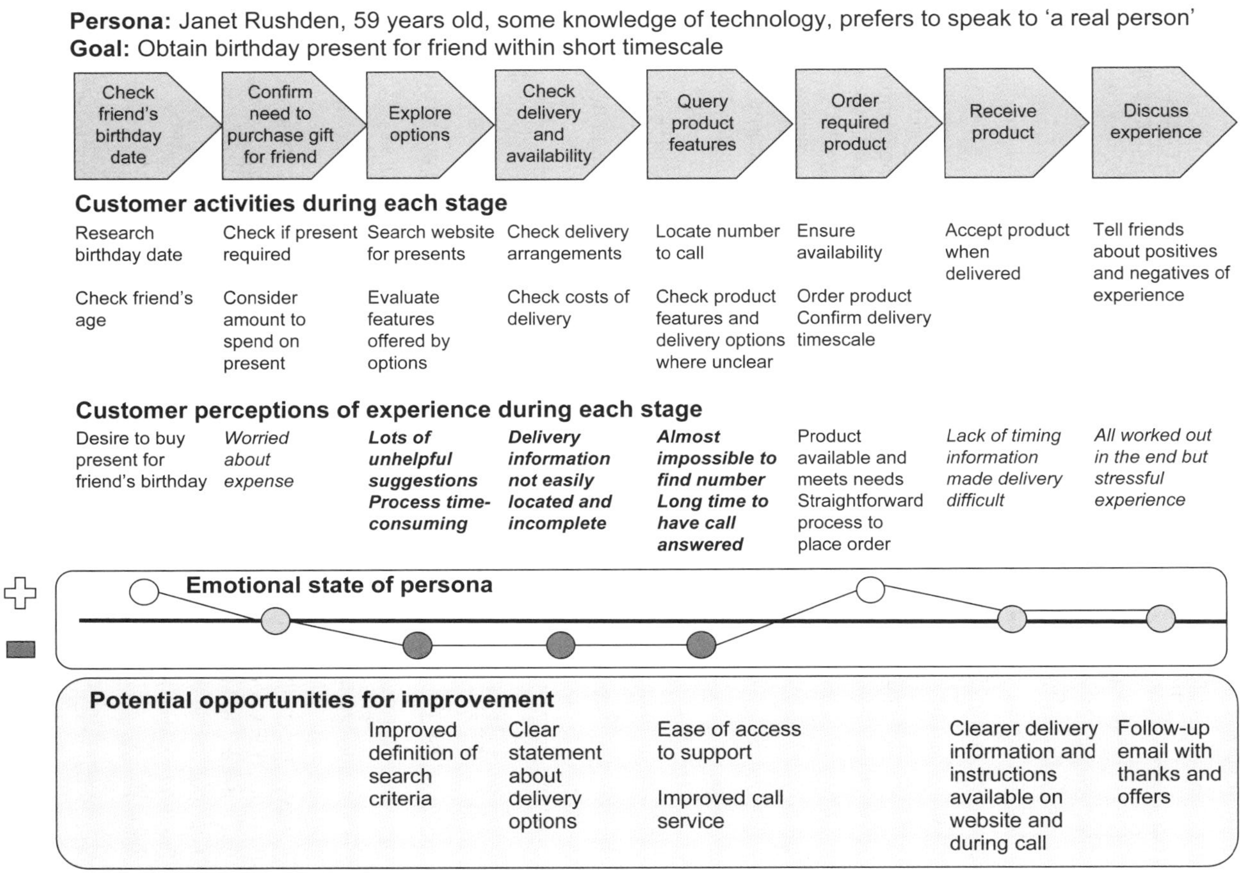

Persona: Janet Rushden, 59 years old, some knowledge of technology, prefers to speak to 'a real person'
Goal: Obtain birthday present for friend within short timescale

Check friend's birthday date	Confirm need to purchase gift for friend	Explore options	Check delivery and availability	Query product features	Order required product	Receive product	Discuss experience

Customer activities during each stage

	Check if present required	Search website for presents	Check delivery arrangements	Locate number to call	Ensure availability	Accept product when delivered	Tell friends about positives and negatives of experience
Research birthday date							
Check friend's age	Consider amount to spend on present	Evaluate features offered by options	Check costs of delivery	Check product features and delivery options where unclear	Order product Confirm delivery timescale		

Customer perceptions of experience during each stage

Desire to buy present for friend's birthday	Worried about expense	*Lots of unhelpful suggestions Process time-consuming*	*Delivery information not easily located and incomplete*	*Almost impossible to find number Long time to have call answered*	Product available and meets needs Straightforward process to place order	*Lack of timing information made delivery difficult*	*All worked out in the end but stressful experience*

Emotional state of persona

Potential opportunities for improvement

	Improved definition of search criteria	Clear statement about delivery options	Ease of access to support Improved call service		Clearer delivery information and instructions available on website and during call	Follow-up email with thanks and offers

199

Table 7.9 Key aspects of customer journey maps

Aspect	Description
Point of view	The role and the persona should be at the heart of the customer journey map. The customer experience perceptions are likely to differ in the majority of touchpoints depending upon the characteristics of the persona. For example, one persona may relish the opportunity to have a general discussion (about the weather, time of year, etc.) when purchasing an item from a store; another persona may just wish to make the purchase without any 'unnecessary chat'.
Structure	The map should be chronological as far as is possible, showing the stages across a logical time flow.
Scope	The concept of a 'journey' is that the persona is considered at every point of engagement, from the initial introduction to the organisation until the need is extinguished. The scope of a customer journey map must reflect the particular persona under consideration. Other personas should be analysed through alternative customer journey maps.
Focus	The customer experience is the primary focus of a customer journey map. Therefore, the external perceptions of the customer are at the heart of this technique rather than the internal process requirements of the organisation.
Uses	It is not sufficient to just draw a customer journey map; it should provide a basis for analysing customer experiences and evaluating touchpoints in order to identify where improvement is necessary and possible.

- Understand the current process and develop the 'as is' business process model.
- Analyse the 'as is' business process to identify where there are problems.
- Consider options to improve the business process.
- Decide on the improvements and document the 'to be' business process model.

However, there are some situations where this sequential approach is not possible. For example, there may not be an existing process or such radical changes may be required that it is best to start from a blank sheet. Where either of these situations is the case, it is helpful to use a process engineering approach to develop a new business process. In this approach, only the business context is known at the outset and the detailed tasks and steps are determined during the analysis process.

Every business process begins with an initiating event and aims to achieve defined outcomes. These two elements provide a good basis for designing a business process where an existing process is not to be used as a start point or where a complete overhaul of a process is needed. Once the initiating event and the process outcomes are understood, options to bridge the route between them may be identified, analysed and modelled. Business process engineering is an iterative approach that allows business analysts to think innovatively, without taking into account the constraints inherent in an existing process. The analysts work with business representatives to explore different ideas and ultimately build a consensus view of the new process.

Wastes of Lean

Lean thinking is concerned with improving business processes, or any type of activity, through applying key principles such as defining value, ensuring flow and removing or reducing waste. The origins of examining 'waste' came from Taiichi Ohno, a Toyota executive who identified 'muda' – the Japanese word for 'waste' – as something to be removed wherever possible.

If the areas where there is waste within a business process are identified, relevant actions to remove waste may be considered. Areas where waste may occur are sometimes known as the 'eight wastes of Lean'. The mnemonic TIMWOODS provides a useful framework for remembering these eight areas; this mnemonic is described in Table 7.10.

Table 7.10 Wastes of Lean using TIMWOODS

Waste	Description
Transport	Where people, materials, products, tasks or information move or are transported unnecessarily.
Inventory	Where more than the required volume of materials, components or unfinished products are held.
Motion	Where the process or layout requires people to make unnecessary movements while conducting their work in order to look for information, items or support.
Waiting	Where there are delays during the process to obtain components, information, instructions, equipment or other resources because an earlier activity has not completed or taken place.
Overproduction	Where a greater quantity of an item or a component part is produced than is required at the time.
Overprocessing	Where higher quality standards are applied than are required or justified, or where the designs, tools or standards are inappropriate. This leads to additional effort being required to perform a task and potentially the production of poor quality outputs.
Defects	Where mistakes are made while conducting the work or where the outputs do not meet quality expectations. If defects are undetected the costs associated with fixing them can escalate. If defects impact a customer this can also lead to a loss of goodwill.
Skills	Where skills are underutilised and are not used to their full advantage. This is sometimes referred to as the waste of 'untapped human potential'.

A Lean mindset can be invaluable when improving processes and the TIMWOODS framework helps analysts to identify areas for improvement that may not be detected otherwise.

PROCESS MEASUREMENT

Process measures are used to monitor the organisation's performance when delivering products and services and to identify where improvements are required. Measurements should be defined at the three levels of the process hierarchy:

- **Enterprise level**: The performance areas and levels to be delivered by a value stream of activities.

- **Event-response level**: The performance requirements for a business process that is initiated by a business event.

- **Actor-task level**: The performance requirements for an individual task within a business process.

All of these performance measures should be concerned with the following areas:

- **Financial**: Such as cost to perform a process or task, income generated by a process or task.

- **Customer experience**: Such as levels of customer satisfaction or net promoter score (NPS) that help to determine whether customers will engage further with the organisation or will recommend the organisation to others.

- **Process efficiency**: Such as timing and accuracy requirements related to the work of the process or task.

Performance measures must be considered from two perspectives: measurement for internal management purposes and measurement relevant to external customers. Organisations may experience problems if they concentrate on internal performance measures at the expense of customer concerns.

These measures need to be defined and communicated. Internal staff need to be aware of the measures against which their performance is monitored and evaluated. Customers need to be aware of the measures that impact upon their customer experience such as timescales and costs.

Internal measures

Internal measures are derived from organisational objectives, CSF and KPIs (see Chapter 3). Business process measures should support the organisational measures and, in turn, should be supported by the task measures.

Internal measures are helpful when monitoring performance but often focus on what the organisation itself wants to achieve rather than on what the customer values. For example, the organisation may define 'low cost of operation' as a CSF for the organisation, setting KPIs that measure specific aspects related to costs, but a focus on costs can conflict with the delivery of the required customer experience.

External measures

External performance measures are concerned with the customers' value expectations regarding the quality of the products and services, and the way in which they are delivered. Analysing customer value expectations helps to identify the performance they require and the level they consider acceptable. Personas offer additional depth of understanding when conducting this analysis as they help to relate performance requirements and measures to different types of customer.

There are three major areas that should be considered in relation to customers and their value expectations of an organisation:

- **Time**: The time it takes to deliver a product or service – what timescale is deemed excellent, desirable or acceptable?
- **Prices**: The financial costs associated with a product or service – how much is acceptable or not acceptable?
- **Quality**: The product or service measures that are concerned with areas such as accuracy, effectiveness, robustness, usability, accessibility and support.

It is important to consider all three areas when improving a business process and to review the performance of each individual task. If performance measures related to timing or quality are not defined and monitored, customers may experience delays, inaccurate information and poor quality products or services. Performance measures should be allocated to each task and these measures should be aggregated to ensure that the entire process meets performance requirements. Where a task suffers from delay, high costs or quality issues, the rest of the business process may be affected and it may not be possible to achieve the defined process measures.

The example business process model in Figure 7.22 includes a timeline indicating the time taken to complete each task. The timeline shows that the first task, *Check availability of product*, must take place within 24 hours of receiving the request from the customer. The second task, *Record customer order*, must take place within a further 12 hours. If available, the customer must receive the item within a further 24 hours. Therefore, product request to product receipt should take no longer than two and a half days. These internal performance measures need to be aligned with the external customer value expectation regarding timescale. If the external performance measure, the customer view, is that ordered items are received within three working days then the internal measures are fine. However, if a customer expects to receive an item within two working days, the internal measures do not support the achievement of the customer's expectations.

Estimating the timeline for a process is difficult. It depends upon a range of factors including:

Figure 7.22 Process model with timeline added

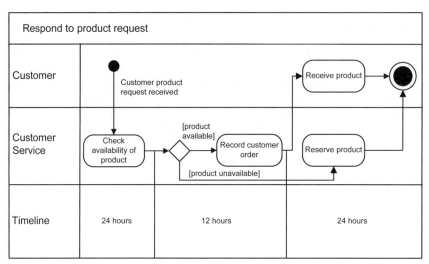

- the length of time required to complete each task within the process;
- the resources available to support the tasks;
- the volume of transactions to be processed and how this varies over time;
- the variety and mix of different transaction types;
- the amount of rework caused by errors;
- the delays and queues at each of the hand-offs;
- the availability, quality and productivity of the staff;
- the potential for interruptions to the task.

It may be possible to estimate task completion times, and link these to the overall process timings, using process modelling software that simulates the behaviour of the process.

Similar issues apply when considering financial performance measures; the cost of conducting a task should be aggregated with other tasks to determine the overall cost of the work to complete a business process. There may also be trade-offs between the three areas. For example, in order to reduce time, it may be desirable to increase resources but this is likely to increase the cost to complete a task or process. In this situation, the costs of the additional resources should be quantified to help decide whether or not the reduced timescale justifies the additional expenditure.

Impact of measures on behaviour

Measures and targets need to be chosen and defined with care as they can dictate how individuals behave, particularly when incentives to achieve targets are set. Targets are designed to change behaviour but a focus on target achievement can often raise problems in associated areas. For example, where sales staff are set sales targets based on volumes of products sold, they may offer discounts that ensure they achieve the targets – but this is at a price. The reduced profit margins may even mean that the overall profit is reduced even though sales figures have increased. This is an example of sub-optimisation where improved performance in one area can result in poorer performance in another.

SUMMARY

Business process models can be used for many purposes, including communication, process improvement and skill development. A process hierarchy offers a clear view of the business processes performed within an organisation and enables business analysts to ensure that any improvements are aligned and consistent. This hierarchy consists of three levels: the enterprise level, representing the set of high level activities required to deliver the organisation's products and services; the event-response level, representing the cross-functional view of a business process that forms the organisation's response to a business event; and the actor-task level, representing the work conducted by one actor in one place at one time.

Business process models may be developed to represent the existing processes – the 'as is' business process models – or the required 'to be' business processes. There are several standard techniques that are helpful when modelling or analysing business processes, some of which consider the customer experience viewpoint. The analysis of the process hierarchy across and between these three levels, and utilising standard modelling and analysis techniques, provides a basis for business process improvement and enhanced customer experience.

8 DEFINING THE SOLUTION

INTRODUCTION

Business analysts apply gap analysis to consider how an organisation might move from a current business situation to a desired future state. The definition of the desired state may be expressed in many different ways, depending upon the organisational context and the specific problem or opportunity to be addressed. For example, any combination of the following may be available:

- a TOM (Chapter 3);
- a BAM (Chapter 6);
- a set of 'to be' business processes (Chapter 7).

Analysing the gap between the current state and desired future state requires critical thinking skills and the application of relevant frameworks and techniques that ensure a holistic view is applied. Actions identified during gap analysis should address any problem areas that have been identified during the analysis process or help to grasp opportunities for business improvement. These actions provide a basis for formulating options, each of which may then require subject to feasibility evaluation and consideration by senior decision-makers within the organisation.

Design thinking is an approach used to identify and develop innovative solutions to business problems. It is based upon engineering design principles and offers business analysts a toolkit of activities and techniques. These are discussed later in this chapter.

THE GAP ANALYSIS PROCESS

Gap analysis is a systematic process, whereby the existing situation is compared with the desired or target system in order to identify where there are differences and where changes need to be made. This process is shown in Figure 8.1; the steps are discussed thereafter.

Figure 8.1 The gap analysis process

Assemble representations of existing and target situations

Gap analysis can apply at different levels, depending upon the situation. For example, it may concern a localised or extensive change. The extent of the change determines the scope of the gap analysis activity and the artefacts used to represent the existing and target situations. Approaches to gap analysis for localised and extensive change are described in Table 8.1.

Table 8.1 Gap analysis approaches and relevant artefacts

Extent of change	Relevant models and artefacts
Localised: a change to a particular task, screen or feature.	Where a change is localised, the desired state is likely to be documented using a task analysis (Chapter 7), prototype or wireframe (Chapter 5) or user story, use case description or requirement description (Chapter 11). Each of these artefacts sets out what should be in place and provides a basis for comparison with the existing situation. While a prototype may be compared with the current screen or feature, it is often the case that there is rarely a formal description of an existing task or scenario so the gap analysis may require input from business staff who understand how the work is done in practice.
Extensive: a change to a business process, product or to an entire business area or organisation.	The gap analysis activity has a broader scope where a change relates to a business process, product or entire business area. There are several different artefacts that may be used to represent the existing situation, including rich pictures, mind maps and fishbone diagrams (Chapter 5) and 'as is' business process models (Chapter 7).
	It may also be helpful to review architectural artefacts such as value stream diagrams, capability maps and information or data models.
	The desired situation may be recorded using any combination of the following documents:
	• TOM (Chapter 3);
	• BAM (Chapter 6);
	• 'to be' business process models and task analyses (Chapter 7).

The models and artefacts identified in Table 8.1 provide a basis for comparison and enable the business analyst to consider where changes need to be made. Most of these items are developed by business analysts although some fall within the responsibility of other roles, such as the enterprise or business architect. The TOM, for example, is an architectural artefact that encompasses many areas and, as such, is likely to be created by a senior executive or enterprise architect.

Compare representations of existing and target situations

The documents representing the existing and target situations are compared in order to identify where there are gaps to be addressed and changes are required. The POPIT™ framework is a popular approach to gap analysis as it serves as an aide-memoire and ensures that a holistic view is taken that encompasses all of the areas where change may be required. This framework is discussed later in this chapter.

Identify gaps to be addressed

Comparison between the representations of the existing and target situations should elicit areas where there is a need for change. The following are possible gaps:

- The organisational structure is not suitable to support the target situation.
- The staff lack the skills to conduct a new task.
- The business processes do not meet the needs of the proposed operating model.
- The business processes are not supported sufficiently by technology.
- The job roles do not cover all aspects of the work.
- Information required for the target situation is not currently captured, recorded or communicated.

Where such gaps are identified, they provide a basis for identifying where action is needed and exploring options.

Consider possible actions to address gaps

There may be many possible actions to address the gaps identified. For example, having identified that there is a gap between the current and required skills held by staff, further work is needed to determine the exact nature of the skills required and the approach that would best enable their development or acquisition. Industry skills frameworks, internal skill descriptions or, possibly, proprietary standards, may be used to define the skills gaps. Similarly, there are options available for skills acquisition including identifying resources for personal study, peer mentoring or attendance at internal seminars or external training courses.

Analysing gaps using BAMs

A BAM (described in Chapter 6), provides a conceptual representation of a desired future business system. A BAM shows 'what' activities would be needed to fulfil a stakeholder perspective, or where this is a consensus BAM, the agreed set of activities to accommodate several perspectives. Each of the activities shown on the BAM may be examined in order to identify where there are gaps and areas for improvement.

The activities on the BAM are inspected, evaluated against the current situation for that area of activity, and categorised in order to identify those requiring further attention. Three categories of activity are used:

- operating satisfactorily: no immediate action;
- some issues to be addressed: action required;
- not in place: urgent consideration.

Another approach, which has a similar basis, is to categorise the activities as RAG. The RAG classifications are used in many business analysis activities and provide a highly visual and easily understood way of identifying where action is needed.

The BAM activities, and the work to improve them, are categorised so that they may be evaluated in the light of the original objectives and scope for the business analysis work, and prioritised accordingly. Once the areas requiring most attention have been identified, the gap analysis activity is undertaken at a more detailed level and the focus shifts from 'what' activity is needed to 'how' the work is undertaken.

Analysing gaps using business process models

The conceptual representation provided by a BAM is supplemented by more detailed definitions, for example, business process models, task descriptions and job designs. These allow for a more detailed gap analysis that examines the differences between:

- the 'as is' and 'to be' business process models and task descriptions;
- the competencies held by an actor and those required to perform a job role;
- the features provided by the current IT systems and those required to support the target situation.

USE OF POPIT IN GAP ANALYSIS

Chapter 5 discussed the techniques that may be used to investigate and represent a current business area or situation. The range of techniques described in Chapter 5 reflects that, too often, the situation investigation service focuses only on problems with business processes or IT systems. Typically, this limits the scope of change proposals and can often result in changes that do not address the underlying problems or fail to grasp where opportunities for improvement may lie. The holistic approach adopted by business analysts helps to avoid such issues and ensures that aspects such as the organisation's structure, culture and management style are considered in addition to the business processes and IT systems.

The POPIT model, shown in Figure 8.2, supports a number of business analysis activities: taking a holistic view of business situations, structuring a gap analysis activity and evaluating the impact of business changes. The five dimensions of the POPIT model, and the aspects considered within each dimension, are described in Table 8.2.

The use of each dimension in gap analysis is discussed.

Figure 8.2 The POPIT model (© Assist Knowledge Development Ltd.)

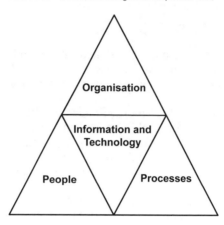

Table 8.2 The five dimensions of the POPIT model

POPIT dimension	Aspects for consideration
People	Skills, motivation, performance objectives, recruitment approach and criteria, appraisal and development approach, salaries and benefits
Organisation	Job roles, management structures, culture, values, standards, policies
Processes	Process and task definitions, business events, business rules
Information	Capture, recording, reporting and distribution of data and information
Technology	Software products, hardware, infrastructure, networking, communication, digital and other forms of technology

Processes

Detailed gap analysis tends to begin with a comparison of the 'as is' and 'to be' business process models. This is because changes made to business processes inevitably have an impact upon other POPIT dimensions. Process changes vary in scope from a relatively minor change to a job description or document, to a significant enhancement of a software product or the revision of an entire team structure. Example impacts include:

- Where a business process improvement requires a new business rule to be applied within a task, there may be a minimal impact upon the task definition and skills requirement.

- Where a business process improvement requires two roles to be merged, then there is likely to be a corresponding impact on organisational structure, job role descriptions, skills requirement and IT support.

The definition of the redesigned business processes needs to be clear and unambiguous if it is to offer a basis for gap analysis. Using a standard modelling technique, such as that described in Chapter 7, to describe the revised processes helps to provide such clarity and reduce ambiguity. A definition of the tasks within the business process is also needed to carry out the detailed gap analysis work effectively. Business process models and supporting documents help to determine where change is required to the remaining POPIT dimensions, in the following areas:

- the elicitation and definition of any information or technology requirements;
- the production of revised job role descriptions;
- the identification of where the actors' skills should be improved.

Information and technology

Business process improvements are often concerned with improving the retrieval and distribution of information. During gap analysis, the information flows shown on the 'to be' business process model may be analysed using techniques such as document analysis and data modelling. These techniques help to identify the information needed to carry out the business processes, clarify how this information is used and determine the information requirements to be fulfilled by an IT system. The information requirements are closely aligned with technology changes as it is usually the case that the information recording, retrieval and distribution is enabled, at least in part, by a software product.

The technology element of the POPIT model is often at the heart of business process redesign. Technological advances such as RPA, AI, mobile apps and other digital services offer opportunities for innovation in process design and are often key elements within a solution architecture.

Redesigned business processes are likely to require additional support from information systems and digital technologies. Business analysts need to identify the functional and non-functional requirements (Chapter 10) to be fulfilled by information and technology.

Awareness of the importance of non-functional areas, such as the accessibility and usability of software products, has increased over recent years. This is largely the case because support for customers has been moved from members of customer service staff to online applications and automated telephony. The redesign of business processes has often involved the introduction of technology to reduce personal contact and increase automated response; however, this has sometimes been at the expense of the customer experience. Analysis of the information and technology gaps needs to be conducted with reference to the needs of the customer and user populations. If there is poor accessibility or usability, the technological support may not be used effectively. If business staff are unable to use a system, or have difficulty in using it, they tend to avoid doing so, which is likely to lead them to develop unauthorised and undesirable workarounds in order to conduct their work. Other stakeholders, such as customers and suppliers, may decide it is easier to work with other, perhaps competing, organisations.

A major problem in many organisations is that software applications are not integrated sufficiently well with each other or with the infrastructure that enables the delivery of the software services. This can lead to problems, such as when transferring data or passing messages, which may result in the same data being entered into several different systems, inconsistent data formats and definitions, and different systems holding differing values for the same data. Many organisations are constrained by legacy systems that are not very adaptable; for example, they are difficult to adjust to new information business needs or have poor scalability so cannot handle increased volumes.

Where redesigned business processes require additional information and technology support, it is important to analyse these gaps and consider where there may be impacts on the existing data, infrastructure and applications architectures. Failure to do this may result in the introduction of additional problems rather than solving those that currently exist.

Organisation

The impact of business process changes on the organisation itself is often the area that is overlooked during gap analysis and option development. However, this can be where gaps exist that have the potential to undermine the new business system and processes. One of the reasons why a holistic view is so important during investigation of the current system is that it places organisational aspects such as structure and culture firmly within the scope of the analysis. McKinsey's 7S model (Peters and Waterman, 1982), shown in Figure 8.3, provides a framework for thinking about the different elements that form the organisational view.

Figure 8.3 McKinsey's 7S model

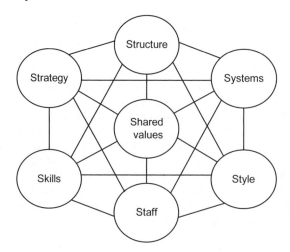

The 7S model provides a representation of seven elements that collectively make up an organisation. Three elements – strategy, structure and systems – are often described as 'hard' because they are tangible, and four elements – shared values, style, staff and skills – are described as 'soft'. These seven elements offer different perspectives that may be analysed to identify areas for improvement or gaps when implementing business change.

All seven elements require attention if changes are to be executed successfully because where one element changes, others are inevitably affected. The elements are described in Table 8.3.

Table 8.3 Elements within McKinsey's 7S model

7S element	Description
Structure	The organisational management structure. There are various forms including functional, divisional, matrix and virtual. Structures may be centralised or decentralised, flat or tall. Each structure determines how information is communicated and distributed, and where management responsibilities lie.
Systems	The processes, tasks, procedures, applications and data that enable the organisation to carry out its work. This element is considered within the Processes POPIT dimension (processes, tasks and procedures) and the Information and Technology dimensions (applications, data).
Style	The leadership approach adopted by senior executives. Possible styles include collaborative or directive.
Skills	The skills of the people within the organisation and the capabilities of the organisation itself. People skills are covered within the People POPIT dimension; capability is part of the Organisation dimension (Chapter 3 includes a discussion about business capability).
Staff	The type of people employed within the organisation and how they are appraised and developed. This is covered within the People POPIT dimension.
Shared values (sometimes known as 'superordinate goals')	This dimension concerns the values, beliefs and behavioural norms of the organisation or business area. They are the guiding concepts and fundamental ideas of the organisation.
Strategy	The actions that an organisation decides upon in order to respond to changes in its external business environment. These changes may include actions taken by competitors or new requests from customers. Strategy concerns the planned approach an organisation adopts in order to improve its competitive position.

Given that some of the 7S elements are explored within the other POPIT dimensions, the Organisation dimension focuses on the remaining four aspects: shared values, style, strategy and structure.

It is sometimes said that the key aspects of the McKinsey model are not the individual elements but the lines that connect them. While analysing each of the individual elements offers opportunities to identify where gaps lie, the connections between them also bear examination. Irrespective of the changes, there must be congruence between the different 7S elements and any misalignment in the organisation must be addressed if changes are to be executed successfully. For example, if there is a disconnect between the management style and the shared values of the organisation this is likely to lead to confusion and reduced productivity.

The shared values are at the core of the organisation. In undertaking a gap analysis, it is vital to ask if these shared values are explicit and communicated, and if they really help to drive the other areas such as the systems and structures. Moving to a new, desired position may require consideration of how inconsistent views in the existing business system are demonstrated and the impact of values upon the work practices.

The style reflected by the management approach and culture that exist within the area of interest also needs to be considered. Is this in line with the values and the strategy and will it help in the introduction of the desired changes or will there need to be some work to ensure this alignment?

More tangibly, the structure of the business area may need to be changed. At a micro level, some job roles may need to be combined but there may also be impacts at a broader level whereby whole teams or even departments need to be merged or reorganised. It is also possible that more fundamental change to the structure may be needed such as moving from a functional to a product-based structure.

People

The gap analysis activity must consider the impact of proposed changes upon the People dimension. In particular, the changes may depend upon the availability of staff with specific skills and, if these skills are not available, this gap will need to be addressed. The following areas are particularly relevant for analysing the People gaps.

Required skills
Consideration must be given to the skills required to conduct the new job roles, and the level of training and support that may be needed during the transition to the new business processes. There may be a need for training in how to carry out any new or revised tasks, including providing guidance on changes to aspects such as process flows, information used, triggering events and business rules.

Skills development processes
Where a skills gap has been identified, the processes applied to develop skills should also be investigated. It is possible that there are skills evaluation and development processes readily available. Sometimes, the current skills development processes are the root cause of problems as they do not help the staff to identify where new skills are

needed or fail to enable staff to acquire new skills. Where this is the case, improved staff development processes may be required to support the development of new skills and, accordingly, the successful introduction of any business changes.

Recruitment processes

In some situations, it may be necessary to recruit new staff to address a skills gap. Where this is the case, the suitability of staff recruitment policies and procedures should be evaluated as part of the gap analysis activity to ensure that they remain relevant and, if this is not the case, to identify any aspects that require revision.

Motivation and reward systems

There may be motivational issues within the organisation that have the potential to undermine change initiatives. For example, if there is a problem with staff motivation, the introduction of a new suite of processes and systems may exacerbate the situation. Where a gap is identified between the current level of motivation and that required to introduce changes successfully, actions for improvement should be considered. The misalignment of reward systems also requires consideration as this can undermine the success of proposed business process changes.

FORMULATING OPTIONS

The result of the gap analysis is a list of business requirements. These requirements are likely to be at the 'what' level rather than dictating the precise ways in which they should be met. Chapters 10–12 discuss the elicitation, analysis, documentation, modelling and management of requirements.

Once the gaps, and the requirements to address them, are understood, the options for change can be explored and formulated. As with all business changes, any proposals must be feasible from the financial, business and technological perspectives. Feasibility assessment and business case development are considered in Chapter 9.

Options must be considered holistically. Proposals that change one or two POPIT areas but neglect to consider the other dimensions are likely to fail. For example, the highest quality software applications are unlikely to work well if they do not align with the goals of the organisation or the people lack the skills to use them. Similarly, it is not possible to change a team structure without considering the impact on individuals and ensuring that they are clear about their roles and responsibilities.

There are two types of option:

- Business options that explore *what* the proposed solution would include in terms of the functionality provided to the business.

- Technical options that consider *how* the solution is to be implemented in terms of the technical infrastructure for the solution.

These two elements may be considered separately with the business options being considered first in order to avoid the technical 'tail' wagging the business 'dog'. However, most business changes involve the use of technology and technological developments often extend the possible business solutions. For example, new business options have emerged from the use of automated payment machines in shops that enable customers to scan their purchases themselves using bar code readers. While business and technical options tend to be intertwined, the business needs should drive the options process and the use of technology for its own sake should be avoided.

Option development

Organisations often benefit from encouraging divergent thinking that generates several ideas for options (see the section on design thinking towards the end of this chapter). Once sufficient ideas have been raised, the focus can switch to convergent thinking and evaluation. This is reflected in the process for developing options shown in Figure 8.4.

Figure 8.4 Process for developing options

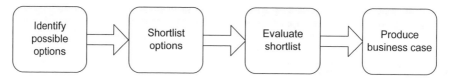

Identifying options is best achieved through discussion, typically in a meeting or workshop, where brainstorming and other creative thinking approaches can be employed. Modelling techniques such as business activity modelling (Chapter 6) or business process modelling (Chapter 7) and the results of the gap analysis, also help to generate options. The aim is to identify a variety of possible options before considering which are most beneficial. Even if some ideas seem unsuitable, they may provide part of the actual solution or give rise to similar, but more workable, suggestions. Options may also be identified by studying what other organisations – possibly competitors – have done to address the same issues.

The suggestions are then examined to identify a shortlist of options that are worth further examination. Some ideas may be rejected quickly, possibly because they are too expensive, or would take too long to implement, or would not align with the prevailing culture of the organisation. Such feasibility criteria are discussed in Chapter 9.

Ideally, the shortlist of options should be reduced to three or four, one of which should be the 'do nothing' option where the status quo is maintained. The 'do nothing' option should always be considered. Sometimes it is a viable option, and may be the best choice for the organisation. Often, though, it is not possible to 'do nothing' as inaction is likely to result in business problems and financial issues. Decision-makers may not be aware that action is imperative and clarifying the risks and consequences of doing nothing may be an important part of making the case for other, more relevant, options.

The options shortlist for a feasibility study or business case usually contains three or four options as it is seldom practical to evaluate a larger number in depth. Each of the shortlisted options should address the major business issues and should offer a distinctive balance between the implementation timescale, the required budget and the range of features offered. Sometimes, the options are 'variations on a theme', with one dealing with the most pressing business issues and others offering various additional features. This situation is illustrated in Figure 8.5.

Figure 8.5 Types of options (© Assist Knowledge Development Ltd.)

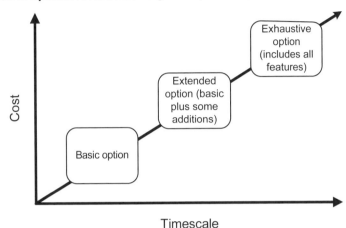

The options shown in Figure 8.5 are at three levels that are often considered during option identification and evaluation.

- The **basic option** deals with the most pressing issues, as quickly as possible and at minimal cost. This option may be based upon business process changes that require little if any technology change, or may involve the purchase of an off-the-shelf software product that can be installed relatively quickly and requires only limited changes to other POPIT dimensions such as the People skills and the Processes. In some circumstances, this may be a short-term option that can be enhanced at a later stage.

- The **extended option** adds some additional features to the solution but costs more and takes longer. This may require the customisation of a purchased software product or the bespoke development or enhancement of an in-house application. The POPIT dimensions may be affected to a greater degree than required by the basic option.

- The **exhaustive option** offers a comprehensive solution but takes the longest time and is the most expensive. This option may involve the purchase or bespoke development of a software product that offers extensive functionality and also meets a wide range of non-functional requirements. The impact on all of the POPIT dimensions is likely to be extensive.

Therefore, options tend to encompass both business and technical aspects.

In defining options, it is also necessary to consider the development and delivery approaches. For example: Would an option be delivered incrementally or as one entire solution? Would an Agile development approach be used? Would there be a direct changeover or a parallel run of both the old and new systems?

The final two stages of the process shown in Figure 8.4, Evaluate shortlist and Produce business case, are discussed in Chapter 9.

DESIGN THINKING

There are various approaches available that may be used to generate options and define solutions. One such approach, which builds on the service thinking philosophy discussed in Chapters 1 and 4, is known as design thinking. Design thinking encourages the use of product design concepts and techniques such as prototyping, learning from trying out ideas, divergent and convergent thinking and, most importantly, keeping a customer focus in mind. The application of a design thinking approach helps to uncover innovative options that may not have been identified when using more traditional approaches.

Design thinking process

The design thinking process is highly iterative as practitioners work through various stages, revisiting each stage as necessary to develop and deliver an outcome or product that will address the defined problem and meet the needs of customers. A linear representation of the key stages is shown in Figure 8.6. It should be noted that there is likely to be extensive iteration between the stages as a solution emerges.

Figure 8.6 Design thinking stages and stage objectives (© Assist Knowledge Development Ltd.)

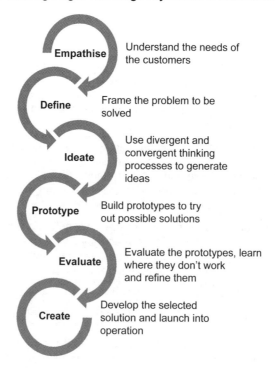

Empathise — Understand the needs of the customers

Define — Frame the problem to be solved

Ideate — Use divergent and convergent thinking processes to generate ideas

Prototype — Build prototypes to try out possible solutions

Evaluate — Evaluate the prototypes, learn where they don't work and refine them

Create — Develop the selected solution and launch into operation

Techniques used to undertake design thinking are numerous and variable. Relevant techniques are found in Chapters 5, 6 and 7 of this book and include the following:

Table 8.4 Design thinking stages and techniques

Stage	Techniques
Empathise	Investigation techniques, personas, empathy mapping and customer journey mapping.
Define	Storytelling and problem framing; perspective analysis.
Ideate	Brainstorming and brainwriting; divergent and convergent thinking; mind mapping.
Prototype	Prototyping and scenario analysis.
Evaluate	Scenario and event analysis; reflective learning.
Create	Experimentation, feedback and review.

Divergent and convergent thinking

A key element of design thinking is concerned with enabling divergent and convergent thinking. Participants in the design thinking process are encouraged to think expansively about various aspects such as where problems exist, the issues that cause concerns, the range of perspectives and personas in play, and ideas for possible solutions. This is then followed by an evaluation session to eliminate, harmonise or summarise ideas into a manageable set. A key factor in successful divergent and convergent thinking concerns identifying the point at which sufficient suggestions have been generated and the focus should shift to reviewing the ideas that appear feasible and offer a potential way forward. This can be difficult to navigate successfully so requires a design thinking facilitator who possesses skill, knowledge and experience.

The Design Council offers a Double Diamond model that represents the use of divergent and convergent thinking at two key points: when defining the challenge to be addressed and when developing the solution that will resolve the challenge and deliver the required outcome. Figure 8.7 shows the Double Diamond model represented within an organisational boundary that provides the context and principles for design thinking.

This model encapsulates the key principles of design thinking.

- The constant focus is on addressing the problem or opportunity to achieve a desired outcome.
- The needs and goals of customers are always kept in mind as this is a customer-centric approach.
- Participants work collaboratively and engage in both divergent and convergent thinking.
- Where possible, customers are involved in the design thinking process in order to support co-creation of products and value.
- The emphasis is on iterating to test, learn and improve.

Figure 8.7 Design thinking Double Diamond model (© Assist Knowledge Development Ltd.)
Business analysis adaptation of the Design Council Framework for Innovation.

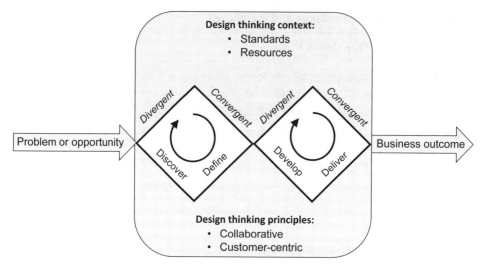

SUMMARY

Gap analysis is concerned with identifying the differences between the current and future business operating models, processes or systems. When analysing the gap, it is important to take a holistic view, considering all of the POPIT dimensions. This work should result in a set of gaps to be addressed and business requirements to be met, both of which provide a basis for identifying options for business change.

Ideas for options should be encouraged so that a wide range of ideas are considered. Once the ideas for options have been exhausted, a shortlist of approximately three to four options should be developed. These options form the basis for feasibility evaluation and the production of a business case.

Design thinking is an approach used to encourage the development of innovative solutions that meet customer needs. Various techniques are used to carry out design thinking. These include customer experience analysis techniques, such as empathy mapping and customer journey mapping, visualisation and experimentation techniques such as prototyping, and idea generation techniques such as brainstorming and divergent/convergent thinking. Together, they form a toolkit that helps the business analyst to define and develop innovative solutions that are focused on offering value to customers.

9   MAKING THE BUSINESS CASE

INTRODUCTION

A business case is a key document in a business change project. It is where the analysts or consultants present their findings and propose actions for senior management to consider. This chapter considers the purpose, structure and content of a business case and provides guidance on how to assemble the information and present the finished product.

It is worth considering why a business case is produced and asking, 'What is the point of a business case?' and 'What is it for?' A business case presents and evaluates one or more courses of action that will address a problem or enable the organisation to grasp a business opportunity. However, this does not necessarily mean that a course of action is recommended. Sometimes, a business case evaluates a poorly conceived idea and demonstrates that it will *not* work.

A business case should, as far as possible, provide a dispassionate and rigorous examination of an issue – and options to address it – so that decisions may be made on the basis of the best possible information and analysis.

Another thing to consider is the importance of examining different options in a business case. There are always options, even if a particular solution is presented as the only way forward, including the option not to do anything (as discussed in Chapter 8). Sometimes, it may appear that an organisation does not have a 'do nothing' option, such as where it is obliged to comply with new legislation. However, there may still be choices as to *how* it complies, each offering a different blend of benefits and costs. For example, if a government organisation is obliged to establish a 'Register of Dangerous Trees' in its area it could comply with this instruction by building, or buying, a software product, which would attract analysis, design and development costs. Another approach might be to buy an exercise book, write 'Register of Dangerous Trees' on the cover and proceed from there. This option would not provide facilities to sift and sort data or to generate reports for central government easily, but it would be cheap and offer a low fidelity option that ensures compliance with the new regulation.

A business case should support decision-making and often needs to persuade stakeholders of a way forward. Therefore, some of the key rules of successful selling apply: stress benefits, not features; sell the benefits before discussing the cost; and ensure the 'buyers' understand the size of the problem – or opportunity – before presenting the amount of time, effort and money that is needed to implement a solution.

WHEN TO PRODUCE A BUSINESS CASE

The conventional view of a business case is that it should be created after a preliminary investigation has been made of a problem or opportunity and before major resources are committed to a project. This is represented in the lifecycle for a business case shown in Figure 9.1.

Figure 9.1 Lifecycle for a business case

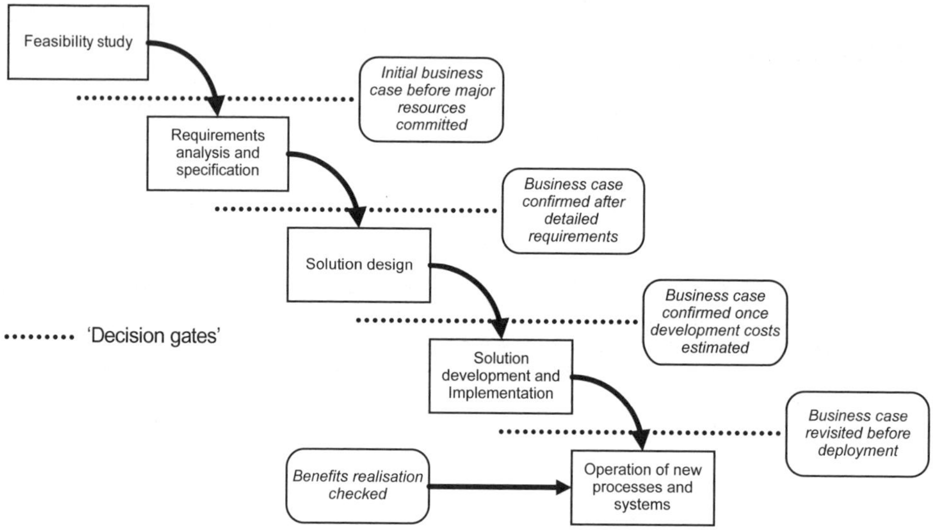

However, many projects today – especially those involving software development – do not apply the linear, or waterfall lifecycle on which Figure 9.1 is based. Instead, where an Agile approach to software development has been adopted, it may not be practical or sensible to create a business case for the entire project as the final destination is not entirely clear and is likely to change as the project progresses. This chapter first examines the conventional, 'linear' approach to business case development, and the general underlying principles of business cases, and then considers business cases within an Agile environment.

THE BUSINESS CASE IN THE LINEAR LIFECYCLE

Whichever lifecycle is used, a business case is – or should be – a living document that should be revised as the project proceeds and more is discovered about the proposed solution and the costs and benefits of introducing it. Organisations and the environments in which they operate are not static and so the business case must be kept under review to ensure that changing circumstances have not invalidated it.

Figure 9.1 explores this ongoing review within the context of a linear lifecycle. It is often the case that a feasibility study is conducted to consider the overview requirements and evaluate any relevant options in terms of their estimated costs, benefits, risks and impacts. This work forms an initial business case that provides a basis for deciding on whether to progress with the change project. The ballpark figures are revisited once more detailed analysis work has been completed and a fuller picture has emerged of the options available. The business case is examined again once the solution has been designed and much more reliable figures are available for the costs of development. It is then reviewed before the solution is deployed, when the costs of deployment have become clear and are now more reliable. Also, business circumstances may have changed and it may not be worth proceeding to implementation. Finally, once the proposed solution has been in operation for a while, there should be a benefits review to determine the degree to which the predicted business benefits have been realised and to identify actions to support the delivery of these benefits.

Figure 9.1 refers to each of these review points as 'decision gates'. The concept shown, now widely used in project management, is that projects should pass certain tests – not least those relating to their business viability – before they can be allowed to proceed to the next stage.

ASSESSING FEASIBILITY

There are many areas to think about when assessing feasibility and they fall under the three broad headings illustrated in Figure 9.2.

Figure 9.2 Areas of feasibility (© Assist Knowledge Development Ltd.)

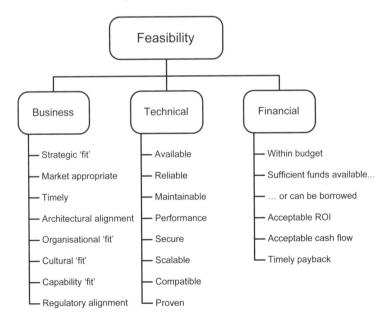

Business feasibility issues include whether the proposal matches the business objectives and strategy of the organisation and – if it is a commercial firm – if the option can be achieved in the current market conditions. There is the question of whether the proposed solution will be delivered in sufficient time to secure the desired business benefits. The solution must 'fit' with the management structure of the organisation and with its culture, as lack of cultural fit is often a cause of projects failing to deliver predicted benefits. The solution must also align with the EA for the organisation. The proposal may be for major process change so may have to align with other processes, including those that are not changing; alignment with the processes defined in the business architecture must also be considered. Whatever is proposed must be possible given the organisation's capabilities. Finally, many sectors are now heavily regulated and the proposed solution must be one that will be acceptable to the regulators and comply with relevant laws.

Assessing **technical feasibility** involves considering whether or not the technology to deliver the solution is available. The proposed solution must meet the organisation's demands in terms of system performance, availability, reliability, maintainability and security. The solution should be scalable to meet changes to the organisation's circumstances. Few IT systems are completely detached from other systems and so the issue of compatibility must be considered. If the solution involves an off-the-shelf software product, thought should be given to the amount of customisation that would be required and whether this would cause technical difficulties. Finally, consideration is needed regarding whether the proposed solution has been proven or, alternatively, if it places excessive reliance on new technological developments. Many organisations would prefer a less ambitious but reliable solution to a more advanced one that comes with a lot of technological risk.

Financial feasibility concerns whether the organisation can afford the proposed solution. The organisation needs either to have the required funds available or to be in a position to borrow them. There may already be a budget imposed. Every organisation has rules or guidelines about what constitutes an acceptable return on its investment (ROI) and methods of calculating this are considered later in this chapter. Even if a project ultimately pays for itself, there may be points where it may have unacceptably high costs and so cash flow must also be considered. Finally, all organisations specify some time period over which payback must occur and, in the case of IT projects, the payback periods are often very short, sometimes within the same accounting year as the investment.

Another tool that can be used in assessing feasibility is a PESTLE analysis. PESTLE examines the environment outside an organisation or within an organisation but outside the area being studied. It can be used to assess feasibility as follows:

- **Political:** Is the proposed solution politically acceptable? The political situation, whether local, national or international, plus the internal politics of the organisation, should be considered.

- **Economic:** Can the organisation afford the solution? Does it represent the best use of scarce funds?

- **Socio-cultural:** Does the solution fit with the organisation's culture? Or, more widely, is it acceptable within the cultural norms of the society in which the organisation operates?

- **Technological:** Can the solution be achieved, technically? This often has to be considered in parallel with the economic question to determine if an available technology is affordable at this point.

- **Legal:** Does it comply with legislation? If relevant, will the regulator allow it?

- **Environmental:** Does it raise any 'green' environmental issues? This is a highly relevant aspect in view of almost universal concerns about the environment and climate change.

Figure 9.3 Force-field analysis overview

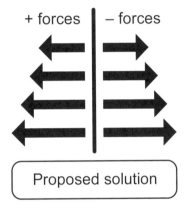

Force-field analysis (Lewin, 1997) may also be used to assess the feasibility of an option. This technique, where the positive and negative forces regarding a solution are identified and analysed, is illustrated in Figure 9.3.

With a force-field analysis, the forces inside and outside the organisation are considered that support adoption of the proposal alongside those that oppose it. The positive forces should outweigh the negative ones if the proposal is to succeed. The forces may include the PESTLE factors mentioned above, the elements identified in Figure 9.2 and also the key stakeholders in the organisation (see Chapter 6). If it is concluded that the negative forces are just too strong, then the proposal is not feasible and must be abandoned or re-cast in a way that increases the positive forces.

Impacts and risks also need to be considered when considering the feasibility of options. They form part of the business case itself and are discussed later in this chapter.

STRUCTURE OF A BUSINESS CASE

Organisations differ in how they like to have business cases presented. Some like large, weighty documents with full analyses of the proposals and all the supporting data.

Others prefer a short, sharp presentation of the main points and may even mandate that business cases are distilled into a single page. Decision-makers are typically busy senior managers with time at a premium, and this needs to be considered when producing a business case.

Whatever their size, the structure and content of most business cases are similar and tend to include these elements:

- Introduction
- Management (or executive) summary
- Description of the current situation
- Options considered
  - Option description
  - Analysis of costs and benefits
  - Impact assessment
  - Risk assessment
- Recommendations
- Appendices, with supporting information

Each of these elements is considered in turn.

Introduction

This sets the scene and explains why the business case is being presented. Where relevant, it should also describe the methods used to examine the business issue and those who have contributed to the study.

Management summary

In many ways, this is the most important part of the document as it is possibly the only part that the senior decision-makers tend to study. It should be written once the rest of the document has been completed and should distil the whole of the business case into a few paragraphs. In an ideal situation, three paragraphs should suffice:

- What the study was about and what was found out about the issues under consideration.
- A survey of the options considered, with their principal advantages and disadvantages.
- A clear statement of the recommendation being made and the decision required.

If it is not possible to summarise the business case in three paragraphs, the management summary should be limited to one or two pages.

Description of the current situation

The current situation is explained and the problems and opportunities are identified. It is good practice to keep this section as short as possible while still explaining the issues, as senior managers often complain of having to read pages and pages to find out what they already knew. Sometimes, the real problems or opportunities uncovered are not what management thought they were when they instigated the study. In that case, more space has to be devoted to explaining the issues and exploring the implications for the business.

Options considered

In this section, the options are presented – again as briefly as possible – and the reasons why some have been rejected are set out. Some organisations require that each business case puts forward a recommended option. Where this is the case, a more detailed description of the recommended solution, including why it is recommended, should be provided. The identification and shortlisting of options is discussed in Chapter 8.

Analysis of costs and benefits

Cost–benefit analysis is a key aspect of a business case. Before examining this subject in detail, it is worth mentioning that it can be more persuasive to present the benefits *before* the costs. In other words, what is presented is actually a benefit–cost analysis even though by convention it is always referred to as a cost–benefit analysis.

Cost-benefit analysis poses a number of challenges:

- identifying where costs will be incurred and where benefits can be expected;
- quantifying the tangible costs and benefits;
- justifying that any benefits will result solely from the changes proposed in the business case;
- explaining the value that may arise from intangible benefits such as 'improved customer satisfaction' or 'better staff morale'.

Costs and benefits are either incurred, or realised, immediately or in the longer term. They are also either tangible, which means that a credible – usually monetary – value can be placed on them, or intangible, where this is not the case. Given these dimensions, costs and benefits fit into one of four categories, as illustrated in Figure 9.4.

Figure 9.4 Categories of cost and benefit

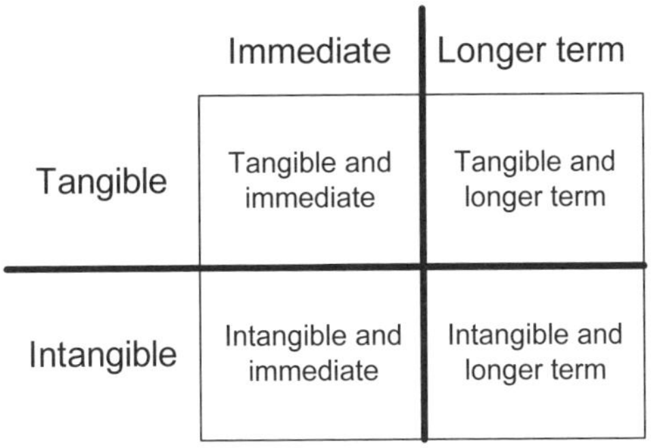

	Immediate	Longer term
Tangible	Tangible and immediate	Tangible and longer term
Intangible	Intangible and immediate	Intangible and longer term

Costs tend to be mainly tangible, whereas benefits are often a mixture of the tangible and intangible. In some organisations, managers do not consider the value of intangible benefits and this often makes it difficult – or even impossible – to make an effective business case. For example, while a more modern company image may be deemed beneficial, it is difficult to quantify what this is worth to an organisation. In theory, it should be possible to put a numeric value on *at least part of a* cost or benefit; the practical problem is that there is seldom the time, or the specialist expertise – for example, from the field of operational research – to do so.

If intangible benefits are allowed, it is vital that they are not over-stated or are allocated a spurious value. Decision-makers are unlikely to believe such values and this is likely to undermine their confidence in other, more soundly based, values. With intangible benefits, it is a better policy to state what they are and clarify why they are beneficial to the organisation, but to leave the decision-makers to put their own valuations on them.

Another pitfall encountered during cost–benefit analysis is basing them on assumptions. For example, a business case that states 'A 20 per cent reduction in the time taken to produce invoices, would amount to 5,000 hours per year or a cost saving of £75,000' will only prove acceptable to the decision-makers if the assumption is plausible. Assumptions should err on the side of conservatism, and under-claim rather than over-claim.

There are some typical costs and benefits that often arise within the four categories of costs and benefits described above: tangible costs; intangible costs; tangible benefits; intangible benefits.

Tangible costs
Tangible costs may include the following:

- **Project staff costs**: In many projects, particularly those that involve developing new processes or IT systems, the costs associated with the project staff are a major cost element. To work them out, a daily rate is needed for the staff concerned – probably available from the HR or finance departments – and an outline project plan showing when and how the resources will be required. If using external consultants, then the costs are likely to be subject to negotiation and contract.

- **Business staff costs**: Business staff have to be available during the initial investigation, solution development and testing, and have to be trained in the new systems and methods of working. Again, daily rates can be used in combination with an outline plan of the level of business staff involvement.

- **Equipment**: There is often a need to purchase new hardware. For this, estimates or quotations can be obtained from potential suppliers.

- **Infrastructure**: There may be a need to purchase items that will establish the infrastructure and, again, estimates may be obtained from suppliers.

- **Packaged software**: Vendors provide details of the costs associated with purchasing and installing software products. Where tailoring of a package is envisaged, estimates of the effort and cost involved are also provided by vendors.

- **Relocation**: These costs include those of new premises, either rented or bought, refurbishment, new furniture and the actual moving costs. There may also be costs associated with surrendering existing leases and so on.

- **Staff training and retraining**: The costs associated with training business staff may be estimated by considering the number of people to be trained and the duration of the training. Training needs analysis may be needed to examine where there are skills gaps and to identify the best way of developing the additional skills. The effort required to develop training material may be estimated by multiplying the proposed training course duration by a factor of 10. For example, a 2-day training course might typically require 20 days of development effort.

- **Ongoing costs**: Any new systems require maintenance and support and quotations for this can be obtained from the vendors. If this is not possible, a very rough rule of thumb is to allow support costs of 15 per cent of operational costs in the first year after installation and then 10 per cent thereafter.

Intangible costs
Intangible costs may include the following:

- **Disruption and loss of productivity**: However good a new process or system is in the long run, there is bound to be some disruption as it is introduced. The level of disruption is very difficult to predict when implementing any business change. Also, if parallel running of old and new IT systems is used to smooth the transition, there will be a tangible cost involved as well.

- **Recruitment**: If new staff or skills are needed, there will be costs involved in recruiting the new staff and inducting them into the organisation. Organisations often have little idea of the total cost to recruit someone although elements of this cost, such as agency fees, are usually available.

Tangible benefits
Tangible benefits may include the following:

- **Staff savings**: This is the most obvious area where savings are made. In calculating the savings, the total cost of employing the people concerned – including salary, national insurance, pension contributions, other benefits, accommodation and equipment costs – should be sought from the HR or finance departments. Where redundancies are to be made, there will be one-off redundancy costs that must be set against the ongoing saved staff costs.

- **Reduced effort and improved speed of working**: If staff posts are not completely eliminated, it may be possible to carry out some tasks in a shorter timescale, thus freeing up time for other work. This is a tangible benefit if the effort to carry out the current task is measured and compared with the expected situation after the change. This is an intangible benefit if it is not possible to predict the expected situation following the change.

- **Faster responses to customers**: Similarly, it is necessary to make a pre-change measurement of the time taken to respond to customers' needs and compare this with the expected response time following the implementation of the changes. This is an intangible benefit if it is not possible to predict the expected response time before the changes are implemented.

- **Reduced accommodation costs**: These may have already been factored into the cost of employing staff (see 'Staff savings' above) but new hardware may also save space and allow staff to work from home some or all of the time. The facilities or finance departments should be able to provide details about the cost of accommodation.

- **Reduced inventory**: New systems – especially 'just in time' systems – often result in the need to hold less stock. Finance and logistics staff should be able to help in quantifying this benefit.

- **Other costs reductions**: These include areas such as reduced overtime working, the ability to avoid basing staffing levels on workload peaks, and reductions in time and costs spent on travel between sites and in the use of consumables. Quantifying the cost reduction depends on the nature of the costs.

Intangible benefits
Intangible benefits may include the following:

- **Increased job satisfaction**: The level of job satisfaction may be observed or identified from anecdotal comments; however, it is difficult to quantify. It is possible that increases in job satisfaction correlate with tangible benefits such as reduced staff turnover or absenteeism, but it is difficult to prove in advance if these things will happen.

- **Improved customer satisfaction**: This is intangible unless there are precise measures that focus on the results obtained from improving customer satisfaction levels; for example, the time taken to respond to customer complaints about the organisation's products or services.

- **Improved management information**: There is a critical distinction between *improved* management information and *more* management information. Better information should lead to better decisions, but this is difficult to quantify and, at least in part, depends upon the abilities of the decision-maker.

- **Greater organisational flexibility**: The ability of the organisation to respond more quickly to changes in the external environment, through having systems, processes and staff who can adapt to new or different work priorities.

- **More creative problem-solving time**: Managers freed from much day-to-day work should have more time to analyse and resolve strategic, tactical or operational issues.

- **Improved presentation or better market image**: New systems often enable an organisation to present itself better to the outside world. It is extremely difficult to quantify how beneficial this is to the organisation.

- **Better communications**: Many people report communication problems within their organisation so improving communications is likely to be beneficial. However, it is difficult to quantify the value of this improvement.

Avoided costs
One particular form of benefit that is worthy of consideration concerns 'avoided costs'. There are often situations where an organisation has to do *something* and has already budgeted for it and that budget can be offset against a more radical solution that would

offer additional business benefits. For example, an organisation has been quoted £2 million to make its legacy systems compliant with new legislation. A business case has been developed that proposes investing in a completely new system for £2.5 million. In this case, the original £2 million can be treated as an avoided cost.

Presenting the financial costs and benefits

Once the various tangible costs and benefits have been assessed, they need to be presented so that management can see whether and when the project pays for itself. As this is a somewhat complex topic, it is examined separately in a later section in this chapter.

Impact assessment

In addition to the costs and benefits already mentioned, for each of the options any impacts that there might be on the organisation need to be explored. Some of these impacts may have costs attached to them but some may not. Impacts include:

- **Organisation structure**: It may be necessary to reorganise departments or functions to exploit the new processes and systems. For example, to create a single point of contact for customers or to create more generalist rather than specialist staff roles. This is likely to be unsettling for both staff and managers and a plan must be made to handle this.

- **Interdepartmental relations**: The relationships between departments may change and there may be a need to introduce service level agreements or redefine these relationships in other ways.

- **Working practices**: New processes and systems invariably lead to changes in working practices and these must be introduced carefully and sensitively.

- **Management style**: Sometimes, the style that managers adopt has to change. For example, if the organisation's management hierarchy is reduced and customer-facing staff are empowered to make decisions, the management style is likely to change.

- **Recruitment policy**: The organisation may have to recruit people using a different recruitment approach.

- **Appraisal and promotion criteria**: It may be necessary to change the targets, objectives and incentives for staff in order to encourage them to display different behaviours, such as increasing their customer-focus.

- **Supplier relations**: The ways of working with suppliers may have to be redefined. For example, implementing a collaborative customer/supplier relationship approach rather than one that is adversarial.

Whatever the impacts from a particular option, they need to be stated in the business case. It must also explain the changes required to exploit fully the opportunities available, and the costs these changes will incur.

Risk assessment

No change comes without risk and it is unrealistic to think otherwise. A business case is immeasurably strengthened if it can be shown that the potential risks have been identified and that suitable countermeasures are available. A comprehensive risk log (sometimes called a risk register) is probably not required until the change project starts but the principal risks should be highlighted in the business case. For each risk, the following should be recorded:

- **Description**: The cause of the risk should be described and also its impact. For example, 'uncertainty over the future leads to the resignation of key staff, leaving the organisation with a lack of experienced staff'.

- **Impact assessment**: This should attempt to assess the extent of the harm that would be suffered if the risk occurred. It is preferable for quantitative measures to be identified but, if this is not possible, a scale of 'small', 'moderate' or 'large' is sufficient.

- **Probability**: How likely it is that the risk will materialise. Precise probabilities may be calculated but it is sufficient to use a scale of 'low', 'medium' or 'high'.

- **Countermeasures**: The countermeasures are concerned with reducing the likelihood of the risk occurring or to lessen its impact if it does. It may also be possible to transfer the impact of the risk onto someone else, for example, through the use of insurance.

- **Ownership**: For each risk, it is necessary to decide who is best placed to take the necessary countermeasures. This may involve asking senior managers within the organisation to take the responsibility.

Where there are many risks associated with an option, it is a good idea to document only the major risks – the potential 'showstoppers' – in the body of the business case and to put the rest into an appendix.

Recommendations

Finally, the business case is summarised and the decisions that the senior managers are being asked to take are set out. An outline of the main tasks and timescales envisaged for the project is also useful to decision-makers. This is best expressed graphically, as a Gantt/bar chart as illustrated in Figure 9.5; this Gantt chart reflects a linear software development lifecycle.

Figure 9.5 Gantt/bar chart for a proposed project

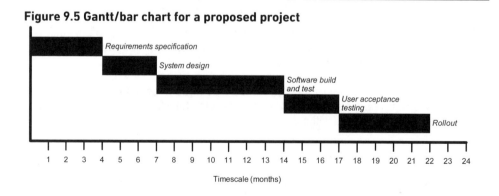

Appendices and supporting information

It is best to place detailed information in appendices to the business case. This separates out the main points that are put in the main body of the document from the supporting detail. If supporting statistics are to be provided, they too should be placed in the appendices, perhaps with a summary graph or chart in the main body. The detailed cost–benefit calculations may also be put into appendices.

INVESTMENT APPRAISAL

Business cases need to include calculations that use the quantified costs and benefits to identify the financial implications of each option. In this part of the business case, the tangible costs and benefits are contrasted so see if, and when, the project will pay for itself.

There are a number of different investment appraisal techniques, three of which – payback calculation, DCF/net present value (NPV) and internal rate of return (IRR) – are described in this section.

Payback (break-even)

The most straightforward technique concerns a 'payback' calculation, which is in effect a cash-flow forecast for the project. An example of a payback calculation is given in Table 9.1. It shows immediate costs of £400,000 for hardware and £300,000 for software for a new system, and ongoing costs of £60,000 for hardware maintenance and £60,000 for software support and upgrades. The tangible benefit concerns the removal of some clerical posts, valued at £300,000 per year. Note that, in these calculations, the convention is to refer to the year in which the investment is made as 'Year 0'.

Table 9.1 Example of a payback calculation

Item	Year 0 (£)	Year 1 (£)	Year 2 (£)	Year 3 (£)	Year 4 (£)
Hardware purchase	400,000				
Hardware maintenance	60,000	60,000	60,000	60,000	60,000
Software purchase	300,000				
Software support	60,000	60,000	60,000	60,000	60,000
Staff savings	300,000	300,000	300,000	300,000	300,000
Cash flow for year (savings less costs)	-520,000	180,000	180,000	180,000	180,000
Cumulative cash flow	-520,000	-340,00	-160,000	+20,000	+200,000

In Year 0, the costs considerably outweigh the benefits, because of the large capital expenditures, but thereafter benefits exceed costs by some £180,000 per year. By working out the cumulative cash-flow positions, the accumulated benefits finally exceed the accumulated costs in Year 3 and thereafter build up at £180,000 per year.

Discounted cash flow and net present value

Payback calculations have the virtue of being easy to understand and relatively easy to construct. Where interest rates and inflation are low, they provide a reasonable forecast of what is likely to happen. However, they do not take account of what accountants call the 'time value of money'. This reflects that money spent or saved today is not worth the same as it will be next year or in several years' time. In part this is the effect of inflation but, even with low or zero inflation, there are other things that could be done with the money besides investing in this project. It might, for instance, be left in the bank to earn interest. Or, conversely, the organisation might have to borrow money and pay interest to finance the project.

A method that takes account of the time value of money is known as DCF and this leads to an NPV for the project. This means that all of the cash flows accumulated in the years after Year 0 are 'discounted' or adjusted to today's value of money.

Management accountants work out the 'discount rate' to use in a DCF calculation by studying a number of factors including the cost of raising capital. The management accountants decide the discount rate and the discount factors by which the cash flows in Years 1 to 4 should be discounted. The discount factors relating to a discount rate are available within spreadsheets or may be found in published tables. For a 10 per cent discount rate, the relevant factors are shown in Table 9.2.

Table 9.2 Example of a NPV calculation

Year	Net cash flow (£)	Discount factor (£)	Present value (£)
0	-520,000	1.000	-520,000
1	180,000	0.909	163,620
2	180,000	0.826	148,680
3	180,000	0.751	135,180
4	180,000	0.683	122,940
NPV of project:			**50,420**

Table 9.2 represents the same project that was analysed in Table 9.1 with the cash flows from Years 1 to 4 adjusted to today's values. It can be seen that the project is not such an attractive investment as the payback calculation suggested. It does pay for itself, but now only in Year 4 and not by as great a margin as before.

A **sensitivity analysis** can also be performed on these results to see how much they would be affected by changes in interest rates. For example, if a discount rate of 5 per cent had been used, the result would have been an NPV of £118,280 and a 15 per cent rate would have produced an NPV of *minus* £5920.

Internal rate of return

One final measure that many organisations use is the IRR. This is a calculation that assesses the ROI from the project in terms of a single percentage figure. This can then be used to compare projects with a set 'hurdle rate' (a minimum level of return) and with other projects to identify the better investment opportunities. It is also possible to compare each IRR with what the money could earn if it was left in a bank account. So, for example, if the IRR of a project is calculated at 1 per cent and current bank interest rates are 2 per cent, then on financial grounds alone it would be better not to spend the money.

IRR is worked out by reversing the DCF/NPV calculations. The question is 'What discount rate should be used to obtain an NPV of zero after n years (where n is the period the organisation mandates should be used for the calculation)?' In other words, 'At what point would financial costs and benefits precisely balance each other?' This is worked out by applying different discount rates until an NPV of zero results. Microsoft Excel has an automated function to do this. In the case of the example project, the result is around 14.42 per cent. If this were being compared with another project offering a lower rate of return, then this project would be the more attractive one.

The IRR may also be compared with the 'cost of money' to the organisation. For example, if a project has an IRR of 3 per cent, but the organisation is borrowing money from its bank at 5 per cent, then on financial grounds alone, the project is not worth proceeding with. (Of course, there may be non-financial reasons for undertaking the project, such as the need to comply with regulations or to improve the organisation's reputation.)

IRR does not take account of the overall size of a project, so that the project with the smaller IRR may produce more actual pounds, or euros or dollars, in the end. For this reason, most accounting textbooks agree that DCF/NPV is the best method of assessing the value of an investment, while acknowledging that many organisations like the simplicity of the single-figure IRR.

PRESENTATION OF A BUSINESS CASE

A business case may be presented both as a written document and as a face-to-face presentation. In both cases, the *way* the business case is presented can often have a major impact on whether it is accepted or not and there are some straightforward rules that apply to both approaches:

- **Think about the audience**: Readers of reports and attendees at presentations have a variety of interests and attitudes. Some like to have all of the details, others prefer an overview. As far as possible, try to address the concerns of each of the decision-makers in the report or presentation. (See Chapter 6 on stakeholder management.)

- **Keep it short**: A pre-set format or template may be mandated for the report that can result in a long document. However, the business case should be as concise as possible.

- **Consider the structure**: This chapter has provided a standard structure for a written business case. For a presentation, the old rule still holds good:

  - Tell 'em what you're going to tell 'em

  - Tell 'em

  - Tell 'em what you've told 'em.

  The presentation should build towards a logical conclusion that starts with the current situation and leads to the decision that needs to be made.

- **Think about appearances**: Organisational standards may constrain the appearance of a business case, but it is still useful to consider how to present the information in an accessible and engaging way. Pictures, diagrams and tables should be used, in colour where appropriate. For a presentation, avoid using bullet point slides, particularly where each bullet point consists of a sentence – audiences are able to read and question the need for a presenter if this approach is used.

BUSINESS CASES WITHIN AN AGILE CONTEXT

The previous sections set out the basic elements of a business case and these are relevant for all project environments. However, organisations now find that they have to respond with ever-increasing speed to changing business environments and this has led to the adoption of Agile approaches to developing solutions. As a result, organisations are tending to avoid large, monolithic projects and are proceeding incrementally. Even when a large project is unavoidable – for example, a bank replacing its core legacy systems – the overall programme is often divided into smaller sub-projects or work streams, each of which is intended to deliver business benefit. This approach stands in stark contrast to the situation where the intention is to realise all of the benefits once the whole change programme has been implemented.

In this context, a modified approach to business case production is required although the basic elements – options, costs, benefits, impacts and risks – still have to be considered.

The key features relevant to the production of a business case when using an Agile approach are:

- Time horizons are shorter and results (positive or negative) appear sooner.

- Budgets are smaller and there is less up-front commitment to large expenditures.

- Risks are accordingly reduced, as the organisation is only proceeding in an incremental way – and they are reduced further by the extensive use of prototyping to try out ideas and make sure they work before implementing them on a large scale.

- Where ROI is concerned, there may be a partial return at an earlier point in time and the gains from earlier phases in a programme can assist in funding the later stages.

It may be argued that a conventional business case isn't needed in an Agile environment since (i) the final destination is uncertain at the start of a programme and (ii) the risks are reduced by the Agile approach. However, this seems an unrealistic argument where large organisations (in any sector) are concerned and where senior managers know they have to account to the 'owners', whether shareholders or taxpayers, for the investments they authorise.

So, how can the business case be adapted for use in an Agile environment? Figure 9.6 illustrates the typical business case approach when using Agile.

Figure 9.6 Generic Agile lifecycle (© Assist Knowledge Development Ltd.)

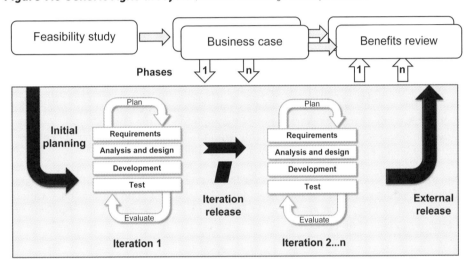

While Agile offers a method of developing and delivering solutions, it is still necessary to define the business needs and identify – at a high level – the main business requirements, at an early stage. The iterations that follow divide up the requirements into deliverable packages, with the most pressing (or mandatory) requirements dealt with first and others being deferred until needed.

The initial business case is produced after the options have been agreed and project feasibility assessed. The MoSCoW approach to prioritisation (see Chapter 10) is used to formulate the options. In respect of the high-level requirements:

- 'Must have' and 'Should have' requirements are both mandatory and so they must form part of any option if it is to be acceptable. The costs of satisfying these requirements form the baseline for the investment appraisal.

- Decision-makers can be offered a 'menu' of 'Could have' requirements, with costings, which can be added to the baseline cost. They can decide to include some, and exclude others, usually on the basis of the organisation's current business strategy and imperatives.

- Any requirements that are left (the 'Want to have but won't have this time' requirements) are outside the scope of the current business case and are 'parked' for consideration at a later date, and probably in a future business case.

Figure 9.6 shows that there may be a series of iterations during which the requirements are refined and the solution is analysed, designed, developed and tested. Figure 9.6 shows that two or more iterations may be associated with a release of the solution. However, it may be the case that just one iteration is sufficient given the content of the release and the nature of the work.

Reviewing a business case in an Agile environment

The delivery of each release is an opportunity for the organisation to revisit or extend the business case and to reprioritise the backlog in the light of any changes to the project or the organisation's business environment. Review of the backlog items may result in the reprioritisation of requirements with a 'Want to have, but won't have this time' priority. Given that this level indicates that requirements are deferred for consideration at a later stage, it is possible that a post-release review may change an individual requirement's priority to 'Must have', 'Should have' or 'Could have'. Alternatively, it is possible that some requirements retain their original 'Want to have but won't have this time' priority and are considered once further work has been completed. Some changes may well have resulted in new requirements being identified and added to the backlog, while others could have been removed because they are no longer relevant.

Given that some work has been completed, the organisation now has better information about the productivity of the development team and the cost of delivering the iterations. This data can be used to refine the estimates of the cost and timescale of proceeding with the remaining requirements.

As with the linear lifecycle, any really significant change in the organisation's environment, whenever it is detected, should trigger a review of the business case to check that proceeding with the project – at least on the original basis – is still justified.

RAID AND CARDI LOGS

A business case documents the risks of a proposed project and it may also set out any constraints, assumptions or dependencies on which it has been based. Since all of these are likely to have ongoing effects throughout the project, this is a good point at which to set up logs that assist in managing them. A RAID log documents risks, assumptions, issues and dependencies. A CARDI log covers these areas and also includes constraints. Table 9.3 describes each element within a CARDI (and RAID) log.

Since a CARDI/RAID log is established at the time that the initial business case is created, its entries are usually at an overview level at this stage and become increasingly detailed as the project proceeds and more is known about its complexities.

Table 9.3 Elements within a CARDI log

CARDI element	Description
Constraints	The main constraints on any project are those of the 'iron triangle' – time, cost (or resources) and product/quality. But other constraints may need to be taken into account as well, such as the need to comply with certain legislation, to use certain standards or to make sure an IT solution runs on a specific platform.
Assumptions	The business case, and thus the project, may rest on certain assumptions. For example, that government funding may be available for part of the project. These assumptions should be documented and actions identified to test whether they are valid.
Risks	The risks documented in the business case form the start of the overall risk log for the project and are augmented as the work progresses. The log should document the risks themselves, their probability of occurrence and scale of impact, the actions proposed to avoid or mitigate them and who should own each risk. As well as new risks arising during the project, others are likely to change and can be retired if they do not arise.
Dependencies	Because modern organisations are so complex, an individual project often has dependencies on other projects, or may be depended upon by other projects. For example, a project to introduce a new IT system may depend on a project to recruit people with the required skills. Capturing details of these dependencies makes sure that they are kept in mind at all times.
Issues	An issue is something that has occurred on a project that could have an effect on it (for good or ill) and therefore needs to be managed. Some issues are risks that have materialised. For example, if it is known at the outset that the project team is inexperienced, this is an issue rather than a risk because it has 100% probability of occurring. As with risks, the issues part of the CARDI or RAID log documents what each issue is, what should be done about it and whose responsibility this is.

DEFINING THE SOLUTION

The business case puts forward options for consideration by senior stakeholders and enables them to make an informed decision. This process allows the decision-makers to decide on the focus and content of the solution, and to allocate the budget required to design and develop the solution components, such as the business processes and the software product. Many organisations employ solution architects to oversee and guide the development of business solutions and ensure that they fulfil the defined requirements. Solution architects are required to take an architectural approach that ensures all aspects of a solution are in alignment with each other and with the relevant architectures deployed across the organisation.

A solution architecture is defined as: 'an architectural description of a specific solution' (Gartner, nd).

There are several elements that should be included in a solution architecture, including definitions of the following:

- the motivation and desired outcome;
- the outputs and deliverables;
- the actors who will engage with the solution;
- the interfaces with other systems, technologies and organisations;
- the solution itself, which should encompass all of the POPIT elements.

The model shown in Figure 9.7 represents a solution architecture lifecycle, providing a conceptual framework for the analysis, development and delivery of a solution. This diagram highlights that the solution architecture should be defined once the business case has been considered and a relevant option, or hybrid of several options, selected.

Figure 9.7 The solution architecture lifecycle (© Assist Knowledge Development Ltd.)

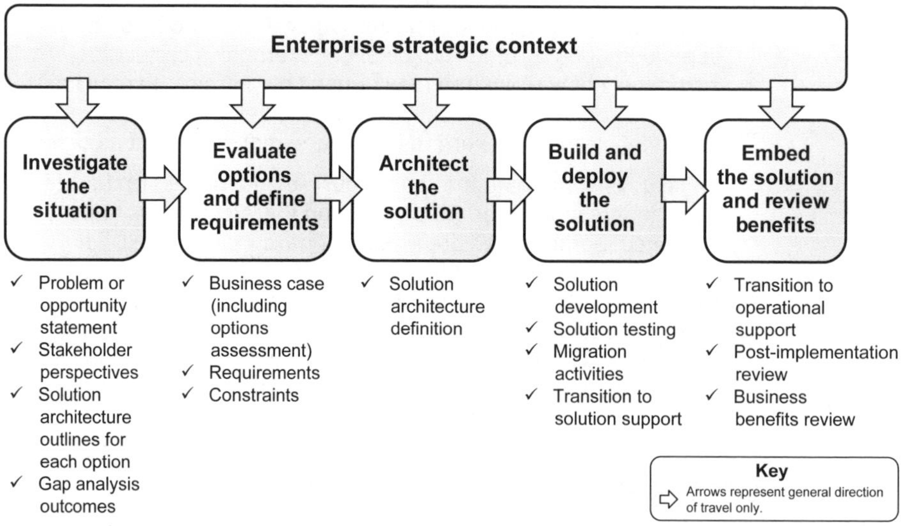

The solution architect takes responsibility for the governance of the build and delivery of the solution and supports the work to embed the solution, review lessons learned and obtain feedback on the business benefits realised.

Solution architecture and business analysis

The business analyst and solution architect roles need to work collaboratively to ensure that the solution fulfils the defined requirements and delivers the changes that are needed. Figure 9.8 represents the areas of activity where business analysts and solution architects work together to deliver the holistic solution.

Figure 9.8 Business analyst and solution architect roles within change projects
(© Assist Knowledge Development Ltd.)

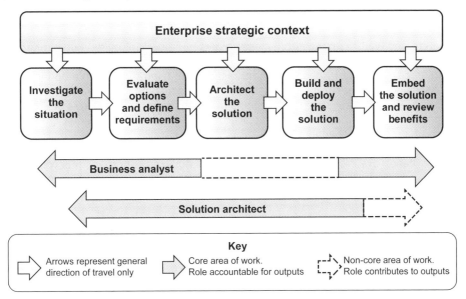

Although they usually have distinct areas of responsibility, the business analyst and solution architect roles have been merged within some organisations. This has resulted in the development of new roles with titles such as functional architect or business designer. The emergence of these roles reflects the need for organisations to ensure that all aspects of their external and internal context are understood and there is a focus on utilising available technologies to innovate, deliver desired outcomes and enable organisational growth. Analytical thinking approaches such as service thinking (see Chapters 1, 4 and 7), CX analysis (see Chapter 7) and design thinking (see Chapter 8) are all highly relevant to those performing these roles.

Defining solution scope

An overview definition of a solution clarifies the scope and helps to enable collaboration and understanding between the project team members and their stakeholders. A standard template for a solution contains the following aspects:

- inputs to the solution;
- outputs from the solution;
- solution components (across all architecture domains);
- actors (this can include both types of actor and the volumes for each type);
- interfaces (with components, software applications and other organisations).

The solution is likely to be recorded in overview at this stage, given that much development work remains. However, such a definition provides a visual representation to ensure that key components of the solution architecture are recorded and are not overlooked and helps to set out a roadmap for the rest of the solution development activity.

SUMMARY

A coherent and well-researched business case is an important guiding document for any change project. Developing a business case involves investigating the change context, uncovering the issues to be addressed, identifying the possible options and then assessing their feasibility. The business case has a standard format and provides a basis that leads to clear recommendations to the decision-makers. There are several investment appraisal approaches that are used to assess the financial costs and benefits of a proposed change project.

Business cases are relevant to both linear and Agile development lifecycles and approaches. A CARDI/RAID log can be developed concurrently with the business case. This log is used to document information about any key areas that could affect the success of the project.

The selected option is developed into an overview solution architecture definition. This incorporates the various elements needed to fulfil the requirements and deliver the business changes.

After the project has been completed, the business case should form the basis for a review to determine whether the expected benefits have been realised in practice and to identify any actions required to support the delivery of those benefits; this is discussed in Chapter 14.

10 ESTABLISHING THE REQUIREMENTS

INTRODUCTION

Requirements are at the very heart of business and IT change. A requirement is a feature or characteristic that has been requested by a stakeholder and may form part of a solution. Requirements are elicited so that they may be recorded for future consideration and are then analysed to determine whether or not they should be included within the solution. Some requirements impose constraints upon the solution and need to be analysed to consider the extent to which compliance is necessary or possible.

Ultimately, requirements determine what a solution should provide and how well the solution should perform. There is a wide range of performance aspects including areas such as security, usability, accessibility and scalability. Some requirements are expressed as outline, vague ideas while others are detailed and specific and provide a firm basis for testing the solution. Sometimes it is necessary to delve into the detail of a requirement at an early stage while on other occasions the requirement can evolve over time as the solution emerges.

The term 'requirement' is sometimes assumed to be relevant only where a linear software development approach applies but this is not correct. Business change solutions are holistic and have to meet business needs that are expressed as requirements. While these requirements may be fulfilled by software products, this is not necessarily the case and, even where software is at the core of the business changes, there are alternatives to developing software. For example, a packaged solution may be purchased or an outsourced service provider may be contracted to supply the required functionality.

There are various standards and techniques used to elicit, analyse and define requirements; these are described later in this chapter and in Chapters 11 and 12.

The approach adopted to define requirements varies according to the business and project context, and the standards applied within the organisation. This variability requires business analysts to be knowledgeable and adaptable, possessing skills that enable them to work effectively across different contexts and with a range of stakeholders.

Requirements definition is often viewed as a straightforward activity that merely requires access to business staff who can advise on what a solution should provide. However, this view has been proven to be a root cause of problems with business change design and software development for many years. In practice, requirements definition is a business analysis service that requires knowledge, experience and analytical skill. A failure to recognise this is likely to be problematic and, as a result, to have far-reaching consequences for both solutions and organisations.

THE PROBLEMS WITH REQUIREMENTS

Studies carried out on IT project failures over the last 30 years tell a familiar story. The problems highlighted include the following:

- A large proportion of errors (over 80 per cent) are introduced at the requirements analysis stage.

- Very few faults (fewer than 10 per cent) are introduced at the development stage; developers are coding things right but too often not coding the right things.

- Most of the project time is allocated to the development and testing phases of the project.

- Less than 12 per cent of the project time is allocated to the requirements analysis phase.

- There is poor alignment of the developed system to business strategy and objectives.

- There is poor requirements management.

The inherent difficulties in understanding and defining requirements has been declared a primary cause of problems with information systems projects. The lack of well-understood and defined requirements is often linked to customer dissatisfaction with delivered systems.

Walia and Carver (2009) identified over 90 causes of requirements errors in a study that reviewed 149 research papers. Key problems with requirements identified during this study include:

- Lack of relevance to the objectives of the project.

- Lack of clarity in the wording, or ambiguity.

- Duplication or conflict between requirements.

- Requirements expressed in such a way that it is difficult to assess whether or not they have been achieved.

- Requirements that assume a technical solution, rather than stating the features to be delivered by the system.

- Uncertainty among business staff about what they need from the new system.

- Business staff failing to identify all requirements.

- Inconsistent levels of detail.

- Business staff and analysts taking certain knowledge for granted and failing to ensure that there is a common understanding.

The conclusion to be drawn is that poor requirements contribute significantly to project problems and failures. This is irrespective of the development and delivery approaches adopted.

THE RE FRAMEWORK

The RE framework was developed to help improve the quality of requirements by clarifying the activities to be carried out when defining requirements. In the same way that 'software engineering' suggests a structured and scientific approach to the development of software, RE encapsulates a more disciplined approach to establishing requirements. The business analyst needs to elicit, analyse and define requirements carefully in order to provide a firm basis for developing business and software solutions. The RE framework helps business analysts to do this.

The RE framework sets out five core activities, and the key interactions between them, that need to take place if requirements are to be well defined. The term 'well defined' does not mean that the requirements need to be specified in exhaustive detail, but it does mean that they should meet certain criteria; primarily, that they are unambiguous, well-structured, correct and relevant.

The scope, depth and timing of the requirements work depends upon the project context, in particular the development and delivery approach adopted. In some circumstances, a detailed, validated and traceable definition of the entire set of requirements is needed before any development work may begin. In other situations, a set of outline requirements may be defined, each of which is decomposed and further elaborated when required. Another possibility is to define requirements in batches, in order to meet the organisation's business priorities. These different approaches, and the contexts in which they apply, are discussed later in this chapter.

The RE framework is set out in Figure 10.1.

Figure 10.1 RE framework

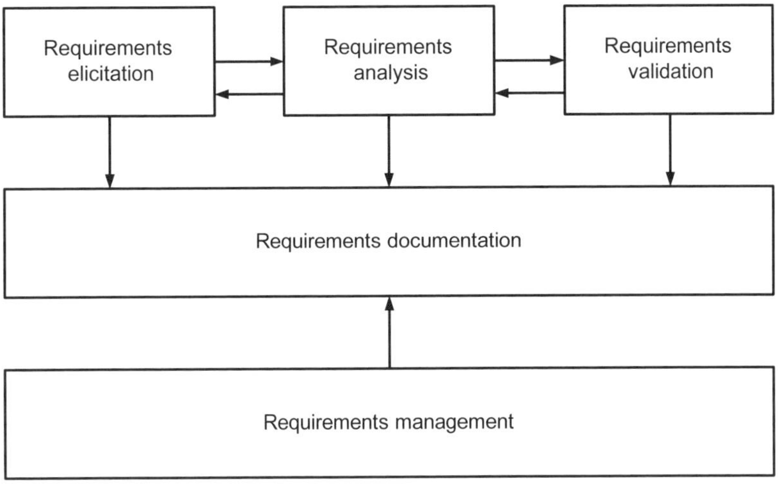

The stages of the RE framework are explained in overview in Table 10.1.

Table 10.1 Stages of the RE framework

Stage	Description
Requirements elicitation	This stage is concerned with drawing out requirements from the stakeholders, in particular those who perform the work of the organisation or are the intended users of the software product.
Requirements analysis	This stage is concerned with reviewing and analysing the elicited requirements to remove duplication or error, negotiate conflicts and contradictions, evaluate feasibility and allocate priorities.
Requirements documentation	This stage is concerned with producing narrative and diagrammatic definitions of the requirements, at varying levels of accuracy and completeness.
Requirements validation	This stage is concerned with reviewing requirements in order to assure that they are defined at the required level of quality.
Requirements management	This stage is concerned with managing changes to the defined requirements and ensuring the desired level of traceability is achieved.

Two stages of the RE framework – requirements elicitation and requirements analysis – are discussed in this chapter. The approaches used to create requirements documentation, including using techniques to model solutions, are described in Chapter 11. The other two stages – requirements validation and requirements management – are discussed in Chapter 12.

The separation of requirements elicitation from requirements analysis is one of the strengths of the RE framework. Analysts are encouraged during elicitation to draw out information, uncover tacit knowledge and discover requirements; during analysis, the business analysts examine the results of the elicitation work in order to define the requirements that the solution should deliver.

The relationship between the elicitation and analysis of requirements is necessarily iterative. Requirements emerge during elicitation, analysis identifies missing information or requirements gaps, further elicitation is required and so on. This connection between these two activities is represented in Figure 10.2.

It is also the case that requirements validation activities (discussed in Chapter 12) may uncover inconsistencies or errors within the requirements. Where this occurs, further requirements analysis – and possibly elicitation – is needed to resolve these issues. This is also reflected in Figure 10.2.

Assumptions and misinterpretations

It is often assumed that the RE framework is onerous and suitable only for projects that have adopted linear development approaches, such as the waterfall lifecycle or 'V' model (see Chapter 13). However, this view is a significant misinterpretation of

Figure 10.2 The relationship between requirements elicitation and analysis

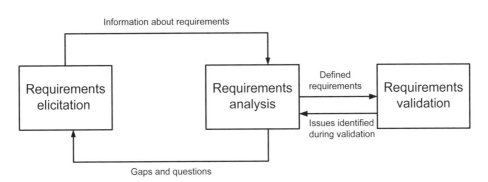

the RE framework and what it offers. Whether a business analyst is defining all of the requirements in detail or is working on a selected batch of requirements, each requirement still needs to be elicited, analysed and validated. Further, each requirement needs to be documented and any changes need to be managed. The techniques and standards used when applying the RE activities need to be relevant given the organisational and project context. Knowledge of the RE framework, and having the ability to determine how and when to carry out the individual activities, are key skills required of business analysts. This is a key reason for the extensive toolkit of skills, described in Chapter 2, that business analysts require.

Adaptability and RE

Business analysts have to adapt their approach to defining requirements as necessary. Factors to be considered when adapting the approach include:

- The standards adopted within the organisation. For example, documentation, modelling or methodological standards.

- The project approach. For example, the required development and delivery standards.

- The type of requirement. For example, non-functional requirements (see later in this chapter) often require in-depth analysis, and documentation needs to be produced that is specific to the needs of the organisation.

- The nature of the solution. For example, which POPIT elements are to be included (solution scope). Are the requirements for a completely new software product or for minor enhancements to an existing software product? Is there an existing legacy system to be taken into account? Is there likely to be a transformative impact upon the organisation's processes, roles and management structure? Will cultural change be required?

Situations and contexts for requirements work can vary considerably from organisation to organisation, and project to project. Business and IT changes can be developed and delivered in many different ways, and the RE framework needs to be applied thoughtfully in order to adapt its application as necessary. Requirements work must always be conducted pragmatically and the RE framework is intended to be as flexible as the situation demands. For example:

- Some projects need the complete set of requirements to be defined before any development work begins. This may be because the solution must comply with extensive regulatory rules, is strategically critical for the organisation or is a replacement for a key legacy system. In such situations, business analysts need to apply the RE framework thoroughly, ensuring the requirements are defined to a granular level of detail.

- Where a project is able to deliver the solution in increments, it is often more productive to document the requirements in outline initially, with each subset of the requirements defined in detail when required. Each stage of the RE framework is applied but the extent of the analysis work varies according to when it is carried out and the depth of definition needed for particular sets of requirements. This approach is sometimes referred to as 'slicing', which is discussed later in this chapter. While it is possible that, ultimately, the majority of the requirements will be defined, the approach taken to aspects of the RE framework – such as how the requirements are documented and managed – depends upon factors such as the development approach, the number of increments developed and deployed, the priority levels allocated to the requirements and the available budget and timescale.

- Many organisations apply an Agile software development approach where the solution is delivered incrementally and requirements are defined in overview initially and evolve during the development process. Where a project adopts an Agile approach to software development, the RE framework is applied to establish an initial set of requirements, typically recorded in a product or solution backlog. The solution or software product is then developed iteratively, allowing for a selected subset of the outline requirements to be elaborated within each iteration through a process of evolutionary development. This ensures that the RE approach is applied without compromising the Agile philosophy and principles. A caveat is that each iteration must be mindful of the integrity of the overall solution architecture and ensure that there are no overlaps or conflicts between requirements that have been developed as part of separate iterations.

The terms 'iteration' and 'increment' are often subject to misinterpretation and the distinction between them is sometimes lost. These terms are defined as follows:

- **Iteration**: A specified time period within which a scoped set of work activities is conducted (for example, a partial solution is developed from a selected set of requirements) by an allocated team of resources (typically, people who fulfil certain roles). This is sometimes referred to as a 'sprint'.

- **Increment**: A partial product (typically a component part of an overall solution) that is ready for release, into either a live or a test environment.

Therefore, all requirements have to be elicited, analysed, validated, documented and managed but how this work is carried out differs depending upon the project context. The depth of the RE work should be tailored according to the philosophy and approach adopted to develop the solution. Where the development requires detailed requirements definitions, these should be provided. Where an evolutionary software development is applied, the requirements need to be defined sufficiently to begin development and to enable the emergence of further detail, typically through prototyping and discussion.

Whichever approach applies, clear high-level requirements are vital as they define the overall goals to be met by the solution and provide context and direction. It is the more detailed lower-level requirements that are subject to the needs of the project. Even within an Agile environment, some requirements may need to be defined in detail. For example, where there is a need for multi-level access restrictions or complex business rules are to be applied, it is likely that the specific details need to be analysed and documented. Depending upon the level of complexity, such requirements may need to be defined at an early stage, possibly in advance of any software development work.

The RE framework also needs to be adapted where the solution includes an off-the-shelf software product. It may not be worthwhile documenting the requirements in exhaustive detail as a purchased product usually imposes functionality and performance constraints. However, it is important to understand the particular needs and requirements of the system in order to produce a requirements document that has enough information to evaluate the package, ensure that there is sufficient 'fit' with the business needs and provide a basis for any necessary customisation.

ACTORS IN RE

An actor is an individual or group who is fulfilling a particular role (see Chapter 7). There are some key roles involved with RE work and they represent two broad stakeholder groups: the business representatives and the project team.

The business representatives

Several actors represent the organisation or business area during a project. The roles that are conducted depend in part on the approach taken to the requirements work and the nature of the project. Key roles are the project sponsor, the product owner, the SME and business stakeholder roles, which may be at a tactical (managerial) or operational (staff) level.

The project sponsor
The **project sponsor** (or **accountable executive**) represents the business in ensuring that business objectives are met. The sponsor has the following responsibilities:

- To agree the PID or ToR for the RE study.

- To make funds and other resources available for the project.

- To rule on any conflicting requirements where the business analyst cannot negotiate agreement.

- To approve any requirements documentation as an accurate statement of the business needs and, where necessary, to provide formal approval and sign off. Some of this authority may be delegated to other roles, such as the product owner or product manager, allowing for ongoing, timely approval.

- To accept the deliverables at the end of the project.
- To deliver the specific and agreed business benefits predicted in the business case.
- To confirm that the benefits in the business case have been realised as promised.

Product owner

The **product owner** role originated from Scrum but has attained wider acceptance across Agile software development and business change projects. The product owner is the custodian of the product or solution backlog, the repository of the requirements, and is empowered to make decisions regarding the product development on behalf of the organisation. The product owner's responsibilities are:

- To manage the product or solution backlog, ensuring that the priorities of the backlog items have been identified and align with business needs.
- To identify the backlog items to be developed in each product development iteration and the features to be included in each incremental release of the product.
- To make decisions on behalf of the organisation regarding the product development and to resolve any conflicts in requirements.
- To ensure that the product development stays on track and timescales are met.

Business analysts sometimes perform the product owner role (the BA as proxy product owner is discussed in Chapter 1) and some business analysts have made a career move to become a product owner. This is because many of the skills required of a product owner overlap with those in the business analyst skill set. On some projects, the product owner may undertake the business analysis work. However, it should be recognised that business analysis is a specialist discipline, requiring analytical skill and expertise in applying a range of frameworks and techniques. Where the product owner – or any other members of the project team – has responsibility for business analysis they need to have the skills and expertise required to perform this work effectively.

Subject matter expert (SME)

The **SME** (sometimes known as the domain expert) should have experience and knowledge of industry best practice and bring a breadth of understanding to the RE work. The knowledge of the business domain offered by an SME helps the other roles to gain a greater depth of understanding of the requirements. For example, the SME may help to distinguish between what the business *needs* and what a particularly forceful stakeholder *wants*.

An SME may be an internal member of staff with extensive knowledge of a particular area or may be an external consultant with specialist industry knowledge who is employed for the duration of the project. There are advantages and disadvantages of employing external SMEs. While they can offer experience, fresh views and insights from across a particular industry, there are some risks associated with their use:

- They may not understand how the organisation itself works, why it operates in a particular way and the type of culture that prevails. This may make their preferred approach to the solution inappropriate or their suggestions irrelevant.

- They may be unaware of political undercurrents in the organisation that can affect the project's success or otherwise.

- They may be regarded as an outsider and internal business staff may resent their interventions, feeling that the expertise they offer is undervalued.

- There may be no knowledge transfer to internal stakeholders so any skills and knowledge gained during the project ceases to be available to the organisation when the consultant SME finishes the work.

The SME's responsibility is to give business advice regarding the requirements. Particular situations when this may be relevant are:

- The organisation wishes to adopt the latest industry best practice, or the latest innovations used within the industry.

- The organisation wishes to introduce a new product or process that the company does not yet fully understand.

Business staff

Business staff are the individuals or groups who carry out the work of the business so will implement the new business processes and use the new or enhanced software product. They work within the operational business areas that are led by **business managers** (who may be requirement owners and also play a key role in defining requirements). They have knowledge and experience of how the organisation operates so are required to describe current processes, procedures and documentation, highlight any difficulties they experience with these processes and identify the requirements for new or improved solution features.

Business staff work with the other roles to define requirements by providing specific, clear information. The way in which they do this varies depending upon the approach adopted by the project, the objectives of the project and the stage of the work. For example:

- During the early, investigation stage for a proposed change project, business staff provide information regarding the issues encountered when performing the work of the business area being studied.

- During the definition of requirements, whether to build a catalogue of requirements or a product backlog, business staff provide details regarding the features and characteristics required from the solution.

- During Agile software development, business staff collaborate with business analysts and developers to elaborate on the user stories and advise on the required features and how they should work within the new product.

One area where business managers may need to be involved concerns the definition of non-functional requirements. These requirements can be difficult to define and, typically, business analysts provide guidance to help with this process. Business staff may be able to assist with the definition of non-functional requirements that apply to specific tasks, such as accessibility requirements; however, some aspects are likely to need management involvement and possibly support from other colleagues. For example, decisions about archiving information and the length of retention of data are likely to require the involvement of business managers and may need reference to data governance specialists. Non-functional requirements are discussed later in this chapter.

Business staff may also represent the 'end customer' or 'consumer' role where the solution under development includes a new or enhanced software product that customers will access directly. This applies to online systems, for example, those used for banking, purchasing or reservation purposes. Techniques such as surveys and focus groups may be needed to support the information provided by business staff and ensure that any requirements that concern the customer experience are defined accurately.

The project team

Project team roles also vary depending upon the context and approach adopted for the project. Key roles include the project manager, the business analyst, developers and software testers.

Business, solution and technical architects support the project work and ensure adherence with architectural principles and standards. Representatives from the project support office ensure that the work aligns with project standards.

Project manager

The **project manager** has overall responsibility for the project as defined in the PID or ToR. In particular, the project manager has to ensure that the project objectives are met and the deliverables are produced. The project manager reports progress to the project sponsor and is concerned to:

- Divide the project work into identifiable and measurable tasks, each with defined deliverables.

- Allocate the tasks to team members.

- Schedule the tasks with their start and end times, recognising dependencies between them.

- Monitor the progress of each task, considering dependencies and the potential for delays.

- Take corrective action where necessary to avoid delays or the risk of non-completion of a task.

- Ensure that the project objectives are achieved in line with the constraints defined in the ToR, typically timescale and budget

Some projects involve making ongoing improvements to the solution in operation. For example, conducting product or platform enhancement or maintenance. In these cases, there may not be a designated project manager and instead there may be a team leader who has responsibility for ensuring that the development team is able to operate effectively; for example, by removing any issues that are delaying the work or hindering progress. Where Scrum is used, the team leader is known as the Scrum Master.

Business analyst

Business analysts are responsible for carrying out the RE work. They must ensure that the requirements are well-formed and defined, in line with the project approach and standards, and provide a basis for a solution that will help to achieve the business objectives and realise the business benefits. Working closely with business staff, they elicit, analyse and document the requirements, applying a range of elicitation, analysis and documentation techniques as appropriate to the project context.

Business analysis is not a passive discipline; instead it is proactive, seeking to uncover root causes of problems and opportunities to improve the business processes and systems. When eliciting and analysing requirements, business analysts have to determine the techniques that are relevant to the situation and offer the insights needed to ensure that the requirements are accurate and that exception situations are not overlooked. For example, requirements modelling techniques (see Chapter 11) may help to define the scope of the solution and clarify particular requirements; or, scenario analysis (see Chapter 5) may help to uncover tacit knowledge about the requirements.

Developer

The **developer** creates the software product in line with business requirements. During this process, developers confirm the technical feasibility of the requirements and help the analysts to appreciate the implications of some of the requests. Developers also assist in the creation of high-fidelity prototypes of the requirements. This helps business staff to visualise what they have requested, identify further requirements and confirm the analysts' understanding.

Typically, the developers collaborate closely with other members of the development team, such as business staff, business analysts, software testers and solution architects, and use evolutionary prototypes to develop the software that fulfils the selected requirements.

Software tester

The **software tester** is responsible for trying to prove that the system does not work and to identify where this is the case. Testing cannot guarantee that a software product is completely error-free; however, when the tester struggles to identify defects it may be declared that the software product is satisfactory.

THE TARGET SOLUTION

All change projects need to have a clearly defined outcome; without this there is no overall direction to the project and it is all too easy for the work to diverge, the scope to 'creep' and problems to emerge.

Desired business outcomes may be expressed as high-level requirements that explain why the project was established. For example, a marketing director might declare that a new website is required to ensure the organisation is able to promote a current, relevant and engaging image. Such requirements fall within the 'general' category, which is discussed within the hierarchy of requirements section later in this chapter.

Beyond overview statements of business need, the rationale and context for a change project may also be clarified using a formal ToR or PID. The ToR/PID may be produced following a feasibility study, whereby options and budget are evaluated (see Chapter 9) and a basis for the project is confirmed. Whichever approach is used, a clear statement of intent for a project is vital if the desired solution is to be delivered and the outcomes achieved.

Clearly stated ToR ensure that everyone involved in defining requirements understands the objectives of the development project and the scope and constraints within which it is to be carried out. The OSCAR acronym, described in Chapter 4, includes the elements objectives, scope, constraints, authority and resources and may be used to structure the ToR for a project. While OSCAR provides a helpful aide-memoire, the project context may require additional items to be included in the ToR/PID, such as dependencies with other projects, external factors or assumptions.

TYPES OF REQUIREMENT

There are four recognised types of requirement, as shown in Figure 10.3.

Figure 10.3 Types of requirement

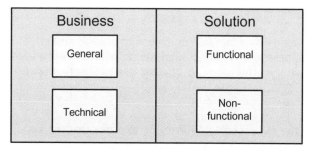

Within each requirement type there are many individual categories to be considered as they provide checklists that help to ensure that areas of requirement are not missed. Figure 10.4 shows the key categories of requirement for each type identified in Figure 10.3.

Each type of requirement, and the categories that fall within it, is described below.

General requirements

These requirements define business policies, standards and compliance areas. They are often very broad in scope and can be decomposed into more specific requirements. For example, a general requirement such as the need to comply with data protection legislation is enacted through functional and non-functional requirements.

Figure 10.4 Categories of requirement

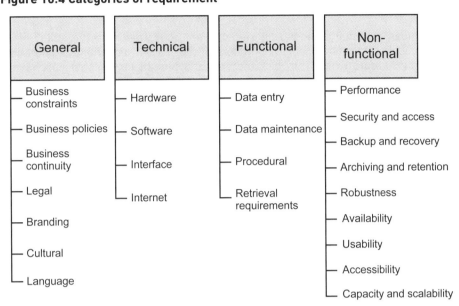

Many general requirements apply to entire business change programmes as they relate to the drivers for change. In some cases, a general requirement may underpin an entire portfolio of change projects.

The defined sub-categories of general requirement are as follows:

- **Business constraints**: These requirements cover aspects such as budget, timescale and resources.

- **Business standards and policies**: These requirements define how work is conducted and the business rules upon which decisions are made. The policies and standards ensure consistency of operation across the organisation and are often linked to the vision and values of the organisation. Examples of business standards and policies include an organisation's customer service standards, environmental policy, inclusion policy or business continuity strategy.

  - Collection and retention of data and information can have environmental impacts so it has been suggested that this is a requirements category that should also be considered (Reed, 2019). Many organisations have adopted a more sustainable approach to collecting, retaining and distributing data and information and have environmental policies. For example, providing guidance that guards against unwarranted printing, transfer of physical documentation or collecting data without good cause. While this guidance is defined at a general level, it generates functional and non-functional requirements with which each process and system should adhere.

- Many organisations also support the need to be inclusive when engaging with stakeholders so have policies on diversity and inclusion that are applied across the organisation's processes and systems.

- **Business continuity**: These requirements are concerned with the ability of an organisation to recover from incidents that may hinder its continued operation. Various threats exist, from both natural and human forces, that can have a detrimental impact on an organisation and its processes and systems. Business continuity requirements typically fall into two categories: preventing an incident from affecting the organisation to an undesirable extent and managing an incident once it has occurred. Prevention requires risk assessment to identify what might be done to avoid the impact of an incident; management requires contingency planning to ensure impacts are alleviated. Some business continuity requirements relate to security or backup and recovery requirements; others may require duplication of operation to ensure a means of recovery exists.

- **Legal**: These are the requirements that state relevant legal and regulatory constraints and may relate to many organisations, often across different business sectors. For example, the General Data Protection Regulation (GDPR) applies to any organisation that holds personal data. Other legal requirements are specific to a business sector or industry; for example, retail organisations must comply with consumer protection legislation.

- **Branding**: These requirements are concerned with the image and style for the organisation. Typically, there is branding documentation and a style guide, which sets out elements such as logos, key words, font, language and colour requirements. These elements are used to ensure a consistent brand and image are established across all forms of communication deployed by the organisation. The style guide sets out the 'look and feel' of any communication collateral, application interfaces, documents and reports used to conduct the organisation's work.

- **Cultural**: These requirements relate to the type of culture required within the organisation. They set out the values that underlie how the organisation operates, the customer experience that is offered and the management style.

- **Language**: Many organisations have specific language requirements as they are operating across international boundaries. These requirements set out the languages to be used internally within the organisation and externally to communicate with customers, suppliers and any other organisations. They may also specify more detailed aspects of this, such as whether screens and documents should be displayed using UK or US spelling, or whether translations are available. Language requirements may be included in a brand style guide or may be defined separately.

Technical requirements

These requirements state the technical policies and constraints to be adopted across the organisation and apply to all change projects. These requirements may refer to the artefacts that describe the technical infrastructure for the organisation. The technical requirement sub-categories are:

- **Hardware**: These requirements cover aspects such as the selected equipment models to be used in the organisation. The requirements cover technology hardware and also include other types of equipment or machinery, such as production, transport or general office equipment.

- **Software**: These requirements cover areas such as operating systems, software applications, networking and communications software. There may also be standards for use of online software such as cloud computing services.

- **Interoperability**: These requirements cover the standards for communicating and exchanging data across applications, networks and various forms of digitally enabled equipment. The interfaces may enable internal communications or those with external organisations.

- **Internet**: These requirements concern the technical policies governing the organisation's use of the internet and web-enabled services. They should stipulate specifics such as the web browsers or sites that are supported or not supported.

Functional requirements

The functional requirements set out the features that a solution should provide; these features typically encompass data entry, processing and reporting. Functional requirements may be delivered by a software product, but this is not necessarily the case – process changes or task enhancements sometimes provide a speedy or cost-effective alternative. Some functional requirements may prove to be too costly or time-consuming to be included in a software product, in which case other options to fulfil the requirements – such as process change – or even their removal, need to be considered.

The functional requirements form the basis for the development of the solution and are, ultimately, explored in detail. The level of detail needed to define the functional requirements, and the point at which this detail is explored, depends upon the project context, as discussed earlier in this chapter.

The requirements documentation to be produced is not always clear-cut. In situations where the development work is outsourced, an iterative development approach may be applied but how the requirements are communicated, given that the developers and business staff are not co-located, requires consideration. A variety of documentation, modelling and visualisation techniques are available to business analysts (see Chapter 11).

Requirements are highly variable in nature. Some are straightforward, while others are more complex. Some may be well-understood by business staff so clarity can evolve during discussion. Some may encompass business rules that require in-depth analysis and the use of techniques that ensure they are expressed with sufficient clarity. The business analyst must be able to think logically and possess a toolkit of skills to ensure that the requirements are defined and managed appropriately given the business and project context (see Chapter 12).

Non-functional requirements

Non-functional requirements are concerned with the level of performance offered by the solution in certain areas. They define the level of service required of a solution by addressing questions such as:

How quickly should the system respond?
How easy will the solution be to use?
What level of security must be offered by the solution?

Non-functional requirements can be difficult to elicit because they are concerned with areas that are intangible – such as usability or robustness – or complex – such as access and security. Business analysts need to be aware of the areas where non-functional requirements may be found and should be able to select the most appropriate analysis and documentation approach for each area of non-functional requirement.

Key areas of non-functional requirement are described in Table 10.2.

Table 10.2 Non-functional requirement categories

Non-functional requirement category	Description
Performance	These requirements concern the speed with which a transaction should be processed. For example, if a customer wishes to order some goods or place a booking, this requirement would define the speed of the processing to handle this. It is vital that these requirements are defined with precision. Comments such as 'this must be done quickly' are not acceptable or helpful. A statement such as 'This transaction must take no more than 1 minute to complete' is clear, specific and offers a basis for testing. Response times can be affected by the volume of transactions being processed so this also needs to be considered. It may be helpful to state a minimum time – 'where there are no exceptional circumstances, this transaction must be completed within 8 seconds' – and a maximum acceptable time – 'during periods of high volume, the transaction must take no longer than 15 seconds'.
Security	These requirements identify the security levels required for the organisation's data. The majority of organisations handle information and data of varying levels of confidentiality, so security levels are likely to differ accordingly. Some data is highly confidential and requires extremely rigorous security while other data may be confidential but subject to less security.

(Continued)

Table 10.2 (Continued)

Non-functional requirement category	Description
	Security requirements do not only apply to structured data; they are also applicable to confidential information that is unstructured. Examples include commercial information, such as financial reports, and intellectual property, such as product designs that are owned by the organisation.
	Security is not purely a technological issue but is a concern across the entire organisation, encompassing the physical environment, people, network, equipment and machinery, application and data elements. All of these elements need to be considered when defining security requirements.
Access permissions and constraints	These requirements are related to security requirements as they define the stakeholder groups and their levels of access to different areas. The access permissions state which stakeholders are able to have access to defined areas of data, information, applications, product designs, equipment or even buildings. Defining access permissions can be a complex task as typically they need detailed analysis to uncover which individuals or roles can access which elements. They may need to be defined at a very granular level. It is not as simple as 'who can access a particular building'; the permissions need to be considered in terms of the rooms within a building – or even a cupboard or filing cabinet. Similarly, a knowledge repository may require access permissions to be assigned at folder or even document level. This analysis can take a great deal of time but is essential if an organisation's security is to be managed adequately.
Backup and recovery	These requirements define the policy and guidance for protecting against the loss of data and information and are linked to the security requirements. While it is necessary to guard against confidentiality breaches, it is also vital to maintain a backup of the data and have a clear means of recovering that data when necessary.
Archiving and retention	The retention of data and information within an organisation may be subject to internal policies and external legal regulations. These requirements define aspects such as the length of time of the retention, the nature of the archiving approach and the approaches to be taken when disposing of information and data.
Robustness	These requirements are concerned with expectations for how well a solution should handle unexpected situations, the service levels to be provided in these cases, and the approaches to problem investigation and correction.

(Continued)

Table 10.2 (Continued)

Non-functional requirement category	Description
Availability	These requirements set out the timeframe during which a solution, or elements of a solution, must be available to stakeholders. For many online systems, this may be 24/7 (24 hours a day, 7 days a week) availability, or there may be communication requirements to inform stakeholders where an availability issue has arisen. Some solutions may not require this level of availability or may include aspects that accept a lesser level of availability. For example, a telephone enquiry service may need to be available from 8.30 a.m. to 6.00 p.m. each day but should be supplemented by a recorded message service outside these hours.
Usability	This area concerns the ease with which a stakeholder can learn, apply and use new processes and systems. It is a critical aspect of many IT solutions because of the increasing use of online information and purchasing services. Internal business stakeholders can be trained to use new processes and systems, but this is not the case for external stakeholders such as customers. Accordingly, ease of learning and use is very important for many organisations and can make the difference between success and failure. Nielsen (1993) identified five key usability dimensions that are helpful to consider when defining usability requirements: • **Learnability**: How easy is it to learn to use the system? • **Efficiency**: How quickly are tasks completed when using the system? • **Memorability**: How easy is it to remember how to use the system when it has not been used for a while? • **Satisfaction**: How pleasant is it to use the system? • **Error**: How likely is it that errors will be made when using the system? There are many specific aspects that can be defined for usability requirements. For example, learnability may focus on ease of navigation (the number of clicks to obtain information).
Accessibility	These are related to the usability requirements. They are concerned with enabling access for those who may wish to use a system or process but may have difficulty due to infirmity or disability. There are four aspects to consider: • **Cognitive disability**: An individual's ability to comprehend, memorise, calculate and interpret. • **Physical or motor disability**: The impaired mobility of an individual.

(Continued)

Table 10.2 (Continued)

Non-functional requirement category	Description
	• **Hearing disability**: An individual's impaired ability to hear.
	• **Visual disability**: An individual's impaired ability to see.
	These requirements state the need for features that enable accessibility for anyone with a disability. The means of meeting accessibility requirements can be numerous and varied. For example, the use of assistive technology, such as screen reading tools, and images rather than text, or the provision of physical facilities such as access ramps and lifts.
Capacity and scalability	These requirements cover areas such as the volumes of data or images to be stored, the volumes of transactions to be processed and the number of stakeholders to be supported. They are also concerned with the potential to increase the scale of coverage of the solution so that it can accommodate additional transactions or stakeholders.

The non-functional requirements encompass areas that are often described just in overview without clear thought and detailed analysis or are left until a late stage of the project. This can be a critical error. There are numerous tales of organisational disasters – or near disasters – resulting from such relaxed thinking.

- Government organisations have been criticised heavily for losing confidential data or making it accessible when not appropriate.

- Commercial organisations have similar issues; some have promoted new services and then failed to establish the staff and systems capacity to handle the level of interest generated.

- Some websites providing online information and services are shockingly unusable, offering unnecessarily complex navigation and time-consuming error handling.

Business analysts have a range of techniques at their disposal to enable them to explore non-functional requirements and ensure that they are clarified at an early stage rather than being considered as a later (and often more expensive) addition. In a competitive commercial world, organisations cannot afford legal transgressions and business mistakes. It is the work of the business analyst to analyse non-functional requirements and ensure that they are considered in the required level of detail and in sufficient time to be fulfilled by the organisation's processes and systems.

Other types of requirement

This section has described a standard requirement taxonomy that is used across organisations and projects. However, there are other types of requirement that are recognised and applied within business analysis. For example, two key areas are:

- User interface requirements, which describe the interaction between a software product and an actor.

- Transition requirements, which describe the aspects that must be addressed to ensure a successful transition from the existing state to operating the deployed solution.

The areas to be explored for these two types of requirement are described in Table 10.3.

Table 10.3 User interface and transition requirements

Category	Areas to explore
User interface requirements	These are typically related to organisational style guides and standards, defined within the general requirements.
	Style guides determine the required 'look and feel' for the products or documents created within the organisation. The key areas to be defined are:
	• display layout, styles, fonts, font sizes;
	• colour palettes;
	• logos including size and resolution;
	• windows and tabs;
	• navigation styles.
	Accessibility standards specify how the organisation must ensure access for all system users, including anyone with a disability. For example, there may be reference to AEGIS Open Accessibility Framework[1] or the Web Content Accessibility Guidelines (W3C, nd).
	Usability standards define factors that support those using a system. They include aspects such as usability testing and measurement, the use of terminology and help guidance. Specific usability requirements are documented as non-functional requirements (described earlier in this chapter).
Transition requirements	These requirements concern areas such as:
	• data migration; specific areas include sources of data, data migration format, data conversion, data standards;
	• stakeholder communication, documentation and training;
	• business continuity planning, customer service and implementation or release strategies.
	These areas are discussed further in Chapter 14.

The hierarchy of requirements

Requirements do not stand alone but are linked through a hierarchy. They are all driven by the organisation's values, strategy, objectives and performance measures. Where this is not the case, requirements may just reflect ideas or opinions and it is possible that, following further exploration, it is established that they are not needed. An example of a general requirement with hierarchical links to functional and non-functional requirements is represented in Figure 10.5.

Figure 10.5 Example hierarchy of requirements

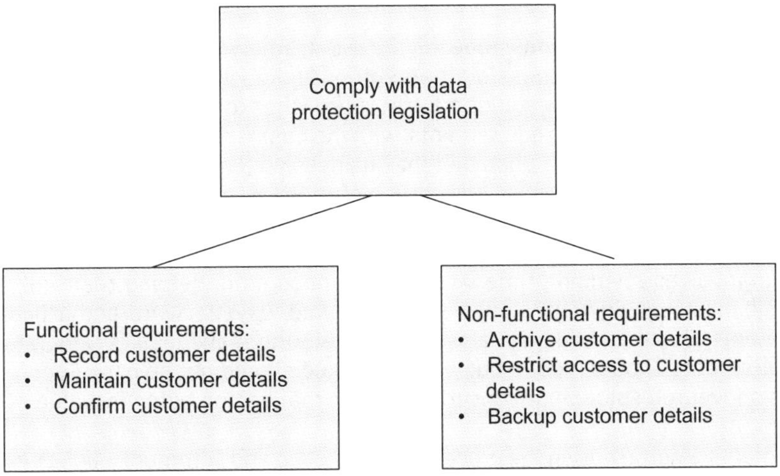

General and technical requirements offer a broad view of the business needs to be met, and the legal and organisational constraints with which solutions should comply. The general requirements set out the overarching vision for any system or business change solution deployed within the organisation; the technical requirements define the infrastructure architecture within which the solution must operate.

The requirements hierarchy has many connections and dependencies and helps to ensure that the requirements are consistent and coherent. The general and technical requirements are elaborated to generate the functional and non-functional requirements to be fulfilled by a solution. As shown in Figure 10.5, data protection legislation defines the principles to be adopted by any organisation that stores personal data. The general requirement to adhere with this legislation is elaborated in the non-functional requirements where the security levels required for specific sets of data, and the requirements concerning access restrictions, backup and recovery, are defined. The functional requirements concerning the data used within a solution are also linked to the security and legal requirements.

Some functional requirements have related non-functional requirements that determine the quality attributes to be achieved; some non-functional requirements apply to several functional requirements.

The hierarchy of requirements, linking functional and non-functional requirements back to the general and technical business requirements, provides a means of tracing the original business driver for the requirements and ensures alignment with business objectives and strategy. This contextual understanding helps to prioritise the requirements, determine the timescale for delivery and assess the possibility of removing a requirement. It also helps to identify the links between requirements when analysing the impact of a change request. While a request may concern just one requirement, it may be that several related or dependent requirements are also affected by the change. The extent of the impact, and the associated costs, must be known before accepting a change.

REQUIREMENTS ELICITATION

The **requirements elicitation** stage of the RE framework is where the business analysts work with the business staff and other stakeholders to 'elicit', or 'draw out' the requirements for the new solution. Early approaches to analysis placed the onus on business staff to identify the requirements, with the business analyst adopting a passive, reactive approach. The assumption that the business staff are readily able to state what is required of a system proved to be a cause of many project challenges and failures. In contrast, requirements elicitation is a proactive approach that seeks to uncover requirements and accepts that it is not possible to merely 'gather' them. Requirements elicitation involves spending time with the business staff, helping them to visualise the possibilities, consider the impacts of suggested ways forward and articulate the requirements. Business analysts also have to help the stakeholders understand that the requirements should meet a business need and should not be based upon opinion, relate to a favoured solution or concern a feature that has no potential value.

Requirements emerge during the process of interaction and communication between the business analyst and project stakeholders. This process is aided by the use of analysis techniques that help to overcome issues such as those related to tacit knowledge and the inability to visualise what an improved system might offer.

Requirements elicitation techniques

Most requirements are based on explicit knowledge and stakeholders are able to articulate them. A **workshop** offers a good forum for beginning the requirements elicitation work and, subsequently, for exploring areas of requirement in further detail. A workshop facilitator needs to select the techniques that will best draw out the requirements from participants; these may be discovery or visualisation techniques, as discussed in Chapter 5. Workshops can be used to initiate requirements elicitation, to help with the analysis of complex requirements, to resolve conflicting requirements or to evaluate prototypes of the proposed solution.

Techniques that have been shown to be particularly effective in eliciting requirements in a workshop include:

- **Visualisation**: Rich pictures, mind maps and fishbone diagrams are extremely useful ways of visualising situations and issues (see Chapter 5).
- **Modelling**: Business process models, data models and use case models are straightforward in drawing and helping to engage participants in discussion.

While the business analyst facilitating the workshop draws the models, business stakeholders provide the information that they represent. Modelling techniques also help to uncover information such as information requirements and business rules. These techniques are described in Chapter 7 (business process models) and Chapter 11 (data and use case models).

- **CSF analysis**: CSFs provide insight into the measures used in an organisation or business area. These measures help to identify the data and reporting requirements for a solution (see Chapter 3).

- **Scenario analysis**: Talking through a step-by-step enactment of a transaction helps to uncover exceptions to the standard process flow and thereby identify alternate pathways and outcomes. Similarly, storytelling offers a way of identifying requirements from exploring stakeholder experiences. Each pathway may be prioritised separately, providing a basis for identifying increments for development or deployment (see Chapter 5).

- **Prototyping**: Prototypes and wireframes may be used in two ways in a workshop: they may be constructed during the workshop as part of an activity to visualise a screen, report or scenario; alternatively a pre-developed prototype may be walked through to validate current thinking, to elicit requirements that have been overlooked or to generate further details about requirements (see Chapter 5).

Interviews provide a structured discussion forum for identifying features and characteristics business managers require. Often, the requirements elicited during interviews are at an overview level and reflect general business needs. These requirements may be decomposed into functional and non-functional requirements that are documented to align with organisational or project standards and can then be prioritised. Reporting and management information requirements also originate from meetings with business managers.

Document analysis helps to explore the stakeholders' specific knowledge of the business area, processes and systems. If the project is to enhance or replace an existing process or system, analysing the current documentation, reports and screens helps to uncover information about actor responsibilities, process flow, reporting requirements and business rules. Documents and screens may well be changed within a new solution, to reflect new business needs and practice, but an analysis of those used currently is likely to cause the analyst to ask specific questions and obtain information. This information assists in the identification and elaboration of requirements, helping in the development of requirements documentation or a solution backlog.

These techniques work well when eliciting requirements that relate to the stakeholders' explicit knowledge. Some techniques, such as **scenario analysis** and **prototyping**, are also sufficiently analytical to assist in uncovering tacit knowledge, as discussed earlier in this chapter.

Tacit knowledge

When eliciting requirements, business staff communicate their explicit knowledge regarding the procedures and data that they can readily identify and easily articulate.

Tacit knowledge refers to other aspects of the work that a stakeholder is unable to articulate or explain. The term derives from the work of Michael Polanyi (1966), whose proposition is succinctly expressed in the maxim 'We can know more than we can tell.' Another way of expressing this is to refer to the 'unknown knowns'.

Requirements are often overlooked because business staff fail to mention them, may be reluctant to state their requirements or may be deterred from doing so because the requirement is complex and not susceptible to a straightforward statement. Business staff often find it difficult to articulate clearly what it is they wish the system to do and problems arise if the analyst fails to use techniques that would have helped to elicit the requirements. The business staff may feel that the need is so self-evident they take it for granted that the analyst is aware of it; this is a **tacit assumption** that is often found to be incorrect. The difficulties associated with taken-for-granted or tacit knowledge are by no means trivial, and in a world of new business practices, business processes and new technology, by no means uncommon. The business analyst is responsible for helping business staff to visualise what they need the new system to do and then to articulate it.

Problems and misunderstandings

Some aspects of tacit knowledge can cause problems and misunderstandings, and include:

- **Skills**: Explaining how to carry out actions using words alone is extremely difficult. For example, conveying the correct sequence of actions required to turn right when driving around a roundabout would be difficult using a narrative description. Even experienced drivers would have difficulty describing this process with complete accuracy largely because they perform the task without having to rationalise each step; they 'know' what to do automatically, without the intervention of conscious thought. Where someone is performing a task with unconscious skill, many steps in the task are performed without the individual being aware that they are done. The introduction of driverless cars has required extensive analysis and questions still remain over the ability of such cars to handle the situations that human drivers encounter regularly.

  When documenting a task that applies unconscious skill, such as driving, a requirements elicitation approach that helps to uncover information about automatic actions is invaluable. **Protocol analysis** is a powerful way to explore unconscious skills and gather the information to document them. This technique involves a member of staff performing the task in discrete steps, talking through each step as it is performed, and repeating this two or three times. This is an approach often used where skills are taught, for example learner drivers shown how to drive a car, and apprentices taught to use equipment.

- **Taken-for-granted information**: Even experienced business staff sometimes fail to mention information or clarify terminology and the analyst may not always realise that further questioning is required. This may result in a gap in understanding and assumptions being made that may not emerge until user acceptance testing or even after implementation; these are likely to be costly and complex to correct. This has also been termed 'not-worth-mentioning' information and is an issue that has been identified as a cause of many project failures. It is not through malice or intention that business staff fail to reveal information about procedure or documentation, they just assume that the information is known. If an analyst fails to ask a question about a particular aspect this may be viewed as confirmation that it does not need to be discussed.

- **Conceptual requirements**: If a study is required to examine a new business area for the organisation, it is very difficult for business stakeholders to conceptualise a relevant solution. There are no existing processes or procedures to describe so it is extremely difficult to produce a detailed definition of the requirements. A visual representation, using a conceptual view such as a BAM or value stream diagram, enables business staff to consider and articulate their requirements more clearly. It may also be helpful to explore possibilities in a **workshop**, using **brainstorming techniques**, **scenarios** and **storytelling**, or building some **wireframes** or **prototypes** to show what a new process or system might offer and how it might look.

- **Tacit assumptions**: This is based upon an apocryphal story about a European explorer who landed in the 17th century on an island and asked a native inhabitant the name of a prominent mountain. He pointed at the landmark he was asking about, but the islanders did not recognise the gesture of pointing to distant objects; the inhabitant assumed that what he was being asked to identify was the outstretched finger. This illustrates the difficulty of an outside party assuming that there is a common language and that the common norms of communication apply. In such situations, cultural and language differences may create many possibilities for confusion and an extended investigation might be required. An **ethnographic study** can be an extremely useful technique in such situations although it requires an extended period of time and a great deal of effort. There are, however, situations where a detailed investigation approach is needed, to ensure that the analysts have sufficient understanding and knowledge to be able to define the business requirements. Without this, the scope for misrepresentation of the situation can grow considerably.

- **Intuitive understanding**, usually born of considerable experience: Decision-makers, such as those working in medical diagnosis or geological surveys, are often thought to follow a logical, linear path of enquiry while making their decisions. In reality though, as individuals acquire decision-making skills and technical knowledge, the linear approach is often abandoned in favour of intuitive pattern recognition. If specialists are asked why they have made a particular judgement, they may talk about the logical thinking process but there is often a point where the logic ends and intuition takes over; this is where knowledge has been applied at a tacit level rather than explicitly. **Protocol analysis** aided by drawing a **decision table** (see Chapter 14) can help with understanding such decisions.

Knowledge categories

There are situations where tacit knowledge is embedded in an organisation and this must be recognised and understood. Examples of organisational tacit knowledge include:

- **Norms of behaviour and communication**: These evolve over time in every organisation. Any new process or system that threatens to conflict with these norms may face resistance.

- **Organisational culture**: The culture of an organisation can be evident through the behaviour of the management and staff. The analyst needs to consider what the behaviour says about the culture of the organisation and ensure that this is taken into consideration when evaluating business changes.

- **Organisation stories**: In an organisation there is typically a shared history of events that have happened in the past. Some of these may relate to projects that have failed or have succeeded in spectacular fashion, and about which stories and humorous tales may have grown over the years. There could be important lessons to learn from these stories, but as they are communicated verbally and are assumed to be widely known, business analysts may not be told the stories and may lack pertinent knowledge, resulting in errors. A **storytelling** session can be fruitful but it needs to happen when situation investigation is under way and before any detailed requirements work is undertaken.

- **Formal and informal networks**: These are discrete groups of workers who may be related by task, department, geographical location or another factor. They have their own sets of experience, norms and practices and, as these are distinct from other groups within the organisation, they are not reflected in the organisation as a whole. A network is likely to have its own body of tacit information, which the members understand well and are not accustomed to sharing openly. If a project involves cross-functional requirements or is company-wide, then it is vital to understand these networks during the elicitation process.

Front story/back story is an explicit knowledge issue that concerns a tendency to frame a description of current working practice more positively than is actually the case – this is known as a favourable 'front story'. This problem may occur if the analysts are perceived to represent business management so are given a favourable version of the business situation. This can be overcome using techniques such as **interviews**, **observation** or **shadowing** to build good working relationships with stakeholders so that the back-story details that clarify the reality of the business operation are revealed.

Table 10.4 categorises areas of tacit and explicit knowledge that apply to individuals and organisations.

Table 10.4 Areas of tacit and explicit knowledge

Level	Tacit	Explicit
Individual	Skills, values, taken-for-granted knowledge, intuitiveness	Task definitions, job descriptions, targets, volumes and frequencies
Corporate	Norms, culture, networks, organisation history, back story	Procedures, style guides, processes, knowledge sharing repositories, manuals, company reports

Techniques to articulate tacit knowledge

Tacit knowledge must be made more explicit if requirements are to be fully understood. The requirement categories, particularly those within the general and technical areas, provide a useful basis for asking specific questions that business staff may not consider relevant or have taken for granted. There are many techniques that business analysts can use to assist business managers and staff to articulate their tacit knowledge and to make this knowledge explicit, through documenting it and disseminating it to the other members of the project team. The process and techniques that help convert tacit knowledge to explicit knowledge are shown in Figure 10.6.

Figure 10.6 Moving from tacit to explicit knowledge

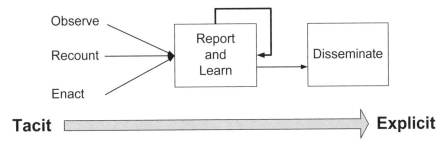

The process for eliciting tacit knowledge shown in Figure 10.6 includes four approaches for uncovering tacit knowledge. These approaches, plus the key techniques used, are:

- **Observe**: observation, shadowing.
- **Recount**: storytelling, scenario analysis.
- **Enact**: prototyping, scenario role-play.

This process reflects that business analysts uncover tacit knowledge using various approaches, allowing their understanding to evolve as they learn more about the particular aspect or requirement.

Business analysts need to possess a toolkit of techniques in order to tailor the requirements elicitation approach to the particular situation and context. Table 10.5 matches some of the most relevant elicitation techniques with the knowledge types that a business analyst may encounter. This mapping of techniques to knowledge types indicates where certain techniques can be particularly useful (✔✔) and where they can still be useful, but to a lesser extent (✔).

Building a requirements list

Initial discussions with stakeholders offer an opportunity to begin identifying requirements. At this point, it is likely that the requirements will be a mix of problems to be addressed, opinion about which changes would be helpful and ideas for new features. These need to be captured so that they aren't overlooked but also need to be reviewed analytically. The initial record may take various forms including outline diagrams, such as context diagrams, more detailed diagrams such as business use case diagrams,

Table 10.5 Techniques and knowledge types (Source: After Eva, 2001, © Assist Knowledge Development Ltd.)

Technique	Explicit knowledge	Tacit knowledge	Taken for granted	Skills	Conceptual requirements	Tacit assumptions
Interviewing	✓✓	✓	✓	✓	✓	✓
Shadowing	✓✓	✓✓	✓✓	✓✓	✓	✓✓
Workshops	✓✓	✓✓	✓✓	✓	✓✓	✓
Prototyping	✓✓	✓✓	✓✓	✓✓	✓✓	✓✓
Scenario analysis	✓✓	✓✓	✓✓	✓	✓✓	✓✓
Protocol analysis	✓✓	✓✓	✓✓	✓✓	✓	✓✓
Storytelling	✓✓	✓✓	✓✓	✓	✓	✓✓

outline user stories or epics, or even partial data models. These documentation styles are discussed in Chapter 11.

A straightforward approach during this early stage is to create a requirements list that captures all of the comments and suggestions that have been elicited. A requirements list is begun following an initial interview or workshop and is extended as more requirements are identified. The requirements identified at this stage are not well-formed and the level and scope may vary considerably; some may be detailed and specific while others may be at an overview level, representing several potential requirements. The requirements list helps to ensure that everything that is raised is recorded and the source identified, and helps to embed traceability in the requirements.

Table 10.6 represents a preliminary requirements list for an inventory project. The comments are added during the first pass at analysis, when each requirement is scrutinised for acceptability. This may be done at any time during elicitation while the list is being compiled. It can be useful to ask another analyst, who was not present at the elicitation session, to review the list as a fresh perspective can often identify questions that may have been missed during the conversation with the stakeholder.

The list of requirements is subject to analysis to ensure that the requirements are well-formed and reflect the business need. The level and type of documentation needed to define requirements depends upon the project context and the organisational standards. For example, the requirements may be defined using user stories, modelled using a use case diagram or data model, or documented as a requirement catalogue entry; this is discussed in Chapter 11.

Table 10.6 Example requirements list

Requirement	Source	Comments
1. We need a customer relationship management (CRM) system	I. Morris	
2. We need to print off a list of expected deliveries	I. Morris	
3. We need to cross-check orders against deliveries	F. Drake	
4. We need to supersede an item	J. Kinder	
5. The system must record the fulfilment of a purchase order on delivery.	J. Kinder	
6. The system must automatically recalculate re-order quantity	J. Kinder	
7. The stores controller must have the facility to adjust re-order quantity	B. Armstrong	
8. We need to create and delete contractors	K. Wyn	
9. We need to return damaged items	F. Drake	
10. We need more accurate stock levels	F. Drake	

REQUIREMENTS ANALYSIS

The **requirements analysis** stage is concerned with ensuring that all of the requirements identified during requirements elicitation have been developed clearly, in a well-organised manner and are appropriately documented. The objective is to identify requirements that overlap, are in conflict with other requirements, are duplicates or need to be separated into individual requirements because they are composite or complex.

Requirements duplication, overlaps and conflicts arise because of different stakeholder viewpoints. Depending upon their role in the organisation, one person might see the solution as providing support for operational business processes, another may think in terms of a 'marketing solution' and a third may view the solution from a customer perspective. All three are describing their perceptions of the same system, but from different viewpoints. It is up to the business analyst to draw the threads together to view the system as a whole, and to meet all three perspectives as well as possible.

Once a set of unique requirements has been identified, each one has to be checked against the business objectives; if a requirement does not support the achievement of a business objective then it is questionable whether or not it is required. This activity highlights where further information must be elicited, which, in turn, is subject to analysis. This iterative process continues until the analyst is content that the requirements have been defined to the desired level of detail and quality.

Some requirements may need to be specified in detail, while others may be defined in outline and developed further through the use of evolutionary prototyping. The extent to which a requirement is defined depends upon several factors including the nature of the requirement, the project context and the approach adopted for the solution development.

Requirements analysis demands a high degree of logical thought, organisation and expertise if the defined requirements are to meet the necessary standard. Only those requirements that are clearly stated, unambiguous, atomic, feasible, aligned with the project objectives, not in conflict with any other requirements and not overlapping with or duplicating other requirements, should be accepted. While the documentation format and level of detail of defined requirements is context-dependent, there remains a need for them to be 'ready' in that they achieve the quality standard that enables further elaboration and solution development.

Whichever solution development approach is adopted for the project, requirements analysis includes the following tasks:

- **Categorising requirements**: It is helpful to categorise requirements into the four specific types of requirement – general, technical, functional and non-functional. Further sub-groupings may be desirable as follows:

  - General, technical and non-functional requirements may be grouped into the categories defined in Figure 10.4.

  - Functional requirements may be grouped by business area or activity, or possibly by use case where this representation of the solution has been created (see Chapter 11 for an explanation of use case diagrams).

  Organising requirements helps the analyst to examine where requirements are related to each other and to check for completeness of the requirements set. Grouping functional requirements by business area, activity or use case helps business stakeholders to prioritise and validate a particular set of requirements and makes it easier to select those to be delivered in an iteration.

- **Modelling requirements**: Various models may be used to represent requirements including use case diagrams and class models. These models enable consistency and completeness to be checked. Modelling techniques are described in Chapter 11.

- **Prioritising requirements**: There are several techniques that may be used to determine the level of priority associated with a requirement. The approach used may vary between organisations but can also vary between different projects within an organisation. Sometimes a straightforward approach of high, medium or low priority is used with the organisation deciding the implications of each level. Similarly, sometimes the categories mandatory, desirable and nice to have are used.

  DSDM defined a richer approach to prioritisation using the acronym MoSCoW. This approach is particularly suitable where several increments of a solution are to be implemented or iterative development is to be used to develop a software product. The MoSCoW acronym stands for the following priority levels (note the 'o' does not denote anything but is used to form the acronym):

- **M**ust have: Mandatory in the current increment under development. It is absolutely essential that these requirements are included as, without them, a solution is not acceptable.

- **S**hould have: Mandatory but may be deferred to the second increment. It is essential that these requirements are included in the solution but their inclusion may be deferred in the short term.

- **C**ould have: Desirable but the solution is acceptable without these requirements as timescale and budget may prevent their inclusion.

- **W**ant to have, but won't have this time: Requirements that are deferred until a later point. There may be business or legal reasons why certain requirements are deferred to be considered at a later point; for example, because they relate to an aspect of the business strategy that is due to be put into operation in the future or to an anticipated legal change. Some requirements are recognised as needing further consideration as they could cause delays to some mandatory requirements if they were implemented earlier.

- **Defining requirements**: Filters may be applied to ensure that the requirements are well defined. These are discussed in the next section.

Requirements filters

The filters listed below are used to examine elicited requirements and build a well-formed set. It is sometimes stated that business analysts working within an Agile project context do not need to consider these filters, as the detail of the requirements is uncovered during the evolutionary product development. However, whether using a formal business requirements document (BRD) or a product backlog, it remains important that any items included are clear, correct and relevant. This can only be achieved if business analysts understand where potential errors may lie and act to ensure that their work achieves the quality standards required to deliver a solution that is fit for purpose and enables the achievement of the desired business outcomes.

Key analysis filters are as follows:

- **Unravelling multiple requirements**: Requirements may have been raised that cover a number of features. These multiple requirements must be split into individual, atomic requirements. An example of a multiple requirement is 'as a receptionist I want to record, amend or cancel a booking'. There are three requirements within this statement and each of them has a level of priority and acceptance criteria. These three requirements need to be defined as individual 'atomic' requirements.

- **Checking for overlapping or duplicate requirements**: Once requirements that cover a similar area are grouped together, it is much easier to find duplicate or overlapping requirements. Where there is duplication, the requirements should be merged; where there are overlapping requirements, they should either be merged or separated into distinct requirements.

- **Confirming relevance of the requirement**: All requirements should be aligned to the business and project objectives. They should also address a root cause of a problem rather than just a symptom of a problem. If this is not the case, it is probable that this is not an actual requirement.

- **Evaluating feasibility**: All requirements should be evaluated to see if they are feasible. There are three aspects that are considered – these are the technical, business and financial feasibility.

  - **Technical feasibility** concerns the availability of technology to fulfil a requirement. Does the technology exist to satisfy the requirement and is it available to the organisation? If the technology is in place, can it cope with the expected volumes and frequency of use? Is it sufficiently robust and secure?

  - **Business feasibility** concerns the likely level of acceptance of the requirement by the business. Does it align with business objectives and strategy? Does it match the organisational culture? Does it contribute to the CSFs?

  - **Financial feasibility** concerns the expenditure required to meet the requirement, the benefits that would accrue from doing so and whether a financial case exists. Is the requirement within the budget? If not, would the extra funding be available? What would be the return on investing in this feature? Imagine a client asking an architect to build a large swimming pool into a new house design without increasing the cost. It is obvious that this would not be possible, but business stakeholders have been known to ask for ambitious additional features without appreciating the cost implications.

- **Removing conflicts**: Some requirements may contradict or conflict with other requirements. When such a conflict is identified, the business analyst is responsible for helping to negotiate a resolution. Sometimes confirming relevance resolves a conflict if only one of the requirements is directly aligned with the business objectives. However, if the sources of the requirements are insistent that they should be delivered, and there is no room for compromise or discussion, then the decision has to be passed to a higher authority. This may be the product owner, the project sponsor or even escalated to a steering committee or project board. Conflicting requirements are often a result of different business perspectives, organisational politics and interpersonal tensions. In these situations, the business analyst needs to tread carefully to avoid alienating any stakeholders. Stakeholder perspective analysis (see Chapter 6) can be very helpful to uncover differences of view at an early stage. Failing to do this is likely to result in conflicting requirements that are difficult to resolve because the stakeholder's opinions are so entrenched.

- **Checking for solutions**: Some requirements do not state a business need to be addressed but instead are a pre-defined solution. Business stakeholders often state how a solution may deliver a feature or characteristic rather than something needed by the business.

- **Confirming quality of expression**: All requirements should meet the following quality criteria:

  - **Clear** – the requirement must be expressed in clear language, avoiding vague adjectives and adverbs and using precise verbs and nouns. Terms such as 'and', 'but', 'except', 'until' should be avoided as they each suggest there is more than one requirement in the statement.

- **Concise** – the requirement must be described concisely. This is not the place to specify data items, triggers or conditions. They are identified at a later point and are often expressed using models. Requirements may be expressed in a sentence or may be defined using formal standards such as use case descriptions or user stories.

- **Consistent** – the requirement must not contradict other requirements and the formats used should be consistent. This reduces ambiguity and confusion and makes requirements validation and solution development much more straightforward.

- **Relevant** – the requirement must be within the scope of the project.

- **Unambiguous** – the description of the requirement must not contain any ambiguity. This can arise because of problems of terminology and jargon, or may result from poor grammar. Common sources of confusion involve the use of synonyms (two words used to mean the same thing) and homonyms (the same word used to mean different things). This is especially relevant when a project crosses a number of business areas. If two people who read a requirement have a different understanding about what should be delivered, then it is ambiguous. Developers and business staff need to compare their understanding of the requirements to be sure that there is no misinterpretation. Use of a glossary of terms within the project helps to guard against such misunderstandings.

- **Correct** – the requirement statement must describe something that is actually required to meet the objectives.

- **Testable** – the requirement should be described such that the solution may be tested to confirm that the requirement has been met. The statement must be worded so that a simple yes or no answer to the question 'Has the requirement been delivered as intended?' makes sense. Non-functional requirements that are relevant to a functional requirement also need to be defined such that they may be tested.

- **Traceable** – information about the requirement must enable the traceability of the requirement. While traceability may be established at different levels, the source of a requirement and the actors to whom it is relevant are usually required. Traceability is discussed in Chapter 12.

The INVEST acronym (Wake, 2003) provides a quality check used to evaluate and improve user stories (see Chapter 11 for discussion of user stories) and other product backlog items. INVEST represents a set of quality attributes, which have similarities to the quality criteria listed above. The original definition is extended in Table 10.7 to incorporate current practice.

Examining the requirements in Table 10.6 in this way yields the following concerns:

1. **We need a CRM system**: This is not a functional requirement relating to CRM but is a strategic decision about the nature of the solution.

Table 10.7 INVEST attributes

INVEST attribute	Each user story/product backlog item:
Independent	Should not be dependent on other user stories but should be discrete and atomic.
Negotiable	Should provide a brief description of a required feature that is a basis for elaboration, clarification and prioritisation through collaborative negotiation.
Valuable to users or customers	Should be outcome or goal focused and offer potential value to customers.
Estimatable	Should be able to be estimated either in terms of its relative size or the amount of development effort it would require.
Small	Should be of a suitable size for iteration planning and development within a timeboxed iteration.
Testable	Should include specific measures that may be tested to evaluate whether or not it has been achieved.

2. **We need to print off a list of expected deliveries**: This is both vague (Who are 'we'? What is meant by 'deliveries'? How soon before they are expected? Why does the list need to be printed?) and is also a solution. The actual requirement is to produce an alert of the deliveries due within the specific time period (today, this week, this afternoon, for instance). The business requirement is not to print the notice. That might well be a good solution, but to put that into the requirement immediately disqualifies other, possibly better, solutions.

3. **We need to cross-check orders against deliveries**: This is unclear – what orders? Deliveries in or out? Cross-check for what? What is the actual business need?

4. **We need to supersede an item**: There is obviously a business function to supersede one item of inventory with another, but it is not clear what the requirement is from this project. This reads like a high-level requirement, and needs a lot of work to understand what information support is needed.

5. **The system must record the fulfilment of a purchase order on delivery of the goods**: This sounds like a clear statement of a business need although 'shall' is preferable to 'must', which could be interpreted as a level of priority.

6. **The system must automatically recalculate re-order quantity (RoQ)**: While this appears to be a clear requirements statement, it sounds like a technically complex operation. There are a series of variables to calculate and the statement does not specify when and how the RoQ is recalculated. Further investigation is needed to elicit this information. Again, 'shall' is preferable to 'must'.

7. **The stores controller must have a facility to adjust RoQ**: This sounds as though it might conflict with requirement no. 6 so negotiation may be needed. Also, 'shall' is preferable to 'must'.

8. **We need to create and delete contractors**: This is a statement of two separate requirements.

9. **We need to return damaged items**: What exactly is the requirement in this instance?

10. **We need more accurate stock levels**: This is both imprecise and a complaint about service rather than a requirement. The problem of inaccurate levels requires investigation; this may be a process or people issue.

If a requirements list is created, it may be updated with these comments so that the way in which the requirement is progressed is clear and traceable. However, it may be that the list is an informal working document that is just used to develop more specific requirements documentation, using the approaches discussed in Chapter 11.

There are several potential outcomes for each requirement from this exercise:

- to accept the requirement as it stands and document it formally so that it may be progressed further;
- to re-word the requirement to remove jargon and ambiguity;
- to merge duplicated or overlapping requirements and re-word them;
- to split composite requirements into their individual entries;
- to raise unclear, ambiguous or conflicting requirements with business staff for clarification.

While this may seem an onerous process, especially when there are numerous requirements, it is necessary to ensure that the requirements are well defined, align with the business and project objectives, and are suitable for further development. Requirements analysis saves time if done well as it results in requirements that are ready for further elaboration whether as input to a formal specification, design and development for a solution, an iteration for timeboxed software development or an evaluation process to support the purchase of an off-the-shelf software product.

Slicing requirements

Requirements are elicited over time and it is not sensible to attempt to complete requirements elicitation before beginning the analysis. Instead, this is an ongoing, iterative process that is likely to be completed in sections rather than focusing on all of the requirements at once. These sections are sometimes referred to as 'slices', and may result in the RE work being completed for a subset of the requirements with others left until a later phase.

When a solution is to be delivered in increments, whether the development approach is linear or uses Agile, it does not make sense to elaborate in detail all of the requirements that have been elicited. Instead, it is more efficient to define and analyse the high priority requirements such that they are in a fit state for the development work to commence.

Requirements analysis is needed for a requirement to be deemed 'ready' as issues, such as a requirement containing multiple requirements, ambiguity, conflicts and duplication, cause problems if they are left unchecked. In the course of this work, it is necessary to carry out three key stages of the RE framework – elicitation, analysis and validation – upon the subset of the requirements, documenting them as appropriate to the project context and type of requirement, and ensuring the required level of traceability.

While this approach in effect 'slices' across the RE framework to break the requirements work into increments, another approach to 'slicing' concerns the requirements themselves. Requirements may be complex, encompassing several scenarios, and it is probable that the scenarios have different levels of priority. For example, a straightforward, typical scenario may be of the highest priority for immediate development and delivery; other scenarios that concern exception situations and happen rarely, may be of much lower priority. In this instance, it may be that only the typical scenario is progressed at the outset, while the other scenarios are deferred to a later release. It is also possible that exception scenarios are removed from the requirements altogether and dealt with through various manual interventions, depending upon the specific circumstances. Viewing requirements through an incremental 'slices' lens that is based upon defined business priorities is often essential if the required timescales for delivery are to be met.

Analysing business rules

Every organisation sets rules that govern how it operates. Business rules are sometimes straightforward to define but there are also rules that are extremely complex. For example:

- An organisation may define a straightforward rule that a customer has to be aged 18 or over to purchase a particular item.

- An organisation may define a complex algorithm for analysing customer purchasing preferences.

Business staff may be aware of some business rules but may not be able to articulate them where the rules have been enforced by software or are complex. It is also the case that some business rules are not mentioned by the business staff because they are taken for granted as tacit knowledge. Business analysts play a key role in uncovering and clarifying business rules and this needs to be done when defining the requirements.

There are two categories of business rule to consider: constraints and operational guidance.

- **Constraints** are rules that govern what may or may not be done. For example, in a car rental organisation, a person may only hire one rental car at a time; a person aged under 21 may not hire a rental car.

- **Operational guidance** sets out the rules that should be applied to decide how a transaction may be conducted, a decision may be made or a figure may be calculated. For example, a set of questions used to determine how a person's identity must be confirmed over the telephone; conditions that determine how a customer complaint should be handled; a series of steps to define how sales commissions should be calculated.

Table 10.8 identifies sub-categories for these two types of business rule and suggests techniques that are helpful to elicit and document the rules.

Table 10.8 Categories of business rule and relevant techniques

Constraints	Techniques
Action governance	Narrative statements that include specific criteria such as those related to age or status
Data constraints	Data models and definitions, CRUD matrices (see Chapter 11)
Operational guidance	**Techniques**
Decision conditions	Activity diagrams, business process models, decision tables, tables, matrices (see Chapters 7 and 14)
Calculations	Arithmetical formulae, Structured English, pseudocode

Business analysts need to be able to elicit and represent business rules in the most appropriate way and need to be able to apply a range of relevant techniques. The techniques listed in Table 10.8 provide a strong basis for business rules analysis.

SUMMARY

RE is a considered approach to uncovering and defining business and solution requirements. The aim of the RE framework is to set out the key activities that should be conducted if the requirements for a solution are to be clearly understood. However, depending on the context, there is considerable variability in the depth and style of the requirements work and the extent to which the requirements are documented and managed.

There is no single way of applying the RE framework. It is not intended to be systematic and prescriptive but to be adapted to different organisational and project contexts as appropriate. While the stages set out in the RE framework are always relevant, the ways in which they are carried out must align with the project context and approach. The business analysts may be tasked with producing a comprehensive requirements document, a set of outline requirements or a backlog of user stories, all of which are ways of defining requirements (see Chapter 11). To do this, they need to possess a good understanding of the different techniques and standards involved in requirements definition and be able to adapt the RE framework as needed.

If a solution is likely to form the backbone of the company's operations for a substantial time or is highly complex, a more disciplined RE approach is likely to be beneficial; if a solution is not replacing a legacy system, is relatively straightforward or is likely to have a short life before needing to be replaced, requirements may be defined in less detail and may evolve during the software development process.

Where organisations place the appropriate emphasis on defining requirements and the business analysts document the requirements according to the needs of the project, there is likely to be a positive impact upon the delivered solutions, enabling business stakeholders to do their jobs effectively and, ultimately, increasing customer satisfaction.

NOTE

1. www.aegis-project.eu/

11 DOCUMENTING AND MODELLING REQUIREMENTS

INTRODUCTION

This chapter introduces some of the most commonly used techniques for documenting and modelling requirements. These techniques are used to record, analyse and specify requirements during solution development. They are extremely useful to clarify understanding and, if cross-checked, to ensure the completeness of the analysis. A model shows only one view, or perspective, of a solution but shows this view very clearly and the process of building a model identifies gaps in understanding. This induces the analyst to ask further questions, often those that have not been identified previously.

A range of documentation styles are described in this chapter. Different styles are relevant depending upon the project context and the approach to solution development. The modelling techniques described have been selected from two distinct approaches to systems modelling: use case diagrams and class modelling from the UML, and entity relationship modelling from the structured, data-driven approaches. The selected techniques model two distinct views of the solution: the functions that the system should offer and the data to be stored within the system.

THE IMPORTANCE OF DOCUMENTATION

There are many reasons for needing good documentation. First, it enables communication within the project team and provides a basis for ensuring that all of the related requirements are consistent with each other. Second, the documentation provides business managers and staff, who are the sources and owners of the requirements, with a firm basis for validating that there is an accurate record of what the solution should provide. Third, any further work to develop and test the business solution uses the documentation as input to these activities. The requirements documentation defines what the solution must offer and the acceptance criteria needed to test that the required features have been delivered correctly. The requirements documentation is also used following the implementation of the solution to support ongoing maintenance and benefits realisation.

The documentation approach differs according to whether the project has applied a linear or Agile approach. When using a linear lifecycle, such as the waterfall lifecycle or 'V' model (see Chapter 13), the requirements are documented prior to the development work, are reviewed and agreed by the business customers and are maintained as changes occur.

When using Agile and the iterative lifecycle, documentation is produced when necessary and to the appropriate level of detail. The requirements are defined in outline at an early stage and changes are applied as more detail emerges during the product development. The documentation is then revised and extended in line with the software product that has been released into operation.

DOCUMENTATION STYLES

There are various ways in which requirements may be recorded. Some are narrative techniques while others are diagrammatic. The skill of the business analyst lies in selecting which techniques are applicable given a particular situation. Factors to consider when deciding the relevant documentation style are as follows:

- The development approach to be applied on the project: Is a linear or Agile approach required? Is a BRD needed or is a backlog of user stories being built?
- The type of requirement: Is this a general requirement that can be summarised in one sentence or a functional data requirement that should be defined using a data model? Is this a non-functional requirement regarding access permissions to be defined at an actor or function level?

The key differences between defining requirements when using a linear approach, whether waterfall or incremental, or where the project is applying Agile, is in the style and level of documentation that is produced. If the former, the aim is to produce a baselined set of good, complete, relevant well-formed requirements before a solution is specified and designed (or purchased). Agile, on the other hand, is concerned with evolving the requirements during development, so much of the detail is not specified in advance; however, it is good practice for the requirements to be defined with sufficient clarity, as this helps to prioritise the requirements, provides a basis for iteration definition and planning, and ensures there is a basis for the development work.

The advantage of Agile is that it reduces the maintenance overhead of managing a detailed requirements document while the solution is being developed. It also removes the redundant work that may be involved in specifying requirements early on, only to see them change, and change again, before implementation. Drawbacks are that it could lead to inconsistencies and scope creep, as focusing on individual requirements can lead the developers to overlook the vision for the solution and the business objectives. Also, unless there is a strong project structure in place, there is a danger that traceability is compromised and, in future years, maintainability could present a problem where the documentation is insufficiently detailed. Agile works particularly well in a dynamic environment where requirements are unclear at the outset, change is likely and a short timescale has been set to deliver some key features.

The key documentation styles available to business analysts are as follows:

- **Text-based**: requirements catalogue; user story.
- **Diagrammatic**: data model; use case model; business process model.

A requirements catalogue is usually produced where a project is applying a linear lifecycle. The depth of the catalogue depends upon the characteristics of the project; for example, whether the software product will be developed internally, outsourced for development or purchased. User stories are the typical documentation style used to define the requirements within an Agile context as they offer a format that supports the collaborative approach. However, it is often the case that other styles, such as models, are needed to supplement text-based descriptions in order to identify gaps in understanding, ensure consistency, clarify business rules or provide additional information.

REQUIREMENTS CATALOGUES

When requirements are elicited, they tend to be unorganised and it is only once requirement analysis takes place that they are structured and formed into an organised set. When building a requirements catalogue, the requirements are defined using a template listing the key characteristics to be described for each requirement. The range of characteristics that may be documented about each individual requirement are defined in Table 11.1. An extensive list of characteristics is described; however, the exact set of characteristics used to define requirements typically depends upon the organisational standards and project context.

Table 11.1 Characteristics documented for requirements

Characteristic	Description
Requirement identifier	The unique identifier allocated to the requirement. This is often a code that is linked to the type of requirement. For example, the technical requirements may be allocated the identifier T-n, such as T-001, T-002, etc. The identifier may also include a version number, including a draft version number for when the requirement is still to be reviewed and agreed. An identifier may be:
	G-006v0-1 to indicate a general requirement in its first draft version;
	F-028v2-0 to indicate a functional requirement in its second reviewed and agreed version.
	Alternatively, the version history for the requirement may include the version number.
Requirement name	The name allocated to a requirement. This is a short descriptive phrase that indicates what the requirement concerns.

(Continued)

283

Table 11.1 (Continued)

Characteristic	Description
Requirement description	The description should provide a clear definition of the requirement. Initially, the description may be at an outline level and elaborated in more detailed versions of the requirement documentation.
	When describing requirements it is good practice to adopt the following structure:
	• actor (or user role); an alternative is to state 'the solution' (or system)
	• verb phrase; it is helpful to use the convention 'shall' as other words, such as 'must' or 'should', may be confused with priority levels
	• object (noun or noun phrase)
	An example functional requirement using this structure is: 'the receptionist shall be able to view the customer name, address and telephone number'.
	An example general requirement using this structure is: 'the solution shall comply with the provisions of the GDPR'.
Source	The originating person or information source for the requirement. This may be a stakeholder or could be a document containing information relevant to the project. For example, a stakeholder may have identified the requirement during an interview or other discussion; or, there may be an earlier document – such as a project brief or feasibility study – that states some of the business requirements.
Owner	The business stakeholder who can make decisions regarding the requirement. Typically, this is the business manager responsible for the business function or department, who has the authority to approve the definition of the requirement.
Author	The analyst who has elicited and documented the requirement.
Type of requirement	The categorisation of the requirement. It may be sufficient to indicate whether the requirement is general, technical, functional or non-functional – although it may not be necessary to state this if the identifier includes a reference to the type. The type of requirement may be defined at sub-category level, for example, a requirement may be 'General, Legal'.
Priority	The level of priority of the requirement. The approach used depends upon the organisational standard and can also vary between different projects within an organisation. Prioritisation approaches are described in Chapter 10.

(Continued)

Table 11.1 (Continued)

Characteristic	Description
Business area	The name of the business area to which the requirement belongs. This may be the name of the business function or department. Alternatively, a more detailed approach may be useful and the name of the relevant business process or use case may be used.
Stakeholders	The job roles or names of any stakeholders with a particular interest in the successful resolution of this requirement, and the details of their interest. Identifying stakeholders and their interests for each requirement provides a useful prompt to the business analyst to ensure that all relevant stakeholders' interests have been considered.
Associated non-functional requirements	Some functional requirements are associated with specific non-functional requirements. For example, the organisation may have a customer service policy that guarantees a speed of response to information requests. As a result, the functional requirement about accessing customer account information may have a performance response time non-functional requirement associated with it. An alternative approach is to document related requirements (described below).
Acceptance criteria	The criteria that enable business staff to formally agree that the requirement has been delivered. For each requirement, the criteria should be identified that will determine if it has been met.
Related requirements	The identifiers of any requirements that are related to this requirement. They may be related for several reasons: there is a higher-level business requirement that provides further business information or justification for a functional or non-functional requirement; there are non-functional requirements concerning areas such as usability or security that affect functional requirements or vice versa; there are other requirements that concern a similar general, technical, functional or non-functional area. The identifier for each of the related requirements should be recorded.
Related documents	The identifiers for any documents that provide further information about this requirement. These documents may be project documentation such as the PID or may be business justification documents such as the business case. Another form of documentation that may be linked to the requirements are the modelling documents that have been created for the business change project. Some of these models may be contained within the requirements document; however, it is still useful to show where there are other requirements that are related to them.
Comments	Additional comments (including questions to be resolved) that the analyst feels are useful to document for a particular requirement.

(Continued)

Table 11.1 (Continued)

Characteristic	Description
Rationale	The business justification for the requirement. The rationale for a requirement may be cross-referenced to specific benefits in the business case.
Resolution	The outcome of a requirement. There are several possible outcomes: a requirement may be implemented, deferred for consideration in a later increment, merged with another requirement or dropped. The resolution is used to record the decision and the timing of this decision. This information is needed to ensure the traceability of a requirement should the business representatives question why a requirement has not been delivered.
Version history	The history of the requirement through the different versions that have been created. This information should include the version number (although as discussed earlier, this may be combined with the identifier) and the date. Each version should also record the reason for the change to the requirement and reference the change control documentation.

Producing a full definition for each requirement can be extremely time-consuming and could waste time and effort if the details provided are not needed. The level of detail of the definition depends upon several factors:

- **The stage of the analysis**: Is this an initial view of the requirements or a more detailed requirements specification?

- **The nature of the solution**: For example, a business process change is likely to require a detailed description of the new tasks and IT support.

- **The level of priority of each requirement**: This is an essential piece of information that is used to prioritise the requirements work. For example, if a requirement is to be deferred for consideration in a later increment, the detailed work to define the requirement should also be deferred until it is to be included in the solution.

- **The approach to be adopted to deliver the solution**: For example, a bespoke development is likely to need more detailed requirement definitions than those needed to evaluate an off-the-shelf software product.

Some aspects of a requirements catalogue definition emerge earlier than others. Initially, only the identifier, name, description, source and author are needed. However, following detailed requirements analysis, additional aspects such as the owner and priority are recorded. After the requirements catalogue has been structured and duplicate or overlapping requirements removed, related requirements are identified. Cross-referencing to other documents or models is typically a later requirements analysis activity and may not be required. The resolution of a requirement is recorded once a decision has been made about if and when a requirement is to be fulfilled. The version history is only required if a requirement changes.

Where a requirements catalogue is developed, it forms a central information repository throughout a business change project. It records what is required, the business justifications, sources of information and a rich network of connections. The level of the descriptions must be sufficient to meet the desired outcomes rather than over-engineered for any eventuality, and this requires business analysts to build a requirements catalogue using analytical skills rather than merely completing a template.

A useful distinction is to separate *what* is required from *how* it will be delivered. Sometimes requirements catalogues stray into solution territory, defining how a requirement should be met rather than focusing on what is actually needed. A typical example is where a 'requirement' states that a 'customer database' is needed rather than identifying the feature, characteristic or output the stakeholders want the solution to offer.

Stakeholders are sometimes criticised for their inability to describe a requirement in extensive and precise detail; however, this is to miss the point of a requirements catalogue. A requirement description should be clear about what is required but is unlikely to contain every detail. The template shown in Table 11.1 offers a clear and exhaustive set of characteristics but this does not mean that each characteristic should be specified for each requirement. It is often the case that business staff have stated in overview what is needed while allowing for some of the finer detail to emerge during further analysis or development activities. Attempting to specify requirements in detail at an early stage can cause errors, inventions and, eventually, substantial change. The requirements catalogue should contain information about what is required, leaving further detail to be explored using other analysis techniques such as modelling or prototyping.

USER STORIES

User stories tend to be used when a project is applying an Agile software development approach, although this is not necessarily the case as they offer a useful approach for discussing requirements. They define, in outline, the features actors require from a system. They are written from an actor, or user role, perspective and set out what is required by an individual or group. They may be written for all types of requirements but are most suitable for functional requirements. Other requirement types often require alternative formats to express the essence of the requirement and, particularly in the case of non-functional requirements, need a more precise definition.

User stories are relatively quick to develop as they do not include several entries found within a requirements catalogue description such as the owner, source and justification. They provide an informal description of a requirement that is explored through further discussion. They are often said to provide a basis for a more detailed conversation, with this conversation taking place between the user role (or a representative) and a software developer. User roles are discussed in Chapter 5.

The intention behind the user story technique is that the outline requirement is identified but the detail of how it is delivered is subject to discussion, prototyping and evolutionary development. This ensures that the software required to fulfil user stories is developed as rapidly as possible and delivered into operation when needed.

Key underlying principles for user story development are summarised in the 3Cs framework:

Card: Each user story is documented using a card format; this limits the amount of information about the user story.

Conversation: Each user story is the basis, or 'placeholder', for a conversation where the user story is explored in further depth.

Confirmation: Each user story can only be deemed to have been fulfilled if it is evaluated against defined acceptance criteria and it is confirmed that these criteria have been met. The acceptance criteria for a user story set out how to determine if the goal of the user story has been fulfilled.

The user story format answers the questions, Who? What? Why? and is expressed in the format: 'As a {user role} I want {feature} so that I can {reason}.' Therefore, when developing user stories, the following standard format is used:

As a ... (who is the user role or actor?)
I want ... (what capability or feature is needed by the user role?)
so that ... (why is the user story beneficial to the user role?)

User stories are recorded in a product backlog, typically in the order of their priority. The priority level determines the relative importance of a user story to the overall product and indicates when it should be selected for inclusion within an iteration.

The effort required to develop user stories is defined using estimated units called 'story points'. The number of story points required to deliver a particular user story is estimated by comparing it with other user stories that have already been delivered. Comparing the relative size and complexity of completed user stories provides a basis for estimating the delivery effort of the user stories still to be delivered.

An example user story, including priority and confirmations, is shown below.

Name: View order
As a registered customer
I want to view the orders I have placed for products
So that I can track when the products will be delivered

Priority: Should have
Story points: 8
Confirmations:

- Only registered customers are able to view orders
- Each registered customer can view orders they have placed
- Only orders placed by the registered customer will be displayed
- Information about product location will be displayed for orders not yet fulfilled
- The delivery date will be displayed for all products that have been delivered

User stories can be extremely complex or contain compound requirements. Where this is the case, they are often referred to as 'epics' and each epic may be decomposed into several individual user stories. It is helpful to do this as it is more straightforward to prioritise, analyse, explore and develop the decomposed user stories. It is also the case that many epics relate to business use cases rather than system use cases and, as a result, reflect a more holistic view. Achievement of the goal of an epic may drive changes to all of the POPIT elements rather than just the software under development.

MODELLING FUNCTIONAL REQUIREMENTS

The saying 'one picture is worth ten thousand words' is always worth bearing in mind when defining requirements. It is extremely difficult, if not impossible, to write textual statements that are completely unambiguous and provide a clear, holistic picture of the target solution. In contrast, models are excellent at providing a picture of the entire solution and confirming that requirements are in scope. Further, the notation used to build models ensures clarity and correctness. Each box, annotation and connection makes a definitive statement about the solution under investigation that cannot be misinterpreted. They can be incorrect if the information provided is not correct but the clarity provided by a model prompts questions to be asked that highlight errors and facilitate corrections.

Some models are more easily understood by business stakeholders than others. Flow charts, such as business process models and activity diagrams, can be interpreted with little knowledge of modelling. Models with a more technical focus, such as use case diagrams and data models, usually require some guidance regarding the notation if they are to be understood. However, if these diagrams are built collaboratively with business stakeholders and use standard business terms, most people can understand them and contribute to their development.

Business process models and activity diagrams are discussed in Chapter 7 and data models are explained later in this chapter. Use case diagrams are described below.

Modelling business use cases

Use case models provide a diagrammatic representation of the actors who will engage with the system and the features the actors need to access. They are an excellent technique to use with business stakeholders as they represent their view of the solution so can be developed during meetings and workshop discussions. They should be developed using an 'outside in' approach, whereby the solution is shown initially as a 'black box' and the actors, and the features they require of the solution, are analysed. This initial diagram is known as a 'context diagram' and it has many uses in that it provides:

- A statement of where the solution fits within an organisation and the wider business context.
- An initial view of the scope of a solution by defining the actors and their interactions with it. The actors may be people, organisations or systems.
- A means of exploring each of the major interactions with the solution.
- A basis for identifying the individual use cases to be available to the actors.

Figure 11.1 shows a context diagram for a retail organisation that sells products via its website.

Figure 11.1 Context diagram for a retail organisation

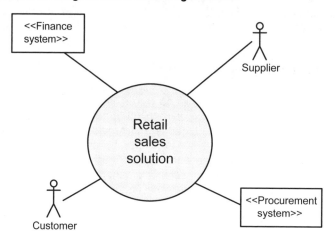

The context diagram is developed into a business use case diagram. This provides a high-level view of an organisation or business system and can be extremely useful when scoping a project or gaining an overview of the areas to be investigated and analysed. A business use case diagram shows the set of features that stakeholders require from a solution. Each individual use case represents a particular feature that an actor wishes to undertake through interacting with a solution. An example business use case diagram is shown in Figure 11.2.

Figure 11.2 Business use case diagram for a retail organisation

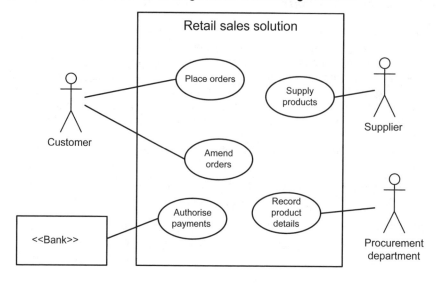

Some of the use cases on a business use case diagram may be fulfilled by a software product but for others this may be only partially the case, and for some the solution may be an entirely manual business process. The use cases that may be delivered by a software product provide a basis for developing a system use case diagram; these are discussed in the next section.

Some business analysts wish to distinguish business use case diagrams from system use case diagrams by drawing a 'stripe' across the actors and use cases. This notation is shown in Figure 11.3.

Figure 11.3 Business use case diagram using additional notation

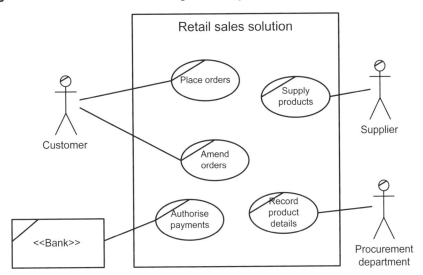

This notation can be helpful where both business and system use case diagrams are developed for a project. The use case diagram notation is discussed in further detail in the next section.

Modelling system use cases

The system use case diagram depicts the functions to be provided by the system and the actors who wish to interact with those functions. A function may be defined as a set of actions that business staff want the system to support in order to achieve a specific goal; for example, a sales manager may wish to access a function that allows customer details to be entered and stored. This may be represented as a use case called 'Record customer' that would include the following actions:

- accept the customer details;
- validate the customer details;
- store the customer details that have been entered.

The UML defines the elements described in Table 11.2 for inclusion in use case diagrams:

Table 11.2 Notation elements for use case diagrams

Use case element	Description
Actors	Whoever or whatever expects a service from the system. They are usually user roles but also may be external systems or time. On a use case diagram, actors are shown interacting with the use cases. As they are external to the system and outside its control, defining the actors and the use cases they are associated with helps to define the system boundary or scope.
	Actors are usually shown as matchstick figures (particularly when drawn by hand); however, the figure notation can vary depending upon the support tool used to draw the diagram and the type of actor. The diagrams in this chapter were drawn using Microsoft Visio® so have used a generic figure. If a software product is an actor, it may be shown using a rectangle with the stereotype <<actor>> shown before the name of the system. Some analysts prefer to show all actors, including the job roles, as rectangles because business staff can feel that matchstick figures trivialise the diagrams. Time can also be an actor and may be shown as a rectangle or figure.
Use case	A use case is something that an actor wants a system to do; it is a 'case of use' of the system by a specific actor and describes the interaction between the actor and the system. Each use case has a stated goal and contains a description of the actions that a system must perform to achieve this goal. Use cases are shown as ovals and represent the functions that the system should perform in response to a triggering event initiated by the actor. The 'verb noun' convention is used to name use cases. For example, 'Set up project' or 'Book room'.
System boundary	The boundary of the system to be delivered is indicated by drawing a large box around all of the use cases, leaving the actors outside the box. This clearly illustrates the boundary of the system and where the interactions cross this boundary. A defined boundary that distinguishes between the work conducted within the system and the external actors is very useful when agreeing the scope of the system.
Associations	The associations indicate which actors need to interact with which use cases. Lines are drawn linking actors with the appropriate use cases.

The use case diagram in Figure 11.4 shows part of the retail sales system. Use case diagrams are often created during a workshop or following interviews with business stakeholders.

Figure 11.4 System use case diagram for a sales system

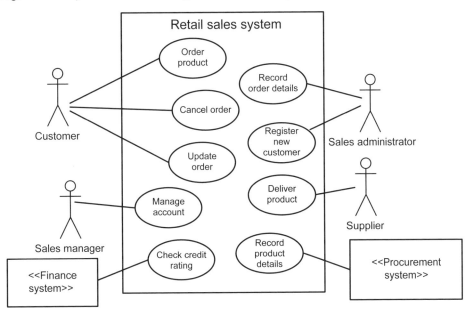

Use case diagrams are very useful during workshop or focus groups discussions because they are so easily understood by the business stakeholders and provide an excellent basis for considering requirements.

Use case descriptions

The detail of an interaction between an actor and a use case is documented in a use case description. Use case descriptions may be defined in outline or in detail. At the outset, the use case diagram shows the actor interacting with a named use case. This information is then supplemented by an outline use case description, which typically includes the following elements:

- Name of the actor interacting with the use case.

- Name and identifier for the use case.

- The goal to be achieved by the use case.

- Overview list of the actions that conduct the work of the use case.

- Exceptions leading to alternative scenarios.

Each use case encompasses different scenarios, each of which results from exchanges of information and requests, and the application of conditions. For example, if a product is requested, the information about the product is provided by the actor and this is then subject to a stock level condition. If the product is available, the order is accepted; if the product is not available, a further information exchange takes place whereby the actor can decide whether to accept an alternative or cancel the original product request.

An example outline use case description is shown in Table 11.3.

Table 11.3 Example outline use case description

Actor name	Sales administrator
Use case name	Register new customer
Goal	Set up customer record
Actions	1. Confirm customer is new to system
	2. Enter customer personal details
	3. Enter customer email address
	4. Confirm customer details
	5. Request issue of customer login and password
Alternative scenarios	1a. Customer already known to system
	3a. Customer does not have email account

Use case descriptions are sometimes extended to include the details of the steps that take place during an interaction. These are sometimes called 'fully described' use case descriptions and comprise structured, text-based descriptions that are similar to a documented scenario. These descriptions define the sequence of interactions using short, precise statements. Quality criteria are typically applied to ensure that the use case description is testable, unambiguous, correct, clear and relevant.

A fully described use case description includes the following elements:

- Name of the actor interacting with the use case
- Name and identifier for the use case.
- The goal to be achieved by the use case.
- The event that triggers the use case.
- The preconditions that need to be satisfied in order for the use case to begin.
- The post-conditions that are in place once the use case has completed.
- The list of actions that comprises the interaction, including the main success scenario ('happy day' scenario).
- The extensions to the scenario; the 'alternative flows' through the use case.

- The priority for the use case. This may be defined for the entire use case or for each of the main success and extension scenarios.
- The frequency and volumes related to the use case.

An example fully described use case is shown in Table 11.4.

Table 11.4 Example of fully described use case description

Actor name	Sales administrator
Use case name	Register new customer
Goal	Set up customer record
Event	Sales administrator receives request to register new customer (from customer unable to register online)
Preconditions	Sales administrator is logged into the system
	Sales administrator has permission to access new customer registration function
Post-conditions	New customer is registered on system
Main success scenario	1. Sales administrator selects 'new customer registration'
	2. System requests customer name and address
	3. Sales administrator enters customer name and address
	4. System confirms customer is new to system and requests additional information
	5. Sales administrator enters additional personal details: date of birth, telephone number, data usage agreement, contact requirements
	6. System accepts additional personal details and requests email address
	7. Sales administrator enters customer email address
	8. System accepts customer email address and requests confirmation of details
	9. Sales administrator confirms customer details
	10. Sales administrator requests issue of customer login and password
	11. System confirms issue of customer login and password
	12. Sales administrator exits 'new customer registration'

(Continued)

Table 11.4 (Continued)

Actor name	Sales administrator
Alternative flows (extensions)	4a. System identifies duplicate customer record and requests confirmation that this is a new customer
	4a1. Sales administrator confirms this is a new customer
	4a2. Return to step 5
	7a. Customer does not have an email address. Sales administrator requests use of alternative contact details.
	7a1. System requests alternative contact details.
	7a2. Sales administrator enters alternative contact details.
	7a3. Return to step 10
	9a. Sales administrator identifies error in customer details
	9a1. Sales administrator re-enters customer details
	9a2. Return to step 9
Priority	Should have
Frequency/volumes	1 request per week

Fully described use case descriptions may also include any non-functional requirements that are associated with the use case. For example, there may be speed of response and security requirements specified for the use case.

Whereas many use case descriptions are text-based (as in the examples above), it is often helpful to represent the processing carried out within a use case using modelling techniques; for example, activity diagrams offer an effective means of representing main success and extension scenarios clearly. Techniques such as decision tables can also be used to represent conditions and actions succinctly and clearly.

The <<include>> and <<extend>> constructs

When exploring the use cases, it often emerges that some processing scenarios are repeated within several use cases. In the retail system, for example, many use cases may confirm the customer identity before commencing the remaining processing. This would require the steps involved in confirming the customer identity to be included in each use case, resulting in significant duplication and the possibility that they are defined differently in the various use cases. An alternative, more efficient, approach is to remove the customer identification processing to a separate use case and show with an 'include' link to the original use cases. This is represented in Figure 11.5 where the <<include>> stereotype is shown on a dotted line with an arrowhead pointing to the included use case.

Figure 11.5 Use case diagram showing <<include>>

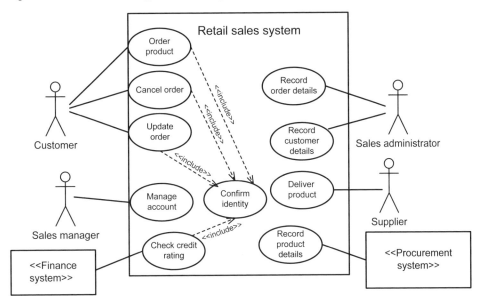

It may also emerge during more detailed investigation and specification that there are some extension scenarios within use cases that have not been prioritised as mandatory (or 'must have' within MoSCoW as described in Chapter 10). This means that this processing will be developed during a later iteration or will be incorporated within a later software release. In this situation, a separate use case can be created to 'extend' the original use case; for example, there may be an extension scenario to record an order for an item that is out of stock but expected to be available in the near future. This extension is shown as an additional use case and is said to 'extend' the original use case. Figure 11.6 shows how this extend relationship should be represented on a use case diagram. In this case, the new use case 'Record out of stock order' is linked to the original use case 'Order product' by a dotted line with an arrowhead.

The <<include>> and <<extend>> concepts allow use cases to be connected to each other under these specific circumstances. This is the only way that use cases are linked as these diagrams are not intended to show the flow – or sequence – of the processing.

MODELLING DATA REQUIREMENTS

A data model allows the stakeholders who use the system, or obtain information from it, to agree the data that is to be recorded and accessed. It also provides the basis for the database design in a bespoke development or helps in the evaluation of a packaged application. Data modelling should not just be the province of system developers or IT professionals; it is a key tool for the business analyst. It helps the analyst to understand the business rules that govern the creation, manipulation and deletion of data within an organisation and the data required to support business process improvements. It also

Figure 11.6 Use case diagram showing <<include>> and <<extend>>

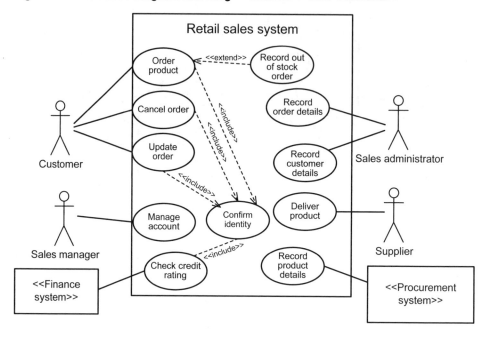

provides a mechanism for communicating the data requirements to those responsible for the design and development of a software product. There are two standard techniques used to model data: entity relationship modelling and class modelling (from UML). Both techniques are described below.

Entity relationship diagrams

Organisations require clear and accurate definitions of the data structures that underlie their information requirements. Data is the raw building block of all information systems and the objective of data modelling is to express this structure in a concise and usable way. Data modelling is concerned with identifying and understanding:

- The data items (attributes) that the organisation (or system) needs to keep.
- The grouping of the attributes (into entities).
- The relationships between entities.

There are several different notation sets used to build entity relationship diagrams (ERDs). The notation used in this chapter is that developed by Harry Ellis and Richard Barker, which is sometimes known as the CACI notation (after the consulting firm where Ellis and Barker worked at the time). This notation was also used within the Structured Systems Analysis and Design Method (SSADM).

Entities

An entity is something that the enterprise recognises in the area under investigation and wishes to collect and store data about. An entity might be:

- **Physical**: For example, Order, Customer, Supplier.
- **Conceptual**: For example, Booking, Appointment.
- **Active**: For example, Meeting, Course.

Entities are represented on the model by a 'soft' box; this is a rectangle with rounded corners. Each entity has a meaningful name, normally a noun, which is always singular. It is necessary to distinguish between two different concepts: the 'entity type' and the 'entity occurrence'. For example, in a bookstore system, if there is an entity type 'Book', then each entity occurrence is a specific instance of a book, such as *Business Analysis* or *Data Analysis for Database Design*. Similarly, in a payroll system, if there is an entity type 'Employee', then each entity occurrence is a specific person employed by the organisation. The physical equivalent of an entity type is a table, and of entity occurrence, a record.

'Entity types' are usually referred to as 'entities' but entity occurrences are referred to using the full term. Individual occurrences of an entity must be uniquely identifiable. For example, in a sales system each Customer or Order would have a unique identifier such as account-number or order-number. This means that an individual customer or order may be found if the identifier is known.

Attributes

Entities contain and are described by 'attributes' (or more accurately, 'attribute types'). For example, the entity 'Book' might be described by the following attributes: title, author-name, publisher, price. Attributes are sometimes known as data items. An attribute's physical equivalent is a field.

A specific entity occurrence should be uniquely identifiable if the value of an attribute or combination of attributes is known. For example, a member may be identified by the attribute member-number, or a specific book recognised from the combination of the two attributes author and title. The identifying attribute or combination of attributes is known as the 'key' to the entity.

The initial entities and some attributes are identified from the interview notes, documents and observations collected during the investigation of the current system. Existing file or database content, current reports and information needs identified by business staff also help to identify entities and their attributes. Attributes may be shown on the ERD itself but this is not usually done as the diagram can become difficult to read. Instead, the attributes are typically defined in supporting documentation (entity descriptions, attribute descriptions) or recorded in a support tool such as a data dictionary.

Relationships

A relationship is a relevant business connection between two entities. A relationship is represented on a data model by a line linking the associated entities. The precise nature of a relationship between two entities is known as the 'cardinality'. The cardinality of a relationship may be:

- One to many (1:m): each instance of entity A is related to many instances of entity B.

- One to one (1:1): each instance of entity A is related to one instance of entity B.

- Many to many (m:m): each instance of entity A is related to many instances of entity B and each instance of entity B is related to many instances of entity A.

It is good practice to name the relationships on the model so as to provide anyone viewing it with more information about the nature of the relationship. This is discussed later in this chapter.

One to many relationships   Relationships are often of the degree one to many (1:m). For example, if modelling a system to hold data about a company, an Employee is allocated to one Office, but each Office must have one or more Employees allocated to it. This is shown in Figure 11.7. A 'crow's foot' notation is used to indicate that an Office is related to between one and many Employees. At the other end, the single solid line indicates that an Employee is related to exactly one Office.

Figure 11.7 One to many relationship between two entities

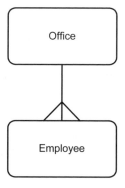

Similarly, in an order processing ERD there is an obvious 1:m relationship between Customer and Order. A customer places one or many orders but a particular order is placed by only one Customer.

One to one relationships   Figure 11.8 shows that an order is related to one invoice and an invoice is concerned with only one order. The relationship between the two entities is exactly one to one. A solid line is used to indicate that the relationship is exactly one.

These relationships are not permitted in some data modelling approaches and, where this is the case, it is usually suggested that the two entities are merged. If this happens, one of the identifiers is selected to identify the merged set and the entity is named accordingly. An identifier is the attribute or set of attributes used to identify the entity.

Figure 11.8 One to one relationship between two entities

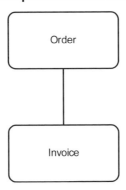

The identifier that is created first is usually used to identify the entity created from the merged entities. If the Order and Invoice entities from the example above were merged, the identifier for the Order entity is likely to be the chosen identifier as the Order is created before the Invoice.

Optionality More detailed information about the business rules that underpin the data model is represented by the optionality of the relationship between two entities. The optionality of the relationship describes whether or not the entities at both ends of the relationship must co-exist or whether one entity can exist without the other. Where there is not optionality and both entities must always co-exist, the relationship is drawn using a solid line. In the examples in Figures 11.7 and 11.8, the entities are joined by a solid line. This indicates that both entities must exist and that neither can be stored on a system without the other being present; this is called a fully mandatory relationship. Another example of this type of relationship is shown in Figure 11.9. In this case, each Order input to the system must always have at least one Order line and each Order line must be related to exactly one Order.

Figure 11.9 Fully mandatory one to many relationship

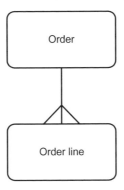

The opposite of a fully mandatory relationship occurs where a relationship is fully optional. This means that both entities can exist completely independently of each other. In the example in Figure 11.10 the relationship is shown using a dotted line. This indicates that an Order can be placed without a Customer call being made and a Customer call need not result in an Order.

Figure 11.10 Fully optional one to many relationship

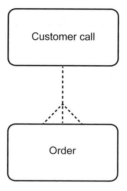

The remaining two alternatives reflect that relationships need to be analysed in two directions: from the 'one' end of the relationship, where the parent or master entity is represented, to the 'many' end of the relationship, where the child or detail entity is shown.

In the example in Figure 11.11, a Customer may not have placed any Orders as yet but an Order must always be placed by a Customer. This means that there is an optional Customer to Order relationship and a mandatory order to customer relationship. In other words, the parent entity (Customer) can exist without any child entities (Order) but a child entity (Order) must have a parent (Customer).

Figure 11.11 Mandatory parent entity with optional child entity

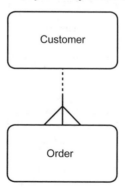

Figure 11.12 shows the opposite situation, where the parent entity (Complaint) must be linked to at least one child entity (Order), but each child entity (Order) can exist without a parent (Complaint). The example in Figure 11.12 shows that an Order need not be related to any Complaints but a Complaint must be linked to at least one Order.

Figure 11.12 Optional parent entity with mandatory child entity

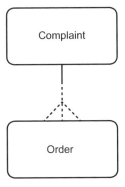

Many to many relationships   Many to many (m:m) relationships occur frequently. For example, as shown in Figure 11.13, an employee may be assigned to one or more projects and a project may have one or more employees assigned to it.

Figure 11.13 Many to many relationship

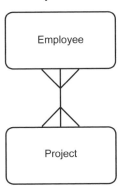

Many to many relationships are normally decomposed into two 1:m relationships with the definition of an additional entity known as a 'link entity'. Figure 11.14 shows how the link entity Assignment has been added so that the many to many relationship can be removed. The extended structure shows the following:

- An Employee is linked to one or more Assignments and an Assignment is for exactly one Employee.

- A Project is linked to one or more Assignments and an Assignment is for exactly one Project.

Figure 11.14 Resolved many to many relationship

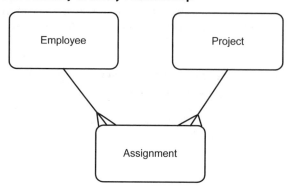

The name of the link entity is normally the noun form of the verb that describes the relationship. Therefore, the relationship between an employee and a project is represented by an Assignment entity. The resultant structure ensures that all of the assignments for an employee may be accessed. It also allows access from the project entity to all of the assignments associated with a specific project.

A link entity provides a means of recording the attributes of the original relationship; for example, 'date employee assigned to the project' and 'duration of each assignment' may be recorded as attributes of the link entity Assignment.

In an order processing system, there is a many to many relationship between the entities Product and Order. An Order may be for one or more Products; each Product may be ordered more than once so would appear on more than one Order. This many to many relationship is resolved by introducing a link entity (Order line) that has one to many relationships with both of the original entities. This structure is shown in Figure 11.17.

Many to many relationships can be problematic for two reasons:

- First, they may mask omitted entities and run the risk of attributes being overlooked.
- Second, most database management systems (DBMS) do not support many to many relationships.

Relationship names The nature of the relationship between two entities is clarified by defining a relationship name. A relationship link phrase is constructed from the perspective of each entity and is shown on the ERD. In the example in Figure 11.15, a Sales region is responsible for zero, one or more Customers and a Customer is allocated to a Sales region.

The full relationship naming convention uses the link phrases and inserts them into a standard sentence structure: 'Each [entity name] must/may be [link phrase] one and only one/one or more [entity name]'.

Figure 11.15 Named relationship between entities

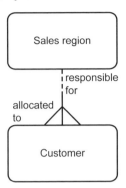

'May be' is used where the relationship is optional; 'Must be' is used where the relationship is mandatory. 'One and only one' is used where the relationship is read from the child to the parent entity; 'One or more' is used where the relationship is read from the parent to the child entity.

Using the example in Figure 11.15, the relationship name from the Sales region entity would be:

Each Sales region may be responsible for one or more Customers

and from the Customer entity:

Each Customer must be allocated to exactly one and only one Sales region

Exclusive relationships In an exclusive relationship, the participation of an entity occurrence in one relationship precludes it from participating in another. This is indicated by an exclusivity arc, as shown in Figure 11.16.

Figure 11.16 Exclusive relationships

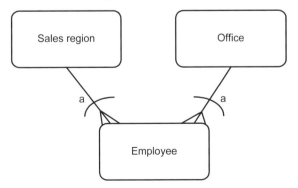

In Figure 11.16, the diagram uses the exclusive arc notation to show that:

- Each Employee must be allocated to one and only one Sales region OR to one and only one Office.
- Each Office must be occupied by one or more Employees.
- Each Sales region must be the employer for one or more Employees.

The exclusive relationship may extend to more than two alternatives. For example, if the Employee could be allocated to a Sales region, Office or Data centre, there would be three entities related to Employee and the exclusive arc would extend across all three relationships.

ERD for the sales system

The ERD shown in Figure 11.17 reflects the data requirements for the entire sales system.

Figure 11.17 ERD for a sales system (© Assist Knowledge Development Ltd.)

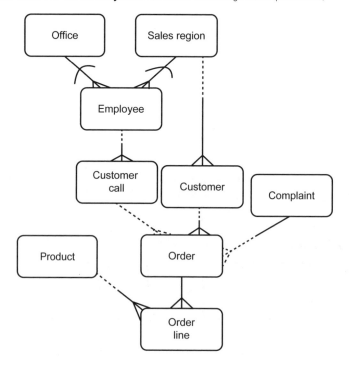

Alternative ERD notation

There are many notations used when modelling data. One alternative notation uses horizontal lines to indicate 'one' and circles to indicate optionality. Examples using this notation are shown in Figure 11.18.

Figure 11.18 Alternative data modelling notation

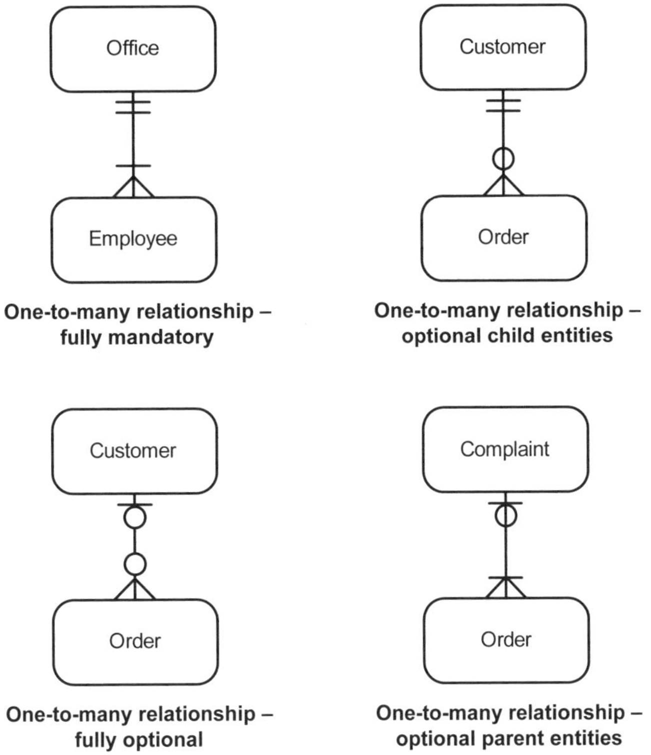
Office
Employee
One-to-many relationship – fully mandatory
Customer
Order
One-to-many relationship – optional child entities
Customer
Order
One-to-many relationship – fully optional
Complaint
Order
One-to-many relationship – optional parent entities

Class models

Class modelling from UML is an alternative data modelling technique. A class is a set of attributes that collectively describe something of interest to a system. A class model is a graphic representation of all of the classes in a business system and their associations with each other.

These models have similarities to ERDs and apply many of the same principles. Examples of the classes for a project control system would include Project, Customer and Team member.

Objects

An object is a particular entity or item for which a system is required to hold data; for example, in an order processing system, there is a class called 'Order' and a corresponding object is a specific instance of an order. The following information about this object could be:

Order number:	UK74563
Customer:	C66430
Date placed:	25 August
Date fulfilled:	1 September
Total value:	£147.50

Within a system, objects are sent messages that invoke them to respond in some way, typically by changing data. A message might be sent to the object UK74563 to change the date the order was fulfilled for example.

Classes

Classes of objects rather than individual objects are represented on a model of the system data. In class modelling, the classes provide the generic definition of the data items or attributes and the objects are the instances of a particular class. This is similar to the difference between entity types and entity occurrences, as described earlier. The example of the particular order shown above has the Order number UK74563 and is an object of the class 'Order'.

Figure 11.19 shows a definition of the class 'Order'. This definition shows that 'Order' has attributes such as orderNumber and totalValue; each object for this class will have values associated with these attributes. When defining a class, the operations that the class performs are also included. These might include updateDateFulfilled and createOrder; these operations are also shown in Figure 11.19.

All orders within the system contain the attributes shown in the definition and are subject to the same operations. A class, therefore, is a template for its object instances in the same way that an entity type is the template for its entity occurrences. Every object is an instance of one class and each class defines the set of features (attributes and operations) that are shared by all objects in that class.

In UML, classes are represented by rectangular boxes with three sections. The name of the class is shown in the top part and is a singular noun. The first letter is capitalised, for example; Order, Customer and Complaint. If the name has more than one word then each word is joined and capitalised in the class name, for example, OrderLine.

The attributes – the individual items of data about the class – are stored in the middle section. The attribute names are usually shown in lower case with constituent parts shown with a capital letter. The first letter of the attribute name is not capitalised, for example; orderNumber, customer and datePlaced.

Operations are stored in the bottom part of the class and are invoked by messages being sent to the class by other classes. It is usual to name the operation in the class with the same name as the message. The detailed content of the operation – what the class does when that operation is invoked – is defined in the *method* associated with the operation; this is usually left to the later stages of the development process.

Attributes held within a class are only accessible to the operations of that class as they are hidden from all other classes in the system. This is known as encapsulation and is a

Figure 11.19 Definition of the class 'Order'

Order
orderNumber customer datePlaced dateFulfilled totalValue
createOrder updateDateFulfilled

key principle of the object-oriented approach. Any other part of the system that needs to access or modify the data of that class has no need to understand how it is structured. It just sends a message and the receiving class responds as required.

For example, in Figure 11.19 the class 'Order' contains the operation updateDateFulfilled that takes place when all of the goods have been despatched to the customer. To ensure that this happens, a message is sent to the relevant Order object to state that the operation updateDateFulfilled must be performed. The message includes parameters stating the orderNumber and newDateFulfilled; these indicate the order in question and the date the order was fulfilled. In the class Order, the operation called updateDateFulfilled responds to the message of the same name by carrying out the required processing. The processing for this operation is specified as 'replace dateFulfilled with new dateFulfilled' so the value of the date contained in the message is used to update the date on the given order.

Associations
As in entity relationship modelling, classes are linked to each other; these connections between classes are called 'associations'. Figure 11.20 shows an association between an Order class and an OrderLine class; this association ensures that the system is able to identify the items purchased on each order.

Figure 11.20 Association between two classes

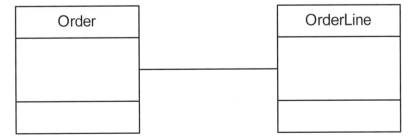

Classes interact through messages moving along the association lines shown on the class model. If there is no association between classes, then they cannot communicate directly.

The class model reflects the business rules that govern the classes and the operations performed upon them. Multiplicity is used to show the business rules for an association between classes. For example, the multiplicity of the association shown in Figure 11.21 indicates that an Order may include many OrderLines (indicated by the asterisk) but an individual OrderLine may only be part of one Order.

Figure 11.21 Association with one to many multiplicity

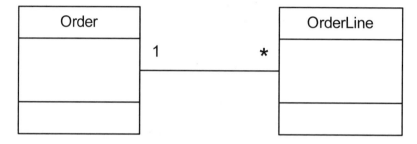

The multiplicity entries can be extended to show the minimum and maximum values in the association. This is shown using two dots between the minimum and maximum values. If the minimum and maximum range for each end of the association in Figure 11.21 was shown, the asterisk would be expanded to represent the range 0..* and the '1' would be shown as 1..1.

The JobSheet to Task association shown in Figure 11.22 shows that an instance of Task has an optional association with JobSheet. In addition, this shows that there may be no JobSheets associated with a Task (the minimum for this association is zero) or there may be one JobSheet for a given Task (the maximum for this association is one).

Figure 11.22 Association with one to zero-to-one multiplicity

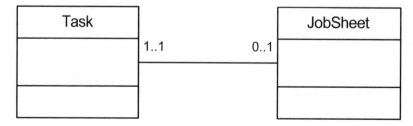

In the example in Figure 11.23, the class 'Customer' has a mandatory association with 'Order'. There must be at least one instance of 'Order' for each instance of 'Customer' (the minimum value for this association) and the asterisk indicates that there is no upper limit (the maximum value for this association is infinity). Reading the association from the other direction, each Order is for one and only one Customer. This example also demonstrates how associations are manifestations of business rules. In this case, the business rule is evidently that in this organisation a customer is defined as someone who has placed at least one order.

Figure 11.23 Association with one to one-to-many multiplicity

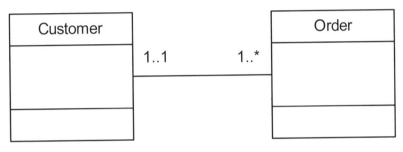

In some circumstances, the minimum and maximum values may be defined precisely. For example, if there is a business rule that no more than 20 people can be allocated to a project, the association would be modelled as shown in Figure 11.24.

Figure 11.24 Association with defined range of multiplicity

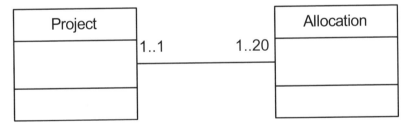

The class modelling technique allows associations where the multiplicity is many to many. For example, Figure 11.25 shows that a Project may have many ProjectManagers and each ProjectManager may control many Projects. It is probable that this business rule reflects what would occur over a period of time. The multiplicity shown in Figure 11.25 indicates that a ProjectManager may be newly appointed so may not have been allocated a Project but, over time, may manage several projects; and that a Project may be set up without having a ProjectManager allocated but, over time, several ProjectManagers may run the Project.

Figure 11.25 Association with many to many multiplicity

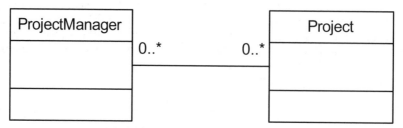

In some circumstances, the association between the classes also holds information. For example, the multiplicity shown in Figure 11.25 indicates that there may be several project managers for a particular project and a project may be managed by several project managers. This situation can occur for several reasons such as a project manager moves to another project, leaves the company, falls ill or changes role.

The structure shown in Figure 11.25 is not acceptable if it is necessary to store data that relates to a time when a specific project manager managed a particular project. This would require the system to record the dates a particular project manager began and ceased managing the project.

Class modelling allows for this situation through the use of an *association class* that is linked directly to the association in question. Figure 11.26 shows this additional class. In this example, an association class, Assignment, is modelled and contains the attributes dateStarted and dateFinished. These attributes provide the start and end date for each ProjectManager's tenure on a Project.

Figure 11.26 Association class structure

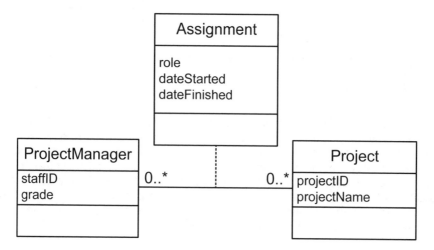

In this example, there is only one instance of the class 'Assignment' for each combination of Project and ProjectManager; this is similar to an intersection on a grid. If there were more than one – for example, if a ProjectManager could be reassigned to a Project they had previously left – then it would be necessary to convert this association class into a class in its own right.

Generalisation and inheritance

Sometimes, there are different sub-categories for a particular class. For example, a permanent employee and a contractor are both members of staff but the information held about them has some similarities and some differences. UML handles this situation through a concept known as generalisation and this is illustrated in Figure 11.27.

Figure 11.27 shows that some attributes are shared by all Employees, whether they are office-based or work in sales. So, these are shown in the general class called 'Employee'. However, other details are very different for office employees and sales employees so different attributes are held for them. The upward-facing arrow indicates that these two sub-classes inherit the attributes of the generalised class.

Figure 11.27 Generalisation structure

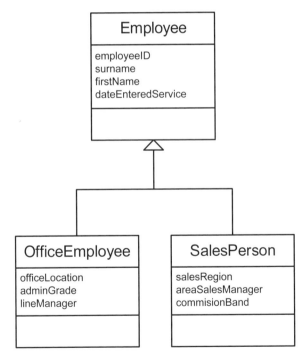

In terms of associations with other classes, some relate to the generalisation class, while others only apply to one of the sub-classes. The associations between 'OfficeEmployee' and 'Office', and 'SalesPerson' and 'SalesRegion' in Figure 11.28 represent associations that only apply to a particular sub-class.

Class model for the sales system

Figure 11.28 represents the sales system as a UML class model; this was modelled previously as an ERD in Figure 11.17.

Figure 11.28 Class model for a sales system (© Assist Knowledge Development Ltd.)

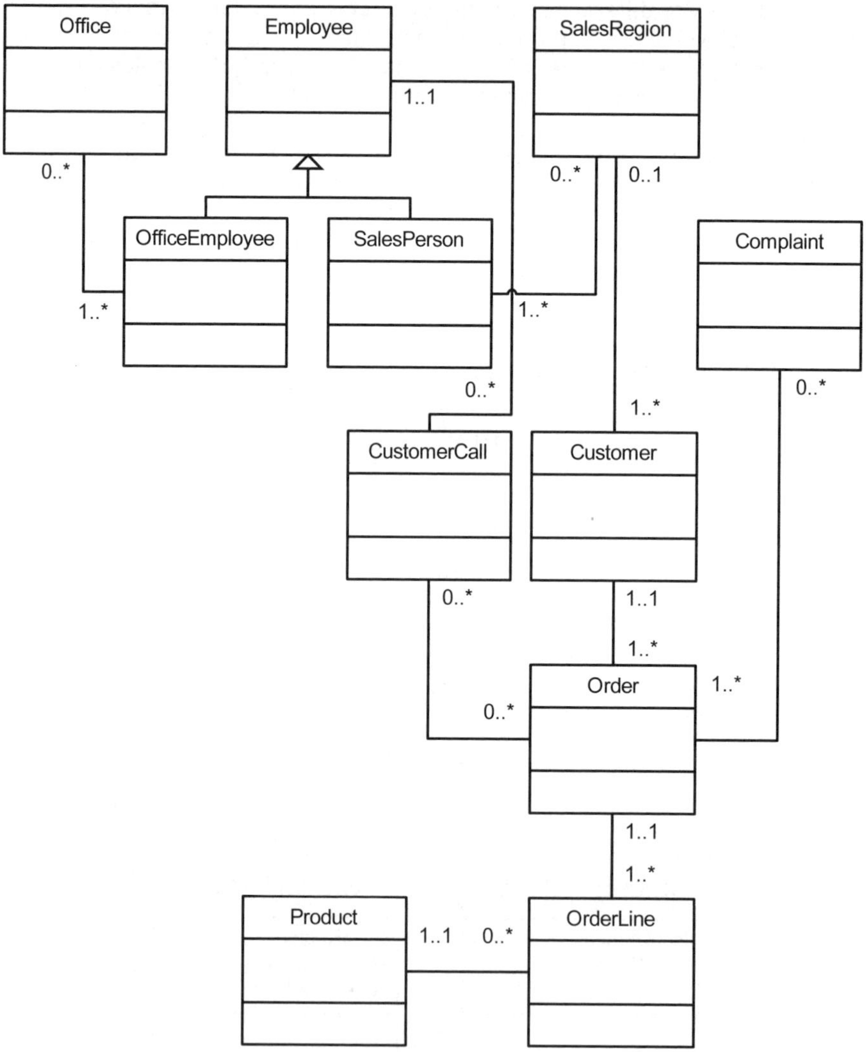

The UML notation does not cover the 'exclusive relationship' between employee and office or region shown in the ERD in Figure 11.17. The UML uses generalisation to represent these relationships and this is reflected in Figure 11.28. 'CustomerCall' is associated with the generalised class 'Employee'; a specific type of employee, 'OfficeEmployee', is associated with 'Office' and, similarly, 'SalesPerson' is associated with 'SalesRegion'.

This shows how a particular issue can be shown in different ways depending on the method or notation that is being used.

CROSS-CHECKING MODELS

Models offer business analysts several benefits. They help the business community to understand the scope and scale of the proposed solution before detailed development commences. The notation set for each model is clearly defined and represents a specific viewpoint, helping business analysts to ensure that ambiguity is minimised.

Questions may be raised during the development of a model. For example:

Which actors wish to access use case xxx?
How many of entity A may be related to entity C?
What information should be held about class X?

Analysts often worry that they may overlook some key piece of information; the questions raised when developing and reviewing models help to ensure that this risk is avoided and the essential details are defined. Cross-checking models offers a further level of assurance. While each model represents a particular viewpoint, they are all concerned with a particular system. The views should therefore align and, if they do not, something has been missed or depicted incorrectly.

Three different viewpoints are:

- A use case diagram defines the scope of the system and the features to be delivered.

- A business process model illustrates how the work is to be conducted and the flow of the process.

- A data model represents the data to be held within a system, the attributes and links between groups of data, and the business rules to be enforced by the data structure.

Cross-checking these models helps to expose where there are omissions or errors. For example:

- A data model does not include the data that a use case needs to deliver a particular feature.

- A task on a process model requires software support but there isn't a use case offering that support on the use case diagram.

- There is a use case to record some data but that data is never updated, accessed or deleted by any other use cases or process tasks.

Created, read, updated or deleted (CRUD) matrices offer a concise and rigorous means for cross-checking models. A CRUD matrix records the event, use case or process that causes an entity or class to be created, read, updated or deleted. An example CRUD matrix is shown in Table 11.5. This matrix is a partial CRUD analysis based on the use case diagram in Figure 11.6 and the class model in Figure 11.28.

Table 11.5 Example CRUD matrix (partial)

Use case \ Class	Customer	Order	OrderLine	Product	Complaint
Register new customer	C				
Order product	R	C	C	U	
Record product details				C	
Cancel order		D	D		
Update order	R	U	U		

Table 11.5 reflects several issues that are identified when a CRUD matrix is used. For example, the Customer class does not appear to be updated or deleted; the Complaint class does not seem to be created, updated, read or deleted. To resolve the issues in this example, the business analyst needs to investigate the following areas:

- Are use cases concerned with updating and deleting customer records missing from the use case diagram shown in Figure 11.6?

- Is the Complaint class required and, if so, how are complaints recorded and managed? This may also reveal a business process problem.

- Should there be a use case that allows product information to be updated or products to be deleted?

- Are reports required that provide information about products, orders and customers?

- Are there situations where updates to products also require orders and order lines to be updated?

If any of these situations are identified, there may be missing or incorrect requirements. Alternatively, data, tasks or use cases may have been modelled that are outside the scope of the solution. Cross-checking models helps to prompt questions that improve analysis and, ultimately, the quality of the solution.

AGILE MODELLING AND DOCUMENTATION

It is sometimes suggested that models are not used in projects that are applying Agile because there is no need to define the requirements 'up front'. This belief is based upon the statement within the Agile Manifesto that working software is valued over comprehensive documentation.

However, the Manifesto does not say that there is *no* value in documentation, only that working software is *more* valuable. When working in an Agile environment, it is not advisable to completely ignore documentation and most projects define requirements in some way. An understanding of the different documentation styles helps the analyst to ensure that the work needed is done and that unnecessary or over-detailed documentation is not produced. Essentially, it is all about relevance. A helpful approach is to develop:

- An initial set of general and technical requirements, possibly using elements of the requirements catalogue template.

- A context diagram to represent the place of the solution within the business context.

- A use case diagram with business staff to offer a clear view of the overall scope of the solution and its required features.

- A backlog of user stories through consulting the actors on the use case diagram to develop the user stories they would like the solution to fulfil.

- Outline definitions of non-functional requirements that require further exploration. Where they apply to the entire project, such as usability requirements, one definition – possibly using the requirements catalogue template – may be developed for each non-functional requirement that can then be applied across all development activity.

- A data model to ensure the data requirements are represented in an effective way.

Documentation should only be produced if it is justified and relevant. Some projects produce documentation because there is an organisational standard stating it is necessary but, unless the documentation offers benefits to the project, such standards should be questioned and possibly ignored. This applies across all documentation styles. User stories are very popular as a way to frame an exploratory conversation during solution development but they are not always the best approach. For example, security requirements are likely to need definitions with greater precision and depth.

USING MODELS TO MAINTAIN A SOLUTION

The question of documentation maintenance arises once a solution has been delivered and is subject to further development, enhancement and maintenance. When the lifetime cost of a system is considered, by far the bulk of the expenditure is incurred after the solution has been implemented. This is partly to fulfil requirements that were deferred or of a lower priority but may also be to correct errors discovered in the software, improve inefficient processes or respond to changing business needs.

A common problem that faces those working to enhance and improve solutions, is understanding the overall scope of a solution and how it all fits together. While detailed investigation, such as shadowing processes or inspecting code, can usually reveal *how* a solution works, the business reasons for it being developed that way are often lost in the mists of time.

It is in these situations that models can prove invaluable in clarifying the intent and business rules that underlie a solution. For example, use case diagrams represent the overall scope and functionality of a system and the stakeholders engaged with it; data models, either ERDs or class models, capture the data definitions and the business rules that control the creation, manipulation and deletion of data; and requirements definitions explain business motivations and priorities.

Models represent information clearly and succinctly so are invaluable during the continuous development and enhancement of a solution. The use of models during the software development process varies according to the approach adopted. Some lifecycles and approaches, such as the UP, rely heavily on models to support and enable the solution development work. However, where Agile software development is applied, the solution features and characteristics may be defined in outline and then elaborated during the development process. While documentation should align with the needs of the project and the solution context, it may not be sufficient to support the continuous development and improvement of a solution. In such situations, function, data and process models should be updated, or even created, in order to ensure that accurate representations of the business and solution requirements are available to inform the solution development work.

THE REQUIREMENTS DOCUMENT

In some situations, a BRD is required to define what should be delivered. The content of a BRD varies from organisation to organisation and project to project. Typically, a BRD is produced when a linear approach has been decided upon for a particular project; however, this is not necessarily the case, as it can be helpful to produce a document that brings together different artefacts as part of the initiation of a project. The style, depth and nature of the artefacts should reflect the project context and be sufficient to meet the needs of the project.

Structure

The clarity and relevance of a BRD is enhanced by a clearly defined structure. A well-structured document helps with the development of the BRD, and enables reviewers to identify errors and omissions and project team members to use the content. The BRD may be partitioned in several ways; a standard structure is represented in Figure 11.29.

Figure 11.29 Possible structure for a BRD

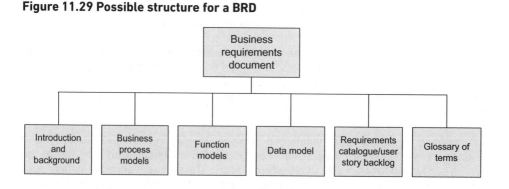

These sections are described in Table 11.6.

Table 11.6 Sections within a BRD

Section	Description
Introduction and background	A description of the business situation and drivers for the project. It serves to clarify the objectives and scope of the work and ensure that all stakeholders are aware of the business context for the requirements and the solution.
Business process models	The 'to be' process models setting out the vision for the new processes and, possibly, detailed 'to be' task models (see Chapter 7). Business requirements often involve changes to business processes and any new or enhanced software product must support the business process changes. The 'as is' processes that are to be revised may also be included, if required for additional clarity or explanation.
Function models	Diagrams such as context diagrams and use case diagrams that represent the scope and required functionality of the proposed solution.
Data model	An ERD or class model, setting out the data requirements for the solution. It is preferable to build a data model rather than describe the data requirements in text as a model is unambiguous and provides a detailed and precise representation of the data and the business rules relevant to the data.
Requirements catalogue/user story backlog	Information about each individual requirement may be defined using text; this may be within a requirements catalogue or a backlog of user stories. It is likely that some requirements are better described using the requirements catalogue format; for example, non-functional requirements tend to require detail beyond that of a user story, and their definition may be enhanced through the use of techniques such as matrices or decision tables.
Glossary of terms	A key quality characteristic for a BRD is that it provides a clear definition of the requirements. However, within any organisation, terminology is used that is understood only by the people working in a particular business area and often this terminology is very precise in conveying information. As a result, while it is important that the requirements use this terminology, this can present a problem for analysts and reviewers who may lack familiarity with these terms. A glossary of terms overcomes this problem and provides a central source of terminology definitions. While this may be a section of the BRD, in practice many organisations have a glossary of terminology that is accessible by all employees. This central repository may provide the required information or could offer a basis for extracting a project glossary of terms.

Some organisations include other areas in their BRD templates, such as a list of assumptions or decisions made regarding a project or solution. It is always important to consider whether a BRD is of use, the different aspects and artefacts that may be included in a BRD, which of these elements would be of benefit to a project and the level of definition needed to support a project in the delivery of the solution.

SUMMARY

This chapter has introduced some of the key techniques used to document and model requirements. Different documentation styles have been discussed to enable the business analyst to build a toolkit of templates and models that help to identify where questions need to be asked and clarify the features a solution should provide.

A model provides an unambiguous view of a system, albeit from one specific perspective. For example, a class diagram provides an unambiguous view of data and a use case diagram clearly represents the actors and the system features they wish to access. A further benefit of using models is that these single perspective views may be compared and cross-checked to identify inconsistencies and gaps. This helps to generate further questions that improve the business analysts' understanding of the requirements that the new solution must satisfy.

12 VALIDATING AND MANAGING REQUIREMENTS

INTRODUCTION

This chapter is concerned with two of the key elements of RE: validating the requirements that have been elicited and analysed, and managing the requirements in such a way that they can be traced from source to delivery. The approaches taken to validating and managing requirements vary depending upon the project context and organisational standards. The requirements validation approach taken may range from 'light touch' to formal sign-off; requirements management may be limited to tracking just critical requirements or may be applied to all baselined requirements. Whichever is the case, the underlying principles, and the extent to which they are executed, need to be understood so that they can be applied where relevant.

REQUIREMENTS VALIDATION

Requirements validation involves a review of the requirements that is conducted by a selected group of stakeholders who are external to the project. The aim is to agree that the defined requirements state the features and characteristics to be fulfilled by the solution. The requirements may be defined using different documentation and modelling techniques, as discussed in Chapter 11. It may be that a formal BRD is produced that includes a complete set of requirement descriptions and models. Alternatively, a product backlog may be developed that contains the requirements, features and other work items that need to be delivered. Validation forms a key part of both approaches and is the responsibility of business representatives such as business staff, the project sponsor and product owner.

When a linear project approach is in use, the documented requirements are reviewed to determine if they may be confirmed as accurate. Where this is the case, they are said to be 'signed off' or 'baselined'. They are then suitable for progression into solution design and development in order for them to be fulfilled and any subsequent changes requested are subject to change control and configuration management. This approach requires a formal requirements validation process, which is discussed in further detail in the next section.

Alternatively, when using an Agile approach, the validation is less formal but there remains a need for the requirements to be expressed with sufficient clarity to be accepted into the backlog. The validation review is likely to accept outline definitions of the requirements, typically in a user story format, and it is accepted that they are likely to evolve as further details emerge during the development process. The requirements within the backlog are subject to ongoing refinement until they achieve 'ready' status and are fit to be allocated to an iteration.

When validating requirements, reviewers examine the descriptions and question whether they are unambiguous, clear and correct. The review applies criteria similar to the filters used during requirements analysis but this time it is the business stakeholders who carry out the checks rather than the analysts. Technical stakeholders such as solution architects, developers and testers, and possibly project support office representatives, may also be involved in the validation process.

Formal requirements validation

Once the analysts have completed the analysis activity and have deemed the BRD to be complete and correct, the business and project representatives need to confirm that the document provides an accurate statement of the requirements. A review group is formed that is responsible for checking the requirements within the BRD and confirming their suitability. The BRD is issued for review once the reviewers have been identified.

The review group

The group responsible for validating requirements should include representatives from the key stakeholder groups. Each reviewer has different responsibilities as they are required to examine the requirements from a particular perspective. The following roles and responsibilities should be represented within the review group.

- The business sponsor, who reviews the BRD to ensure that the requirements are all in alignment with the business objectives and do not concern areas that are outside the scope of the project.

- The business owners of the individual requirements, or their representatives, who review the requirements to ensure that they express the business needs clearly and correctly, without ambiguity. It is the business representatives' responsibility – and their last opportunity – to be satisfied with the requirements before accepting them.

- The SME, who reviews the requirements to ensure that they reflect correct business practice.

- The solution architect, who reviews the requirements to ensure that they provide a firm basis for developing and delivering the solution within the architectural context for the organisation.

- The developers, who review the requirements to ensure that they are technically feasible.

- The testers, who review the requirements to ensure that they are testable.

- Project office representatives, who ensure that the requirements are compliant with business standards and policies, and that correct quality review procedures have been followed.

Collating review comments

There are several ways to collate review comments on the BRD: reviewers may attend a meeting, submit comments via a shared online forum or provide individual responses via email. If a meeting is held, this may be face to face, online or a combination of the two. Where reviewers are able to provide feedback in a formal meeting or via a shared forum, all of the comments are available to the entire group. This provides an opportunity to consider other perspectives and allows the reviewers to analyse, discuss and provide feedback on each other's comments. The use of individual emails tends to provide a more limited approach as there can be a lack of shared review and comment and it is more difficult to collate responses and reach conclusions. However, email responses can provide valuable information and this approach is preferable to not reviewing at all.

Whichever approach is taken to the BRD review, there are two key roles to be filled: there should be a chairperson, who is responsible for controlling the review, and a business analyst, who is responsible for providing information about the requirements, which may involve presenting it to the review meeting.

Different representatives should review different aspects of the requirements. A common validation problem is that the stakeholders are too busy to study the BRD and conduct a formal review. The analyst and project manager need to emphasise the importance of this task and must stress the impact and risks associated with incorrect or inadequate requirements. It is possible that reviewers feel they need to review every aspect of the BRD; identifying that they need to fulfil their responsibilities (discussed above) can help alleviate any time pressures.

Where a key stakeholder is unable to conduct their part of the BRD review, it may be necessary for the business analyst to support this work, possibly by holding a less formal one-to-one meeting. While this is not ideal, an informal review that focuses on a particular perspective may still help to identify where there may be errors in the requirements. Any problems with the BRD are likely to cause difficulties, delays and expense at a later stage in the development process.

Another requirements validation problem concerns the size of the BRD. Where it is large, a section-by-section review can be an effective approach. If the BRD is a well-organised document and the requirements have been organised, possibly by business area or use case, the review process may consist of a set of shorter review meetings or online discussions. Only relevant stakeholders (the business owners of the particular area under discussion) need be invited to review each section of the BRD, which helps to save time for everyone.

Review outcomes

There are three possible outcomes to a review:

1. The BRD needs significant rework and should be reviewed again once this rework has been carried out.

2. The BRD requires some amendment and, once any changes have been completed, can be signed off by the review chairperson. This is typically the business sponsor.

3. The BRD is confirmed as a satisfactory statement of the business requirements. Once the document has been agreed, it is signed off and the requirements are baselined.

Once a BRD has been signed off, any subsequent changes are subject to formal change and version control. This is described in the 'Managing requirements' section, below.

The outcome of the review should be an agreement that the BRD is complete, consistent and conformant, and provides a firm basis for the development and delivery of the solution.

Agile requirements validation

If the project is applying an Agile approach, the approach taken to requirements definition is different and this is reflected in the requirements validation process. There are two stages to Agile requirements validation:

- When initiating the project: the outline solution is determined and the backlog is established.
- When maintaining the backlog: work items are refined until they are deemed 'ready' to progress into development.

Formal review processes may be conducted during the project inception as this helps to ensure that the general requirements, and key solution requirements, are understood and a solution outline is available. Informal review of work items and user stories also helps to ensure that the solution backlog is sufficiently well-formed.

Once a backlog has been established, the items held in the backlog are subject to ongoing refinement to ensure they are fit for further development; at this point they are said to be in a 'ready' state. The refinement process involves various activities, including:

- Ensuring individual requirements align with any models developed to represent a solution.
- Producing initial, possibly low fidelity, prototypes of requirements; this helps stakeholders to identify any missing or incorrect features.
- Developing and discussing scenarios for use cases or user stories, particularly where they are complex or compound.
- Building models such as swimlane or activity diagrams to represent workflow for a particular task.
- Defining acceptance criteria for requirements and confirmations for user stories.

It is important that validation is conducted to the extent that is helpful and necessary. Some requirements are highly complex and need detailed analysis in order for them to be defined sufficiently that they may be selected for further development. Examples of such requirements are as follows:

- Compound requirements that should be decomposed into smaller items. Many non-functional requirements may fall into this category, in particular, security and access requirements, accessibility requirements, usability requirements.
- Complex requirements where the business rules need to be determined clearly. These requirements are often difficult to express and may require discussions

with SMEs in order to uncover the potential scenarios, combinations of rules and actions. Analytical and modelling techniques should be used where rules are complex. Data models and data definitions offer precise clarification of the business rules related to the data; activity diagrams, decision tables and state machine diagrams are effective in clarifying business rules related to processes and decisions.

Essentially, Agile requirements validation is concerned with ensuring that any requirements allocated to an iteration are in a sufficiently defined state for development work to commence. This may be a relatively straightforward process or may require detailed analysis and validation. The approach taken has to align with the nature and complexity of the requirement.

MANAGING REQUIREMENTS

A failure to understand, document and manage requirements often lies at the heart of problems with business and IT change projects.

While a structured, well-defined set of requirements provides a firm basis for business change, problems can occur if the requirements are not traceable. The extent of the traceability may differ depending upon the project context; however, this needs to be considered at an early stage if the required level of traceability is to be achieved.

The traceability of the requirements is a critical quality characteristic. It is concerned with the origin and ownership of a requirement, and the eventual outcome achieved. There are two forms of traceability: horizontal and vertical. Horizontal traceability concerns tracing the requirement from inception to delivery. There are two forms of horizontal traceability: 'backwards from' and 'forwards to' traceability.

- **Backwards from** traceability involves the ability to trace the source of a feature or requirement from any later point in the business change or software development lifecycle. It answers the question 'What was the source for this requirement or solution feature and who raised it?' The ability to identify where a requirement originated helps when clarification is needed. This is particularly relevant when requirements are in conflict or there are conflicting views as to the priority of a requirement.

- **Forwards to** traceability involves the ability to identify any requirement and track where it has been developed and implemented. It answers the question 'What happened to this requirement?' and shows that each requirement has been resolved satisfactorily. There are various ways of confirming that a requirement has been fulfilled: if a requirements catalogue has been developed, the resolution should identify the point at which the requirement was implemented or dropped; if a solution backlog has been established, a requirement is noted as 'done' once it has been developed or remains in the backlog if it has not been fulfilled.

These two forms of horizontal traceability are reflected in Figure 12.1.

Figure 12.1 Horizontal traceability

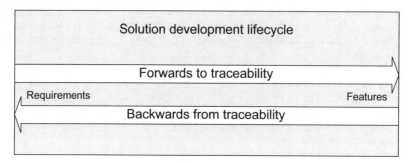

Vertical traceability concerns tracing a requirement up or down the requirements hierarchy, answering questions about alignment with general or technical requirements and, ultimately, business values, policies, strategy and objectives. This is represented in Figure 12.2.

Figure 12.2 Vertical traceability

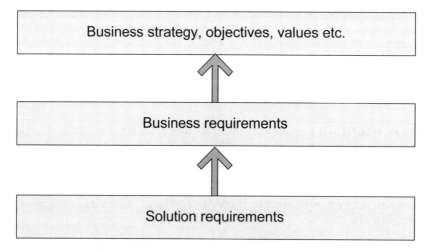

Requirements management enables requirements traceability. There are several elements involved in managing requirements as shown in Figure 12.3. Each of these elements is described below.

Requirements identification

Each requirement is identified uniquely in order that any reference to that requirement corresponds to only one requirement. This is relevant to all requirements, irrespective of the style used or project context. It is important to know which requirement, work item or user story is under discussion or being developed.

Figure 12.3 Elements of requirements management

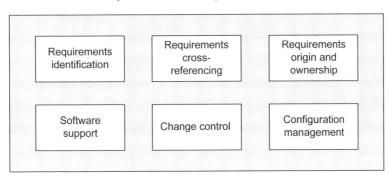

Cross-referencing

Related requirements and documents should be cross-referenced so that further elaboration or information concerning the requirement can be accessed easily. This guards against inconsistency or fragmentation. Cross-referencing also supports the impact analysis of proposed changes, enabling business analysts to identify which other requirements are related to the requirement that is the subject of the change, and to consider whether the change will affect the other requirements.

Origin and ownership

The origin of the requirement is the person or document responsible for raising the requirement. Requirements should be traced back to the origin (or source) during 'backwards from' traceability. Whether this was a person or a document, the origin should be able to provide additional information about the requirement and justify its existence. When considering changes to the requirement, the origin can help to clarify the impact of the change and support any decisions made about the change.

It may also be helpful to identify an owner for a requirement. The owner typically has responsibility for the business area affected by the requirement so may be called upon to make decisions about the requirement. Owners are usually key stakeholders so may not be involved in the project on a daily basis. They may be represented by other members of business staff who can make decisions on their behalf. Where a project has an established backlog, the product owner should be empowered to act on behalf of the business stakeholders. However, where there are disagreements, options or major proposed changes relating to a requirement, it may be necessary to seek guidance from the business actor who owns the requirement. In addition, fundamental business changes such as budget reductions or timescale changes may require requirements to be discontinued, reprioritised or delayed; the owner is the senior person in the decision-making process for the requirement and has the ultimate authority.

Configuration management

Configuration management is concerned with managing configurations of items or components. A configuration is a collection of items that together make up a composite item such as a deliverable or product increment. Whether requirements are documented in a BRD or held in a solution backlog, configuration management is essential to understand which version of each requirement forms part of a particular configuration. Configuration management ensures that project artefacts are updated in a disciplined manner, the latest version for an item is clearly identified and traceability is sustained.

There can be confusion between change control and configuration management. Change control is about managing changes that have been requested whereas configuration management is about managing the items that make up the deliverables or product. There is a relationship between change control and configuration management because, in assessing the potential significance of a proposed change, the configuration management records indicate which items are affected and if there are any corresponding effects on other items. Change control is described later in this chapter.

Without effective configuration management, configurations of requirements can become inaccurate as the following problems can occur:

- There may be difficulty in identifying the latest version of a requirement or the content of a configuration.
- Out-of-date requirements may be reintroduced.
- Incorrect requirements may be used during product development work.

While there needs to be flexibility and openness to change during the product development process, it is important to ensure that configuration management is applied where necessary to avoid the problems listed above.

Agile approaches accept that requirements often change during the product development work so state that requirements should be defined in outline and provide a basis for discussion and further exploration. The discussion, prototyping and elaboration of requirements allows for details to emerge during development and minimises the need for formal change and version control. However, appropriate mechanisms need to be developed to ensure that each configuration of items developed during an iteration is clearly recorded and to manage changes to the requirements where this is necessary.

There are two key configuration management areas to consider: configuration identification and configuration control.

Configuration identification
Configuration identification is concerned with the following:

- The deliverables to be brought under configuration control. These are known as the configuration items (CIs). During requirements management, deliverables include the individual requirements, the composite set of requirements within a catalogue or the BRD, iteration or release, and the models that elaborate and define the requirements. There may also be a structure showing how these CIs relate to each other.
- The identifier and version numbering scheme to be applied to the CIs. While each requirement has a unique identifier, it is also helpful to assign an identifier or name

to other CIs; for example, a BRD should be allocated a document identifier. Where a CI has been identified, and has an identifier, it also requires a version number. The approach to be adopted for allocating version numbers should be defined; organisational or project standards may be available. Version numbers apply to each individual CI; for example, a requirement, an entire requirements catalogue and a released product should all be allocated a version number.

Configuration control

A version control process is needed to control the CIs and ensure they are not changed without formal approval and version numbering. There are several elements to this.

First, a CI is created in draft form. While the CI is allocated an identifier, the version number needs to indicate the draft status. One approach is to number initial drafts using the format 0.n. For example, a draft requirement with an identifier T-007 could be numbered T-007v0.3 indicating that this is the third draft version of the technical requirement numbered 007.

Second, validation is carried out to review and agree the requirements. Where formal requirements validation is appropriate, each requirement description becomes a 'baselined' CI so is not in a draft form any longer. This means that it is brought under configuration control and cannot be changed by anyone without following the formal configuration management procedure. When a CI is brought under configuration control it is allocated a version number reflecting its baselined status. Using the example above, the technical requirement would be allocated the identifier/version number T-007v1.0.

Third, once a CI is baselined, no changes can be made to the content without approval of the configuration manager. A distinction needs to be made between the elaboration of a requirement and a change to a requirement. It is typically the case that requirements state 'what' is to be achieved and contain acceptance criteria or confirmation that determine when this is the case; however, they do not state 'how' a requirement is fulfilled within a solution – this level of detail emerges during the development process. This raises the question of when a change is actually a change. The most straightforward way of clarifying this is to consider when a change needs to be made to a defined requirement, whatever the documentation style adopted. Where a 'change' is actually an emergent detail, then the original requirement – or CI – does not need to be subject to configuration management. Where the original CI does need to be changed, then an absence of configuration management control is likely to cause confusion.

CIs should be stored securely so that they cannot be accessed and revised at will. If a change to an item is approved, the configuration manager releases it for revision. Once the item has been amended and the revised version brought under configuration control, the new version is renumbered. In the example, an update to the technical requirement would result in a new identifier T-007v2.0.

Configuration management in an Agile environment

Configuration management needs particular consideration when an Agile development approach such as DSDM or Scrum is used. Because these approaches tend to embrace change and explore requirements using prototyping approaches, much of the information about the requirements is captured within prototypes rather than a BRD;

however, the initial requirement is likely to be stated in some form, typically a user story or use case.

While these descriptions are relatively stable, the prototypes used to elaborate and develop the requirements are likely to change regularly. This detail focuses in the main on the fulfilment of the requirement rather than the stated requirement itself, as discussed above. There are instances where changes to a requirement are made though and, in these situations, it may be necessary to maintain the requirement description in order to aid traceability and support maintenance of the product. Changes to the requirements may be added at a later stage so configuration management may take place following deployment of the product, or a release, in order not to delay progress. This may include baselining and controlling versions of the prototypes, as these provide a form of requirements definition. There are several possibilities for baselining prototypes during Agile software development including:

- **Baselining every prototype before demonstration**: this has the virtue of clarifying the version that has been demonstrated to the business users.
- **Baselining daily**: this is highly disciplined but can prove onerous and unnecessary.
- **Baselining at the end of a timebox**.

Each baselined prototype is placed under configuration control as this is the only way to ensure that the up-to-date version of the prototype is available. The CI consists of the actual prototype, the tests run on it and the record of comments made about the prototype. Where prototypes are refined and extended as a basis for product development, controlling them as CIs ensures that a complete audit trail is created of the changes made and the rationale for doing so.

Change control

Changes occur frequently on projects. This may be because of external factors such as legal or regulatory changes or competitive forces, or may result from internal changes, such as strategies, policies or people. These drivers may cause any requirement to change during a project. Requirements management encompasses change control, which involves defining and implementing a process to manage changes. This process is invoked where a change arises that causes a CI to be updated and a new version to be created.

The stages of a change control process are as follows:

- **Documenting the proposed change**: Each change is documented as a 'change request', stating who raised the change, a description of the change and a justification for requesting it.
- **Analysing the proposed change**: Each change request is analysed to consider the impact of the change and the time and costs associated with making the change.
- **Consulting the stakeholders**: Each change request is sent to representative stakeholders to consider the impact of the proposed change, including the effort to make the change and the corresponding cost.

- **Deciding on the change**: Each change request, and the associated impact assessment, is reviewed by the designated approval authority. If the change is approved for implementation, the CI is released by the configuration librarian so that the change can be applied and the new version created.

The combination of the configuration management, version control and change control mechanisms provide a means of creating a version history of the requirements and the developed product. Each change that has been applied is recorded and explains why a CI was changed to create the new version. Over time, a complete audit trail will be created explaining what actions were taken, why this was done and when.

Software support

Most BRDs or product backlogs contain many requirements or work items so are best managed using an automated support tool. There are many such support tools available and they typically provide the following features:

- **Documentation creation and storage**: Editing tools that provide facilities such as word processing and modelling. Some tools provide document management features such as publishing documentation for access by authorised stakeholders, allowing online reviewing and tracking revisions.

- **Secure storage and access**: If the requirement artefacts are to be placed under configuration control, it is essential that access to them is restricted.

- **Documentation linkage**: Cross-references between CIs are recorded, allowing for related documents to be accessed easily. This helps with requirements management activities such as impact analysis and tracing version histories.

- **Version numbering**: The allocation of identifiers and version numbers to CIs.

There are some specialist requirements management support tools that provide a range of features, including those above, and are designed to support requirements management. There are also integrated tools that provide functionality to support both requirements management and later activities such as code generation and automated testing. Many organisations use support tools that are not designed for requirements management specifically and just offer generic features such as diagram creation and word processing. These tools, when supplemented by manual tasks, may assist with some aspects of requirements management.

SUMMARY

Well-defined and traceable requirements are undeniably key to a successful business change project. The requirements set out the features a solution needs to deliver and their relative priorities, and may be defined within a BRD or a product backlog. While there are different approaches to validating and defining requirements, there is little point in developing features that are incorrect, inconsistent or irrelevant. Therefore, some level of review and agreement is needed whatever the project context.

Traceability of requirements enables the business actors to confirm that their needs have been met and ensures that all decisions regarding the requirements are transparent and auditable.

Requirements management encompasses several areas, including change control and configuration management, and provides a disciplined approach to requirements fulfilment and solution deployment. Business analysts need to understand the rationale, principles and processes involved in requirements management if they are to make or support informed decisions regarding business or solution changes.

13 DELIVERING THE REQUIREMENTS

INTRODUCTION

Once the requirements have been defined, attention shifts to considering how they will be delivered. Business analysis work could provide the basis for a large-scale, broad scope business change programme or could concern a solution with a narrower focus, such as the introduction of updates to a software product. As a result, delivering the requirements could include any or all of the following changes:

- **Business process change**: Changes to business processes so that they are more accurate, efficient or effective.

- **People changes**: Redefinition of roles and jobs with new tasks and skills added. This may give rise to further requirements regarding skill development, recruitment and appraisal.

- **Changes to organisational structure**: The creation of new jobs, roles or teams, the reorganisation of sections or departments or the adoption of new structures or business models.

- **Changes to the IT systems**: The enhancement, development or procurement of software products, to support business processes and provide the features and information needed by the organisation. New technology may also be needed to provide the infrastructure that will support delivery of the solution.

These elements are interdependent so should not be considered in isolation. A holistic approach to defining a solution is essential if the desired changes are to deliver beneficial outcomes for the organisation.

THE DELIVERY STYLE

There are numerous lifecycles, methods and standards that may be used when developing the solutions to fulfil the defined requirements. The factors to consider when deciding how to develop a solution are summarised in Figure 13.1.

These factors concern the following areas:

- **Context:** The characteristics of the organisation, including the business domain and structure, and the project provide the basis for deciding how the solution will be delivered.

Figure 13.1 Factors in deciding the solution development style (© Assist Knowledge Development Ltd.)

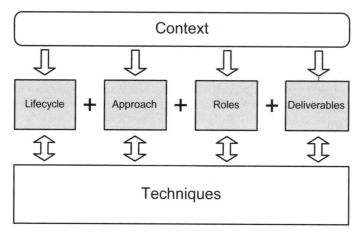

- **Lifecycle:** The process adopted for developing and implementing the solution.
- **Approach:** The methods and standards that are used during the lifecycle.
- **Roles:** The key roles to be performed during the project.
- **Deliverables:** The artefacts to be delivered by the project team.
- **Techniques:** The project management and solution development techniques used to plan, monitor, organise, analyse and record the work of the project team.

These areas are described in further detail in the following sections.

CONTEXT

The organisational and project contexts provide the basis for deciding the solution development approach. Organisations are subject to external pressures from customers, competitors and other forces within the business environment. These pressures drive the need for change and determine the constraints within which changes need to be made. For example, if an organisation works in a safety-critical or highly regulated environment it may be necessary for the entire set of requirements to be defined precisely and for all aspects of the solution to be deployed at the same time. Alternatively, if an organisation operates in a highly competitive, fast-moving business environment, it is likely that a rapid response to change is required and small increments are deployed as they become available.

The key contextual factors to take into account are shown in Table 13.1.

The context is likely to vary from project to project or across change programmes. Understanding the context helps to determine which delivery approach is most suitable for the project.

Table 13.1 Contextual factors

Factor	Description
Culture and philosophy	The culture and philosophy of the organisation that are based upon the core values and beliefs held by senior management. These factors determine the way in which the organisation is structured and underlie the behaviours demonstrated by management and staff.
Business context	The characteristics of the business domain within which the organisation operates and the pressures presented by the business environment. These factors drive the need for change and determine the desired outcomes.
Constraints	The factors that limit the project, such as the required timescale for delivering the solution, the budget and resources available, the standards to be applied.
Prioritised business needs	The priorities of the senior management and the balance between those priorities. For example, improving an organisation's reputation for customer service may be more important than reducing costs – or vice versa.
Project drivers	The basis for the project, such as a need to comply with new legislation or to offer an enhanced customer experience.

DELIVERY LIFECYCLES

The business change lifecycle defined in Chapter 1 is reproduced in Figure 13.2. This lifecycle shows an overview of the stages to be carried out when analysing, developing and delivering business changes.

While this lifecycle represents the areas of activity needed to deliver business change, it does not indicate *how* a solution is developed and delivered. There has been a great deal of research devoted to defining software development lifecycles and there are several in use. These lifecycles provide a clear basis for conducting development projects. Although they focus on software development, the lifecycles can be adapted for use on more holistic business change projects. The major lifecycles in use are:

- the waterfall lifecycle;
- the 'V' model;
- the incremental lifecycle;
- the iterative lifecycle.

These lifecycles are described in further detail below.

Figure 13.2 Business change lifecycle (© Assist Knowledge Development Ltd.)

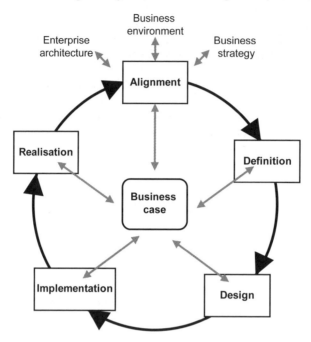

The concept of an SDLC

The standard approaches used to develop software products are known as SDLCs. These approaches have evolved over many years and are based upon underpinning philosophies that determine the route taken from the elicitation and analysis of requirements through to the deployment of system solutions.

An SDLC sets out the sequence of stages required to define, develop and deploy an IT system. The lifecycle covers the entire life of a system, from feasibility study to operation. There are two major philosophies that underpin SDLCs. First, in the linear paradigm steps are carried out in sequence; each step is completed before progressing to the next step and the solution is typically deployed in one release. Second, in the evolutionary paradigm the solution emerges during iterative periods of software development based upon the use of prototyping and multi-disciplinary teams and is typically deployed in incremental releases.

The earliest established model of a linear SDLC is the waterfall lifecycle but, over the years, variants and alternatives have been devised, each of which has advantages and disadvantages.

The waterfall lifecycle

The waterfall lifecycle, illustrated in Figure 13.3, shows software development proceeding through a series of sequential stages. In theory, each is reviewed and signed off before the next starts so analysis would begin once a feasibility study has been approved, and design is based on an agreed set of requirements delivered by the analysis stage.

Figure 13.3 The waterfall lifecycle

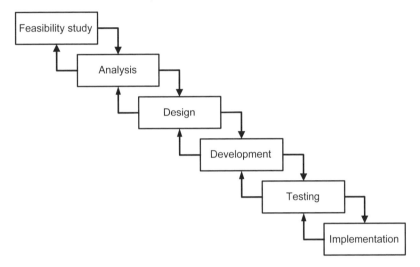

The backwards-facing arrows in the lifecycle indicate the need to check back at each stage to ensure that the project has not expanded its defined scope, that the present stage builds logically on its predecessor and that modifications to the deliverables from the previous stage may be made where required.

Business analysts are typically involved in the feasibility study and analysis stages of the lifecycle. They are also likely to assist in the user acceptance activity that forms part of the testing stage and to help business staff during the implementation stage. They may also be involved in the design and development stages, answering queries about the business and solution requirements and offering support to the software designer and developers where needed.

The principal benefit of the waterfall lifecycle is that it provides a strong basis for firm and clear management of the project. In addition, the need to sign off the deliverables from each stage before starting the subsequent stage should support the delivery of a high-quality solution, whether a software product or set of holistic business changes. However, the highly structured nature of this lifecycle is also its weakness, as it can create an environment where stage deliverables are not progressed to the next stage until all quality requirements have been met. This emphasis on exhaustive quality can lead to a drawn-out development process that can cause delays to the delivery of required business changes. In addition, this lifecycle does not enable adaptation and change well because of the focus on the delivery of high-quality deliverables at each stage. This may mean that a whole sequence of deliverables may require adjustments to adapt to a change. Should a change occur during the development stage for example, this would require adjustments to the analysis and design documentation and possibly to a feasibility study report as well.

337

The 'V' model

The 'V' model, shown in Figure 13.4, is a variant of the waterfall model. It consists of similar stages to those within the waterfall lifecycle and they follow the same sequence. However, in this model, the testing stages are shown explicitly and are linked to the deliverables that determine the basis for the different levels of testing.

Figure 13.4 The 'V' model

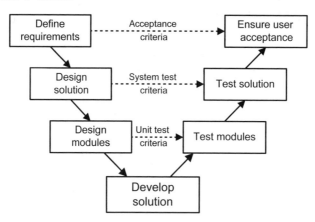

While the 'V' model is based upon the same principles as the waterfall lifecycle, in effect the waterfall has been bent back on itself following the development activity. This adds another dimension, showing explicitly the connection between the earlier developmental stages of the project and the later stages where testing is conducted. The derivation and usage of the test criteria is made explicit at each stage; for example, the model shows the acceptance criteria being defined within the requirements documentation and used during user acceptance testing.

An extended 'V' model has been developed to show the context and nature of business analysis work within this lifecycle. This model is shown in Figure 13.5.

In the extended 'V' model, the initial stage concerns an analysis of the business needs and the development of the business case that justifies the recommended solution. The selected solution sets out the scope of the business change work to be explored further in the requirements definition stage. The corresponding leg of the extended 'V' model shows that the business case is used during the post-implementation review to test the success of the recommended solution. This is done by reviewing the predicted business benefits against what has been realised by the new business system. The aim is to confirm that the benefits have been achieved and to identify further actions needed to enable benefits realisation if this has not yet happened.

The extended 'V' model is also used to clarify the range of business analysis work. As can be seen in Figure 13.5, the business analyst is involved at the outset in assessing the business needs and defining the requirements to be fulfilled by the solution. The later activities that are concerned with ensuring user acceptance and reviewing the benefits

Figure 13.5 The extended 'V' model (© Assist Knowledge Development Ltd.)

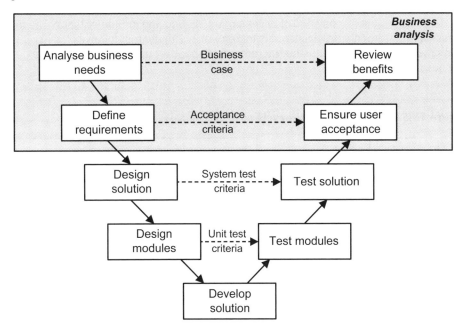

also form part of the business analyst role. Business analysts do not play such a major role within the stages of the lifecycle that are focused on the design, development and testing of the solution, as these stages are primarily the remit of solution architects, technical architects, developers and software testers. However, the business analyst should still be involved during these stages and offer the following services:

- Provision of information about the business domain and stakeholder perspectives.
- Clarification of the requirements.
- Facilitation of discussions between more technical staff and business representatives.
- Development of any additional artefacts, such as process and job role definitions, that support business readiness and efficient deployment of the solution.
- Assessment of the impact of proposed changes.

The incremental lifecycle

Some requirements are more important, or more urgent, than others; for example, a regulatory deadline or an expected competitor tactic may make it imperative that some requirements are implemented quickly. Other requirements may not be needed urgently so can be delivered at a later point. Developing and delivering the solution in a series of increments ensures that high priority requirements are fulfilled at an earlier stage while those of a lower priority are deferred.

The incremental delivery lifecycle is illustrated in Figure 13.6. This lifecycle is based upon early work to establish feasibility and conduct the analysis and design for the solution. In this version of the model, these stages are followed by two incremental delivery phases, each consisting of development, testing and implementation. The most pressing requirements are delivered in Increment 1 with the rest following in Increment 2. In practice, there may be further increments, depending upon the project context and the business requirements.

Figure 13.6 The incremental lifecycle (© Assist Knowledge Development Ltd.)

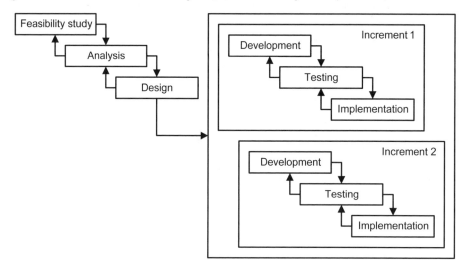

A disadvantage of using the incremental lifecycle is that the total cost of delivering the solution is likely to be higher than delivering the solution in one release. This is due to the need to ensure that each increment delivered does not compromise the solution when it is implemented. Also, in the second and subsequent increments, it is necessary to carry out a specific form of testing known as regression testing, to make sure that the additional features do not cause problems within the delivered solution. The high level analysis and design for the solution is defined such that the design is future-proofed and can accommodate the later increments. If this is not done, inconsistencies, errors and conflicts may arise that diminish the quality and effectiveness of the solution.

This lifecycle utilises the linear structure defined in the waterfall lifecycle but also allows for incremental development and delivery. The need for a complete set of requirements and an overall design is one of the fundamental differences between the incremental lifecycle and the iterative approach described below.

The iterative lifecycle

A feature common to the waterfall, 'V' and incremental models is that a complete set of requirements is gathered at the start of the project, which then forms the basis for all subsequent work. An alternative approach is represented by a spiral model as originally devised by Barry Boehm (1986) in his article: 'A spiral model of software development and enhancement'. Boehm's original perception of the spiral model incorporated the concept of iterations (or 'rounds' as Boehm called them) and used prototyping to reduce risk when developing software for complex situations. This developed into the basis for early Agile approaches such as RAD.

With the advent of Agile methods, such as DSDM and Scrum, iterative development has increasingly used prototyping and related techniques in order to evolve the detailed requirements and the corresponding software features. The Agile methods apply the generic principles shown in Figure 13.7.

Figure 13.7 Principles underlying the Agile approach (© Assist Knowledge Development Ltd.)

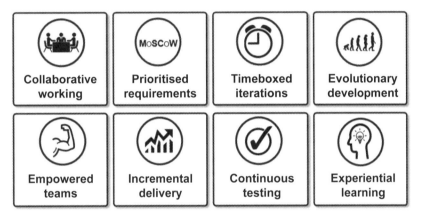

These principles focus on the following:

- **Collaborative working**: The development team members, from both business and technical domains, work together collaboratively.

- **Prioritised requirements**: A prioritisation approach, such as MoSCoW (see Chapter 10), is used to identify the different levels of priority among the features to be delivered.

- **Timeboxed iterations**: The concept of a 'timebox', where a time limit is set for an iteration or 'sprint', during which an iterative approach is used to complete an identified set of work items.

- **Evolutionary development**: Detailed requirements evolve through a series of product development iterations, typically using exploratory techniques such as prototyping.

- **Empowered teams**: The development team, which includes business staff and software developers, is self-organising and empowered to make decisions about the software development work.

- **Incremental delivery**: The solution is deployed in increments, with each subsequent increment providing additional functionality or improved performance. This allows for early delivery of product features that offer benefit to customers.

- **Continuous testing**: The software is tested continuously as testing is an integral part of the iterative development approach. Automated testing tools may be used to support this.

- **Experiential learning**: Learned experience informs the approach to the development work. Where this work does not deliver a desired outcome it is not perceived as a waste of time but instead as an integral part of the iterative learning process.

It is essential that business analysts understand these key principles and that they are able to adapt their skills and toolkit as necessary.

A generic Agile model that encompasses the key aspects of iterative software development is shown in Figure 13.8.

Figure 13.8 The generic Agile lifecycle (© Assist Knowledge Development Ltd.)

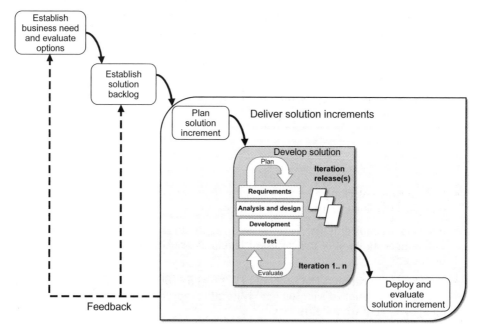

The model begins with understanding and establishing the business need; a perceived business need initiates the generic Agile lifecycle. The stages within this lifecycle are described in Table 13.2. The arrows on Figure 13.8 show the overall sequence. The dotted arrows show optional revisiting of previous stages in the light of feedback generated during solution planning, development and deployment.

Table 13.2 Stages of the generic Agile model

Stage	Description
Establish business need and evaluate options	Each change initiative is initiated by an identified business need. This may originate from the external environment, where a change requires an organisational response, or may reflect an internal requirement resulting from strategic or tactical change. It is often the case that a stated business need is revised following the investigation of the situation (see Chapter 5). Understanding the issue to be addressed and expressing it clearly is vital to ensure that any proposed solution will deliver the required outcome.
	A feasibility study is usually conducted to determine the options that the business might pursue in order to meet the business need and to evaluate the costs, benefits, impacts and risks of each option. The feasibility study may also recommend a preferred option.
	Once a solution increment has been deployed, there may be feedback that requires the solution to be reconsidered. The benefits review may also identify where additional features or changes are required if the business benefits are to be realised. This may mean further consideration of options to deliver the outcomes required by the organisation.
Establish solution backlog	Once an option has been selected, the high-level business requirements are defined from which more detailed solution requirements can be derived. The business requirements are explored and defined as solution requirements, using techniques such as user stories, use cases, storyboards, wireframes and prototyping. A product/solution backlog is established as a repository for these requirements.
	The backlog is maintained as the solution development progresses. This involves prioritising and reprioritising the work items within the backlog and determining when they are to be fulfilled. Feedback from deployed increments is also considered and used to update the backlog as necessary.
Plan solution increment	The increment, or release, of the solution is planned in advance of the development work. This involves deciding on the features and characteristics, documented as solution functional and non-functional requirements within the product backlog, that are to be deployed within the increment. A release backlog, containing the requirements selected for inclusion within the increment, may be formed.

(Continued)

Table 13.2 (Continued)

Stage	Description
Develop solution	An iterative approach is applied to elaborate and analyse the requirements, and design and test the solution. Each iteration is planned so that the requirements to be addressed within that iteration are identified and prioritised. Typically, these requirements include some that have a 'must have' priority, some that have a 'should have' priority and possibly some with a 'could have' priority. The different prioritisation levels are used to provide contingency in the timebox. For example, where some 'must have' requirements are found to be complex and require more time than initially allocated, features of a 'should have' or 'could have' priority may be deferred or dropped, in order to ensure that the timebox delivers the mandatory requirements.

Several iterations may be required to develop working software that may be deployed into operation. The working software should address both functional and non-functional requirements.

Once the planned increment has been developed and agreed, a production-ready solution is built that can be deployed into the live environment. |
| **Deploy and evaluate solution increment** | The tasks necessary to deploy the working solution into the live operational environment are conducted, including data take-on, data conversion, preparation of documentation, end-user training, installation of the live environment and transition to the service delivery team.

Once the solution has been in operation for a period of time, an evaluation is undertaken to determine whether it has met the business objectives and is working satisfactorily. This review may lead to perfective maintenance to improve aspects of the solution such as performance and usability. Where sufficient functionality has been deployed, a benefits review is conducted to examine whether or not the benefits have been realised and, if not, to identify further actions required to enable their realisation. |

Disadvantages of the lifecycles

The waterfall, 'V' model and incremental lifecycles consist of a sequence of stages and, as a result, incorporate a high level of control. While this offers many advantages, in practice, the use of these lifecycles also has disadvantages:

- There may not be time to define all the requirements at the outset. This may result in a poor BRD containing requirements that are not of sufficient quality or inconsistent documentation where only the most important or urgent requirements are well defined.

- It is unlikely that the business actors know exactly what they want at the outset of a project, particularly if the organisation is moving into a new area of business or offering new services. Even if they are reasonably knowledgeable about some requirements, it is likely that there are areas where they are less certain. These areas could concern specific details regarding functional or non-functional requirements; for example, the business rules underpinning some decisions or the exact nature of the disaster recovery procedures.

- It may not be possible to implement some of the business changes at the time required, which may cause stakeholder dissatisfaction.

- The pace of business change is rapid so a completely defined set of requirements is likely to be out of date very quickly. This can result in significant work to maintain an up-to-date set of requirements.

Iterative software development addresses many of the disadvantages associated with the linear lifecycles. It applies Agile principles whereby requirements are not defined in detail at the outset of a project but are elaborated during a process of evolutionary development. This approach accepts and expects changes during the development process and, as a result, there may be limited focus on maintaining documentation and ensuring traceability of requirements. The iterative lifecycle is based upon incremental delivery but differs from the incremental lifecycle in that the requirements evolve rather than being defined in detail as a precursor to the design and delivery of each increment.

However, an iterative approach has some disadvantages, as follows:

- Where there are requirements that concern complex business rules or legal constraints, it is not always possible to allow the requirements to evolve – they have to be defined accurately, often at an early stage. Failing to recognise this can diminish the quality of the product, risking aspects such as business compliance and user acceptance.

- Requirements are defined without an overview understanding of the intended solution or increment, resulting in a fragmented view and a product that is inconsistent or fails to address key non-functional issues.

- Too frequent product releases can be unacceptable to customers as this may require them to change their ways of working more often than they feel is necessary.

Developing the business solution

While the lifecycles described above are concerned with software development, the basic principles also apply to other business changes. For example, where there is a business process improvement project, the requirements for the new processes may be defined prior to the development of the processes or an explorative, evolutionary approach may be adopted. Similarly, process changes may be deployed simultaneously or incrementally. Given that most requirements are delivered through a combination of software and process change, the lifecycle chosen for the software elements is likely to impose development and delivery constraints on the other aspects of the business solution. For example, where a software product is delivered in increments, the corresponding set of process, task and job changes that make that increment workable in practice must be defined for each increment. Where there is a direct changeover to an entire solution, the full set of process, task and job definitions is required.

APPROACH

Whichever lifecycle is adopted, it is necessary to decide on an approach to the project work. The approach concerns the method, standards, events and documentation styles that are adopted on the project. There are several published approaches to business process improvement and software development that offer techniques and standards. The UML is a popular approach, providing a range of modelling techniques that may be used to represent different views of a system.

Figure 13.1 reflects the need to consider the context and the lifecycle when deciding which approach to adopt. In deciding this, there are two key areas that should be considered: the approaches to the development and the delivery of the solution.

Development

When considering the development approach, there are two key questions to answer:

1. Will it be possible to have ongoing close collaboration with the business representatives during the development of the solution?

2. Will it be acceptable for the detailed requirements to evolve during the development work or is it essential that the detailed requirements are defined and agreed up front?

Where it is acceptable, if not preferable, for the detailed requirements to evolve during the development of the solution, it is vital that the business representatives are available to work closely and collaboratively with the development team. If both of these conditions are met, many of the requirements may be defined using techniques such as use cases, user stories, scenarios and prototypes. These techniques provide a basis for exploratory conversations and requirements clarification.

However, if the requirements need to be defined in depth prior to the solution development work, or there is likely to be limited contact with the business representatives while the development work is under way, formal documentation that includes a well-formed BRD, business process models and a data model is needed (see Chapter 11).

Delivery

The delivery of the solution may be done incrementally or in one major release. The approach taken depends upon the context, in particular the status of the existing solution and whether the organisation requires an entire new solution. Where a legacy system is to be replaced, it is probable that a direct changeover to a complete replacement solution will be required and an incremental delivery approach will not be acceptable. Where this is a new application, or an existing product that is to be improved in some way, there aren't legacy concerns and the organisation requires speedy delivery of some features, a phased delivery using incremental releases is preferable. The context section earlier in this chapter provides the basis for deciding whether the organisation requires the delivery of all of the requirements in one release, or if a phased approach that delivers incremental change is necessary.

Software development approaches

There are several published, defined approaches to developing software products, each of which provides a framework and standards. Two key approaches are described below.

The UP

The **UP** from the OMG offers a generic software development process that can be configured to meet the requirements of an organisation. Its structure acknowledges that no single development process fits all organisations, development environments and cultures. It is designed to be suitable for small releases such as enhancements to existing software products as well as large solution development projects. The UP provides a guide on where and how to use the modelling techniques from the UML effectively; techniques from UML are discussed in Chapter 11. The UP is both an iterative and incremental approach. It is based upon the principle of using UML modelling techniques to explore and elaborate requirements through a series of iterations. Increments are developed that may be combined for one release of the entire solution or may be implemented as phased releases.

Scrum

Agile approaches have become increasingly popular for a number of reasons:

- The need for organisations to respond quickly to fast-changing business situations.

- The difficulty – indeed, sometimes the impossibility – of knowing what is wanted at an early stage of the project.

- The importance of flexibility when deciding how to fulfil requirements. For example, there may be a requirement to protect certain areas of system data but there may be several possible ways to achieve this, each of which may be considered before deciding on the most appropriate approach.

Scrum is a widely used Agile software development approach, which is based upon some key roles and principles. The key roles are described in Table 13.3.

Table 13.3 Roles used in Scrum

Development team	Responsible for developing the product. This team should be empowered to be self-organising and should include software development professionals and business representatives.
Scrum Master	Responsible for ensuring that the development team can perform the work by removing any impediments to progress and providing required resources.
Product owner	Responsible for the governance of the product backlog and acts as the VoC. This includes the prioritisation of the items within the backlog and the selection of items for development within a specific iteration (sprint).

In a Scrum project, the development work proceeds in a series of 'sprints', which are timeboxed iterations typically between one week and one month in duration. The aim of the sprints is to deliver working software using evolutionary prototyping. Close collaboration with the business representatives is vital for this approach to be effective as the requirements are often defined as user stories (see Chapter 11) so need to be further elaborated through discussion between developers and business staff.

The product backlog is the prioritised repository for the user stories, and any requirements defined using alternative styles. The product owner directs the work by allocating the items from the product backlog that are to be developed during each sprint. At the start of each sprint, there is a sprint planning meeting where the backlog items are considered and the work of the sprint is designed. An important issue concerns the quality of the items held within the product backlog. There is little point in the development team working on backlog items that are unclear or insufficiently defined as this can cause a great deal of work for the development team and can result in wasted effort. This may be avoided if the Scrum team agree on a set of criteria that determines whether or not a backlog item is 'ready' for development. Where an item does not meet the agreed criteria, the development team may decline to accept it for development within a sprint.

A daily scrum (a meeting) is held to review the progress of the sprint. These meetings are intended to last for a maximum of 15 minutes and are sometimes referred to as 'daily stand-ups' because the attendees usually stand up, which helps to ensure adherence to the time allocation. The Scrum Master is the facilitator for these meetings. The daily scrum meetings focus on what was accomplished yesterday, what is planned for today and what obstacles have been encountered.

The working software that is available at the end of a sprint is presented to the business community during a 'sprint retrospective'. This is a timeboxed event that should last up to three hours. A retrospective enables the development team to evaluate the work completed during the sprint and plan the work of the next sprint.

The rationale underlying Agile approaches assumes that it is impractical for the set of requirements to be defined completely at an early stage in the project and for the system to be developed and implemented in its entirety. Products developed using Scrum are delivered incrementally into live operation. Scrum applies the concept 'Definition of Done', which is a 'shared understanding of expectations that the Increment must live up to in order to be releasable into production'.[1] The software developed during a sprint may not be sufficient to be implemented into operation as it may form only part of an increment. Software developed during several sprints may need to be combined to form a releasable increment.

Agile approaches, such as Scrum, run the risk that the emerging prototypes are not documented sufficiently, may cover only a limited number of potential scenarios or are fragmented. All of these factors can lead to considerable difficulties when the software product is in live operation. This is, however, often a result of how these approaches are applied. The Agile Manifesto prioritises working software as the product from the development process; however, it also states clearly that there is value in documenting systems and that testing is needed throughout the development activity.

Scrum depends on close cooperation between the business community, the product owner and the developers, and on the ability to prioritise the work to be done. Prioritisation is explored in more detail in the next section.

The importance of prioritisation

Prioritisation is extremely important during solution development as there are always many requirements and limitations on time and budget. Clearly, all requirements are not deemed of equal importance, and prioritisation helps to determine what should be worked on during each iteration or should be released into live operation.

There are many prioritisation approaches. Some are relatively simple to define, for example, high, medium or low, while others have greater depth and complexity. It is notable that the major issue regarding prioritisation concerns the ability of the team to agree on a prioritisation level and, if a simple structure is used, to agree on what the levels mean.

The MoSCoW prioritisation scheme, which was introduced in Chapter 10, is particularly helpful as the levels are clearly defined (although gaining agreement on allocation of levels to requirements is still likely to present challenges). The MoSCoW prioritisation categories are related to the development and delivery of the solution as follows:

- **Must have** requirements are delivered in the first deployed increment. These form the 'minimum usable subset' of requirements and may be developed iteratively using evolutionary prototyping.

- **Should have** requirements provide one of the mechanisms for introducing contingency and flexibility. Where they are included in the plan for a particular increment, they may be deferred to the following increment if difficulties are encountered and they cannot be delivered within the defined timescale. They could be implemented as manual 'workarounds' in the short term, which is extremely helpful when deadlines are tight. 'Should have' requirements that have not been delivered in the first release are allocated a 'must have' priority in the second increment.

- **Could have** requirements may be included in the set of requirements under development, particularly if they are relatively easy and inexpensive to incorporate with the higher priority requirements. Where timeboxes are used, these requirements provide some contingency, as they can be left out should the development team run out of time.

- **Want to have, but won't have this time** requirements are recognised as those that should be set aside and considered during one of the later increments. This is an essential element for incremental delivery approaches as it provides a means of identifying requirements for later phases of the solution and specifically annotating them as such. These requirements may be allocated a different priority once the point arrives for their delivery to be considered. For example, there may be a specific date when some of these requirements become mandatory and, when planning for that release, the prioritisation may be changed to Must have.

The MoSCoW approach is also extremely useful for prioritising other types of business changes. For example, when developing process documentation, MoSCoW prioritisation helps to identify the elements that must be included at the outset, those that can wait for the next version and those that could be dropped if there is insufficient time; or when developing team capability, the MoSCoW categories may be used to prioritise the different skills in order to highlight those that are most important and those that are not needed until later.

Use cases, described in Chapter 11, are useful during prioritisation as they can provide a highly visual way for business actors and developers to understand the level of priority assigned to each of the use cases. While modelling the potential scope of the entire solution, a use case diagram can be used to partition the solution into practical implementation packages for the short or longer term and provide a means of considering the different options available to deliver the business requirements. Use case descriptions are also helpful as they define alternative scenarios through a use case and identify the main success scenario. Each scenario may be allocated a different priority level to aid the development work and early delivery of key product features.

Software package approach

This chapter has considered the lifecycles and approaches that may be used when developing a software product, using either an in-house development team or an outsourced software development supplier. However, in many situations, organisations prefer to adopt commercial off-the-shelf (COTS) solutions where possible, using these to implement best practice within business processes and software applications. The reasons are not hard to identify:

- A COTS solution is almost certainly going to be less expensive than the cost of a bespoke software development process since, by definition, the development costs for a COTS are shared among the purchasers and users, typically through the use of licence fees.

- Implementation should be faster, as the solution exists and only has to be set up as required by the organisation.

- Standard support and maintenance packages are available from the software vendors so a dedicated in-house team is not required and costs are clearly defined.

- COTS vendors keep their software up to date, for example, in line with legislative changes, and the costs associated with these updates are shared among the user community.

However, there are some drawbacks associated with using COTS including:

- No COTS package is likely to be a perfect fit with the requirements, so either the organisation must adapt their processes to what the package can do or they must pay for expensive tailoring and customisation, thereby partly negating one of the benefits of the COTS approach.

- If competitive advantage is required, it is unlikely to come from a software package, since all organisations working in a particular business domain can buy the same software and adopt the same work practices. However, most COTS offer built-in customisation features and, if the deployment and use of the software is done effectively, these may offer an opportunity for differentiation from competitors.

If a COTS solutions is desired, care must be taken that the defined requirements, in the main, focus on *what* the system is required to do, rather than *how* it is expected to work (unless there are non-functional requirements where the 'how' encompasses factors such as performance and security). The most effective use of a software package requires a willingness to change business processes and procedures where necessary to align with how the package works.

ROLES IN DELIVERING REQUIREMENTS

The roles required to deliver a solution depend upon these three factors:

- the context of the organisation and project;
- the nature of the lifecycle selected;
- the approach adopted.

Typically, a project team is set up that includes some or all of the following roles:

- project manager;
- business analyst;
- product owner;
- solution architect;
- developer;
- tester.

The point at which these roles are required differs depending upon the nature of the solution, the lifecycle to be used and the approach chosen. Example situations are as follows:

- Where a solution is concerned with changes to business processes rather than to software applications, the business analyst is needed to provide a business process improvement service (see Chapter 4). This involves analysis of the business processes and definition and design of the business process improvements. Roles such as developer and tester are unlikely to be required for this work. If the work is complex or extensive, a project manager is likely to be needed to plan, monitor and control the project.
- Where a software product is to be developed or procured, the business analyst role is needed to complete much of the early requirements definition work. The business analyst is also needed to elaborate the initial requirements so may develop a fully formed BRD or may define the items within a product backlog and ensure that they are in a sufficiently ready state for development. A product owner is needed to govern the product backlog (where this approach is used). Developer and tester roles are needed once the product moves into a development phase. There may be a need for a solution architect to oversee the different elements of the entire solution and ensure that they work coherently. Business analysts are required during product development to facilitate communication between developers and business staff, clarify requirements, analyse scenarios and impacts, and define business rules.

Whichever approach is adopted, there may also be a need for other roles. For example, a technical architect may be needed where the solution to be developed is complex and needs to be integrated with existing applications and infrastructure architectures. A data analyst may be needed where the software is underpinned by a complex data structure that requires careful design to ensure that all of the requirements are fulfilled and the business rules are met.

The key roles from within the business community, such as the project sponsor and business staff members, play an essential part in the development of business change and software solutions. The project sponsor is the business representative who is the point of contact for the project manager and is responsible for providing the resources to the project team. Business staff provide the details of the requirements. The nature of the work carried out by these roles varies depending upon the approach adopted. Where a waterfall, 'V' model or incremental lifecycle is adopted, the business staff are involved in the definition and validation of the requirements and the acceptance of the solution. Where an Agile approach is adopted, the business staff have to work collaboratively with the development team during the development process.

DELIVERABLES

The products that are to be delivered vary depending upon the nature of the solution, the standards of the organisation and the lifecycle and approach adopted. Sometimes, the requirements have arisen through a procedural change or a need to improve task efficiency. In this case, they may be delivered through a training exercise to improve the skills and understanding of business staff and the deliverables are procedure descriptions and training manuals. Where the changes are more extensive and encompass business processes and software changes, the deliverables are more extensive and are linked to the business process design standards and software development lifecycle and approach.

Some organisations develop extensive requirements documentation prior to deciding upon the development and delivery approach, and maintain the documentation throughout the development lifecycle. Where an Agile environment exists, projects document requirements in overview before exploring them further through the use of prototyping. In this situation, the key deliverables are the prototypes developed during each iteration. However, many organisations also enhance the requirements documentation as part of the iterative development work (in order to safeguard longer-term maintenance and support) and ultimately may produce similar deliverables to those resulting from a waterfall-style lifecycle.

One key aspect about any deliverables is that they should always be fit for purpose. Where documentation standards exist – whether they are organisational standards or are determined by a particular approach – it is useful to adhere to the standards as long as the deliverables are valuable in the particular project context. There is little benefit to be gained (and potentially a lot of time to be wasted) in developing deliverables that do not contribute to the goals of the project.

TECHNIQUES

The techniques to be adopted during the development of the solution can vary considerably from project to project. They depend upon the scope of the solution, the standards of the organisation and the lifecycle and approach adopted. Some typical situations are described below:

- The use of a waterfall lifecycle (or variant) requires comprehensive documentation that has been reviewed and 'signed off'. This necessitates the use of formal techniques for documenting and modelling requirements. For example, techniques such as use case modelling or class modelling from UML are likely to be required.

- An Agile approach also determines the techniques to be used. While prototyping is a vital element of Agile approaches, techniques such as wireframes, scenarios and user stories are also extremely useful. The UML techniques have much to offer within an Agile project as they help to provide a coherent view of the solution and to uncover errors, inconsistencies and omissions.

- Organisations may have defined templates for requirements documentation that include standards for modelling business processes, system features and data. They may also have templates for organisational documents such as task descriptions and job role definitions.

- Many organisations have adopted support tools that impose both a development process and a set of modelling standards.

SUMMARY

This chapter has described the aspects to be considered when deciding the approach to deliver requirements. These aspects include the context for both the organisation and the project. Selection of a development lifecycle and approach that do not align with the context is likely to undermine the predicted business benefits and result in wasted time and budget. This may even lead to the failure of the change initiative.

The standard lifecycles and approaches are used primarily to develop software although some stages and activities are also relevant when procuring a COTS. Solutions are typically holistic, encompassing aspects such as business processes and procedures, and new jobs and people skills. Therefore, consideration of the lifecycle, approach and techniques required to deliver these aspects is also necessary.

In many situations, it is not possible to deliver all of the requirements in one release; for example, there may be business constraints that require some requirements to be delivered at an early stage while others can be deferred. The role for the business analyst is to identify what is required and when, and seek out the options for delivering the requirements in line with business needs.

NOTE

1. https://www.scrum.org/resources/scrum-glossary

14 DELIVERING THE BUSINESS SOLUTION

INTRODUCTION

This chapter considers the work of the business analyst following the initial problem investigation and the definition of requirements. Although utilised mainly during the early stages of the business change lifecycle, business analysis skills are also required to support the delivery and operation of solutions in order to enable the successful implementation of the changes and the realisation of the business benefits.

THE BUSINESS CHANGE LIFECYCLE

While business analysis is critical at the outset of a change project, there remains a lot of work to be done as the project progresses through the business change lifecycle. This may involve the engagement of stakeholders in order to ensure their continued buy-in to the detailed design, development and deployment of the new processes and systems. To do this successfully requires a great deal of thought, preparation and planning – and all of these activities are facilitated by the involvement of business analysts.

There are five stages in the business change lifecycle shown in Figure 14.1. These stages represent the key areas of activity required to enable successful business change for an organisation.

The concerns addressed by the five stages within this lifecycle are as follows:

- **Alignment** is concerned with ensuring that the organisation's objectives and strategy are aligned with the external business world and that any changes to this environment are considered and, if appropriate, accommodated. This stage also aims to ensure that any proposed business changes are aligned with internal policies and architectures. The work of this stage, including the involvement of the business analyst, is discussed in Chapter 3.

- **Definition** is concerned with taking a closer look at a proposed business situation in order to uncover root causes of problems, conduct a thorough analysis, recommend relevant, feasible changes and define requirements. Business analysts define the business and solution requirements during the definition stage. This stage is the topic of much of this book and is not explored further in this chapter.

- **Design and development** is concerned with the detailed specification, development and testing of the solution, including business processes and related tasks, and the software that is needed to support them.

Figure 14.1 The business change lifecycle (© Assist Knowledge Development Ltd.)

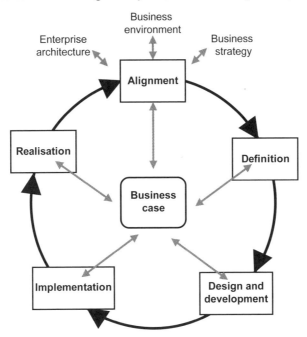

- **Implementation** is concerned with planning, preparation and deployment of the business changes.

- **Realisation** is concerned with review of the predicted business benefits with a view to identifying those that have been achieved and identifying where further action is needed to achieve those benefits still to be realised.

While the lifecycle stages are shown in a sequence, in practice, it is likely that there are overlaps and that some stages are revisited as changes arise and issues occur. Therefore, it is preferable to consider the lifecycle as providing an overall direction for a change project rather than enforcing a strict sequence.

BA ROLE IN THE BUSINESS CHANGE LIFECYCLE

Business analysis helps organisations to understand where changes are needed and to develop and implement these changes successfully; the role of the business analyst is therefore relevant across the entire change lifecycle. The frameworks, principles and techniques described throughout this book form an invaluable toolkit for business analysts when working within business change projects. The alignment and definition stages in the lifecycle have been explored in Chapters 3–13 and the application of key frameworks and techniques in the remaining stages is discussed in the rest of this chapter.

Design and development stage

The design and development stage encompasses several major tasks: the design of the solution and development and testing of the software to support the solution. If the changes are complex, there may be a need for extensive testing or piloting of the revised business processes in order to ensure that they are effective and efficient in meeting the needs of the organisation. The POPIT model, shown in Figure 14.2, was introduced in Chapter 8 as a useful aid for gap analysis; however, it is also used within the design stage as a basis for identifying the different elements required within a solution.

An alternative view of the POPIT model is shown in Figure 14.2 to reflect the importance of putting people at the heart of business change design and implementation.

Figure 14.2 An alternative view of the POPIT model (© Assist Knowledge Development Ltd.)

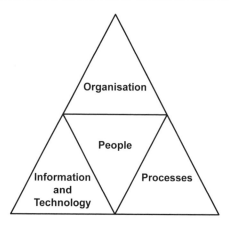

The perspectives shown in the POPIT model should be considered during the design and development stage. It is not possible to change processes and systems without considering their impact upon people and their skill requirements, plus the organisation's management structure and job roles.

Particular considerations in this regard are:

- The people and their emotional responses to change (see 'Implementation stage' discussion below).
- The new skills required to carry out the new work practices.
- The impact of merged roles and teams on the structure of the organisation or business area.
- The changes made to the tasks performed by staff and the corresponding need to redefine roles.
- The relevance of existing performance measures and whether changes are required.

All of the POPIT areas need to be thought through, not only in terms of what the changes might be but also how the changes may be delivered.

People

Any new skills required of team members should be identified and a gap analysis should be conducted to identify where skill development is needed. Having identified the skill gaps, the means of achieving them is determined, which may involve the design and development of training events. Business analysts are often involved in work to extend and improve the skills held by business staff, delivering the training and support to business users to enable them to conduct their new work practices.

Organisation

Where the revised processes have resulted in roles being merged or changed in other ways, a new organisation structure must be defined and the impact upon the management approach considered. Changes to business processes typically result in revised or new job roles for which role descriptions are required. The business analyst should collaborate with specialists from other disciplines, such as organisational design, to produce these role descriptions. There may also be a need to review and define performance measures, such as CSFs and KPIs (see Chapter 3).

Processes

The design of the 'to be' business processes was described in Chapter 7; this is a core business analysis service and is concerned with developing a key element of a holistic business change solution. The implementation of a 'to be' process requires much detailed work and it is often the case that this detail is overlooked or postponed; for example, creating the task definitions and the documents to be used in the new process. All of this needs to be considered at an early stage in order to ensure that the solution is well defined and ready for deployment.

Information and technology

Chapter 13 set out software development lifecycles that are used to develop the software product that should fulfil the defined requirements and support the business processes. While other chapters have discussed in detail what business analysts do to define the requirements for the information and technology aspects of the solution, it is also worthwhile considering the business analyst role during the design, development and testing of the software product. This is discussed in Table 14.1.

The business analyst may also be involved in documenting the outcome of the user acceptance testing and, in some cases, may provide advice on how the issues that arise may be addressed.

Implementation stage

The implementation of a business change programme requires a great deal of planning and any changes need to be executed with care. Business change deployment is an accepted business analysis service (see Chapter 4) and business analysts often conduct or support the work of this stage.

Table 14.1 The role of the business analyst during software design and development

Design and development task	Role of the business analyst
Design	The requirements documentation produced by the business analysts provides a basis for the design of the software product. During design, the business analysts: • facilitate communication between the business and technical staff to help ensure that the requirements are clearly understood; • where required, develop models and enhance documentation to ensure that there is clarity and consistency; • clarify aspects relating to some requirements, possibly by applying techniques such as scenario and impact analysis; • work with solution architects to ensure that the information and technology requirements will be fulfilled successfully.
Development	The business analysts work with the business staff and development team to help with any detailed queries about the requirements and to support them in making decisions about the software functionality. Given that business analysts have an overall understanding of the solution, they can offer a vital service during this discussion as they are able to assess the impact of proposed software features across the holistic solution, identifying where there may be problems and suggesting alternatives.
Testing	User acceptance testing is an accepted business analysis service (see Chapter 4). Once the software has been developed and tested by the IT team, business analysts provide support to the business staff as they undertake the user acceptance testing. The business analysts define the acceptance criteria used to confirm a requirement has been met, within the user stories, use case descriptions and requirements catalogue (see Chapter 11). They also use a variety of techniques to define test cases and test scenarios, including the following: • **Use case descriptions**: Developed for each use case within the use case diagram and to define the system response to the occurrence of an event. A main success scenario or 'happy day' is documented as a series of steps and is augmented by descriptions of any alternative scenarios that may occur. • **Decision tables**: Defined to set out clearly the range of conditions given a particular situation and the actions to be taken given a specific set of conditions. An example is shown in Figure 14.3, which concerns a decision about the level of service to be offered to a retail organisation's customers. • **State charts** (also known as state transition diagrams and state machines): Representing the different states a particular entity or class may take on during its lifetime in the system and the valid transitions between these states. An example is shown in Figure 14.4, which concerns a person who registers to attend an event.

Figure 14.3 Example decision table to decide level of customer service

Conditions:								
C1: No outstanding balance?	Y	Y	Y	Y	N	N	N	N
C2: Order value > £250?	Y	Y	N	N	Y	Y	N	N
C3: Cardholder > 3 years?	Y	N	Y	N	Y	N	Y	N
Actions:								
A1: Priority treatment	X	X	X		X			
A2: Standard service				X		X	X	X

Figure 14.4 Example state chart for person registering to attend an event

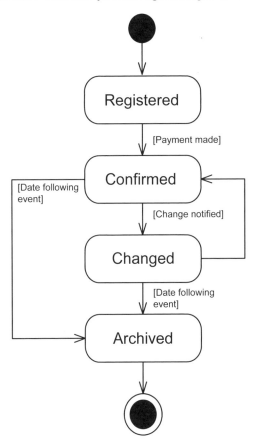

There are three major implementation aspects to consider – business readiness assessment, transition and migration, and people's response to change – and the business analysts may contribute to all of them.

Business readiness assessment

The business analyst is well-placed to conduct a business readiness assessment. This involves analysing if the business area where changes are to be made is sufficiently prepared to accept and operate the new ways of working. There are several frameworks that suggest aspects to consider when assessing business readiness for change.

The **McKinsey 7S framework**, shown in Figure 14.5, may be used to analyse the impact of proposed business changes (see Chapter 8) but also helps when assessing business readiness for change. The framework suggests a number of key areas to review and highlights the need to evaluate the 'fit' between these areas. While the shared values are often shown at the heart of this model, this element was originally labelled 'superordinate goals' (Waterman et al., 1980). This is the version that is shown in Figure 14.5 as it emphasises the importance of assessing the other six elements within the overarching context of the superordinate goals for the change project.

Figure 14.5 McKinsey 7S framework

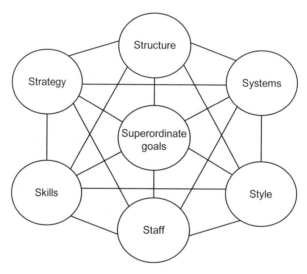

The **CPPOLDAT** framework suggests several key areas to be evaluated. Key questions to be asked when applying this framework are shown in Table 14.2.

The **POPIT** model, discussed earlier in this chapter, may also be used to assess how well prepared a business area is regarding a set of changes. This model covers many of the areas identified within CPPOLDAT but also highlights two additional key aspects to be included in the business readiness assessment:

Table 14.2 The CPPOLDAT framework

CPPOLDAT element	Description
Customer	Have the different customer groups been identified? Are the customers (in each group) aware of the forthcoming changes? Is there a need for further communication with customers to clarify how the organisation, processes and systems are changing? Do some customers, for example, internal customers, need training in the new processes and systems? Is there any resistance to the changes that needs to be addressed?
Product	Is the product ready for deployment? Will this be done in increments? What is the implementation strategy (see later in this section)? Are there any known risks or issues with the product? Is documentation available that describes the product?
Process	Do the changes align with the process architecture? Have the new processes been designed and communicated? Have the tasks within the processes been documented and communicated?
Organisation	Are any role changes needed? Are any management structure changes needed? Have organisational changes been agreed, defined and communicated?
Location	Have any changes to offices or venues been analysed and agreed? Have the changes that are needed been made or are they planned and under way?
Data	Do the changes align with the data architecture? Are the data in a fit state for migration and conversion? Has the data migration and conversion process been defined? Is this process planned within the change deployment timetable?
Application	Do the changes align with the applications architecture? Are any new or enhanced applications in place or planned for implementation? Have the required interfaces between applications been identified and implemented?
Technology	Do the changes align with the infrastructure architecture? Is any required technology available?

- the culture of the organisation and whether this will conflict with the proposed changes;
- the people working within the organisation, in particular the level of resistance they may offer and any skill gaps that could undermine the successful deployment of the changes.

Migration and transition

The transition requirements (see Chapter 10) set out the key areas to be addressed for a successful change implementation. These areas may fall within the scope of the business analyst role or the work may be supported by business analysts. They are concerned with:

- Analysing the data to be migrated to the new system, ensuring the data is in a fit state to be migrated, defining the format of the data in the new system, and setting up the migration processes.

- Supporting the business staff to learn about the new system, possibly by delivering formal training sessions, and providing information and guidance to help embed the new ways of working.

- Creating user guides, procedure descriptions, checklists and other aids for people using the new business processes and systems.

- Evaluating the possible implementation strategies and determining which is most appropriate given the context. Possible strategies are:

  - **Direct changeover** (sometimes known as 'big bang'): This is where the old systems and processes are removed and they are replaced by the new system and processes. This is a risky approach because there is little opportunity for contingency. However, it may be the only viable transition strategy in some circumstances, such as where there is a need to comply with legislation or where a system has become obsolete.

  - **Parallel running**: The old systems and processes are run alongside the new systems and processes for an agreed period of time. This strategy removes or reduces the risks associated with a direct changeover implementation as it is possible to revert to the previous ways of working. However, this is an expensive strategy because of the need to maintain two different approaches to carrying out the work.

  - **Pilot running**: The new systems and processes are deployed in a specific part of the business or location. This allows the organisation to test how well the solution works in an operational environment and to learn where adjustments are required. Any changes may then be made before the new solution is deployed more widely.

  - **Phased implementation**: The new systems and processes are deployed in phases (or increments). This means that only part of the solution is implemented at one time, possibly across the entire organisation, and other phases are delayed until the implemented changes are working well. This strategy also allows the organisation to learn where adjustments are to be made but, in this case, to just part of the whole solution.

The human response to change

The emotional impact experienced by business staff during the implementation stage is a major concern. A failure to consider this may cause resistance and undermine the changes. In extreme cases, this may cause the entire change programme to fail. The shock, anger, rejection, acceptance, hope (SARAH) curve in Figure 14.6 sets out the emotional curve that may affect anyone experiencing the introduction of business change.

Figure 14.6 The SARAH curve

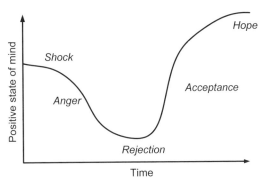

The SARAH curve sets out five stages of the emotions experienced when someone is faced with a change.

- **Shock**: The initial reaction to a change initiative is often shock. This may be due to a lack of awareness of the need for change. This may be particularly the case if most of the staff feel the organisation is doing well.

- **Anger**: Shock then moves to anger as people begin to understand what the change may mean for them. This anger may be directed at the senior managers who have initiated the change and also at others, such as the business analysts or developers, who are involved in the change process.

- **Rejection**: When someone feels angry about the change, the next stage is to reject the ideas and direction. A sense of avoiding the change can develop along with the desire to be left to continue as normal.

- **Acceptance**: Eventually an acceptance of the change develops. This may not mean that there is wholehearted support for the change but, as a minimum, a sense that the change is definitely happening, so it is best to accept it.

- **Hope**: Ultimately, people begin to see the positive benefits brought about by the change.

Business analysts must recognise that these reactions to change are to be expected in those affected by a business change programme. It is important to be sensitive to these reactions and to try to help people move through the different emotional stages. Business analysts can help business staff to cope with any business changes by providing coaching, training and ongoing support. They may also be able to offer reassurance to help business staff gain confidence in using the new processes and systems. To do this requires a high degree of interpersonal and stakeholder engagement skill during the deployment of the changes.

Realisation stage

Benefits are only likely to be realised if they are well defined, their delivery is planned and they are managed carefully throughout the business change lifecycle. However, it is often the case that a lot of thought goes into planning the technical aspects of change projects so that the solution is defined, developed and delivered successfully but there is less emphasis on how the expected business benefits are to be achieved. A comprehensive benefits plan that supplements the business case should be developed to provide a firm basis for tracking the business benefits and managing their realisation.

The benefits plan

A benefits plan should include the elements shown in Table 14.3.

Table 14.3 Elements of a benefits plan

Benefits plan element	Description
Context/vision	The background for the change project that provides a wider business context for the predicted benefits.
Benefits profiles	A full description of each of the benefits, including the type of benefit and the identified benefit owner (see below). Each benefit profile includes: a benefit identifier and name, the benefit owner, the stakeholders involved or interested in the benefit, relevant measures and dependencies associated with the benefit.
Benefits dependency network	The benefits dependency network shows the enabling and lasting business changes required to deliver the predicted business benefits. The dependencies between the benefits and the ultimate business objectives are also shown; see Figure 14.7.
Responsibilities	A list of the benefit owners and their responsibilities.
Tracking procedures	The process for monitoring and reporting on the benefits.

The **benefit owner** is a named individual who is tasked with ensuring that a benefit is achieved. To discharge this role effectively, the person nominated must be in a position to take the actions needed to secure the benefit. This implies that they are a senior manager with responsibility for the area in which the benefit is to be achieved. For example, if the main benefit of a project concerns savings related to staffing expenditure, then the benefit owner has to be a manager who is in a position to ensure these savings are made. Sometimes – and particularly in large organisations – benefit ownership has to be shared among a number of people but this brings with it the problem of divided responsibility. The risk is that some managers make the required changes to secure the benefits while others do not and so the project is less successful overall than it could have been.

Benefits dependency network

A benefits dependency network (or benefits map) is a diagrammatic representation of what needs to be done on a project in order to achieve its expected benefits. It also sets out how the benefits contribute towards the project's ultimate (business) objectives. An example of such a framework – for an organisation that wishes to raise its public profile – is shown in Figure 14.7.

Figure 14.7 Example benefits dependency network (Source: Adapted from Ward and Daniel, 2012. © Assist Knowledge Development Ltd.)

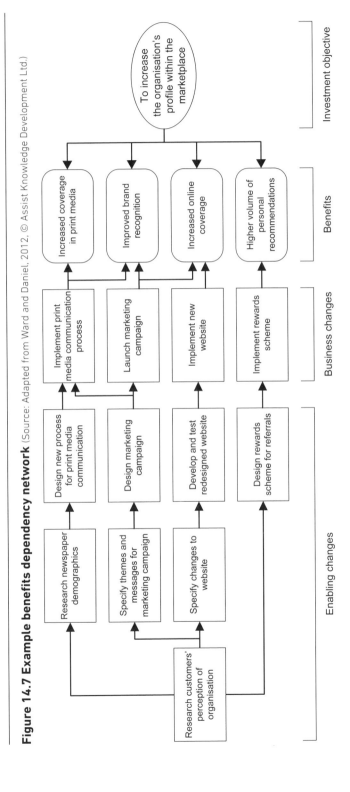

Although the arrows run from left to right, a benefits dependency network is best created right to left, starting with the overall business objectives that the change project is designed to achieve. Once the business objectives have been identified, the benefits that are required to contribute to the delivery of those objectives are represented on the diagram. Next, the business changes that are required to secure those benefits are shown, and finally the enabling changes that are needed for the business changes to be deployed.

The advantage of constructing a benefits dependency network such as that in Figure 14.7 is that it requires consideration of the work that is needed to realise the project's business benefits. This encompasses all of the areas of business change, not just those related to software or other technical products. The example in Figure 14.7 shows that only one 'stream' of enabling/business changes represents the technical aspects of the project; the other 'streams' highlight the non-IT changes that are required to achieve the benefits and objectives.

The network also helps to identify who should take responsibility for each stream. For example, the technical stream relating to the website redevelopment is the responsibility of the designated (IT) project manager, whereas the stream relating to improved press coverage would be managed by a PR function or marketing team.

Managing the business case

The business case needs to be managed throughout the business change lifecycle. The central and ongoing nature of the business case is shown clearly in Figure 14.1. The business case should be reviewed each time a request for change arises, to ensure that it is still valid and that the impact of the change is indicated. There may be an impact upon several aspects of the business case, such as the solution description, costs, benefits and risks. It is also usual to review the business case at key points during the business change lifecycle and also if there has been a significant change in the business environment. The review takes into account the detailed work that has taken place up to a particular stage and may require changes to the costs, benefits and risks. If these changes are required, the case for the investment must be checked to ensure continuing viability.

Benefits reviews

Management processes are needed to ensure that the benefits are reviewed in two circumstances:

- **Scheduled reviews**: At each of the 'decision gates' in the project (see Figure 9.1), the expected benefits should be examined as part of the review. At each stage, careful consideration is needed regarding whether the expected benefits are still available and are still sufficient to compensate for any increase in the expected costs of the project. In the light of such a review, it may be necessary to rework the financial case in order to define the expected ROI or even to re-scope the project and thereby improve the prospects of securing the maximum business benefit.

- **Unscheduled reviews**: These should be triggered whenever a significant event occurs that could potentially affect the expected benefits. Major requests for change are an example of such a situation as they could cause the project to cost more, take longer or deliver something different; all of these might affect the benefits. Other significant events could include a change to the key stakeholders (especially the project sponsor), developments in the external business environment or a revision of the organisation's business strategy.

The business case should be reviewed frequently during the project in order to check if it is still possible to achieve the predicted benefits and to identify any changes required to the project in order to enable those benefits to be delivered. The main evaluation, however, takes place after the project has finished and has been in operation for a designated period of time. Consideration should be given to the timescale required for the expected benefits to have materialised. Depending on the type and scale of the project, this could happen months, or even years, after the project ends. The evaluation should also examine the progress being made towards achieving the benefits and consider whether any further action needs to be taken to enable the benefits to be achieved.

Benefits realisation report

A benefits realisation report should be produced once the business changes have been implemented. This report provides a clear assessment of whether the predicted benefits have been realised or not. This report has four key uses:

1. To identify any additional actions that could be taken to realise any predicted benefits that have not yet been achieved. For example, additional training or support may be required if business staff are not making full use of a new system.

2. To reassure the decision-makers, and the wider organisation, that the time, effort and cost of the project has been justified.

3. To provide input to future business cases and future projects, in order to improve success rates.

4. To enable the organisation, over time, to improve the capability for choosing which projects to undertake.

A benefits review is conducted at a designated point following the deployment of the business changes. The review focuses on the predicted benefits and assesses whether or not they have been realised. During the review, benefits that have not been fully realised are analysed to identify where the required business changes have not taken place or where additional changes are needed. Where further changes are required to realise the benefits, the benefits plan should be updated and a further benefits review should be scheduled.

It is also possible that additional benefits that were not predicted in the business case but may now be available are identified during the benefits review. The benefits review includes an analysis of the actions to be taken to deliver these additional benefits, which may result in changes to the benefits plan and the scheduling of a further benefits review.

SUMMARY

This chapter has provided an overview of the contribution made by business analysts during the design, implementation and realisation stages of the business change lifecycle. It is often said that the successful implementation of business changes, and the realisation of business benefits from these changes, are difficult to achieve successfully. The techniques and concepts in this chapter are intended to help business analysts conduct their work during these stages and, accordingly, to support their organisations when adopting business changes.

Business analysis is a discipline that offers organisations insight, options, guidance and support, and it can help to ensure the wise investment of limited financial resources. Throughout this book, the portfolio of services offered by business analysts has been explored. Understanding these business analysis services, and their corresponding value propositions, activities and techniques, enables the identification, development and delivery of business solutions that help organisations to compete effectively in today's fast-moving business and digital world.

SUPPLEMENTARY CHAPTER: BCS BUSINESS ANALYSIS CERTIFICATION PORTFOLIO

INTRODUCTION

BCS has offered certifications in business analysis since February 1999. Over the years, the original certifications have been updated or replaced, and the portfolio has been extended such that BCS now offers an entire career development pathway for business analysts. This chapter describes the BCS business analysis certification portfolio and explains the different levels of qualification individual business analysts may achieve.

BLOOM'S ASSESSMENT LEVELS

The BCS business analysis certifications are aligned with levels of assessment defined in Bloom's taxonomy of cognitive domains. This taxonomy, adapted from the updated version (Krathwohl, 2002) is described in Table SC.1.

Table SC.1 Bloom's assessment levels

Bloom's level	Assessment description
1. Remember (Knowledge level)	The ability to retrieve relevant knowledge from long-term memory. This z involve recognizing or recalling information. For example, a question that requires a candidate to remember information about a framework or technique.
2. Understand (Comprehension level)	The ability to determine the meaning of messages and instructions. This may involve interpreting, classifying, comparing or explaining information. For example, a question that requires a candidate to explain or interpret the meaning of a statement or classify a statement.
3. Apply (Application level)	The ability to apply acquired knowledge, or use a technique or procedure in a defined situation. This may involve using knowledge to solve a problem or employing a modelling technique. For example, a question may require a candidate to employ a specified technique in order to represent certain information from a scenario description.

(Continued)

Table SC.1 (Continued)

Bloom's level	Assessment description
4. Analyze (Analysis)	The ability to separate material into its constituent parts, uncover information or assumptions and detect how the parts relate to one another and to an overall structure or purpose. For example, a question that requires a candidate to analyse a scenario to identify different elements, highlight areas for further investigation, uncover problems and suggest potential ways forward. Competence in analysing scenarios is demonstrated through the identification and application of relevant techniques plus the provision of appropriate justifications.
5. Evaluate (Evaluation level)	The ability to use criteria and standards to critique proposed options, make judgements and decide actions or solutions. For example, a question that requires a candidate to evaluate a proposed course of action against defined criteria. This level of assessment is likely to require subjective judgement.
6. Create (Creation level)	The ability to generate a new and original product, concept or service. This level is not concerned with the application of standard frameworks, concepts or techniques but entails the generation of something entirely new. For example, an assessment that requires a candidate to create a new and relevant framework or technique.

OVERVIEW OF THE BUSINESS ANALYSIS CERTIFICATIONS

There are six levels of certification offered by BCS and they are represented in Figure SC.1.

Figure SC.1 The BCS business analysis certifications

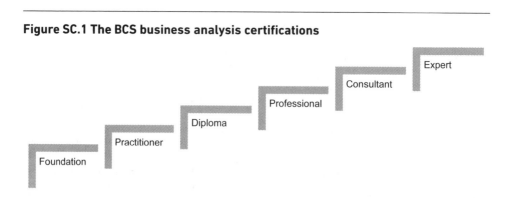

Each certification is assessed using an approach that is suitable for the particular level. Business analysts gain the certifications by meeting the required assessment criteria. The aim of the BCS business analysis certification portfolio is to offer business analysts a defined career development pathway, help them to acquire a toolkit of skills and techniques, and provide recognition of their skills and experience.

Foundation level

BCS offers foundation level certifications that are relevant to business analysis.

Each of these certifications offers a broad syllabus that covers a range of frameworks, concepts and techniques. For example, the Foundation in Business Analysis syllabus covers a broad range of business analysis principles and techniques and is based upon a subset of the topics discussed in this book.

The foundation level certifications are assessed at Bloom's levels 1–2 so the questions assess knowledge and understanding. These examinations consist of 40 multiple-choice questions and there are no pre-requisites for sitting them.

Examples of foundation level questions for the Foundation Certificate in Business Analysis are as follows.

Foundation Q1
Which of the following elements of a SWOT analysis are identified by an examination of the internal environment for an organisation?

    A. Weaknesses and Threats
    B. Opportunities and Threats
    C. Strengths and Opportunities
    D. **Strengths and Weaknesses**

Foundation Q2
Which of the following stakeholders is not in favour of the project but is not actively opposed to it?

    A. Opponent
    B. Neutral
    C. **Critic**
    D. Blocker

Foundation Q3
Which of the following is an investment appraisal technique that results in a net present value?

    A. **Discounted cash flow analysis**
    B. Gap analysis
    C. Payback analysis
    D. Scenario analysis

Practitioner level

BCS offers practitioner level certifications that are relevant to business analysts. These certifications are classified as core or optional according to how they contribute towards the next level – the International Diploma in Business Analysis. For the full range of certifications available visit: bcs.org/businessanalysis.

The practitioner level certifications are assessed at Bloom's levels 1–3 so the questions assess knowledge, understanding and application, although the majority of the questions are at the application level. These examinations are scenario-based and are either based on narrative and modelling questions or consist of 40 multiple-choice questions. There are no pre-requisites for sitting the examinations.

Examples of practitioner level questions for the Practitioner Certificate in Business Analysis Practice are as follows.

Practitioner Q1
Karen is an experienced business analyst who has just joined a new firm where the IT department is starting a new project. As a preliminary to commencing work, Karen has performed a stakeholder analysis and has concluded that the Managing Director, Lawrence, does not seem particularly interested in the project at the moment.

What should be Karen's stakeholder management strategy with regard to Lawrence?

Possible answers (correct answer in bold):

    A. Largely ignore
    B. Keep satisfied
    C. Keep onside
    D. **Watch**

Bar-B-Q is a chain of restaurants offering mainly barbequed food in town centres. Each restaurant has a 'food store' where customers select their ingredients which they then take to the 'campfire', a large barbecue where they can cook them. Accompaniments, such as chips, are prepared in a kitchen by professional cooks and delivered to the customers' tables, with a refund guaranteed if these are not available on time. Clive, the Managing Director, has told Angelica, the Lead Business Analyst that Bar-B-Q offers "fun, companionship and good food".

Practitioner Q2
Where, in a CATWOE analysis of Clive's business perspective, would Angelica document Clive's statement?

Possible answers (correct answer in bold):

    A. In the Transformation
    B. **In the World view (Weltanschauung)**
    C. In the Environment
    D. In the Actor

Practitioner Q3
Develop a CATWOE for Clive.

Possible answer:

Customer	People who like barbecued food and want a fun experience.
Actor	Food suppliers; food store staff; professional cooks.
Transformation	Offer meat for selection and provide barbecue meals.
World view	Bar-B-Q exists to allow customers to select their meat, and offer good barbecue-style meals in a fun, companionable environment.
Owner	Clive.
Environment	Willingness of customers to engage with the Bar-B-Q experience; health and safety legislation; fire safety legislation; environmental concerns regarding pollution.

Diploma level

Business analysts may apply for the BCS International Diploma in Business Analysis once they hold the following from the available foundation and practitioner certificates:

- A knowledge-based specialism: one BCS foundation certificate.
- Two mandatory practitioner certificates: the core BCS practitioner certificates.
- A practitioner specialism: one further BCS practitioner certificate.

The Diploma is assessed via an oral examination that is conducted by two BCS examiners and lasts approximately 50 minutes. The questions are primarily at Bloom's levels 4–5 so the majority of the questions are at the analyse and evaluate levels.

Diploma questions are typically contextual and are intended to invoke discussion. Examples of Diploma questions are:

- What are the benefits an organisation can realise from employing business analysts?
- Why is it important to analyse the stakeholder perspectives (for a given scenario)?
- What types of non-functional requirements would be relevant (within a given scenario)?

Professional level

BCS offers six professional level certifications that are relevant to business analysts. These certifications are categorised as Analytical, Business or Personal. For the full range of certifications available visit: bcs.org/businessanalysis.

The professional level certifications are assessed at Bloom's levels 3–5 so the questions assess application, analysis and evaluation. These examinations are scenario-based and are either a mix of multiple-choice and narrative questions or consist of 40 multiple-choice questions. There are no pre-requisites for sitting the examinations. Examples of professional level questions are shown in Table SC.2.

Table SC.2 Example questions: professional level certifications

Analytical	**Q1: Advanced Requirements Engineering**

The Chief Operations Officer for an organisation has raised a new requirement for the core application within the business transformation project. He has insisted that the system is accessible 24 hours a day, even though the offices are only open currently between 08:00 and 20:00. His rationale for this request is that this will future-proof the solution because there have been requests for longer opening hours which will require longer access to the system. Which category of non-functional requirement is this?

A. Robustness

B. **Availability**

C. Longevity

D. Scalability

Business	**Q2: Benefits Planning and Realisation**

What are dis-benefits?

A. Negative cash flows during the project

B. Benefits that have high associated costs

C. Projects with a negative net present value

D. **Negative impacts on particular stakeholders**

Personal	**Q3: Stakeholder Engagement**

A senior business analysts has decided to use De Bono's six hats technique to structure a meeting. The analyst has decided to start the meeting with the red hat and then follow it with the white hat. Which of the following perspectives will the meeting consider when using the hats in this sequence?

A. Process and emotion

B. Ideas and facts

C. **Emotion and facts**

D. Ideas and criticism

Consultant (Advanced Diploma) level

Business analysts may apply for the BCS Advanced International Diploma in Business Analysis once they hold the following from the available analytical, business and personal certificates:

- One BCS professional certificate from each of the three categories.
- One additional BCS professional certificate from either the analytical or business categories.

There are three other prerequisites for the Advanced Diploma. Applicants must:

- hold the International Diploma in Business Analysis
- have a minimum of 5 years' experience of business analysis work
- be able to demonstrate a contribution to the business analysis profession.

The Advanced Diploma application requires candidates to provide evidence of their experience in a variety of areas. Each application is reviewed by a BCS Advanced Diploma assessor. The assessment is primarily at Bloom's levels 4–6 and candidates are required to provide evidence of extensive analytical ability and the ability to offer something additional to the business analysis community.

Expert level

Senior, experienced business analysts may apply for the Expert BA Award, which is offered by BCS in collaboration with the BA Manager Forum. The BCS International Diploma in Business Analysis is a pre-requisite for this Award. There are two possible routes to achieving the Expert BA Award:

1. Completion of the Expert BA Award application, setting out extensive experience across a range of mandatory and optional areas of business analysis work, submission of a project abstract and description, and attendance at an assessment interview.

2. Attainment of the BCS Advanced International Diploma in Business Analysis, submission of a project abstract and description, and attendance at an assessment interview.

The assessment interview is conducted by two assessors. Candidates are required to deliver a presentation about their selected project and are then questioned about their work on the project and their experience as a senior business analyst.

CONCLUSION

This book supports the BCS business analysis certification portfolio and is the textbook for the BCS Foundation Certificate in Business Analysis. It is also used as the study guide for the BCS International Diploma in Business Analysis and provides valuable information and insights for the entire BCS business analysis certification portfolio.

For the full range of certifications available visit: bcs.org/businessanalysis

GLOSSARY

Activity diagram: A form of flow chart defined in the **Unified Modeling Language** that is used to represent diagrammatically a process and the differing paths through it. Can be used as a visual alternative to text to describe the **tasks** in a **swimlane diagram** in more detail.

Activity sampling: An investigation technique carried out to determine the amount of time individuals spend on different aspects of their work. Activity sampling is a **quantitative approach** to **observation** and involves the collection of data that may be used for statistical analysis.

Actor: A role that performs areas of work within a business system. Actors are modelled on swimlane diagrams and use case diagrams. Actors are usually user roles and show the individual or group of individuals responsible for carrying out the work or interacting with a system. An actor may also be an IT system or time.

Adaptive strategy development: The iterative development of an organisation's **strategy** in response to market or stakeholder feedback.

Agile: An approach to software development based upon the Agile Manifesto and using evolutionary development and incremental delivery approaches.

Analytical skills: A **competency** required of a **business analyst** that allows them to dig deeply into a business problem or issue until its real nature and its **root cause** is properly and fully understood.

APM: The Association for Project Management; aims to develop and promote project management.

Applications architecture: The portfolio of applications used within an organisation and their alignment with the **business architecture**.

'As is' business process model: A representation of a business process within an organisation as it is currently performed.

Association: On a **class model**, a line indicating a relevant business connection between two **classes**. Or, on a **use case diagram**, a line indicating a relevant business connection between an **actor** and a **use case**.

Attribute: An individual item of data to be held about an **entity** or **class**.

Background research: Preliminary work undertaken by business analysts to familiarise themselves with a business **domain** prior to starting more detailed investigation of a problem or issue.

Backwards from traceability: A form of **traceability** involving tracing the source of a requirement from any later point in a business change or software development project.

Balanced scorecard (balanced business scorecard): A balanced business scorecard supports a strategic management system by capturing both financial and non-financial measures of performance. There are usually four quadrants – Financial, Customer, Process, Learning and Growth. The balanced scorecard was developed by R.S. Kaplan and D.P. Norton.

BCS, The Chartered Institute for IT: BCS is the leading international professional body for the IT industry. BCS is responsible for setting standards for the IT profession and advises and informs industry and government on the use of technology across society and business.

Benefit: A positive gain to an organisation expected to follow from carrying out a business change **programme** or **project**.

Benefit owner: A named person responsible for securing a **benefit**.

Benefits dependency network: A visual representation of the actions needed to secure the benefits from a proposed change initiative.

Benefits management: A process that is concerned with the delivery of the predicted business benefits defined in a **business case**. This process includes managing projects so that they are able to deliver the predicted benefits and, after the project has been implemented, checking progress on the achievement of these benefits and taking any actions required to enable their delivery.

Benefits map: See **benefits dependency network**.

Benefits realisation report: The deliverable from carrying out a **benefits review**.

Benefits review: A formal examination of the benefits expected to flow from a business change initiative and of any further actions that are needed to harvest those benefits.

Bespoke (software): A suite of programs that are constructed to meet a specified business need and fulfil a defined set of requirements.

Big bang: See **direct changeover**.

Boston box: See **growth share matrix**.

Brainstorming: A technique used during meetings and workshops whereby participants suggest ideas relating to a problem or issue. Brainstorming is based on the principles that an idea from one person will generate suggestions from others and that more suggestions will be generated if judgement is suspended initially.

Brainwriting: A technique used during meetings and workshops whereby participants are invited to write down ideas relating to a problem or issue. Brainwriting is based on the principles that an idea from one person will generate suggestions from others and that more suggestions will be generated if judgement is suspended initially.

Breakeven analysis/breakeven calculation: See **payback calculation**.

Break-out groups: A technique used in meetings and workshops whereby participants are put into small teams and asked to discuss aspects of an issue, and bring their conclusions back to the entire group.

Business acceptance testing: A service within the **Business Analysis Service Framework** that is concerned with supporting business staff in testing new business and IT changes to ensure their acceptability.

Business activity model (BAM): A conceptual model that shows the set of business activities that are required to fulfil a particular stakeholder perspective. There are five types of business activity represented on a BAM. These are: planning, enabling, doing, monitoring and controlling activities. See **stakeholder perspective**.

Business actor: Someone who has an interest in a project, either because they have commissioned it, they work within the business system being studied or they will be the users of a proposed new IT system. See **stakeholder**.

Business analysis: Business analysis is a specialist service that co-creates value for organisations through offering the following services:

- Situation investigation and problem analysis.
- Feasibility assessment and business case development.
- Business process improvement.
- Requirements definition.
- Business acceptance testing.
- Business change deployment.

Business Analysis Manager Forum (BAMF): A networking forum that enables anyone with **business analysis** managerial responsibility to engage with their peers and share information at a strategic level.

Business Analysis Maturity Model™ (BAMM): A model that illustrates the increasing maturity of the use of business analysis in terms of the scope of business analysis work and the authority wielded by the business analysis function.

Business analysis service: An internal service function that provides **business analysis** capabilities to its organisation.

Business Analysis Service Framework: A framework that identifies a standard portfolio of services that may be offered by an internal **business analysis service**. The standard services are: situation investigation and problem analysis; feasibility assessment and business case development; business process improvement; requirements definition; business acceptance testing; and business change deployment. These services may be subject to adaptation and customisation in order to meet the needs of a particular organisation.

Business analyst: A person who performs **business analysis**. Most people in a business analysis role are employed by organisations but others work for consultancy companies, IT services firms and as freelance contractors. The scope of the business analyst role varies between organisations and includes: business BA or enterprise BA; technical BA or business systems analyst; digital business analyst; project business analyst; and proxy product owner.

Business analyst role: An advisory role that carries out some or all of the services within the BASF in order to ensure the effective deployment of business changes and use of technology in line with the needs of an organisation.

Business architecture: A set of artefacts that define several views of an organisation.

Business-as-usual (BAU): The normal, ongoing, day-to-day activities carried out by an organisation.

Business capability model: An abstract and conceptual representation of what an organisation is able to do.

Business case: A document that describes the findings from a business analysis study and presents a recommended course of action for senior management to consider. A business case normally includes an introduction, management summary, description of the current situation, options considered, analysis of costs and benefits, impact assessment, risk assessment, recommendations, plus appendices that provide detailed supporting information.

Business change deployment: A service within the **Business Analysis Service Framework** that is concerned with supporting the deployment of business and IT changes to ensure a smooth transition.

Business change lifecycle: A visual representation of the stages that an organisation carries out to identify, evaluate, specify and implement business change. The stages involved are Alignment, Definition, Design, Implementation and Realisation. Each stage is governed by and contributes to the development of the **business case** for change.

Business environment: See **external business environment**; **internal business environment**.

Business event: A business event initiates a business process, which is an organisation's response to the occurrence of an event. There are three types of business event: external, internal and time-based.

Business feasibility: The degree to which a proposed course of action is compatible with the strategy, structure and culture of an organisation and the business domain within which it operates.

Business model canvas: An overall, generic, model template for an organisation, developed by Osterwalder and Pigneur (2010).

Business option: A business option describes the scope and content of a proposed business solution and states what it is intended to achieve in business terms. See **technical option**.

Business perspective: See **stakeholder perspective**.

Business process: A linked set of tasks performed by an organisation in response to a business event. The business process receives, manipulates and transfers information or physical items, in order to produce an output that offers value to a customer. See **business process model**.

Business process engineering: A technique used to design or redesign a business process, which is concerned with analysing a business event and defining an effective and efficient process to respond to this event and achieve the desired outcome.

Business process hierarchy: A structure used to decompose business processes into lower levels of detail. The levels of the hierarchy are enterprise, event-response (business process) and actor-task.

Business process improvement: A service within the **Business Analysis Service Framework** that is concerned with researching, analysing and defining current and proposed business processes, and applying gap analysis to identify actions required to implement the revised processes.

Business process model: A diagram showing the tasks that need to be carried out in response to a business event and in order to achieve a specific goal. See **swimlane diagram**.

Business readiness assessment: An analysis of the readiness of an organisation to accept business changes, and identification of the actions required to ensure that the organisation is ready.

Business rule: An instruction or procedure that determines how an activity, process, task or step should be conducted. There are two main types of business rule: constraints that restrict how an activity is performed; and operational guidance that describes the procedures for performing activities.

Business sponsor: A senior person in an organisation who is accountable for delivering the benefits from a business change. The sponsor is also responsible for providing resources to the project team.

Business staff: The individuals or groups who carry out the work of an organisation and who will implement and use new business processes and/or systems.

Business strategy: The long-term direction defined for an organisation in order to achieve the vision, mission and objectives.

Business system: A set of business components working together in order to achieve a defined purpose. These components are defined in the POPIT model. See **IT system**.

Business use case: A feature to be provided in a proposed business system. Each business use case encompasses the POPIT elements.

Capability Maturity Model Integration (CMMI): A model developed by the Software Engineering Institute of Carnegie Mellon University that consists of five stages, showing increasing maturity of operation. Provides guidance for improving the quality of processes.

CARDI log: A record of the constraints, assumptions, risks, dependencies and issues on a proposed or actual project. See also **RAID log**.

CATWOE: A technique from the Soft Systems Methodology that provides a framework for defining and analysing business perspectives. The mnemonic stands for: C – customer, A – actor, T – transformation, W – world view, O – owner, E – environment. See **stakeholder perspective**, **Soft Systems Methodology**.

CBAP®: The Certified Business Analysis Professional awarded by the International Institute of Business Analysis (IIBA®).

CCBA®: Certificate of Capability in Business Analysis.

Change control: A process whereby changes to requirements are handled in a controlled fashion. The change control process defines the process steps to be carried out when dealing with a proposed change. These steps include documenting the change, analysing the impact of the change, evaluating the impact of the change in order to decide upon the course of action to take, and deciding whether or not to apply the change. The analysis and decisions should be documented in order to provide an audit trail relating to the proposed change.

Class: A class is a definition of the attributes and operations shared by a set of objects within a business system. Each object is an instance of a particular class. See **object**.

Class model: A technique from the UML. A class model describes the classes in a system and their associations with each other.

Cloud computing: A general term for the delivery of hosted services over the internet.

Cognitive flexibility: The ability of the brain to transition between thinking about one concept to another.

Competency (or competence): A competency is a skill or quality an individual needs to perform his or her job effectively.

Compliance architecture: A definition of the compliance obligations of an organisation and the means by which they are met.

Configuration management: A formal process for organising and managing the configuration of individual products within a project and the relationships between them.

Consensus model: The definitive, agreed BAM derived from the individual stakeholder BAMs.

Context diagram: An outline visual representation of a business or IT system, comprising a box or circle and the interactions the system has with external actors and systems.

Control activity: The activity within a **business activity model (BAM)** that indicates the need for actions to correct where performance standards have not been met.

Convergent thinking: A thought process that encourages the development of ideas by using techniques to find the 'right' answer to a question.

Cost–benefit analysis: A technique that involves identifying the initial and ongoing costs and benefits associated with a business change initiative. Costs and benefits are categorised as tangible or intangible and a financial value calculated for those that are tangible. The financial values are analysed over a forward period in order to assess the potential financial return to the organisation. This analysis may be carried out using investment appraisal techniques. See **payback period** (or **break-even analysis**) and **discounted cash flow/net present value analysis**.

CPPOLDAT: A framework for carrying out a **business readiness assessment**. The elements of CPPOLDAT are: Customer, Product, Process, Organisation, Location, Data, Application, and Technology.

Creative problem solving: An approach to finding innovative solutions to problems.

Critical success factors: The areas in which an organisation must succeed in order to achieve positive organisational performance.

Critical thinking: The objective analysis and evaluation of an issue.

CRUD matrix: A comparison of the functional and data vies of a system to show which functions create, read, update and delete which entities.

Customer experience (CX) analysis and design: An approach to business improvement that focuses on the customer's experience of engaging with an organisation to determine how it may be improved or enhanced.

Customer journey map: A representation of the way a customer interacts with an organisation, including their activities and perceptions at each stage of the interaction.

Data architecture: A representation of the data held and used within an organisation.

Data modelling: An approach used to analyse and represent data items.

Design thinking: An approach to generating options and solutions that encourages the use of product design concepts and techniques such as prototyping, trying out new ideas and **convergent** or **divergent thinking**. Design thinking is focused on outcomes and the customer's views and needs.

Developer: A person possessing the technical skills needed to design and create a software product.

Direct changeover: A method of introducing new business processes or systems whereby the existing processes and systems are discontinued at the same time as the changes are deployed into use. Sometimes also referred to as 'big bang'.

Discounted cash flow (DCF): An investment appraisal technique that takes account of the time value of money. The annual net cash flow for each year following the implementation of the change is reduced (discounted) in line with the estimated reduction in the value of money. The discounted cash flows are then added to produce an NPV. See **net present value**.

Divergent thinking: A thought process that encourages the generation of novel ideas.

Document analysis: A requirements elicitation technique where samples of documents are examined in order to analyse the data recorded and the usage made of that data.

Doing activities: The activities in a **business activity model (BAM)** that carry out the transformation defined in the corresponding **CATWOE** analysis.

Domain: A business domain is a sector of the economy or industry.

Domain knowledge: A general understanding of the business drivers, issues, pressures, dynamics, finances and technologies of a business domain. See also **subject matter expertise**.

DSDM Agile Project Framework: A project delivery framework that emphasises continuous user involvement and the importance of delivering the right solution at the right time.

Enabling activities: The activities in a **business activity model (BAM)** that acquire and replenish the resources needed to carry out the transformation as defined in a corresponding **CATWOE** analysis.

Enterprise architecture: 'The fundamental concepts or properties of a system in its environment embodied in its elements, relationships, and in the principles of its design and evolution' (ISO/IEC/IEEE 42010:2011)

Entity: Something of interest to a system about which data will be held.

Entity relationship diagram: A diagram produced using the entity relationship modelling technique. The diagram provides a representation of the data to be held in the system under investigation. See **entity relationship modelling**.

Entity relationship modelling: A technique used to model the data required within a system. The technique models the data groupings, known as 'entities', and the relationships between those entities.

Ethnographic study: A form of **observation** concerned with spending an extended period of time within an organisation, community or society in order to obtain a detailed understanding of its culture and behaviours.

Exclusive relationship: A relationship on an **entity relationship diagram** where an **entity** can be connected to only one of a set of other related entities.

Executive summary: See **management summary**.

Explicit knowledge: The knowledge of procedures and data that is foremost in the business users' minds, and which they can easily articulate. See **tacit knowledge**.

External business environment: The business environment that is external to an organisation and is the source of forces that may impact the organisation. Types of forces may include the introduction of new laws, social trends or competitor actions. See **PESTLE analysis**, **Five Forces analysis**.

Facilitation: An interpersonal **competency** required of **business analysts** that allows them to prepare for and manage a meeting or workshop.

Feasibility: The degree to which a proposed course of action is viable given the business, technical and financial constraints imposed by the organisation and the environment in which it operates.

Feasibility assessment and business case development: A service within the **Business Analysis Service Framework** that is concerned with evaluating the options to meet the business need and supporting the development of the business case for change.

Financial feasibility: The degree to which a proposed course of action is compatible with the financial constraints and objectives of an organisation.

Fishbone diagram: A visual technique developed by Dr Kaoru Ishikawa whereby a problem and its causes are represented as the skeleton of a fish. The head shows the problem and the spines radiating from the backbone represent the causes.

Five Forces analysis: See **Porter's Five Forces analysis**.

Focus group: An elicitation technique where a group of people with a common understanding of, or interest in, a topic are brought together to discuss it and provide insights and ideas about the topic.

Force-field analysis: A technique to consider those forces inside and outside the organisation that will support adoption of a proposal and those that will oppose it. This technique was developed originally by Kurt Lewin and may be used in evaluating options for change and in managing proposed changes.

Formal observation: A form of **observation** where an analyst watches and documents a specific task being performed.

Forwards to traceability: A form of **traceability** involving tracing how a **requirement** has been resolved or implemented in a business change or software project.

Functional requirement: A type of **requirement** that is concerned with a feature or function that the system should provide.

Gap analysis: The comparison of two views of a business system: the current situation and the desired future. The aim of gap analysis is to determine where the current situation has problems or 'gaps' that need to be resolved. This leads to the identification of actions to improve the situation. The business activity modelling technique may be used to provide an ideal future view that can then be compared with a view of the current situation. An alternative, more detailed approach is to use the business process modelling technique, using 'as is' and 'to be' process models.

General requirement: A type of **requirement** that documents high-level business constraints and policies.

Growth share matrix: A two-by-two matrix used to analyse the market potential of the products and services provided by an organisation. The technique was defined by the Boston Consulting Group. The two axes represented within the matrix concern market growth and relative market share.

Hand-off: The point within a **swimlane diagram** where a process passes from a task within one swimlane to a task in another swimlane.

Holistic approach: The consideration of all aspects of a business system and their interactions. This encompasses the POPIT elements.

Hothousing/hothouse workshop: An intensive form of workshop whereby analysts and other stakeholders focus on solving a limited range of business problems in a short period of time.

Hybrid strategy development: A blend of **adaptive** and **linear strategy development**.

Impact analysis: The consideration of the impact a proposed change will have on a business system including on the people working within it.

Incremental lifecycle: A variant of the **waterfall lifecycle** where the analysis and design stages are followed by two or more sub-projects to create and deliver the software product in increments.

Infrastructure architecture: The technical platforms and standards that enable an organisation's applications and data to be run and stored, and include the hardware, operating systems, communication and networks.

Intangible benefit: A benefit to be realised by a business change project for which a credible, usually monetary, value cannot be predicted. See **tangible benefit**.

Intangible cost: A cost incurred by a business change project for which a credible, usually monetary, value cannot be predicted. See **tangible cost**.

Internal business environment: The internal capability of the organisation that affects its ability to respond to external environment forces. Techniques such as MOST analysis or the resource audit may be used to analyse the capability of the internal business environment. See **MOST analysis** and **resource audit**.

Internal rate of return (IRR): A calculation that assesses the ROI from a project, defined as a percentage rate. This percentage is the discount rate at which the NPV is equal to zero and can be used to compare projects to see which are the better investment opportunities. Alternatively, this rate may be used to compare all projects with the return that could be earned if the amount invested was left in the bank.

International Institute of Business Analysis™: A professional body that represents **business analysts** and the practice of **business analysis**.

Interview: An investigation technique to elicit information from business users. An interview agenda is prepared prior to the interview and distributed to participants. The interview is carried out in an organised manner and a report of the interview is produced once the interview has been concluded.

INVEST: An acronym used to validate the quality of a **user story** or other product backlog items. The acronym stands for independent, negotiable, valuable (to users), estimatable, small and testable.

Ishikawa diagram: See **fishbone diagram**.

Iterative lifecycle: An approach to software development where a solution evolves through a series of iterations each of which adds features, functionality or performance to what has been developed before. See also **Agile**.

IT system: A set of automated components hosted on a computer that work together in order to provide services to the system users. See **business system**.

IT systems analysis: See **systems analysis/systems analyst**.

Key performance indicators (KPIs): Specific areas of performance that are monitored in order to assess the performance of an organisation. KPIs are often identified in order to monitor progress of the critical success factors. Measurable targets are set for KPIs. See **critical success factors**.

Lean: An approach to business process improvement focused on cutting out the wastes in the process.

Linear lifecycle: See **waterfall lifecycle**.

Linear strategy development: The gradual, systematic development of an organisation's **strategy**, particularly where the business environment is relatively stable.

Management summary: A short summary that provides an overview of the background, findings and recommendations of a document.

McKinsey 7S: A framework developed by the McKinsey consultancy organisation. The 7S model is used to analyse organisations and identify areas where change is needed.

Migration: The process of moving an organisation from an existing business process or IT system to a new one.

Mind map: A technique pioneered by Tony Buzan that represents an issue as a diagram with the name of the issue in the centre and aspects associated with it as radiating branches.

Monitoring activities: The activities in a **business activity model (BAM)** that assess performance against standards set in the **planning activities**.

MoSCoW: An approach to prioritising requirements. MoSCoW stands for:

- Must have: A mandatory requirement without which the system offers no value.

- Should have: An important requirement that must be delivered, but, where time is short, could be delayed for a future delivery. This should involve a short-term delay.

- Could have: A requirement that would be beneficial to include if it does not cost too much or take too long to deliver, but it is not central to the project objectives.

- Want to have (but won't have this time): A requirement that will be needed in the future but is not required for this delivery.

MOST analysis: An analysis of an organisation's mission, objectives, strategy and tactics to identify any inherent strengths or weaknesses, for example from a lack of strategic direction or unclear objectives. See **internal business environment**.

Net present value (NPV): The amount an investment is worth once all of the net annual cash flows in the years following the current one are adjusted to today's value of money. The NPV is calculated using the discounted cash flow approach to investment appraisal. See **discounted cash flow**, **internal rate of return.**

Net present value analysis: An approach to investment appraisal that seeks to establish the **net present value** of a proposed project or other investment.

Non-functional requirement: A type of **requirement** that defines a quality or performance characteristic for a system or specified functional requirements.

Object: An object is something within a business system for which a set of attributes and functions can be specified. An object is an instance of a class. See **class**.

Observation: A technique used within **requirements elicitation** where an analyst observes work being performed with a view to identifying issues and/or requirements to improve a business situation.

Optionality: An indication of whether or not a relationship between one **entity** and another must always exist.

Options: The alternative courses of action considered in a **business case**.

Organisation model: A model showing the place of an organisation within the wider world and in relation to the external business environment within which it operates. The external environment encompasses the organisation's competitors, suppliers and customers.

OSCAR: An acronym that helps to identify the areas to be addressed in a **project initiation document** or **terms of reference** for a project. The OSCAR elements are objectives, scope, constraints, authority and resources.

Outsourcing: A process by which an organisation entrusts certain aspects of its operations to other organisations. Organisations outsource for various reasons including to lower costs or to secure specialist expertise not available internally.

Parallel running: A method of introducing new business processes or systems whereby the existing and the new are run in parallel for a time until the effectiveness of the new processes or systems have been established.

Payback calculation: An investment appraisal technique where a cash-flow forecast for a project is produced using the current values of the incoming and outgoing cash-flows; no attempt is made to adjust them for the declining value of money over time. See **discounted cash flow.**

Payback period: The length of time it takes a project to recoup its initial investment.

Persona: An artefact associated with **user role analysis** whereby a **user role** is given more realism by the creation of a fictitious profile that comprises a named individual, and their personality characteristics and abilities.

PESTLE analysis: A technique used to analyse the external business environment of an organisation. The technique involves the analysis of the political, economic, socio-cultural, technological, legal and environmental forces that may impact upon an organisation. See **business environment**.

Phased implementation: A method of implementing new business processes or systems where they are introduced to an organisation one phase (collection of features) at a time until the entire solution has been deployed.

Pilot running: A method of introducing new business processes or systems where they are tried out in one area first and then, if successful, are implemented more widely across the organisation.

Planning activities: The activities in a **business activity model (BAM)** where decisions are made about the resources required to conduct the **doing activity** (or activities). Planning activities also include devising measures against which performance can be assessed.

POPIT™ model: A model that illustrates the elements that need to be considered by business analysts in order to provide a **holistic** view of a business situation. The elements are people, organisation, process, information and technology. The POPIT model is also used to conduct gap analysis and business readiness assessment and provides a basis for a **target operating model**.

Porter's Five Forces analysis: A technique used to analyse the industry or business domain within which an organisation operates.

Portfolio: The suite of business change **projects** or **programmes** for an organisation.

Post-it™ exercise: A technique used during meetings or workshops where participants are asked to write down possible ideas on sticky notes and then display and discuss them.

Power/interest grid: A visual representation of the relative importance of a project's stakeholders. They are shown in the position that represents the power or influence they can wield over the project and the level of interest they have exhibited in it. Their position on the grid suggests suitable strategies for the management of each stakeholder.

Prioritisation: The ordering of requirements or product backlog items in terms of their importance and the urgency with which they must be satisfied.

Problem solving: A systematic approach to uncovering the root causes of a business problem or issue and developing workable and acceptable solutions.

Process: See **business process**.

Process measurement: A process to monitor how well a **business process** is performed against defined measures, in order to assess its efficiency and effectiveness and identify where corrective action or improvement is required.

Process model: See **business process model.**

Product backlog: In Agile software development, a repository of the requirements and work items to be considered during the project.

Product owner: In Agile software development, a role that is the custodian of the **product backlog** or **solution backlog**.

Professional body: An organisation that offers standards, qualifications, codes of practice and other resources to people working within a field. With regard to **business analysis**, the two leading professional bodies worldwide are BCS, The Chartered Institute for IT, based in the UK, and the IIBA, based in Canada.

Programme: A group of **projects** that all contribute towards the achievement of a business objective and that, because of their interdependence, must be coordinated.

Programme manager: A role responsible for planning, directing and managing a **programme**.

Project: A discrete piece of work with a defined start and end date and specific deliverables, which is designed to achieve a defined objective.

Project initiation document (PID): A document that defines the business context for a project and clarifies the objectives, scope, deliverables, timescale, budget, authority and available resources.

Project manager: A role responsible for planning, directing and managing a **project**.

Project sponsor: A senior manager within an organisation who 'owns' a project as a business undertaking and who is responsible for making major decisions about its scope and direction and making resources available for its execution.

Protocol analysis: A form of **observation** used to elicit, analyse and validate requirements. Protocol analysis involves requesting the users to perform a task and describe each step as they perform it.

Prototyping: A technique used to elicit, analyse and validate requirements. Prototyping involves building simulations of documents, processes or systems in order to enable the business users to visualise any proposed changes and hence increase understanding about the system requirements.

Quantitative approaches: In **requirements elicitation**, techniques that aim to uncover quantifiable data.

Questionnaires: See **survey**.

RACI or RASCI: A linear responsibility matrix that identifies stakeholder roles and responsibilities either during an organisational change process or to support business-as-usual operations.

RAID log: A record of the risks, assumptions, issues and dependencies for a proposed or actual project. See also **CARDI log**.

Relationship: A line that indicates a relevant business connection between two **entities** on an **entity relationship diagram**.

Requirement: A feature that the business staff need the new system (business or IT) to provide.

Requirements analysis: The systematic examination of requirements discovered during **requirements elicitation** with a view to checking their correctness and completeness.

Requirements catalogue: An organised set of requirements where each individual requirement is documented using a standard template.

Requirements definition: A service within the **Business Analysis Service Framework** concerned with the elicitation, analysis and definition of requirements for business and IT change initiatives.

Requirements document: A generic name for a document containing information about the requirements for a proposed information system. Typical contents include: introduction, business process models, function models, data model, requirements catalogue or user story backlog, and a glossary of terms.

Requirements elicitation: A stage of the **requirements engineering** framework, this is a proactive approach to investigating requirements required to resolve a business problem or enable a business opportunity. It involves working with the business staff and helping them to visualise and articulate their requirements.

Requirements engineering: A framework for the elicitation, analysis, validation, documentation and management of requirements.

Requirements filters: These are used during **requirements analysis** to check the quality of the documented requirements. They consist of a checklist of questions to ask about the requirements.

Requirements list: A list of the requirements captured during **requirements elicitation**. The list may later be expanded into a **requirements catalogue** or, in an Agile project, form the basis for a **product backlog**.

Requirements management: A stage of the **requirements engineering** framework and a governance approach that aims to ensure that each requirement is tracked from inception to implementation (or withdrawal) through all of the changes that have been applied to it.

Requirements validation: A stage of the **requirements engineering** framework where the requirements are reviewed and approved by selected external stakeholders.

Resource audit: A technique to analyse the assets held by an organisation. The resource audit considers five areas of organisational resource: tangible resources – physical, financial and human; intangible resources – know-how and reputation.

Rich picture: A pictorial technique offering a free format approach that allows analysts to document whatever is of interest or significance in the business situation. This technique originated from the Soft Systems Methodology. See **Soft Systems Methodology**.

Risk management: The identification, assessment, monitoring and control of significant risks during the development, design and implementation of IT systems.

Risk/risk analysis: A problem situation that may arise with regard to a project or business situation. Potential risks are identified for each option in a business case, the probability of the risk occurring and the likely impact of the risk are assessed, and suitable countermeasures are identified. See **business case**.

Root cause/root cause analysis: The systematic examination of a perceived problem to identify the real underlying causes.

Round robin: A technique used within a meeting or workshop where each participant in turn is invited to offer a fact, comment, idea or opinion.

SARAH curve: A model that shows the typical stages people experience when faced with a change in their situation, including the introduction of new business processes and IT systems. The stages in the SARAH curve are: shock, anger, rejection, acceptance and hope.

Scenarios: A technique used to elicit, analyse and validate requirements. A scenario will trace the course of a transaction from an initial business trigger through each of the steps needed to achieve a successful outcome. Alternative scenarios, for example, where specific conditions are not met, are also traced.

Scrum: An **Agile** method used for software development.

Security architecture: A definition of the components and systems through which the enterprise protects its assets from harm, loss or danger.

SFIA and SFIA*plus*: The Skills Framework for the Information Age (SFIA) and the extended version provided by BCS (SFIA*plus*). Standard frameworks setting out the definition of skills and levels of competency for anyone working in the information systems industry.

Shadowing: A form of **observation** used to find out what a particular job entails. Shadowing involves following an individual as they carry out their job for a period of time.

Situation investigation and problem analysis: A service within the **Business Analysis Service Framework** concerned with investigating the root causes of problems, identifying where a business need exists and shaping a project to address this need.

Six Sigma: An approach to identifying process improvements with a view to decreasing the variability and improving the consistency with which a process is performed. The steps involved in a Six Sigma project are: define (the problem); measure (the data); analyse (the problem); improve (the process); control (the effectiveness of the solution).

Six Thinking Hats: A thinking tool developed by Edward de Bono for individuals and for groups to improve the thinking process by considering different perspectives.

SMART: A mnemonic used to ensure that objectives are clearly defined in that they are specific, measurable, achievable, relevant and time-bound.

Soft Systems Methodology: A methodology that provides an approach to analysing business situations devised by Peter Checkland and his team at Lancaster University.

Software tester: A person within a development project who conducts tests to ensure that software performs according to its specification.

Solution architecture: The practice of defining and describing the architecture for a holistic business solution.

Solution backlog: See **product backlog**.

Special purpose records: A technique that requires individuals to keep a record about a specific issue or task. Typically the record is based on a simple structure, for example a five bar gate record. Special purpose records are one of the **quantitative approaches to requirements elicitation**.

Stakeholder: An individual, group of individuals or organisation with an interest in the change. Categories of stakeholder include customers, employees, managers, partners, regulators, owners, suppliers and contractors.

Stakeholder analysis: An approach to evaluating stakeholders in terms of their levels of power and interest, areas of concern and attitudes. This technique provides a means of categorising stakeholders in order to identify the most appropriate stakeholder management approach.

Stakeholder engagement: An activity associated with the **Business Analysis Service Framework** that is concerned with supporting the achievement of business change and IT project success through stakeholder collaboration, communication and effective stakeholder relationship management.

Stakeholder management: The definition of the most appropriate means to be adopted in order to engage with different categories of stakeholder.

Stakeholder management plan: A formal documentation of the strategy to be adopted to manage a specific project **stakeholder**.

Stakeholder perspective: A view of the business system held by a stakeholder. The business perspective will be based upon the values and beliefs of the stakeholder. These values and beliefs will be encapsulated in a defined world view. There may be several divergent business perspectives for any given business situation. See **CATWOE**.

Stand-up: A short daily meeting of an Agile development team where progress is reviewed and problems identified. The term refers to the fact that such meetings are held standing up, which is designed to promote brevity and to stress urgency.

Stepwise refinement: A technique used in a meeting or workshop whereby the facilitator keeps asking 'why?' until the real facts are uncovered.

Storytelling: A technique used within **requirements elicitation** where **stakeholders** discuss their experiences and situations, and information and insights are uncovered.

Strategic analysis: The application of techniques in order to analyse the pressures within an organisation's external business environment and the level of internal organisational capability to respond to these pressures.

Strategy: The direction and scope of an organisation over the longer term. The strategy is defined in order to achieve competitive advantage for the organisation through its configuration of resources within a changing business environment.

Subject matter expert: A person within a project who offers **subject matter expertise**.

Subject matter expertise: A detailed understanding of the terminology, processes, constraints and technology of a specific business area, product line or service. See also **domain, domain knowledge**.

Survey: A **requirements elicitation** approach used to obtain quantitative data during an investigation of a business situation. Surveys are useful to obtain a limited amount of information from a large group of people.

Swimlane: A row on a business process diagram/model that indicates the actor responsible for a particular task. Actors may be departments, teams, individuals or IT systems.

Swimlane diagram: A technique used to model business processes. A swimlane diagram models the business system response to a business event. The model shows the triggering event, the business actors, the tasks they carry out, the flow between the tasks, the decisions and the business outcome. See **business process model**.

SWOT analysis: A technique used to summarise the external pressures facing an organisation and the internal capability the organisation has available to respond to those pressures. The mnemonic stands for strengths, weaknesses, opportunities and threats.

System use case: A **use case diagram** showing the detailed features or functions to be provided by a proposed software product.

Systems analysis/systems analyst: A role within IT responsible for specifying the requirements for software solutions. Systems analysis is an older discipline than **business analysis** and differs from it in that, if a systems analyst is required, there is a presumption that an IT solution is required; business analysis takes a more holistic view of the business problem or issue.

Systems development lifecycle: A model of the stages and steps to be taken to develop and implement a software product.

T-shaped professional: A concept that represents the need for individuals to have deep skills in their own professional discipline and broad, generic skills that span other disciplines and enable them to interact effectively with anyone working in those disciplines.

Tacit assumption: A belief on the part of an individual that information they hold is correct, without checking to ensure that this is the case. See **explicit knowledge** and **tacit knowledge**.

Tacit knowledge: Information held about business procedures and operations that an individual does not articulate or explain. This may be due to a failure to recognise that the information is required or because there is an assumption that the information is already known to the analyst. See **explicit knowledge** and **tacit assumption**.

Tactics: Short-term actions taken by an organisation in order to execute its longer-term **strategy**.

Tangible benefit: A benefit to be realised by a business change project for which a credible, usually monetary, value can be predicted. See **intangible benefit**.

Tangible cost: A cost incurred by a business change project for which a credible, usually monetary, value can be predicted. See **intangible cost**.

Target operating model (TOM): A model that illustrates how an organisation must be established in order to support the execution of its **strategy**.

Task: A work activity carried out by a single actor in one place at a specific moment in time (one person, one place, one time also known as OPOPOT). Tasks are represented within swimlanes on a **business process model** or **swimlane diagram**.

Task analysis: A technique used to analyse the work conducted during a given task. The analysis considers the event that triggers the task, the input information, outputs, steps, measures and decisions.

Task scenario: See **scenarios**.

Technical feasibility: The degree to which a proposed course of action is compatible with the technical constraints and infrastructure available to an organisation.

Technical option: A technical option describes how the business solution may be implemented using available technology.

Technical requirement: A type of **requirement** that documents high-level technical constraints and policies.

Terms of reference (ToR): An alternative name for a **project initiation document (PID)**, sometimes preferred for consultancy assignments such as a feasibility study. The **OSCAR** acronym may be used to develop a ToR.

Tester: See **software tester**.

'To be' business process model: A representation of a business process within an organisation as it is to be performed in the future.

Traceability: A fundamental principle of **requirements engineering** whereby requirements can be traced from their origin to their resolution, and back from the resolution to the origin, and to the strategic context that gave rise to the requirement.

Transition requirement: A type of **requirement** that documents features or actions that will be required during the transition to new processes and systems.

Unified Modeling Language: The Unified Modeling Language (UML) is a suite of diagrammatic techniques that are used to model business and IT systems.

Unified process: A process model that underpins the **Unified Modeling Language**.

Use case: A feature that an actor wants a system to offer; it is a 'case of use' of the system by a specific actor and describes the interaction between an actor and the system.

Use case description: A use case description defines the interaction between an actor and a use case. It may take the form of text or a diagram such as an **activity diagram**.

Use case diagram: A diagram showing the **use cases** within the scope of a business or IT system and the interaction of these with business actors.

Use case model: A technique from the UML. A use case model is made up of a diagram showing the actors, the boundary of the system, the use cases and the associations between them, plus a set of use case descriptions.

User interface requirement: A type of **requirement** that documents the style and nature of elements of the solution that will be used by **business staff**.

User role: A generic title (for example, 'customer') for a role taken by an individual or group who will interact with a business or IT system.

User role analysis: A technique used to identify and understand the actors who need to interact with a proposed business or IT system.

User story: A technique used within Agile development approaches where a feature required by a **user role** is stated in terms of what a system should do and why the delivery of the required feature would be beneficial.

'V' model lifecycle: A variant of the **waterfall lifecycle** where the earlier analysis and design stages of a project are represented by the left, downwards-facing side of a letter 'V' and the testing stages by the right, upwards-facing side.

Value chain: A concept developed by Michael Porter to identify the primary and support activities deployed within organisations to create a value proposition to their customers.

Value network analysis: A technique devised by Verna Allee (2002) that defines a 'network of relationships' between the various actors and stakeholders in an organisation as a series of exchanges of value.

Value proposition: A clear statement of the value that an organisation offers customers through the delivery of a product or service.

Value stream: A representation of the activities carried out by an organisation that collectively offer a product or service to internal or external stakeholders.

Version control: See **configuration management**.

Vertical traceability: A form of **traceability** where the link is evident between the business strategy and objectives, and the business and solution requirements.

VMOST: An extension of the **MOST** technique for an organisation where vision is added to the mission, objectives, strategy and tactics.

Waste: Several areas, defined in **Lean**, where possible process improvements may be identified. These areas are: transport; inventory; motion; waiting; overproduction; overprocessing; defects; and skills. They form the acronym TIMWOODS.

Waterfall lifecycle: A form of **systems development lifecycle** where the work is undertaken in discrete, sequential stages.

Workshop: A meeting attended by business actors from a range of business areas and run by a facilitator, for the purpose of eliciting, analysing or validating information. An agenda is prepared prior to the workshop and distributed to participants. The actions and decisions are recorded by a scribe.

REFERENCES

Allee, V. (2002) *The Future of Knowledge: Increasing Prosperity through Value Networks*, Abingdon-on-Thames, Routledge.

Boehm, B. (1986) A spiral model of software development and enhancement. *ACM SIGSOFT Software Engineering Notes*, 11(4), 22–42.

Business Architecture Guild (2020) *A Guide to the Business Architecture Body of Knowledge®* (BIZBOK® Guide), V8.5

Buzan, T. and Buzan, B. (2000) *The Mind Map Book*, London, BC Worldwide Ltd.

Cadle, J., Paul, D. and Turner, P. (2014) *Business Analysis Techniques*, 2nd edition, Swindon, BCS.

Chandler, A.D. Jr (1962) *Strategy and Structure: Chapters in the History of the Industrial Enterprise*, Cambridge, MA, Massachusetts Institute of Technology.

Checkland, P. (1999) *Systems Thinking, Systems Practice: Includes a 30 Year Retrospective*, Chichester, UK, John Wiley.

De Bono, E. (2016) *Six Thinking Hats*, London, Penguin Books.

De Ville, H.G. (1986) *Review of Vocational Qualifications in England and Wales: A Report by the Working Group, April 1986*, Sheffield, Manpower Services Commission and Dept. of Education and Science.

Eva, M. (2001) Requirements acquisition for rapid applications development. *Information & Management*, 39, 101.

Gartner (no date) Gartner glossary: Solution architecture. https://www.gartner.com/en/information-technology/glossary/solution-architecture

Gray, A. (2016, 19 January) The 10 skills you need to thrive in the Fourth Industrial Revolution. World Economic Forum. https://www.weforum.org/agenda/2016/01/the-10-skills-you-need-to-thrive-in-the-fourth-industrial-revolution/

Harmon, P. (2019) *Business Process Change*, 4th edition, Upper Saddle River, NJ, Morgan Kaufmann.

Hofer, C.W. (1973) Some preliminary research on patterns of strategic behavior. *Academy of Management Proceedings*, 1973(1), 46–54. doi: 10.5465/AMBPP.1973.4981180

Institute for the Future for the University of Phoenix Research Institute (2011) *Future Work Skills 2020*, Palo Alto, CA.

International Institute of Business Analysis (IIBA) (2015) *BABOK V3: A Guide to the Business Analysis Body of Knowledge*, Toronto, IIBA®.

Isaksen, S. and Treffinger, D. (1985) *Creative Problem Solving: The Basic Course*, Buffalo, NJ, Bearly Limited.

Ishikawa, K. (1985) *What is Total Quality Control? The Japanese Way*, Englewood Cliffs, NJ, Prentice Hall Direct.

ISO/IEC/IEEE 42010:2011 (2011) Systems and software engineering – Architecture description. https://www.iso.org/standard/50508.html

Johnson, G., Whittington, R., Scholes, K., Angwin, D. and Regner, P. (2017) *Exploring Corporate Strategy*, 11th edition, Harlow, UK, Pearson.

Kaplan, D. and Norton, R. (1996) *The Balanced Scorecard*, Boston, MA, Harvard Business School Press.

Kim, W. and Mauborgne, R. (2015) *Blue Ocean Strategy: How to Create Uncontested Market Space and Make the Competition Irrelevant*, Boston, MA, Harvard Business School Press.

Krathwohl, D.R. (2002) A revision of Bloom's taxonomy: An overview. *Theory Into Practice*, 41(4), 212–218.

Lencioni, P. (2012) *The Advantage*, Chichester, UK, John Wiley & Sons.

Lewin, K. (1997) *Resolving Social Conflicts: Field Theory in Social Science*, Washington, DC, American Psychological Association.

Mance, H. (2013) Why big IT projects crash, *Financial Times*, 18 September. https://www.ft.com/content/794bbb56-1f8e-11e3-8861-00144feab7de#axzz2jL208Sjj

Newcombe, R. (2003) From client to project stakeholders: a stakeholder mapping approach. *Construction Management and Economics*, 21(8), 841–848.

Nielsen, J. (1993) *Usability Engineering*, Upper Saddle River, NJ, Morgan Kaufmann.

Osterwalder, A. and Pigneur, Y. (2010) *Business Model Generation*, Chichester, UK, John Wiley & Sons.

Paul, D.E. (2018) *Defining the Role of the Business Analyst*, doctoral thesis, Henley Business School, UK.

Paul, D. and Lovelock, C. (2019) *Delivering Business Analysis: The BA Service Handbook*, Swindon, BCS.

Peters, T.J. and Waterman, R.H. (1982) *In Search of Excellence*, London, Harper & Row.

Polanyi, M. (1966) *The Logic of Tacit Inference*, London, Macmillan.

Porter, M. (1980) *Competitive Strategy*, New York, The Free Press.

Porter, M. (1985) *Competitive Advantage*, New York, The Free Press.

Pullan, P. and Archer, J. (2013) *Business Analysis and Leadership: Influencing Change*, London, Kogan Page.

Reed, A. (2018) *Business Analyst: Careers in Business Analysis (BCS Guides to IT Roles)*, Swindon, BCS.

Reed, A. (2019) It's time we revisited our NFRs: let's add sustainability and diversity & inclusion. Adrian Reed's Blog. https://www.adrianreed.co.uk/2019/09/02/its-time-we-revisited-our-nfrs-lets-add-sustainability-diversity-inclusion/

Ross, J.W., Weill, P. and Robertson, D.C. (2006) *Enterprise Architecture as Strategy: Creating a Foundation for Business Execution*, Boston, MA, Harvard Business Review Press.

Ross, J.W., Beath, C.M. and Mocker, M. (2019) *Designed for Digital: How to Architect your Business for Sustained Success*, Cambridge, MA, Massachusetts Institute of Technology.

Senge, P.M. (2006) *The Fifth Discipline: The Art and Practice of The Learning Organisation*, London, Random House Business Books.

Silver, B. (2011) *BPMN Method and Style with BPMN Implementer's Guide*, 2nd edition, Norwood, CA, Cody-Cassidy Press.

Thomas, P., Paul, D. and Cadle, J. (2012) *The Human Touch: Personal Skills for Professional Success*, Swindon: BCS Learning and Development Ltd.

W3C (no date) Web design and applications: accessibility. https://www.w3.org/standards/webdesign/accessibility

Wake, B. (2003) INVEST in good stories, and SMART tasks. XP123. https://xp123.com/articles/invest-in-good-stories-and-smart-tasks/

Walia, G. and Carver, J. (2009) A systematic literature review to identify and classify software requirement errors. *Information and Software Technology*, 51, 1087–1109.

Ward, J. and Daniel, E. (2012) *Benefits Management: How to Increase the Business Value of Your IT Projects*, 2nd edition, Chichester, UK, John Wiley & Sons.

Waterman, R.H. Jr, Peters, T.J. and Phillips, J.R. (1980) Structure is not organization, *McKinsey Quarterly*, 3, 2–20.

FURTHER READING

Alexander, I. and Stevens, R. (2002) *Writing Better Requirements*, Upper Saddle River, NJ, Addison Wesley.

Arlow, J. and Neustadt, I. (2005) *UML 2 and the Unified Process*, 2nd edition, Upper Saddle River, NJ, Addison Wesley.

Cockburn, A. (2001) *Writing Effective Use Cases,* Upper Saddle River, NJ, Addison Wesley.

Hammer, M. and Champy, J. (2001) *Reenginering the Corporation: A Manifesto for Business Revolution*, London, Nicholas Brealey Publishing Ltd.

Rummler, G. and Brache, A. (2013) *Improving Performance: How to Manage the White Space on the Organisation Chart*, San Francisco, CA, John Wiley.

Schwaber, K. (2004) *Agile Project Management with Scrum*, Redmond, WA, Microsoft Press.

Simsion, G. and Witt, G. (2004) *Data Modelling Essentials*, 3rd edition, Burlington, MA, Morgan Kaufmann.

INDEX

domain knowledge 13, 26, 27, 35

Double Diamond model 219–20

DSDM (Dynamic Systems Development Method) 12, 36, 129, 272, 329, 341

duplication
  of processes 84, 140, 190, 191, 192
  of requirements 244, 246, 256, 271–2, 273, 277, 278, 286, 296

Economic factor (PESTLE analysis) 54, 173, 189, 224, 225

Empathise (design thinking stage) 218–19

Employees (stakeholder category) 145, 146

empowered teams 341

Enabling activities (business activity model) 160–1, 162

enterprise architecture 1, 3, 8, 27, 28, 37, 59, 78–82, 224, 336

enterprise level (business process hierarchy) 164, 165, 166–76, 187, 189, 202, 205

entity relationship diagrams (ERDs) 38, 281, 298–307, 314, 317–18, 319

Environment (CATWOE technique) 157, 158, 372–3

Environmental factor (PESTLE analysis) 55, 173, 189, 225

ethnographic studies 118, 267

Evaluate (design thinking stage) 218–19

Event (UML activity diagrams) 165, 178–80, 183

event-response level (business process hierarchy) 164, 165, 176–85, 187, 189, 202, 205

evolutionary development 12, 248, 287, 341, 345

exhaustive option 217

experiential learning 342

explicit knowledge 264, 265, 268–9, 270

<<extend>> construct 296–7, 298

extended option 217

external environment analysis 38, 49, 52, 53–60, 70, 72, 84, 86, 157, 173, 175–6

external performance measures 203–4

facilitation 26, 27, 30, 38, 111, 339

feasibility assessment and business case development 18, 19, 88, 90–1, 99, 215
  see also business case development

financial costs and benefits, presenting 231

financial feasibility 91, 223–4, 274

financial resources 5, 12, 64, 100, 368

fishbone diagrams 90, 101–2, 123, 140, 142–3

Five Forces Model 53, 56–60, 71, 86, 189

focus groups 38, 252, 293
  situation investigation 107, 114–15, 132, 137

force-field analysis 225

Fork and join (UML activity diagrams) 179, 180

formal observation 116–17

formal requirements validation 321, 322–4, 329

formal/informal networks 29, 268

'forwards to' traceability 325, 326

functional requirements 211, 343–5
  documenting and modelling requirements 283, 284, 285, 287, 289–97
  establishing requirements 254, 255, 257, 263–4, 265, 272, 275

future of business analysis 22–4

gain creators 172

gap analysis 77, 161, 356, 357, 371
  approaches and relevant artefacts 207
  BASF 88–9, 92, 93
  business activity models 208–9, 216
  business analyst competencies 27, 39, 40
  POPIT model 208, 209–15, 217, 220
  solution definition 206–15, 216, 220

gateways 184

general requirements 254–6, 262, 263, 282, 283, 284, 324, 326

generalisation (class modelling) 313, 314

growth share matrix 53, 69–70, 86

hand-offs 36, 190–1, 192, 204

holistic approaches 32, 155, 241, 243, 289, 357, 358
  business analysis overview 1, 5, 6, 9, 10–12
  business process improvement 164–5, 167, 173, 196
  requirements delivery 333, 335, 337, 353
  solution definition 206, 208, 209, 212, 215, 220

horizontal traceability 325, 326

hothouse workshops 113–14, 137

human resources 36, 40, 64, 75, 100, 130, 166, 169, 228, 229

human response to change 362–3

hybrid strategy development 52

idea generation 27, 38, 76, 102–3, 112, 218, 220

Ideate (design thinking stage) 218–19

identifying problems (business processes) 190

IIBA (International Institute of Business Analysis) 21, 41, 44, 45

impact assessment 231, 232, 331

Implementation stage (business change lifecycle) 3, 336, 355, 356, 357, 360, 361–2, 368

inappropriate measures 191, 201

<<include>> construct 296–7, 298

incremental lifecycle 12, 339–40, 342, 344, 345, 352

individuals/groups of stakeholders 151

industry competitors (Five Forces Model) 56, 57, 58

industry engagement 41

inefficient work practices/processes 143, 165, 191, 192, 317

influencing 27, 29–30, 32

Information and Technology (POPIT model) 11–12, 77–8, 210, 211–12, 213, 356, 357

infrastructure architecture 37, 81, 82, 263, 352, 361